Communications
in Computer and Information Science   555

Commenced Publication in 2007
Founding and Former Series Editors:
Alfredo Cuzzocrea, Dominik Ślęzak, and Xiaokang Yang

More information about this series at http://www.springer.com/series/7899

Andreas Holzinger · Jorge Cardoso
José Cordeiro · Therese Libourel
Leszek A. Maciaszek · Marten van Sinderen (Eds.)

Software Technologies

9th International Joint Conference, ICSOFT 2014
Vienna, Austria, August 29–31, 2014
Revised Selected Papers

 Springer

Editors

Andreas Holzinger
Medical Informatis, Statistics, Document
Medical University Graz
Graz
Austria

Jorge Cardoso
Engenharia Informática Department
Universidade de Coimbra
Coimbra
Portugal

José Cordeiro
INSTICC and IPS
Setúbal
Portugal

Therese Libourel
Département Informatique
Université de Montpellier
Montpellier
France

Leszek A. Maciaszek
Wroclaw University of Economics
Wroclaw
Poland

Marten van Sinderen
Department of Computer Science
University of Twente
Enschede, Overijssel
The Netherlands

ISSN 1865-0929   ISSN 1865-0937 (electronic)
Communications in Computer and Information Science
ISBN 978-3-319-25578-1   ISBN 978-3-319-25579-8 (eBook)
DOI 10.1007/978-3-319-25579-8

Library of Congress Control Number: 2015952534

Springer Cham Heidelberg New York Dordrecht London

Printed on acid-free paper

Springer International Publishing AG Switzerland is part of Springer Science+Business Media
(www.springer.com)

Preface

The present book includes extended and revised versions of a set of selected papers from the 9th International Joint Conference on Software Technologies (ICSOFT 2014), which was sponsored by the Institute for Systems and Technologies of Information, Control and Communication (INSTICC) and co-organized by the Austrian Computer Society and the Vienna University of Technology – TU Wien (TUW). ICSOFT 2014 was held in cooperation with the IEICE Special Interest Group on Software Interprise Modelling (SWIM) and technically co-sponsored by the IEEE Computer Society and IEEE Computer Society's Technical Council on Software Engineering (TCSE).

The purpose of ICSOFT is to bring together researchers, engineers, and practitioners working in areas that are related to software engineering and applications. ICSOFT is composed of two co-located conferences: ICSOFT-PT, which specializes in new software paradigm trends, and ICSOFT-EA, which specializes in mainstream software engineering and applications. Together, these conferences aim at becoming a major meeting point for software engineers worldwide.

ICSOFT-PT (9th International Conference on Software Paradigm Trends) focused on four main paradigms that have been intensively studied during the last decade for software and system design, namely, Models, Aspects, Services, and Context.

ICSOFT-EA (9th International Conference on Software Engineering and Applications) had a practical focus on software engineering and applications. The conference tracks were Enterprise Software Technologies, Software Engineering and Systems Security, Distributed Systems, and Software Project Management.

ICSOFT 2014 received 145 paper submissions from 46 countries in all continents, of which 14 % were presented as full papers. To evaluate each submission, a double-blind paper evaluation method was used: each paper was reviewed by at least two internationally known experts from the ICSOFT Program Committee.

The quality of the papers presented here stems directly from the dedicated effort of the Steering and Scientific Committees and the INSTICC team responsible for handling all secretariat and logistics details. We are further indebted to the conference keynote speakers, who presented their valuable insights and visions regarding areas of interest to the conference. Finally, we would like to thank all authors and attendants for their contribution to the conference and the scientific community.

We hope that you will find these papers interesting and consider them a helpful reference in the future when addressing any of the aforementioned research areas.

April 2015

Andreas Holzinger
Jorge Cardoso
José Cordeiro
Therese Libourel
Leszek A. Maciaszek
Marten van Sinderen

Organization

Conference Co-chairs

Andreas Holzinger	Medical University Graz, Austria
Stephen Mellor	Freeter, UK
(honorary)	

Program Co-chairs

ICSOFT-EA

Therese Libourel	University of Montpellier II (IRD, UR, UAG), France
Leszek A. Maciaszek	Wroclaw University of Economics, Poland and Macquarie University, Sydney, Australia

ICSOFT-PT

Jorge Cardoso	University of Coimbra, Portugal and Karlsruhe Institute of Technology, Germany
José Cordeiro	Polytechnic Institute of Setúbal/INSTICC, Portugal
Marten van Sinderen	University of Twente, The Netherlands

Organizing Committee

Marina Carvalho	INSTICC, Portugal
Helder Coelhas	INSTICC, Portugal
João Francisco	INSTICC, Portugal
Lucia Gomes	INSTICC, Portugal
Rúben Gonçalves	INSTICC, Portugal
Ana Guerreiro	INSTICC, Portugal
André Lista	INSTICC, Portugal
Filipe Mariano	INSTICC, Portugal
Andreia Moita	INSTICC, Portugal
Raquel Pedrosa	INSTICC, Portugal
Vitor Pedrosa	INSTICC, Portugal
Cátia Pires	INSTICC, Portugal
Carolina Ribeiro	INSTICC, Portugal
João Ribeiro	INSTICC, Portugal
Susana Ribeiro	INSTICC, Portugal
Sara Santiago	INSTICC, Portugal
Fábio Santos	INSTICC, Portugal
Mara Silva	INSTICC, Portugal

José Varela   INSTICC, Portugal
Pedro Varela   INSTICC, Portugal

ICSOFT-EA Program Committee

Hamideh Afsarmanesh   University of Amsterdam, The Netherlands
Markus Aleksy   ABB Corporate Research Center, Germany
Waleed Alsabhan   University of Brunel, UK
Toshiaki Aoki   Japan Advanced Institute of Science and Technology,
                            Japan
Gabriela Noemí Aranda   Universidad Nacional Del Comahue, Argentina
Farhad Arbab   CWI, The Netherlands
Jocelyn Armarego   Murdoch University, Australia
Cyrille Artho   AIST, Japan
Fevzi Belli   University of Paderborn, Germany
Jorge Bernardino   Polytechnic Institute of Coimbra - ISEC, Portugal
Marcello Bonsangue   Leiden University, The Netherlands
Dumitru Burdescu   University of Craiova, Romania
Antoni Lluís Mesquida   Universitat de les Illes Balears (UIB), Spain
  Calafat
Jose Antonio   Universidad Politécnica de Madrid, Spain
  Calvo-Manzano
Mauro Caporuscio   Politecnico di Milano, Italy
Luiz Fernando Capretz   University of Western Ontario, Canada
Kung Chen   National Chengchi University, Taiwan
Marta Cimitile   UNITELMA Sapienza, Italy
Peter Clarke   Florida International University, USA
François Coallier   École de technologie supérieure, Canada
Kendra Cooper   The University of Texas at Dallas, USA
António Miguel Rosado   Instituto Politécnico de Viana do Castelo, Portugal
  da Cruz
Aldo Dagnino   ABB Corporate Research, USA
Ferruccio Damiani   Università degli Studi di Torino, Italy
Steven Demurjian   University of Connecticut, USA
Juan C. Dueñas   Universidad Politécnica de Madrid, Spain
Philippe Dugerdil   Geneva School of Business Administration, University of
                            Applied Sciences of Western Switzerland, Switzerland
Fikret Ercal   Missouri University of Science and Technology, USA
João Faria   FEUP - University of Porto, Portugal
Rita Francese   Università degli Studi di Salerno, Italy
Matthias Galster   University of Canterbury, New Zealand
Nikolaos Georgantas   Inria, France
Hamza Gharsellaoui   INSAT Institute – University of Carthage, Tunisia, Al-Jouf
                            College of Technology, TVTC, KSA, Saudi Arabia
Paola Giannini   Università del Piemonte Orientale, Italy
J. Paul Gibson   TSP - Telecom SudParis, France

Slimane Hammoudi	ESEO, MODESTE, France
Brian Henderson-Sellers	University of Technology, Sydney, Australia
Pedro Rangel Henriques	University of Minho, Portugal
Jose Luis Arciniegas Herrera	Universidad del Cauca, Colombia
Yoshiki Higo	Osaka University, Japan
Jose R. Hilera	University of Alcala, Spain
Andreas Holzinger	Medical University Graz, Austria
Jang-eui Hong	Chungbuk National University, Korea, Republic of
Ivan Ivanov	SUNY Empire State College, USA
Bo Nørregaard Jørgensen	University of Southern Denmark, Denmark
Dimitris Karagiannis	University of Vienna, Austria
Carlos Kavka	ESTECO SpA, Italy
Foutse Khomh	École Polytechnique, Canada
Mieczyslaw Kokar	Northeastern University, USA
Jitka Komarkova	University of Pardubice, Czech Republic
Jun Kong	North Dakota State University, USA
Dimitri Konstantas	University of Geneva, Switzerland
Nicholas Kraft	The University of Alabama, USA
Martin Kropp	University of Applied Sciences Northwestern Switzerland, Switzerland
Konstantin Läufer	Loyola University Chicago, USA
David Lorenz	Open University, Israel
Ricardo J. Machado	Universidade do Minho, Portugal
Leszek A. Maciaszek	Wroclaw University of Economics, Poland and Macquarie University, Sydney, Australia
Ahmad Kamran Malik	Quaid-i-Azam University, Pakistan
Eda Marchetti	ISTI-CNR, Italy
Cristina Marinescu	Universitatea Politehnica Timisoara, Romania
Katsuhisa Maruyama	Ritsumeikan University, Japan
Tom McBride	University of Technology Sydney, Australia
Emilia Mendes	Blekinge Institute of Technology, Sweden
Marian Cristian Mihaescu	University of Craiova, Romania
Dimitris Mitrakos	Aristotle University of Thessaloniki, Greece
Mattia Monga	Università degli Studi di Milano, Italy
José Arturo Mora-Soto	Carlos III University of Madrid, Spain
Antao Moura	Federal Universisty of Campina Grande (UFCG), Brazil
Henry Muccini	University of L'Aquila, Italy
Yuko Murayama	Iwate Prefectural University, Japan
Takako Nakatani	University of Tsukuba, Japan
Paolo Nesi	University of Florence, Italy
Jianwei Niu	University of Texas at San Antonio, USA
Rory O'Connor	Dublin City University, Ireland
Hanna Oktaba	Universidad National Autonoma de Mexico, Mexico

Xin Peng   Fudan University, China
Dewayne E. Perry   ARiSE, UT Austin, USA
Giuseppe Polese   Università degli Studi di Salerno, Italy
Anders Ravn   Aalborg University, Denmark
Claudio de la Riva   University of Oviedo, Spain
Colette Rolland   Université Paris 1 Panthéon-Sorbonne, France
Gustavo Rossi   Lifia, Argentina
Chanchal Roy   University of Saskatchewan, Canada
Chandan Rupakheti   Rose-Hulman Institute of Technology, USA
Krzysztof Sacha   Warsaw University of Technology, Poland
Francesca Saglietti   University of Erlangen-Nuremberg, Germany
Maria-Isabel   Carlos III University of Madrid, Spain
  Sanchez-Segura
Luis Fernandez Sanz   University of Alcala, Spain
Riccardo Scandariato   iMinds-DistriNet, KU Leuven, Belgium
Giuseppe Scanniello   University of Basilicata, Italy
Bradley Schmerl   Carnegie Mellon University, USA
Beijun Shen   Shanghai Jiaotong University, China
Istvan Siket   Hungarian Academy of Science, Research Group on
                                    Artificial Intelligence, Hungary
Harvey Siy   University of Nebraska at Omaha, USA
Anongnart Srivihok   Kasetsart University, Thailand
Bedir Tekinerdogan   Bilkent University, Turkey
Massimo Tivoli   University of L'Aquila, Italy
Davide Tosi   University of Insubria, Italy
Yuh-Min Tseng   National Changhua University of Education, Taiwan
Burak Turhan   University of Oulu, Finland
László Vidács   University of Szeged, Hungary
Sergiy Vilkomir   East Carolina University, USA
Gianluigi Viscusi   EPFL-CDM, Switzerland
Christiane Gresse von   UFSC - Federal University of Santa Catarina, Brazil
  Wangenheim
Bin Xu   Tsinghua University, China
Hong Zhu   Oxford Brookes University, UK

ICSOFT-EA Additional Reviewers

Mariano Di Claudio   University of Florence, Italy
Estrela Ferreira Cruz   Instituto Politécnico de Viana do Castelo, Portugal
Huseyin Ergin   University of Alabama, USA
Cynthya García   UC3M, Spain
Ana Lima   Associação CCG/ZGDV - Centro de Computação Gráfica,
                                    Portugal
Bernardi Mario Luca   University of Sannio, Italy
Giacomo Martelli   Università degli Studi di Firenze, Italy
João Moreira   University of Porto, Portugal

Alvaro Navas   Universidad Politécnica de Madrid, Spain
Ana Cristina Ramada   Feup, Portugal
  Paiva
Hugo Parada   UPM, Spain
Yu Sun   Vanderbilt University, USA
Juliana Teixeira   Minho University, Portugal
George K.   Loyola University Chicago, USA
  Thiruvathukal
Robert Yacobellis   Loyola University, Chicago, USA

ICSOFT-PT Program Committee

Markus Aleksy   ABB Corporate Research Center, Germany
Toshiaki Aoki   Japan Advanced Institute of Science and Technology,
                             Japan
Colin Atkinson   University of Mannheim, Germany
Xiaoying Bai   Tsinghua University, China
Alexandre Bergel   Pleiad Lab, University of Chile, Santiago, Chile
Jorge Bernardino   Polytechnic Institute of Coimbra - ISEC, Portugal
Marcello Bonsangue   Leiden University, The Netherlands
Thomas Buchmann   University of Bayreuth, Germany
Dumitru Burdescu   University of Craiova, Romania
Nelio Cacho   Federal University of Rio Grande do Norte, Brazil
Fergal Mc Caffery   Dundalk Institute of Technology, Ireland
Jose Antonio   Universidad Politécnica de Madrid, Spain
  Calvo-Manzano
Mauro Caporuscio   Politecnico di Milano, Italy
Cinzia Cappiello   Politecnico di Milano, Italy
Sergio de Cesare   Brunel University, UK
Kung Chen   National Chengchi University, Taiwan
Marta Cimitile   UNITELMA Sapienza, Italy
Peter Clarke   Florida International University, USA
Kendra Cooper   The University of Texas at Dallas, USA
Sergiu Dascalu   University of Nevada, Reno, USA
Steven Demurjian   University of Connecticut, USA
Juan C. Dueñas   Universidad Politécnica de Madrid, Spain
Maria Jose Escalona   University of Seville, Spain
Jean-Rémy Falleri   Institut Polytechnique de Bordeaux, France
João Faria   FEUP - University of Porto, Portugal
Rita Francese   Università degli Studi di Salerno, Italy
Nikolaos Georgantas   Inria, France
Paola Giannini   Università del Piemonte Orientale, Italy
J. Paul Gibson   TSP - Telecom SudParis, France
Cesar Gonzalez-Perez   Institute of Heritage Sciences (Incipit), Spanish National
                             Research Council (CSIC), Spain
Gregor Grambow   University of Ulm, Germany

Esther Guerra   Universidad Autónoma de Madrid, Spain
Christian Heinlein   Aalen University, Germany
Markus Helfert   Dublin City University, Ireland
Brian Henderson-Sellers   University of Technology, Sydney, Australia
Jose Luis Arciniegas   Universidad del Cauca, Colombia
  Herrera
Jose R. Hilera   University of Alcala, Spain
Andreas Holzinger   Medical University Graz, Austria
Jang-eui Hong   Chungbuk National University, Korea, Republic of
Milan Ignjatovic   Prosoftwarica GmbH, Switzerland
Ivan Ivanov   SUNY Empire State College, USA
Edson A. Oliveira Junior   State University of Maringá, Brazil
Hermann Kaindl   Vienna University of Technology, Austria
Bill Karakostas   City University, UK
Mieczyslaw Kokar   Northeastern University, USA
Jun Kong   North Dakota State University, USA
Martin Kropp   University of Applied Sciences Northwestern Switzerland,
                                   Switzerland
Juan de Lara   Universidad Autónoma de Madrid, Spain
Konstantin Läufer   Loyola University Chicago, USA
Jonathan Lee   National Taiwan University, Taiwan
David Lorenz   Open University, Israel
Ricardo J. Machado   Universidade do Minho, Portugal
Ahmad Kamran Malik   Quaid-i-Azam University, Pakistan
Eda Marchetti   ISTI-CNR, Italy
Jasen Markovski   Eindhoven University of Technology, The Netherlands
Manuel Mazzara   Polytechnic of Milan, Italy
Gergely Mezei   Budapest University of Technology and Economics,
                                   Hungary
Marian Cristian   University of Craiova, Romania
  Mihaescu
Tommi Mikkonen   Institute of Software Systems, Tampere University
                                   of Technology, Finland
Raffaela Mirandola   Politecnico di Milano, Italy
Dimitris Mitrakos   Aristotle University of Thessaloniki, Greece
Mattia Monga   Università degli Studi di Milano, Italy
José Arturo Mora-Soto   Carlos III University of Madrid, Spain
Claude Moulin   JRU CNRS Heudiasyc, University of Compiègne, France
Elena Navarro   University of Castilla-La Mancha, Spain
Paolo Nesi   University of Florence, Italy
Rory O'Connor   Dublin City University, Ireland
Marcos Palacios   University of Oviedo, Spain
Fiona Polack   University of York, UK
Giuseppe Polese   Università degli Studi di Salerno, Italy
Jolita Ralyte   University of Geneva, Switzerland
Anders Ravn   Aalborg University, Denmark

Claudio de la Riva	University of Oviedo, Spain
Colette Rolland	Université Paris 1 Panthéon-Sorbonne, France
Carlos Rossi	Universidad de Málaga, Spain
Gustavo Rossi	Lifia, Argentina
Gunter Saake	Institute of Technical and Business Information Systems, Germany
Maria-Isabel Sanchez-Segura	Carlos III University of Madrid, Spain
Marian Fernández de Sevilla	Alcalá University, Spain
Harvey Siy	University of Nebraska at Omaha, USA
Peter Stanchev	Kettering University, USA
Ernest Teniente	Polytechnic University of Catalonia, Spain
Davide Tosi	University of Insubria, Italy
Gianluigi Viscusi	EPFL-CDM, Switzerland
Christiane Gresse von Wangenheim	UFSC - Federal University of Santa Catarina, Brazil
Andreas Winter	Carl von Ossietzky University Oldenburg, Germany
Jinhui Yao	Xerox Research, USA
Jingyu Zhang	Macquarie University, Australia
Elena Zucca	University of Genova, Italy

ICSOFT-PT Additional Reviewers

Saverio Giallorenzo	Università di Bologna, Italy
Carlos Salgado	Universidade do Minho, Portugal
Reimar Schröter	University of Magdeburg, Germany

Invited Speakers

Emilia Mendes	Blekinge Institute of Technology, Sweden
J.C. (Hans) van Vliet	Vrije Universiteit, The Netherlands
Ivona Brandic	Vienna UT, Austria
Dimitris Karagiannis	University of Vienna, Austria

Contents

Software Paradigm Trends

Software Engineering and Applications

BPMN 2.0 and the Service Interaction Patterns: Can We Support Them All?

Dario Campagna[(✉)], Carlos Kavka, and Luka Onesti

Research and Development Department, ESTECO SPA, Area Science Park,
Padriciano 99, Trieste, Italy
{campagna,kavka,onesti}@esteco.com

Abstract. The Business Process Model and Notation (BPMN) specification version 2.0 represents the amalgamation of best practices within the business modeling community to define the notation and semantics of collaboration diagrams, process diagrams and choreography diagrams. Capturing and managing collaborative processes became a hot topic in the past years, and different choreography modeling languages have emerged. The advancement of such languages let to the definition of the service interaction patterns, a framework for the benchmarking of choreography languages against abstracted forms of representative scenarios. In this paper, we present an assessment of BPMN 2.0 support for service interaction patterns. We evidence the issues that limit the set of supported patterns, and propose enhancements to overcome them.

Keywords: BPMN 2.0 · Collaboration diagrams · Service interaction patterns

1 Introduction

In the past years there has been much activity in developing languages for Business Process Management systems. In particular, languages suited for describing interaction behavior between different services, i.e., for modeling service choreography, have emerged as a key instrument for achieving integration of business applications in a service-oriented architecture (SOA) setting. Examples of such languages are Lets'Dance [1], WS-CDL [2], and WS-BPEL [3].

With the advancement of service choreography languages came the need for consolidated insights into the capability and exploitation of the resulting standard specifications and associated implementations in terms of business requirements. In 2005, Barros et al. concluded that for service-oriented architectures to move forward, it was necessary to shift from thinking in terms of request-response and buyer-seller-shipper interaction scenarios into addressing complex, large-scale, multi-party interactions in a systematic manner. They thus presented in [4] a set of thirteen patterns of service interactions, the *service interaction patterns*. These patterns aim to contribute to the gathering of requirements needed to shed light into the nature of service interactions in collaborative business

© Springer International Publishing Switzerland 2015
A. Holzinger et al. (Eds.): ICSOFT 2014, CCIS 555, pp. 3–20, 2015.
DOI: 10.1007/978-3-319-25579-8_1

processes, where a number of parties, each with its own internal processes, need to interact with one another according to certain pre-agreed rules [4]. The patterns capture different peculiar characteristics of such collaborative processes. The number of involved parties may be in the order of tens or even hundreds, and thus the nature of interactions is rarely only bilateral but rather multilateral. Furthermore, the assumption of strict synchronization of all responses before the next steps in a process breaks down due to the independence of the parties. More realistically, responses are accepted as they arrive. Also, while it is conventional to think of multi-cast interactions as a party sending a request to several other parties, the reverse may also apply, several parties send messages from autonomous events to a party which correlates these into a single request. Finally, not all interactions in dynamic marketplaces follow a requester-respondent-requester structure. Rather, a sender may re-direct interactions to nominated delegates. Receivers may outsource requests, choosing to "stay in the loop" and observe parts of responses. More generally, it may only be possibly to determine the order of interaction at run-time, given, for example, the content of messages passed.

The collected service interaction patterns have been derived and extrapolated from insights into real-scale B2B transaction processing, use cases gathered by standardization committees, generic scenarios identified in industry standards, and case studies reported in the literature. The patterns consolidate recurrent scenarios and abstract them in a way that provides reusable knowledge. They range from simple message exchanges to scenarios involving multiple participants and multiple message exchanges. On the one hand, the service interaction patterns consolidate the nature of service interactions through generalized functional classification. On the other hand, they clear the track for further and ongoing extensions. These patterns allow the assessment of web services standards, and the benchmarking of choreography and orchestration languages, making it possible for SOA technologies to progress further [4].

Since their introduction, the service interaction patterns have been used to evaluate different choreography languages. In this paper, we focus on the latest version of the Business Process Model and Notation, i.e., BPMN version 2.0 [5], and present an assessment of BPMN 2.0 collaboration diagrams support for the service interaction patterns.

The remainder of this paper is structured as follows. In Sect. 2 we recall some of the choreography language analysis based on the service interaction patterns. In Sect. 3, we evaluate BPMN 2.0 for its pattern support, and point out issues that limit the set of representable patterns. To overcome such issues, we propose in Sect. 4 a set of enhancements for BPMN 2.0. The paper conclusions are presented in Sect. 5.

2   Related Work

WS-BPEL [3] has been the first language to be analyzed in terms of service interaction patterns. In [4,6] the authors show that WS-BPEL directly supports

Single Transmission Bilateral Interaction Patterns. For *Single Transmission Multilateral Interaction Patterns*, WS-BPEL imposes some restrictions to the *Send/Receive* pattern and requires "house-keeping" code for correlation and for capturing stop and success conditions. WS-BPEL provides support for two of the three *Multi Transmission Interaction Patterns*. Lack of sufficient transaction support compromises a WS-BPEL solution for *Atomic Multicast Notification*. All the *Routing Patterns* are supported with the exception of *Dynamic Routing*, which is outside the scope of WS-BPEL.

In [7] the authors show that BPMN 1.0 directly supports only five of the thirteen service interaction patterns, and present extensions for BPMN 1.0 that allow the representation of multiple participants, reference passing, and correlation. They introduce the concept of *participant set* in order to represent a set of participants of the same type involved in the same conversation, and the concept of *reference* to distinguish individual participant out of a participant set. A reference is a special data object, it can be connected to flow objects via directed associations, and can be passed to other participants connecting it to message flows with undirected associations. Thanks to these extensions, the number of patterns supported by BPMN 1.0 increases to ten. *Contingent Request* is only partially supported, while *Dynamic Routing* is excluded from the analysis.

The BPMN 2.0 specification extends the scope and capabilities of BPMN 1.0 in several areas. Among other improvements, it describes the execution semantics for all BPMN elements, defines an extensibility mechanism for process model extensions, and defines a choreography model. BPMN 2.0 choreographies are evaluated in [8] by using an extended quality framework, which includes the service interaction patterns. Since the patterns only cover one perspective of the requirements for choreography definition languages, the framework also includes other perspectives paying special attention to graphical notations. The evaluation identifies a number of issues in BPMN 2.0 that affects the perceptual discriminability of certain choreography modeling constructs. To address these deficiencies, the authors propose the introduction of new concepts in choreography diagrams. Examples are the concept of channel annotations, message multiplicity for message flows, and annotations for message flows to indicate which participant initiates a conversation. In [9] the authors considered a precise analysis of the support of the service interaction patterns in BPMN 2.0 as an important future work. However, such a study is still missing.

3   Pattern Analysis

We present in this section an assessment of BPMN 2.0 support for the service interaction patterns introduced by Barros et al. in [4]. This section is organized by following the structure of [4]. For each pattern, we present its description and issues, and propose a BPMN 2.0 implementation. The implementations and their semantics are described in natural language. For most of the patterns, we include a BPMN 2.0 graphical representation of the implementation. We provide no formal validation of the proposed solutions, since the only complete BPMN 2.0 semantics specification is presented in [5] by using natural language.

As we will show, BPMN 2.0 directly supports the *Single Transmission Bilateral Interaction Patterns*, two of the three *Single Transmission Multilateral Interaction Patterns*, the *Multi-responses* pattern, and two of the three *Routing Patterns*. With the addition of a BPMN 2.0 extension for collaborations and message queuing, it is possible to support the *One-to-many Send/Receive* pattern and the *Contingent Requests* pattern too. The *Atomic Multicast Notification* pattern can only be partially supported. We excluded from this assessment the *Dynamic Routing* pattern since its description is too imprecise, as already noted in [7,10].

From now on, with the term *party* we indicate a BPMN 2.0 participant instance, and with the term *parties* we indicate a set of heterogeneous BPMN 2.0 participant instances, i.e., instances of one or more BPMN 2.0 participants.

3.1   Single Transmission Bilateral Interaction Patterns

Single transmission bilateral interaction patterns correspond to elementary interactions where a party sends (receives) a message, and as a result expects a reply (sends a reply). These patterns cover one-way and round-trip non-routed bilateral interactions.

Send

Description. A party X sends a message to another party.
Issues. The counter-party may or may not be known at design time.

The *Send* interaction pattern can be modeled as shown in Fig. 1(a). A *send task* in a participant X sends a message to a participant Y. If participant Y has multiplicity greater than one (i.e., there may be more than one instance of Y in execution at the same time), then we can add a reference for Y to the sent message payload, and use context-based correlation in Y to route the message to the correct instance. It is assumed that the sender gains knowledge about the receiver reference and stores it in, e.g., a data object.

Receive

Description. A party X receives a message from another party.

The *Receive* interaction pattern can be modeled by using a *receive task* in a participant X. The task receives a message from a participant Y, as shown in Fig. 1(b). If Y has multiplicity greater than one, then we can use context-based correlation in X to accept only messages from a particular instance of Y.

Send/Receive

Description. A party X engages in two casually related interactions: in the first interaction X sends a message to another party Y, while in the second one X receives a message from Y.

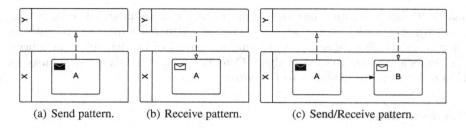

(a) Send pattern. (b) Receive pattern. (c) Send/Receive pattern.

Fig. 1. Single transmission bilateral interaction patterns.

Issues. The counter-party may or may not be known in advance. The outgoing and incoming messages must be correlated.

The *Send/Receive* interaction pattern is depicted in Fig. 1(c). It can be modeled with a *send task* followed by a *receive task* in a participant X. The former task sends a message to a participant Y, the latter receives a message from Y. If Y has multiplicity greater than one, then we can make use of context-based correlation for communicating with the desired instance of Y, and take advantage of key-based correlation to correlate outgoing and incoming messages in X.

3.2 Single Transmission Multilateral Interaction Patterns

Single transmission multilateral interaction patterns cover non-routed interactions where a party may send or receive multiple messages, but as part of different interaction threads dedicated to different parties.

Racing Incoming Messages

Description. A party X expects to receive one among a set of messages. Messages may be structurally different and may come from different parties. The way a message is processed depends on its type and/or the party from which it comes.

The *Racing Incoming Messages* interaction pattern can be modeled by using an *event based gateway* connected to *catch message events* in a participant X, as depicted in Fig. 2(a). Each catch message event receives messages of a certain type, or from a particular participant.

One-to-many Send

Description. A party X sends a message to several other parties. All the messages have the same type (although their contents may differ).
Issues. The number of parties to whom the message is sent may or may not be known at design time.

Under the assumption that receiving parties are instances of a single participant, this pattern can be thought as variant of the *Send* pattern when participant Y

has multiplicity greater than one. The pattern can be modeled as shown in Fig. 2(b). A *parallel multi-instance send task* A in participant X receives as input a *data object collection* containing references of participant Y instances, and sends a message to each of them. Context-based correlation can be used in Y in order to route messages to the correct instances.

One-from-many Receive

Description. A party X receives several logically related messages arising from autonomous events occurring at different parties. The arrival of messages needs to be timely so that they can be correlated as a single logical request.

Issues. Since messages originate from autonomous parties, a mechanism is needed to determine which incoming messages should be grouped together.

Under the assumption that sending parties are instances of a single participant, this pattern can be viewed as a variant of the *Receive* pattern when the sending participant Y has multiplicity greater than one. The pattern can be modeled as depicted in Fig. 2(c). A *loop receive task* A with an *interrupting boundary timer event* is used in participant X to receive messages from participant Y instances. Context-based correlation can be used in X to accept only messages from certain instances of participant Y.

One-to-many Send/Receive

Description. A party X sends a request to several other parties, which may be all identical or logically related. Responses are expected within a given time-frame. However, some responses may not arrive within the time-frame and some parties may even not respond at all.

Issues. The number of parties to which messages are sent may or may not be known at design time. Responses need to be correlated to their corresponding requests.

A BPMN 2.0 representation of this pattern is shown in Fig. 2(d). We use in participant X a *multi-instance sub-process* with an *interrupting boundary timer event*, and whose *loop data input* is a *data object collection* containing references to instances of a participant Y. The sub-process contains a *send task* followed by a *receive task*. Each instance of the sub-process sends a message to an instance of Y (context-based correlation is used in Y), and then waits for a response. Responses could be correlated to their corresponding request by using key-based correlation in X. However, BPMN 2.0 correlation works at process instance level, i.e., we can only correlate a message to a specific instance of a process. To support this pattern we need to correlate received messages to a particular instance of the sub-process, and this is not possible in BPMN 2.0. To overcome this limitation, we propose a BPMN 2.0 extension for collaboration/conversations, and a modification of message correlation semantics, which will be described in Sect. 4.

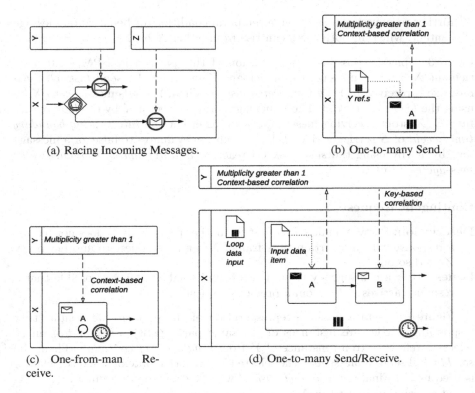

(a) Racing Incoming Messages.   (b) One-to-many Send.

(c) One-from-man   Re-   (d) One-to-many Send/Receive.
ceive.

Fig. 2. Single transmission multilateral interaction patterns.

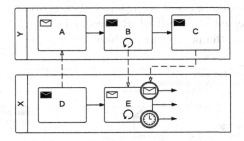

Fig. 3. Multi-responses pattern.

3.3   Multi Transmission Interaction Patterns

Multi transmission interaction patterns are dedicated to non-routed interactions
in which a party sends (receives) messages to (from) the same party.

Multi-responses

Description. Party X sends a request to party Y, then X receives any number
of responses from Y until no further responses are required. The trigger of no

further responses can rise from a temporal condition, or be based on message content, which in both cases can rise from either X or Y.

Figure 3 depicts a possible representation of this pattern in BPMN 2.0. Participant X sends a message to participant Y by using the *send task D*. Such message is received in Y by the *receive task A*. Then, Y sends messages to X by using the *loop send task B*. These messages are received in X by the *loop receive task E*. X stops receiving message as soon as either the *interrupting boundary timer event* of E is triggered, or E loop condition evaluates to false, or a message sent by Y (by using the *send task C*) reaches the *interrupting boundary catch message event* of E.

Contingent Requests

Description. Party X makes a request to another party Y. If X does not receive a response within a certain time-frame, X sends a request to another party Z, and so on.

Issues. After a contingency request has been issued, it may be possible that a response arrives (late) from a previous request.

Figure 4 depicts a possible representation of the pattern (we assume that responding parties are instances of the same participant). First, a *task* in X selects a reference to an instance of Y from a *data object collection*. Then, the *send task A* sends a message to the selected Y instance (context-based correlation is used in Y). Finally, the *receive task B* waits for a response from Y. Context-based correlation is used in X to accept only messages containing the selected Y instance reference in their payloads. If no response is received before the *interrupting timer boundary event* is triggered, then another Y instance reference is selected and processed as described. Responses that arrive late from previous requests are discarded thanks to context-based correlation.

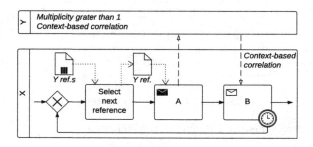

Fig. 4. Contingent Requests pattern, solution (1).

The just described implementation of the pattern exploits one of the three available solutions to handle the late response issue. The first solution (1) is to disallow late arrivals altogether, and receive only the response of the current request. Another solution (2) is to accept the first response even if it is late and

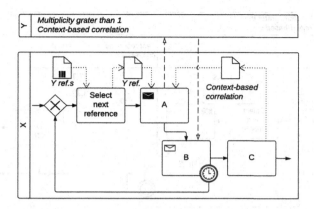

Fig. 5. Contingent Requests pattern, solution (2).

stop outstanding requests. The last solution (3) is to accept the first arriving response, trigger the end of outstanding request, but receive any further response that arrives (before X terminates). The pattern does not predispose which of the three solutions prevails. Solution (1) is the one adopted in Fig. 4.

To support solution (2) we modify the workflow in Fig. 4 adding to it a *data object* and a *task C*. The resulting workflow is shown in Fig. 5. We use the new data object for context-based correlation in X. We initialize this data object with some value, and add this value to the payload of messages sent to Y instances. Only messages from Y instances containing the chosen value in their payload are accepted in X. As soon as a response is received by B, the task C executes and changes the value of the new data object. Any other message coming from Y instances will then be discarded by context-based correlation. With the workflow in Fig. 5 we accept late responses, but we may lose messages that arrive after the interrupting boundary timer event has been triggered and before the activation of B. Hence, the response we receive in X may not be the first sent from Y. To avoid losing responses, we propose a modification to the message semantics. This modification will be described in Sect. 4.2.

Solution (3) does not specify how late responses arriving after the first one should be managed upon receipt. Assuming that such responses can all be managed in the same way, Solution (3) can be supported by modifying the workflow in Fig. 5 adding to it a *data object collection*, a *multi-instance receive task*, and defining two *conversations*. Figure 6 depicts the resulting workflow. We store in the new data object collection the references of Y instances that will receive a message. The first conversation, named *First response*, groups the message flow exiting from A and the message flow entering in B, and is associated to a correlation key based on the data object *Key*. The second conversation, named *Other responses*, groups the message flow exiting from A and the one entering into the multi instance receive task D. *Other responses* is associated to a correlation key based on the payload of messages sent from A. The two correlation keys will be such that messages that correlate with one keys do not correlate with the other key. As soon as a response is received by B, the task C executes and changes the

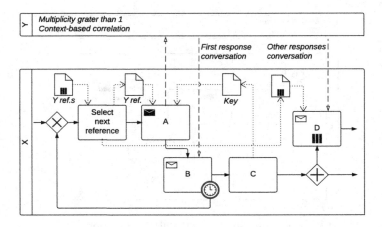

Fig. 6. Contingent Requests pattern, solution (3).

value of the new data object. Any other message coming from Y instances will be correlated to the *Other responses* conversation, and received by an instance of task D. Since we are assuming that late responses succeeding the first response from Y can all be treated in the same way, we do not care which instance of D receives a particular response from Y. With the workflow in Fig. 6, we accept late responses but again we may lose messages that arrive when no receive task is active. Hence, the response received by B may not be the first sent from Y, and D instances may not receive all other late responses. The modification to the message semantics that will be described in Sect. 4.2 will help to solve these issues. If we want a response from Y to be received by a particular instance of D, then deep changes to the BPMN 2.0 message correlation mechanism are needed. A precise analysis of such changes is out of the scope of this assessment.

Atomic Multicast Notification

Description. A party sends notifications to several parties such that a certain number of parties are required to accept the notification within a certain time-frame. For example, all parties or just one party are required to accept the notification. In general, the constraint for successful notification applies over a range between a minimum and maximum number.

Issues. The constraint that all parties should have received the notification, means that if any one party received the notification, all the other parties also received it. Thus, some kind of transactional support is required.

The main issue of this pattern relates to atomic transactions. Atomic transactions have an all-or-nothing property: the actions taken by a transaction participant prior to commit are only tentative (typically they are neither persistent nor made visible outside the transaction); if all participants were able to execute successfully then transactions are committed; if a participant aborts or does not respond at all, all transactions are aborted. Web Service Atomic Transaction [11] is an OASIS standard that defines protocols for atomic transactions, one of them is Two-Phase Commit (2PC). The 2PC protocol coordinates registered participants to reach a commit or abort decision, and ensures that all participants are informed of the final result.

BPMN 2.0 provides built-in support for business transaction through the notion of *transaction sub-process*. A sub-process marked as transactional means that its component activities must either all complete successfully or the sub-process must be restored to its original consistent state. However, business transactions are usually not ACID transactions coordinated via the 2PC protocol. The reason is they fail the isolation requirement. In order to isolate, or lock, the resource performing the component activities of the transaction, the transaction must be short-running, taking milliseconds to complete. For business transactions it is not possible to make that assumption. Business transactions are long-running, and the resources associated with their component tasks are not locked while the transaction is in progress. Instead, each activity in the transaction executes normally in its turn, but if the transaction as a whole fails to complete successfully, each of its activities that has completed already is undone by executing its defined compensating activity. Hence, BPMN 2.0 provides no support for atomic transactions, but different workarounds can be provided for the *Atomic Multicast Notification* pattern. These workarounds will be described in Sect. 4.3.

3.4   Routing Patterns

Routing patterns cover routed interactions, i.e., interactions involving transfers of party references.

Request with Referral

Description. Party X sends a request to party Y indicating that any follow-up should be sent to a number of other parties $(Z_1, Z_2, \ldots, Z_n)$ depending on the evaluation of a certain condition.

Issues. Party Y may or may not have a prior knowledge of the identity of the other parties. The information transferred from X to Y must therefore allow Y to interact with the other parties.

This pattern can be represented in BPMN 2.0 as shown in Fig. 7. A *data object collection* in participant X contains references to instances of participant Z that should receive the follow-ups (we assume that the referred parties are all instances of the same participant). The data object collection is transferred to participant Y through a message sent by the *send task A* in X. The *receive task B* in Y receives the message from A, and stores its payload (i.e., the collection of references) into a data object collection. Then, the *multi-instance send task C* in Y sends a message to each instance of Z referenced in the data object collection (context-based correlation is used in Z).

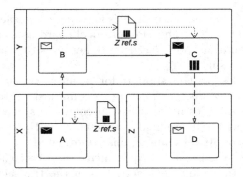

Fig. 7. Request with Referral pattern.

Relayed Request

Description. Party X makes a request to party Y which delegates the request
to other parties $(Z_1, Z_2, \ldots, Z_n)$. $Z_1, Z_2, \ldots, Z_n$ then continue interactions
with X while Y observes a view of the interactions including faults.

Issues. The delegated parties $(Z_1, Z_2, \ldots, Z_n)$ may or may not have prior knowledge of the identity of the request originator, i.e., party X. The information
transferred from party Y to the delegated parties must therefore allow these
to fully identify and interact with X.

Figure 8 depicts the BPMN 2.0 representation of this pattern. The *send task*
A in participant X sends a message containing the reference of X in its payload
to participant Y. The message is received by an *intermediate catch message event*
and its payload is stored into a *data object*. Subsequently, the *multi-instance send
task* C in Y sends a message containing the reference of X in its payload to each
instance of participant Z referenced in a *data object collection* (context-based
correlation is used in Z, we assume that delegated parties are all instances of
the same participant). Each message sent by task C reaches a different instance
of the *receive task* E, that in its turn transfers the payload into a data object.
The *send task* F and G in Z executes in parallel. The task F sends messages
to Y, allowing it to monitor interactions between Z and X through the *loop
receive task* D. The task G sends messages to the *loop receive task* B in order
to continue the interaction with the participant X. Context-based correlation is
used in X to receive messages from the delegated parties.

4   BPMN 2.0 Enhancements

We describe in this section the proposed set of enhancements for BPMN 2.0 that
improve its support for service interaction patterns.

4.1   Initiator Extension

In this section, we introduce the concept of collaboration/conversation *initiator*,
and modify the message correlation semantics in order to move message routing

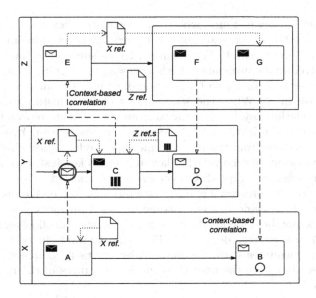

Fig. 8. Relayed Request pattern.

at the initiator level. Then, we show how such extensions help supporting the *One-to-many Send/Receive* pattern with the BPMN 2.0 workflow described in Sect. 3.2.

Business processes typically can run for days or even months, requiring asynchronous communication via messages. Moreover, many instances of a particular process will typically run in parallel, e.g., many instances of an order process, each representing a particular order. Correlation is used to associate a particular message to an ongoing conversation between two particular process instances. BPMN 2.0 allows using existing message data for correlation purposes, rather than requiring the introduction of technical correlation data [5].

The concept of correlation facilitates the association of a message to a process instance send task (throw message event) or receive task (catch message event) often in the context of a conversation, which is also known as instance routing. This association can be viewed at multiple levels, namely the collaboration (conversation), choreography, and process level. However, the actual correlation happens during runtime (e.g., at the process level). Correlations describe a set of predicates on a message (generally on the payload) that need to be satisfied in order for that message to be associated to a distinct process instance send task (throw message event) or receive task (catch message event).

In plain key-based correlation, messages that are exchanged within a conversation are logically correlated by means of one or more common correlation keys. A correlation key represents a composite key out of one or many correlation properties. A correlation property essentially specifies an extraction expressions atop a message. At run time, the first sent or received message in a conversation populates at least one of the correlation key instances. If a follow-up message derives a correlation key instance, where that correlation key had previously been initialized within the conversation, then the correlation key value in the message and conversation must match. For example, let us suppose to have participant X and Y involved in a conversation with a message flow going from a send task in X to a receive task in Y, and a message flow going from a send task in Y to a receive task in X. When the send task of the i-th instance of X sends a message, a correlation key is instantiated from the message payload. When the receive task of the i-th instance of X receives a message from Y, a correlation key instance is derived from the received message payload, and checked against the previously instantiated correlation key. If the two key instances match, then the received message is accepted. Otherwise, it is discarded.

Key-based correlation allows one to route messages to receive tasks (or catch message events) in specific process instances, based on messages payloads. In some cases, this may be not enough. For example, in the workflow for the *One-to-many Send/Receive* pattern depicted in Fig. 2(d), we want the task B to receive a message that correlates with the one sent by the task A. Hence, we want to route messages from Y to the task B in specific instances of the multi-instance sub-process in X.

BPMN 2.0 does not provide a way to indicate which element (e.g., participant, activity, etc.) involved in a conversation initiates the communication. Such information can be useful to better understand the sequence of interactions determined by message flows in a conversation. Moreover, the knowledge of the conversation initiator is fundamental for moving message correlation to a level different from the one of process instances. We propose a BPMN 2.0 extension, called *initiator*, which allows one to specify the id of the element initiating a conversation.

The following is the XSD schema for the initiator extension.

```
<xsd:schema ...>
  <xsd:element name="initiator" type="tInitiator"/>
  <xsd:complexType name="tInitiator">
    <xsd:attribute name="initiatorId" type="xsd:string" use="required"/>
  </xsd:complexType>
</xsd:schema>
```

The initiator element can be used to specify the initiator of a collaboration as follows.

```
<bpmn:definitions ...>
  ...
  <bpmn:extension mustUnderstand="false" definition="esteco:initiator"/>
  ...
  <bpmn:collaboration ...>
    <bpmn:extensionElements>
      <esteco:initiator initiatorId="_11"/>
    </bpmn:extensionElements>
    ...
  </bpmn:collaboration>
  ...
</bpmn:definitions>
```

In key-based correlation, correlation key instances are associated to conversation instances. A conversation instance is associated to the process instances that it involves. We propose to associate conversation instances to their initiators. Thanks to this association, a received message can be routed to a specific initiator instance. The modified key-based correlation mechanism works as follows. When a message is sent by an initiator instance, a correlation key is instantiated and associated to the corresponding conversation instance. When a message reaches the initiator, the correlation key instance derived from the message payload is matched with correlation key instances associated to conversation instances. If a match is found, the message is routed to the initiator instance associated to the matching conversation.

Let us now consider the *One-to-many Send/Receive* workflow depicted in Fig. 2(d). The initiator in the conversation between X and Y is the sub-process in X. At run-time, for each message sent by task A, a correlation key is instantiated and associated to an instance of the conversation. Each sub-process instance is associated to a different conversation instance. Each message sent by Y generates a correlation key instance that is matched with the correlation key instances of conversation instances. When a match is found, the message is routed to the sub-process instance associated to the matching conversation, and received by the correct instance of task B.

4.2   Message Queuing

In Sect. 3.3 we proposed three BPMN 2.0 representation of *Contingent Requests*. The representation depicted in Fig. 5 and the one shown in Fig. 6 have a flaw, i.e., late responses may be lost.

In order to overcome this limitation, we propose the introduction of *message queuing*. We associate a queue to each message flow. A message directed to a receive task or catch message event in a process, is stored in the queue of the message flow it is traversing when it cannot be received (e.g., when the receive task to which it is directed to is not yet active). As soon as a receive task or catch message event becomes active, it looks for messages in the message queue. If message correlation is used, only messages that correlate with some key are stored in queues.

Thanks to message queuing, responses that reach participant X when the receive task B in Fig. 5 is not yet active are not lost. Let us suppose a message from Y reaches X just after the interrupting timer boundary events of B has been triggered. The message is stored in a queue for the message flow entering task B. After the selection of the next Y reference and the execution of A, B becomes active and immediately receives the message that was previously stored in the queue. Message queuing also avoid losing messages in the workflow depicted in Fig. 6.

4.3   Workarounds for Atomic Transactions

As we already pointed out in Sect. 3.3, BPMN 2.0 provides no support for atomic transactions. Nevertheless, different workarounds can be provided for the *Atomic Multicast Notification* pattern.

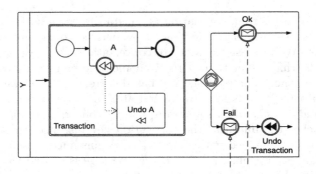

Fig. 9. Example of usage of transaction sub-process, compensating activity, and compensation events.

The first workaround consists in enforcing *quasi-atomicity* [12]. Quasi-atomicity is related to the ability to undo certain parts of a process execution. Using this mechanism, receiving parties can perform the work associated to received requests, and compensate for it in case of failure. However, the effect of the performed work is visible to other parties, thus violating the principle of atomicity. Quasi-atomicity can be enforced in BPMN 2.0 by exploiting its built-in support for business transactions. Each receiving party can use a *transaction sub-process* to perform the work associated to the received request. Activities within the transaction that need to be undone if the transaction fails can be connected with their respective *compensating activities* by using *compensating boundary events*. Figure 9 depicts an example of usage of such BPMN 2.0 elements. Participant Y executes a transaction through a transaction sub-process. The transaction only consists of a task A connected to its respective compensating activity. After the execution of the transaction sub-process, Y awaits for an "Ok" or a "Fail" message. If a "Fail" message is received, the *compensation event* "Undo Transaction", targeted to the transaction sub-process, triggers the compensating activity of A and rolls back the transaction to its initial state.

The second workaround is a BPMN 2.0 encoding of the 2PC protocol as a sequence of sub-interactions, in a way similar to the one proposed in [4]. In the first phase, a "prepare" message is sent from the coordinating party to each receiving party. Each receiver deals with this message with a separate sub-process, which eventually will send back a "ready" message to the coordinator. After the timeout, the responses are counted to determine whether the minimum and maximum constraint are satisfied. Then, the second phase has a related set of sub-processes for each party providing a "commit" or "reject" message. Different payloads may be included in the first and second phase messages. As part of the first phase of interactions, contacted parties might only see a limited content of the message, enough to decide whether they are ready to accept the request or not. In the second phase, selected parties see all details needed to act on the request. Transaction sub-processes, compensating activities, and compensation events may be used to enforce quasi-atomicity in the second phase.

The third workaround is a variant of *One-to-many Send/Receive* pattern with a completion condition at the notifying side, as proposed in [7].

5   Conclusions

In this paper, we investigated BPMN 2.0 support for the service interaction patterns [4], and proposed a set of enhancements to broaden it.

We assessed that BPMN 2.0 collaboration diagrams directly supports nine of the thirteen patterns, i.e., the three *Single Transmission Bilateral Interaction Patterns*, *Racing Incoming Messages*, *One-to-many Send*, *One-from-many Receive*, *Multi-responses*, *Request with Referral*, and *Relayed Request*. Standard BPMN 2.0 supports *Contingent Requests* when we choose to disallow late responses altogether. The BPMN 1.0 extensions presented in [7] are not necessary in BPMN 2.0, since it supports multiple participants and message correlation out of the box, and since reference passing [7] can be modeled by using data objects/data inputs/data outputs, messages, and context-based correlation.

We proposed three enhancements to broaden BPMN 2.0 support for service interaction patterns. The first is an extension called *initiator* that together with a modification of the key-based message correlation semantics allows the representation of the *One-to-many Send/Receive* pattern. The second enhancement consists in the use of *message queues* to fully support the *Contingent requests* pattern. The last enhancement is a set of workarounds for *Atomic Multicast Notification*. Thanks to these enhancements, BPMN 2.0 supports eleven of the thirteen patterns.

Future work will include the study of BPMN 2.0 extensions to further improve the *Contingent request* pattern support. We also plan to evaluate BPMN 2.0 as a whole, comparing and combining our results with the ones presented in [8]. Moreover, we consider a π-calculus formalization of the BPMN 2.0 semantics as an important future work. Such a formalization would make it possible for a formal validation of the proposed pattern representations, since a π-calculus formalization of the service interaction patterns has already been presented in [13].

Acknowledgements. The authors thank the reviewers for the very useful comments that have contributed to enhance the paper.

References

1. Zaha, J.M., Barros, A., Dumas, M., ter Hofstede, A.: Let's dance: a language for service behavior modeling. In: Meersman, R., Tari, Z. (eds.) OTM 2006. LNCS, vol. 4275, pp. 145–162. Springer, Heidelberg (2006)
2. W3C: Web Services Choreography Description Language Version 1.0. http://www.w3.org/TR/ws-cdl-10/ (2005)
3. OASIS: Web Services Business Process Execution Language Version 2.0. http://docs.oasis-open.org/wsbpel/2.0/OS/wsbpel-v2.0-OS.html (2007)

4. Barros, A., Dumas, M., Hofstede, A.: Service interaction patterns: towards a reference framework for service-based business process interconnection. Technical report FIT-TR-2005-02, Faculty of IT, Queensland University of Technology (2005)
5. OMG: Business Process Model and Notation (BPMN) Version 2.0 (2011). http://www.omg.org/spec/BPMN/2.0
6. Barros, A., Dumas, M., ter Hofstede, A.H.M.: Service interaction patterns. In: van der Aalst, W.M.P., Benatallah, B., Casati, F., Curbera, F. (eds.) BPM 2005. LNCS, vol. 3649, pp. 302–318. Springer, Heidelberg (2005)
7. Decker, G., Puhlmann, F.: Extending BPMN for modeling complex choreographies. In: Tari, Z., Meersman, R. (eds.) OTM 2007, Part I. LNCS, vol. 4803, pp. 24–40. Springer, Heidelberg (2007)
8. Cortes-Cornax, M., Dupuy-Chessa, S., Rieu, D., Dumas, M.: Evaluating choreographies in BPMN 2.0 using an extended quality framework. In: Dijkman, R., Hofstetter, J., Koehler, J. (eds.) BPMN 2011. LNBIP, vol. 95, pp. 103–117. Springer, Heidelberg (2011)
9. Cortes-Cornax, M., Dupuy-Chessa, S., Rieu, D.: Choreographies in BPMN 2.0: new challenges and open questions. In: Proceedings of the 4th Central-European Workshop on Services and their Composition, ZEUS-2012, vol. 847, pp. 50–57 (2012)
10. Decker, G., Overdick, H., Zaha, J.M.: On the suitability of WS-CDL for choreography modeling. In: Proceedings of Methoden, Konzepte und Technologien für die Entwicklung von dienstebasierten Informationssystemen, EMISA 2006 (2006)
11. OASIS: Web Services Atomic Transaction (WS-AtomicTransaction) Version 1.2 (2009). http://docs.oasis-open.org/ws-tx/wstx-wsat-1.2-spec-os/wstx-wsat-1.2-spec-os.html
12. Hagen, C., Alonso, G.: Exception handling in workflow management systems. IEEE Trans. Softw. Eng. **26**, 943–958 (2000)
13. Decker, G., Puhlmann, F., Weske, M.: Formalizing service interactions. In: Dustdar, S., Fiadeiro, J.L., Sheth, A.P. (eds.) BPM 2006. LNCS, vol. 4102, pp. 414–419. Springer, Heidelberg (2006)

Design Patterns for Model-Driven Development

Timo Vepsäläinen[✉] and Seppo Kuikka

Department of Automation Science and Engineering, Tampere University
of Technology, P.O Box 692, 33101 Tampere, Finland
{timo.vepsalainen,seppo.kuikka}@tut.fi

Abstract. Design patterns document solutions to recurring design and
development challenges. UML, which is the de-facto modeling language
in software development, supports defining and using patterns with its
Collaboration concepts. However, as is demonstrated in the paper, the
support is not sufficient for all kinds of patterns and all meaningful ways
to use patterns. In this paper, the use of design patterns is suggested
for documentation purposes in Model-Driven Development. The pattern
support of UML is complemented with an approach that does not con-
strain the nature of pattern solutions. The approach is tool-supported
in a model-driven development tool environment for basic control and
safety-related control applications, UML AP tool. The developed tool
support includes instantiating and highlighting patterns in models as
well as gathering documentation on use of patterns, which could especially benefit safety system development.

Keywords: Design pattern · Model-driven development · Safety · Tool
support

1 Introduction

Design patterns document proven solutions to recurring challenges in design and
development work. Patterns capture expert solutions for reuse purposes and aid
communication by giving names to known solutions. Support for patterns is
included also in UML, which is the de-facto modeling language in software development. The support is based on Collaboration and CollaborationUse concepts
[21] that have been developed along the entire language, from parameterized
collaborations [24].

However, in addition to the standard approach, many tool vendors, e.g. No
Magic [20], have implemented additional pattern support in a more ad hoc manner. Such pattern support is in many tools based on informal templates that can
be copied to models to create instances of the patterns. Copying the templates
may also utilize wizards that enable modifying pattern occurrences by selecting
existing elements for pattern-specific roles, for instance. However, without explicitly indicating pattern instances, the information about them is endangered to
vanish. With application specific names of classes and interfaces, for instance,
the pattern instances can be difficult to notice for both developers and the tools.

© Springer International Publishing Switzerland 2015
A. Holzinger et al. (Eds.): ICSOFT 2014, CCIS 555, pp. 21–38, 2015.
DOI: 10.1007/978-3-319-25579-8_2

UML, thus, aims to support defining patterns and their instances in models. It appears that the UML pattern concepts have been designed with traditional GoF (Gang of Four) [12] patterns in mind: with focus on classes and their contents. However, as will be demonstrated, the UML Collaborations may not be sufficient for all kinds of patterns and foreseeable, meaningful ways to use patterns. Nevertheless, when patterns are utilized in software projects, documenting their use in models could be of great value. Especially this is the case with development processes that emphasize the use of models in place of written documentation, e.g. Model-Driven Development (MDD). In MDD, the information that is required for producing documentation should be in the models.

In some domains of applications, the information content of documentation is even governed by regulations and standards, in addition to development needs. For example, the development processes and techniques of safety systems and applications are governed by standards such as IEC 61508 [15]. In addition to using standard-compliant methods and techniques, a developer of such a system must be able to prove the compliance of the developed system. This is where the relevant documentation is needed.

This paper addresses the aforementioned issues by extending the work in [28] with support for design patterns of safety systems [29]. A pattern modeling approach is presented that is not restricted to the contents of UML classifiers only. Safety Systems are supported with specific pattern concepts and means for organizing related patterns to catalogues. The approach is tool-supported in UML AP (UML Automation Profile) tool environment [26] for MDD of control applications. The contributions of this paper are as follows. Shortcomings in UML pattern support are demonstrated. A set of non-restrictive patterns concepts is presented and rationalized. The Use of the pattern concepts for documenting the solutions of safety systems and producing documentation is demonstrated.

The rest of this paper is organized as follows. Section 2 reviews work related to modeling and using design patterns in UML context. Section 3 outlines and discusses how the use of patterns could benefit specifically MDD and safety system development. The means of UML for pattern modeling are presented in Sect. 4, in addition to pointing out shortcomings in the approach. Section 5 presents the new patterns modeling concepts. Tool support for using patterns is presented in Sect. 6. Conclusions are drawn in Sect. 7.

2   Related Work

The roots of design patterns, as a concept, lie in building architecture and in the work of Christopher Alexander, see [2,3]. In software development, the use of patterns began to gain popularity after the publication of the GoF patterns [12]. The application area of the GoF patterns was object oriented programming. However, support for patterns was also developed into UML in the form of the collaborations.

In addition to area of expertise, e.g. building and software engineering, design patterns vary with respect to their abstraction levels and detailedness. For example, Lasater [19] describes patterns as design tools for improving existing code (on the programming language level) whereas [6] focuses on architectural patterns that can have varying implementations. Patterns for safety system development can be found e.g. in [22], the patterns mainly describing the roles of their elements and their responsibilities in basic control and safety systems.

The need for automated tool support to define and use design patterns in models has been identified by several researchers. Support has also been developed for specifying patterns, detecting pattern instances, detecting parts in models where to apply patterns and for instantiating and visualizing patterns in models. For example, [10] presents a formal pattern specification technique that is based on UML. It is intended for specifying design patterns and checking the conformance of pattern instances to their specifications. In publication [11], automatic transformations are developed for refactoring patterns into models. The approach is based on the specifications of pattern-specific problems, solutions and model transformations to apply the solutions.

Detection of points in models where to apply design patterns has been studied, among others, in [5]. Detection rules are specified with Object Constraint Language (OCL) and combined with decision trees. Detecting design pattern instances has been studied in [25]. The approach is based on representing both the models and patterns with graphs and applying graph similarity scoring.

Automating the application and evolution of design patterns has been proposed and studied e.g. in [8,18,30]. In [8], QVT (Query/View/Transformation) transformations are developed for evolving pattern applications to new ones, by e.g. adding new observers to an Observer pattern instance. Publication [30] uses XSLT (Extensible Stylesheet Language Transformations) for pattern-specific transformations to add patterns. In [18] model transformations (to apply patterns) are guided with UML stereotypes that mark appropriate points in models.

Visualizing design patterns in models and diagrams has been addressed in [7,17]. Publication [7] presents several notations to highlight patterns and pattern-related elements in diagrams. Among the notations is the collaboration notation that is also used in this work. In [17], a UML profile is developed for the specification of pattern specific roles that elements in models play. Based on the profile, the authors have developed a web service tool that integrates e.g. to Rational Rose to visualize patterns.

Among other domains of applications, design patterns have been developed to document the recurring solutions of safety applications, e.g. redundancy. Douglass [9] presents 4 patterns to implement redundancy or redundancy-like behavior so that a task is performed in several channels or that another computing channel is used to observe the behavior of the main channel. Also IEC 61508 [15] (part 6) presents several M out of N solutions in which the idea is to perform a calculation redundantly and to use voting to acquire a reliable result for it. In its recommendation tables, IEC 61508 also refers to a range of solutions that have already been described in pattern literary. For example, the standard recommends the use of backward recovery (from faults) [13,23] and cyclic program execution [9].

Because of the documentation requirements, safety system development could also benefit from ability to indicate the use of the standard solutions in models.

Instead of detecting pattern instances as e.g. in [25], a starting point should be that uses of patterns are design decisions of developers. Developers apply standard solutions with a reason and they should be explicitly marked in models. In this way, reliable documentation, which is of special importance in the domain, could be gathered from models.

3   Design Patterns to Facilitate MDD

Design patterns provide many general, well-known benefits to development work. For example, patterns encapsulate knowledge and experience, provide common vocabulary for developers and enhance documentation of designs [1].

Design patterns can be seen to mark points in models in which developers have been faced with challenges. Patterns can be considered as predefined, reusable design decisions. However, they often require configuring for specific applications [16]. Patterns are proven and general whereas design decisions are more tentative, specific to an application and possibly choices between possible solutions [14]. By applying a pattern and marking the instance, a developer thus not only instantiates and configures a solution. The model is enriched with architectural information.

The use of patterns can thus extend models with architectural knowledge. However, especially patterns could be valuable in MDD in which the purpose is in shifting development efforts from documents to models. To demonstrate this point, we discuss their use to a few selected purposes.

When patterns are marked in models that are used throughout the development process, it is possible to gather statistics on the use of the patterns. Pattern markings promote traceability between the solutions and their uses in individual systems. The work and preferred solutions of developers can be compared by comparing the patterns that they use in the models. Companies and teams can set up rules for using patterns in order to unify practices. For example, a specific challenge could be agreed to be solved always in a standard way. Also metrics could be defined to evaluate software products. Extensibility and modifiability, for example, are quality attributes that many classic design patterns aim to improve. As a consequence, it is possible that similar software products could be compared in terms of preferred quality attributes by comparing the patterns that are used in the products.

Design patterns can promote learning of new developers, too. When best practices and expert solutions are documented as patterns and pattern instances marked in design models, the models can be used as training material. New developers can look for pattern instances, in which kinds of contexts they have been used and how they have been used by experienced developers. Optimally, design pattern instances could be highlighted in models and diagrams in order to ensure their discovery. Diagrams with pattern annotations could also be used as parts of written documents when copied to such documents, when necessary.

It can be argued that the mentioned benefits are not restricted to the use of patterns in MDD only. However, improving the documentation value of models is of special importance in model-driven approaches, such as MDD. This is because one of the objectives of MDD is to gain benefits by changing the focus of development efforts from documents to models. However, if the aim is not to produce written documents in which challenges and decisions could be included, the only places where they can be added are the models.

As mentioned, documentation plays an especially important part in safety system development. In special application areas it could be possible to maintain separate documents. However, that would be against the essential idea of MDD and lead to splitting information to several places. It could also require additional work. A more appropriate approach would be to include the documentation in the models, in the first place. A possible challenge for this objective is that models tend to be more applicable to representing solutions than rationale behind them. However, at least the use of patterns could provide general rationale for the solutions and, in case of safety systems, could also indicate compliance to standards.

4   Design Patterns in UML

In UML, patterns are defined with the Collaboration concept that extends both the StructuredClassifier and BehavioredClassifier concepts, similarly to the Class concept of the language. A pattern definition is a set of cooperating participants that are owned by a Collaboration as its properties, similarly to properties of a class. For each role of the pattern there should be a property owned by the Collaboration. Required relationships between the participants can be specified with connectors between the properties. The features required from the participants are defined by UML Classifiers (e.g. classes or interfaces) that are used as types of the properties.

Pattern instances are represented with CollaborationUses. A CollaborationUse represents an application of a Collaboration (pattern) to a specific situation. CollaborationUses are owned by classifiers to the contents of which the Collaborations (patterns) are applied. Properties of the applying classifiers are bound to the roles (properties) of the Collaborations with Dependencies. The properties that play roles in a pattern instance must be owned by the classifier that owns the CollaborationUse element.

Graphically, Collaborations and CollaborationUses can be used in composite structure diagrams (CSDs). In case of defining a Collaboration (pattern), the root element of the diagram is the Collaboration, whereas in case of a CollaborationUse the classifier owning it. In other diagrams, CollaborationUses can be visible in compartments related to the applying classes, if supported by the tool being used.

4.1   Challenges with the UML Approach

The approach of UML for defining and using design patterns is formal and well-defined. However, with the approach, for example, the literature presentations of many well-known patterns cannot be re-produced in models. A CollaborationUse

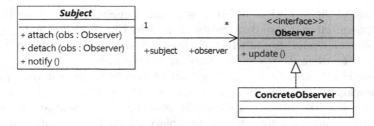

Fig. 1. A class diagram illustrating the Observer pattern.

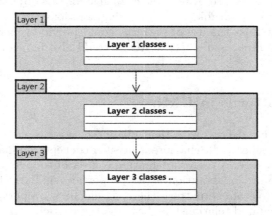

Fig. 2. A layered architecture pattern illustration in a class diagram.

cannot be used e.g. in a class diagram describing the classes of a package because the participants would be classes (instead of properties) and owned by a package (instead of a class). For example, the classes in Fig. 1 could not be marked as an Observer [12] pattern instance.

A rationale for claiming that the familiar structure in the figure is not an Observer instance could be that a class diagram does not yet indicate occurrences and uses of instances of the classes in the pattern specific way. Instead, the UML approach would be to define another class, create instances of the classes (of the figure) as properties of the other class and connect them to use the services of each other. Graphically this could be done with CSDs that were not available at the time e.g. Observer pattern was authored. This is a possible explanation for the UML support to differ from the literature (or vice versa). However, from a pragmatic point of view, it may not be worthwhile to limit patterns strictly to describe classifiers, only. On one hand, CSDs are not used as commonly (e.g. in industry) as class diagrams are. On the other hand, if a developer deliberately designs classes so that they can be used according to a pattern, it should be possible for her to mark the decision, e.g. for documentation purposes.

Another example related to the lack of pattern modeling capabilities in UML is related to architectural patterns. A well-known example of such a pattern is the Layers pattern [6]. An intuitive means to illustrate the use of Layers

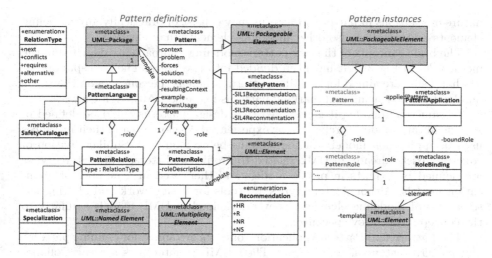

Fig. 3. The metamodel of the new pattern modeling concepts; UML concepts are highlighted with grey colour.

in a UML model could be the presenting of the packages and classes that an application is built of in a layered-like orientation as in Fig. 2. One could also use component diagrams and arrange the components to a layered like orientation, like in [6], pp. 35. However, neither of these approaches could be marked as a Layers instance. Packages, which both the diagram types are used to describe, cannot own CollaborationUses. And if they could, the packages and components would not be properties of a class.

Related to pattern languages, UML does not define means to specify relations between patterns. According to the language specification [21], Collaborations can extend others. However, there is no means to specify, for example, that after applying a pattern it could be advisable to apply another, related pattern. Lastly, the means of UML for defining the information content of patterns other than solutions, e.g. context and problem, are limited. The Collaboration concept does not include textual or other kinds of properties for such purposes.

5   The General Pattern Modeling Approach

Generally, the concepts that can be used in models conforming to a modeling language are defined in the metamodel of the language. The concepts that are available in UML models, for example, are defined in the UML metamodel [21]. The UML metamodel, in turn, has been defined with Meta Object Facility (MOF). The metamodel of the new pattern modeling concepts is presented next.

What pieces of information a pattern is obviously required to include are a name (identifier), problem (that the pattern solves), context (in which the pattern can be used) and the solution, as also suggested in [3]. On the other hand, as argued in the previous section, the modeling approach should not restrict the nature of solutions in patterns. Patterns may consist of practically any modeling elements and describe also other modeling elements than classes.

The basic concepts of the new pattern modeling approach are depicted in the metamodel in Fig. 3 that has been divided into two parts. The concepts on the left-hand side are aimed for defining patterns whereas the concepts on the right-hand side are for using and marking patterns instances. Although they are part of the same metamodel, it is assumed that design patterns could be defined in specific library models (preferably by experienced developers) and their instances used in application models (of the systems being modeled). Similar division of concepts exists already in UML related to profiles and stereotypes. Stereotypes are defined by experts in profile models and then used in a number of application models. Although stereotypes are tools for design work and altering the semantics of modeling elements, they are defined in UML models similarly to the concepts that they specialize.

The Pattern and PatternApplication concepts are aimed for defining patterns and pattern instances, respectively. Their UML counterparts are the Collaboration and CollaborationUse concepts. However, instead of defining (only) the contents of a classifier, Patterns contain textual information which has been structured based on the canonical form of patterns [4] with an addition of consequences from the Alexandrian form [2].

The Pattern concept is extended from the UML PackageableElement so that Patterns can be defined within package hierarchies. The main contents of Patterns are PatternRoles that are used to specify structural and behavioral roles specific to the Patterns. Multiplicities define the limitations to numbers of modeling elements playing the roles in pattern instances. PatternRoles can also refer to template elements that are specific to the roles. Their purpose is to enable the development of tool support to facilitate the creation of pattern instances.

RoleBindings are owned by PatternApplications and they bind pattern instance specific elements to the roles of the patterns. The approach does not restrict the metaclasses of bound elements since the (concrete) elements of UML all extend the abstract Element concept that is used as the type of the meta-reference. The same applies to SysML and UML AP modeling elements in the supporting tool; they can be used in patterns and pattern instances as well.

The patternLanguage concept is a lightweight approach to pattern languages, allowing patterns to be organized into hierarchies. With PatternRelations, patterns can be organized into (pattern) sequences describing meaningful orders of using patterns, and sequences combined to simple languages. Relations also allow the specification of alternatives, patterns requiring other patterns and patterns that conflict with each other. This aspect is yet to be defined in more detail.

The safety-related concepts of the metamodel include support for distinguishing the patterns of safety systems and for specifying their applicability for different levels of safety. A SafetyPattern is, thus, a design pattern that has been identified to be related to safety and that may have recommendations for safety systems of different Safety Integrity Levels (SILs).

With safety systems, we refer to systems that perform safety functions, which are required to ensure the safety of a controlled process. The SILs in the metamodel refer to the 4 Safety Integrity Levels in IEC 61508, SIL1 being the lowest and SIL4 the highest level [15]. In general, SILs determine the probabilities of correct behavior. However, for software systems, it may be difficult to provide probabilities. The focus of the standard is thus on development techniques and measures. For each SIL and for each development phase, the standard specifies a set of techniques that can be highly recommended (HR), recommended (R) or non-recommended (NR) or with non-specified recommendation (NS). The alternatives in the Recommendation (enumeration) in the metamodel correspond to these alternatives.

The purpose of the SafetyCatalogues is to collect together (from various pattern sources) related SafetyPatterns. Catalogues are aimed to contain patterns that should be used together and to which sets of patterns that are used in models can be compared. Patterns in a catalogue can be related to, e.g., a phase in development. For example, IEC 61508 [15] includes the lists of recommended techniques to be used during specific software development phases. For software architecture design, for instance, the standard mentions 27 techniques and/or measures, some of which are alternatives to each other.

The background of the Specialization relation is that many solutions (e.g. redundancy) that are recommended by safety standards have numerous specialized pattern versions in pattern literature. With the Specialization relation, the purpose is to enable the use of general SafetyPatterns in SafetyCatalogues but in such a way that patterns specializing the general patterns can be considered as their alternatives, for example when comparing the patterns of a model with SafetyCatalogues.

The major differences of the general pattern modeling approach in comparison to the UML approach are as follows. The roles of patterns have been separated from their template elements in the template packages. Pattern definitions contain textual information. The model elements playing the roles in patterns and their instances are not restricted to be properties or instances of any specific UML (or e.g. SysML) metaclass. PatternApplications are owned by packages that are used in models in any case. In addition, specific safety-related concepts have been defined for safety application development.

The concepts relieve the restrictions of UML so that, for example, the patterns of the examples presented in Sect. 4.1 could be marked as instances of appropriate pattern definitions. Since elements playing roles in a pattern need not be properties, for example the class definitions of Fig. 1 could be marked as parts of an Observer instance. A structure like that could also be marked as a pattern instance regardless of whether the constructs would be defined in the same or different package. It would only affect to which package should own the PatternApplication element. Constructing patterns from classes, packages and components is also possible, which enables marking the structure of Fig. 2 as a Layers instance.

As a downside, the approach is less formal than that of UML. Because of the freedom to define patterns to consist of practically any elements, it is more difficult to confirm the correctness of pattern applications. Since the approach does not restrict the elements that play roles in a pattern instance to be owned

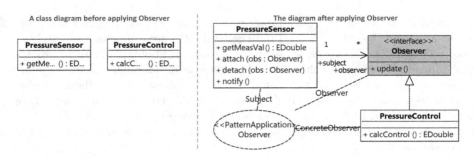

Fig. 4. A visualization of an Observer pattern instance.

by a single model element, it is also possible for pattern instances to disperse to several places in models due to, for example, model refactoring. That is, although some simple checks of consistency can be automated, more responsibility over the correctness of pattern definitions and instances is left for developers. Another restriction of the approach is related to the portability of it to other tools. This aspect is discussed in more detail in Sect. 7.

6   Tool Support to Use and Benefit from Patterns

To demonstrate the use of the concepts and tool support developed based on them, the concepts are used in two example models. First of the models illustrates the use of the pattern concepts with Observer [12] as an example. The second model, then, demonstrates the use of the safety-related concepts. It presents a SafetyCatalogue and how a model of a safety application complies with the catalogue.

6.1   General Pattern Concepts

The starting point in the Observer example is a situation in which a class (PressureControl) should be made capable of receiving notifications of new (pressure) measurements from another class (PressureMeasurement). A class diagram illustrating the starting point is shown on the left-hand side of Fig. 4. However, in order to apply Observer, it needs to be first defined with the pattern concepts. A tree view of a model defining the pattern with the concepts is shown on the left-hand side of Fig. 5.

The pattern is in the example defined in a Package that contains the Pattern element (Observer) as well as a template Package. The pattern element contains the roles related to it (Observer, Subject and ConcreteObserver). The classes and interfaces of the template package were illustrated in Fig. 1; they also define several operations that are hidden from the figure below. Textual information related to the pattern, e.g. context and problem, is stored in the properties of the Pattern element.

The example class diagram, after applying the pattern, is illustrated on the right-hand side of Fig. 4. The diagram also illustrates how pattern instances are

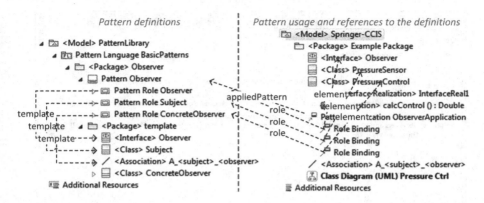

Fig. 5. References in a pattern definition and from a pattern instance to its definition.

visualized with the collaboration notation. The modifications from applying the pattern include an addition of an interface (Observer), an interface realization as well as several operations specific to the role elements of the pattern, e.g. update(). These elements have been added based on the template elements illustrated in Fig. 1.

Another view to the results is presented on the right-hand side of Fig. 5 that illustrates the references between the model trees related to the pattern definition and pattern instance. The operations and other added model elements are contained in the model in a similar manner than any model elements. The information about the pattern instance, on the other hand, is stored in a PatternApplication element. The PatternApplication contains the RoleBindings that link the pattern instance specific elements to the general roles of the pattern definition.

Tool support has been developed to facilitate the use of patterns and to demonstrate the benefits from their use. The metamodel extensions to UML AP and UML modeling concepts, see Fig. 3, were defined with Eclipse Modeling Framework (EMF) that is a Meta Object Facility (MOF) implementation used by the UML AP tool [26]. In addition to implementing the concepts, tool support has been developed to instantiate and visualize patterns in models as well as to generate documentation from models. For the first two purposes, support has been implemented into the core tool whereas the latter extends the documentation generation work in [27].

Instantiating Patterns. Compared with instantiating patterns from templates in an ad hoc manner, the use of the pattern concepts requires additional work. Defining patterns with the Pattern and PatternRole elements has to be done only once for each pattern. PatternApplications, however, need to be created and configured for each new pattern instance. As such, it is natural that this task should be facilitated with tool support. In the tool, this task has been integrated into a wizard. Compared with existing pattern wizards in UML tools, the novelty of the wizard is in managing the new concepts.

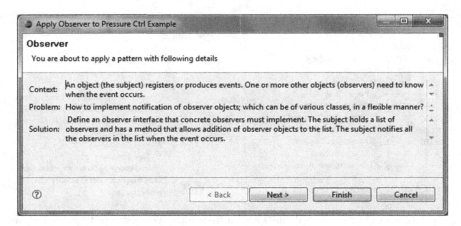

Fig. 6. The pattern information page of the pattern application wizard.

The process of instantiating patterns is performed as follows. The user of the tool initiates the wizard from a tool menu. As a response, the tool scans through available pattern libraries in order to find available patterns. New libraries can be added to the tool by registering them with an (Eclipse) extension point that has been developed for this purpose. The user of the tool is provided with a list of available patterns. When selecting a pattern to apply, part of the textual information (problem, context and solution) related to the patterns are shown to the user, as illustrated in Fig. 6. After selecting a pattern, the pattern (definition) that should be referenced by the PatternApplication to be created is known. In case of the diagram root element being a package, the PatternApplication to be created can be owned by the package. Otherwise, it can be created to be owned by the package closest to the diagram root in the model hierarchy. The wizard proceeds to processing (iterating through) the pattern roles.

For each role, the wizard enables the user to select an existing element from the active diagram to act in the role. If the pattern in question defines a template, it is also possible to copy an element for the role from the template. For PatternRoles that the user has either selected an element for or copied it from the template, the wizard creates RoleBindings that bind the elements to the roles of the pattern. In case of using existing elements in roles of a pattern, their contents (elements owned by them) are compared and completed to correspond to those of the templates by copying missing contents.

Technically, the wizard only collects the information from the user whereas actual model changes are performed all at the same time after completing the wizard. The purpose of this is to enable collecting model modifications to a single (undoable) command. However, currently undoing a pattern application requires manual work.

It is also possible to modify pattern instances after creating them. PatternApplications and RoleBindings can be selected from the outline view of the tool and modified with the properties view. Elements related to a pattern instance can be reorganized and it is possible to apply more (compatible) patterns. Information

Design pattern usage in Springer-CCIS model

Statistics on design pattern applications:

Design Pattern	Pattern applications
Observer	1
Total number of patterns	1
Total number of pattern instances	1

Package --> design pattern traceability:

Package -->	Applied pattern(s)
Example Package	Observer

Design pattern --> package traceability:

Design Pattern -->	Applying package(s)
Observer	Example Package

Design pattern --> Element traceability:

Design Pattern (Package) -->	Element with a role (role)
Observer (Example Package)	PressureSensor (Subject)
	PressureControl (ConcreteObserver)
	Observer (Observer)

Fig. 7. An exemplary automatically generated traceability sheet.

on which elements are part of a pattern instance is stored in a PatternApplication specific to the instance and the RoleBindings of it. They are not affected by the additions of new elements or simple changes to the bound elements, e.g. re-naming or moving them.

Visualizing Patterns. Although pattern instances are always visible in the outline view of the tool, they are not visible in diagrams by default. This is in order to keep the amount of details in diagrams relatively small to keep them understandable. Patterns can also be considered as explanatory information that may not be required all the time. However, when pattern applications are necessary to be shown, e.g. for documentation or teaching purposes, it should be possible to visualize them in diagrams.

Visualization of a pattern is initialized from a menu of the Eclipse outline view while at the same time selecting the pattern instance (PatternApplication) to be shown. As a response, a dotted ellipse shape with lines to the elements, which play the roles in the pattern instance, is created. The ellipse represents a pattern instance and contains the name of the pattern (definition). Connections to the role elements show the names of the corresponding pattern roles.

The graphical presentation of pattern instances is similar to CollaborationUses in UML CSDs, with addition of <<PatternApplication>> to distinguish between them. An example graphical presentation of an Observer pattern application was presented at the right-hand side of Fig. 4. In the figure, the pattern has been applied to a client application model so that the names of the concrete classes are different from the names of the template classes, which were shown in Fig. 1.

Patterns as a Part of Documentation. One of the main motivations of the work has been to use patterns for documentation purposes in MDD, for both safety-related and non-safety related applications. Since design patterns

Safety Sequence: "IEC 61508 Architecture Design"

#	Pattern	SIL 1	SIL 2	SIL 3	SIL 4
1	Fault detection	NS	R	HR	HR
2	Error detecting codes	R	R	R	HR
3a	Failure assertion programming	R	R	R	HR
3b	Diverse monitor techniques (with independence)	NS	R	R	NS
3c	Diverse monitor techniques (with separation)	NS	R	R	HR
3d	Diverse redundancy	NS	NS	NS	R
3e	Functionally diverse redundancy	NS	NS	R	HR
3f	Backward recovery	R	R	NS	NR
3g	Stateless software design	NS	NS	R	HR
4a	Re-try fault recovery mechanism	R	R	NS	NS
4b	Graceful degradation	R	R	HR	HR
5	Artificial intelligence - fault correction	NS	NR	NR	NR
6	Dynamic reconfiguration	NS	NR	NR	NR
7	Modular approach	HR	HR	HR	HR
8	Use of trusted/verified software elements (if available)	R	HR	HR	HR

Fig. 8. An example safety catalogue sheet presenting architecture design techniques.

and their instances are modeled with dedicated elements, it is possible to track the patterns that are used in a model of an application as well as the numbers of pattern instances. Since PatternApplications are owned by packages, it is possible to trace the parts of models in which design patterns are used. Starting from packages, it is again possible to track the patterns that are used in the packages.

Exporting documentation on pattern usage is initiated by the user of the tool that selects the root of the model from the outline view, selects export functionality and then traceability information. The documentation sheet generation, for safety-related and non-safety-related applications, has been developed to extend the work presented in [27].

The first of the new sheets, pattern traceability sheet, lists the design patterns that are used in the exported model. The sheet is collected by searching all PatternApplication instances in the model. The sheet presents the numbers of instances for each design pattern and totally. With traceability matrices, the sheet presents package to design pattern traceability (the patterns that are used in each package), design pattern to package traceability (in which packages each design pattern is used) and lastly design pattern to element traceability. In the latter matrix, each design pattern instance is traced to all elements that play roles in the instance. An example sheet presenting traceability for the pressure sensor example of Fig. 4 is presented in Fig. 7.

Another new sheet, pattern sheet, focuses on the design patterns themselves. At the beginning of the sheet, a list of patterns, instances of which can be found in the model, is repeated with the numbers of pattern instances. After this table, the sheet presents the printouts of information for each design pattern used in the model including context, problem, forces, solution (textually), consequences, resulting context, example, and known usage.

6.2 Patterns of Safety Systems

Documentation sheets for safety system development are illustrated with two examples. The first of the sheet types is for presenting SafetyCatalogues that can be defined to correspond to recommendations tables of safety standards, for

Conformability to "IEC 61508 Software safety requirements specification"

#	Pattern	SIL 1	SIL 2	SIL 3	SIL 4
1a	Semi-formal methods	R	R	HR	HR
1b	Formal methods	NS	R	R	HR
2	Forward traceability between the system safety requirements and the software safety requirements	R	R	HR	HR
3	Backward traceability between the safety requirements and the perceived safety needs	R	R	HR	HR
4	Computer-aided specification tools to support appropriate techniques/measures above	R	R	HR	HR
	Pattern usage:	4/4	4/4	4/4	4/4
	Pattern usage (%):	100.0	100.0	100.0	100.0

Fig. 9. An example safety catalogue conformability sheet (Color figure online).

example. The latter sheet type is intended for comparing the sets of SafetyPatterns that are used in models with SafetyCatalogues.

Safety catalogue sheets are intended for printing SafetyCatalogues. Selected catalogues are printed to separate tables starting from their first patterns, which are assigned number 1 in the tables. The next and alternative SafetyPatterns can be found with the use of the corresponding PatternRelations (of the metamodel). Alternatives are in the tables assigned same numbers but different letters, to indicate them being alternatives to each other. Recommendations of the patterns to all SILs are also printed into the tables.

An example safety catalogue sheet can be seen in Fig. 8 that presents a part of a printout of a catalogue of techniques and measures that IEC 61508 [15] recommends for software architecture design. In the table, patterns can be highly recommended (HR), recommended (R), non-recommended (NR) or with non-specified recommendation (NS). To avoid repeating standard material, the table includes only 15 techniques that have been modeled as patterns to produce the example. By looking at the table, however, it becomes clear that pattern literature already includes specialized versions of many of the techniques, for example to implement redundancy [9].

Safety catalogue conformability sheets are intended for presenting how SafetyPatterns that are used in a model conform to SafetyCatalogues. To compile the sheet, SafetyCatalogues related to the model are collected into a list from which the user may select the desired ones. The general structure of the sheet is similar to the previous sheet. However, the SafetyPatterns of the catalogue that are used in the model are indicated with a grey colour. In addition, the table presents whether the used patterns are compatible with each SIL. The compatibility of the (used) patterns is illustrated with a green colour and incompatibility with a red colour. Incompatibility can result from both using a non-recommended pattern or not-using a recommended (or highly recommended) technique or any of its recommended alternatives. The last rows of the table present the numbers of patterns (excluding alternatives) that would be recommended for each SIL and how many of them have been actually used.

An example safety catalogue conformability sheet can be found in Fig. 9. It presents the conformability of SafetyPatterns used in an example model to the software safety requirement specification techniques of IEC 61508 [15] that have been modeled as a SafetyCatalogue. According to the table (grey highlighting), semi-formal modeling techniques and computer-aided specification tools have been used and the software safety requirements specification supports both backward and forward traceability. The table also illustrates (with the green colour) that these choices would be appropriate to all SILs.

7   Conclusions and Discussion

This paper has discussed the use of design patterns in UML based modeling and their potential benefits in model-driven development. Shortcomings in UML design pattern support have been pointed out and an additional set of modeling concepts has been presented.

Design patterns document solutions and capture expert knowledge to recurring challenges in design and development work. They enable including additional documentation in models. Patterns enrich models with information on challenges, the points of decisions as well as traceability between solutions and their use in specific applications. Visualizing patterns in diagrams may support learning of developers and increase the value of diagrams in written documents. Knowledge on pattern usage can be gathered to documentation and to compare applications and the work of developers.

Related to safety systems and application, patterns enable specifying the applicability of solutions to applications of different integrity levels. SafetyPatterns, i.e. the patterns of systems, can be collected into collections with which it is possible to model both recommendation tables of safety standards and custom collections of patterns. Safety-related information can then be used to generate documentation from models and to compare models with catalogues. Safety application development is also an application domain that could specifically benefit from possibilities to export documentation. Without automated documentation support, the documentation would have to be produced manually.

The scope of design patterns that can be found in literature varies in terms of area of expertise and abstraction level of patterns. Many patterns present rather conceptual solutions than concrete structures that could be copied or modeled always in the same way. However, although the UML concepts have been enriched along the entire language, the pattern support is still restricted to the collaborating properties of classifiers.

The information content of actual published patterns is not restricted to such narrow scope. For example, the solutions of patterns may consist of packages, components or even use cases. Thus, patterns may not always even concern programming language level aspects and their information content is not restricted to solutions only. In addition, patterns include information about their contexts and problems for which the patterns provide the solutions.

In this work, these issues have been addressed by defining and implementing a set of pattern modeling concepts that can be used to complement the UML concepts. The presented, simple set of modeling concepts enhances the UML limitations by enabling patterns to include textual information and to consist of practically any elements that a pattern author finds useful. As a downside, the approach leaves more responsibility over the correctness of patterns and pattern applications to developers. The portability of the approach to other tools is also questionable, which is caused by metamodel modifications.

The approach introduces new metaclasses to the UML metamodel that has been defined with MOF. Implementing the approach in other tools would require similar additions to their metamodels. The other extension mechanism of UML, light weight profiles, however, would not have enabled all the required additions. UML specification [21], for example, denies stereotypes to be used to insert new metaclasses or metareferences between the existing metaclasses of UML. That is, with stereotypes it would have been possible to include the suggested textual information in the Collaborations of UML. However, CollaborationUses would still have to be owned by classifiers and the other mentioned constraints would still apply.

Tool support for automating the use of the new concepts has been developed for instantiating patterns, visualizing patterns in diagrams as well as collecting documentation and statistics from models. SafetyCatalogues can be presented in standard-like tables with which models and their patterns can be compared. Such safety sheets can be used also during development as guidance to present the standard-compliant selections that still have to be addressed.

The tool and the concepts have been used by researchers working in Re-Use project at the Tampere University of Technology (TUT). They have been found useful and will be used to gather more use experience in software engineering courses in the department of Automation Science and Engineering at TUT.

References

1. Agerbo, E., Cornils, A.: How to preserve the benefits of design patterns. ACM SIGPLAN Not. **33**, 134–143 (1998)
2. Alexander, C., Ishikawa, S., Silverstein, M.: Pattern Language: Towns, Buildings Construction. Oxford University Press, Oxford (1977)
3. Alexander, C.: The Timeless Way of Building. Oxford University Press, Oxford (1979)
4. Appleton, B.: Patterns and software: essential concepts and terminology. Object Mag. Online **3**, 20–25 (1997)
5. Briand, L.C., Labiche, Y., Sauve, A.: Guiding the application of design patterns based on UML models. In: The 22nd IEEE International Conference on Software Maintenance, ICSM 2006, pp. 234–243 (2006)
6. Buschmann, F., Meunier, R., Rohnert, H., et al.: Pattern Oriented Software Architecture: A System of Patters. Wiley, New York (1996)
7. Dong, J.: UML extensions for design pattern compositions. J. Object Technol. **1**, 151–163 (2002)
8. Dong, J., Yang, S.: QVT based model transformation for design pattern evolutions. In: 10th IASTED International Conference on Internet and Multimedia Systems and Applications (2006)
9. Douglass, B.P.: Real-time design patterns. In: Real-Time UML: Developing Efficient Objects for Embedded Systems. Addison-Wesley, Reading (1998)

10. France, R.B., Kim, D., Ghosh, S., et al.: A UML-based pattern specification technique. IEEE Trans. Softw. Eng. **30**, 193–206 (2004)
11. France, R., Chosh, S., Song, E., et al.: A metamodeling approach to pattern-based model refactoring. IEEE Softw. **20**, 52–58 (2003)
12. Gamma, E., Helm, R., Johnson, R., Vlissides, J.: Design Patterns: Elements of Reusable Object-Oriented Software. Pearson Education, Upper Saddle River (1994)
13. Hanmer, R.: Patterns for Fault Tolerant Software. Wiley, Chichester (2013)
14. Harrison, N.B., Avgeriou, P., Zdlin, U.: Using patterns to capture architectural decisions. IEEE Softw. **24**, 38–45 (2007)
15. IEC: 61508 Functional Safety of electrical/electronic/programmable Electronic Safety-Related Systems. International Electrotechnical Commission (2010)
16. Jansen, A., Bosch, J.: Software architecture as a set of architectural design decisions. In: The 5th working IEEE/IFIP Conference onSoftware Architecture, pp. 109–120 (2005)
17. Jing, D., Sheng, Y., Kang, Z.: Visualizing design patterns in their applications and compositions. IEEE Trans. Softw. Eng. **33**, 433–453 (2007)
18. Kajsa, P., Majtás, L.: Design patterns instantiation based on semantics and model transformations. In: van Leeuwen, J., Muscholl, A., Peleg, D., Pokorný, J., Rumpe, B. (eds.) SOFSEM 2010. LNCS, vol. 5901, pp. 540–551. Springer, Heidelberg (2010)
19. Lasater, C.G.: Design Patterns. Jones & Bartlett Publishers, Boston (2010)
20. No Magic, Inc., MagicDraw (2014). http://www.nomagic.com/products/magicdraw.html
21. OMG: Unified Modeling Language Specification 2.4.1: SuperStructure. Object Management Group (2011)
22. Rauhamäki, J., Vepsäläinen, T., Kuikka, S.: Patterns for safety and control system cooperation. In: VikingPlop (2013)
23. Saridakis, T.: Design patterns for checkpoint-based rollback recovery. In: The 10th Conference on Pattern Languages of Programs (PLoP) (2003)
24. Sunyé, G., Le Guennec, A., Jézéquel, J.-M.: Design patterns application in UML. In: Bertino, E. (ed.) ECOOP 2000. LNCS, vol. 1850, pp. 44–62. Springer, Heidelberg (2000)
25. Tsantalis, N., Chatzigeorgiou, A., Stephanides, G., et al.: Design pattern detection using similarity scoring. IEEE Trans. Softw. Eng. **32**, 896–909 (2006)
26. Vepsäläinen, T., Hästbacka, D., Kuikka, S.: Tool support for the UML automation profile - for domain-specific software development in manufacturing. In: The Third International Conference on Software Engineering Advances, ICSEA 2008, pp. 43–50 (2008)
27. Vepsäläinen, T. and Kuikka, S.: Towards model-based development of safety-related control applications. In: 2011 IEEE 16th Conference on Emerging Technologies and Factory Automation (ETFA) (2011)
28. Vepsäläinen, T., Kuikka, S.: Design pattern support for model-driven development. In: 9th International Conference on Software Engineering and Applications, pp. 277–286 (2014)
29. Vepsäläinen, T., Kuikka, S.: Safety patterns in model-driven development. In: 9th International Conference on Software Engineering Advances, pp. 233–239 (2014)
30. Xue-Bin, W., Quan-Yuan, W., Huai-Min, W., et al.: Research and implementation of design pattern-oriented model transformation. In: The International Multi-Conference on Computing in the Global Information Technology, ICCGI 2007 (2007)

Measuring the Quality of Open Source Software Ecosystems Using QuESo

Oscar Franco-Bedoya[1,2](✉), David Ameller[1], Dolors Costal[1],
and Xavier Franch[1]

[1] Group of Software and Service Engineering (GESSI), Universitat Politècnica de
Catalunya, Barcelona, Spain
{ohernan,dameller,dolors,franch}@essi.upc.edu
http://www.essi.upc.edu/~gessi/
[2] Universidad de Caldas, Manizales, Colombia

Abstract. Open source software has witnessed an exponential growth
in the last two decades and it is playing an increasingly important role
in many companies and organizations leading to the formation of open
source software ecosystems. In this paper we present a quality model
that will allow the evaluation of those ecosystems in terms of their relevant quality characteristics such as health or activeness. To design this
quality model we started by analysing the quality measures found during
the execution of a systematic literature review on open source software
ecosystems and, then, we classified and reorganized the set of measures
in order to build a solid quality model. Finally, we test the suitability of
the constructed quality model using the GNOME ecosystem.

Keywords: Quality model · Software ecosystem · Quality measures ·
Open source software

1 Introduction

Software ecosystems are emerging in the last years as a new way to understand
the relationships between software projects, products, and organizations. There
are two widespread definitions:

- A software ecosystem is *"a set of actors functioning as a unit and interacting
  with a shared market for software and services. A software ecosystem consists
  of actors such as independent software vendors (ISV), outsourcers, and customers. A software ecosystem typically is interconnected with institutions such
  as standardization organizations, open source software communities, research
  communities, and related ecosystems"* [1].
- A software ecosystem is *"a collection of software projects which are developed
  and evolve together in the same environment"* [2].

In the first definition software ecosystems are understood from a holistic business oriented perspective as a network of actors, organizations and companies,

© Springer International Publishing Switzerland 2015
A. Holzinger et al. (Eds.): ICSOFT 2014, CCIS 555, pp. 39–62, 2015.
DOI: 10.1007/978-3-319-25579-8_3

while the second definition focuses on technical and social aspects of a set of software projects and their communities. In this paper we try to reconcile both visions and consider the business oriented perspective together with the technical and social perspectives in order to assess software ecosystem quality in its broader sense.

We focus on a particular kind of software ecosystems, i.e., those that are built around an Open Source Software (OSS) initiative (e.g., Android, GNOME, and Eclipse ecosystems), namely OSS ecosystems. We have identified three dimensions of quality in OSS ecosystems: the first dimension is the quality of the software platform in which the projects of the ecosystem are built upon (e.g., the Android ecosystem provides the Android platform used by all the Android mobile apps); the second dimension, as mentioned Jansen and Cusumano [1], is the quality of the OSS communities that grow inside the ecosystem and ecosystem's projects (e.g., the *GNOME* community itself, i.e., the community of the platform, but also the communities of the projects that belong to the ecosystem such as Anjuta, Banshee, and Abi Word communities); the third dimension of quality is inherent to the ecosystems themselves, i.e., the quality derived from the understanding of the OSS ecosystem as a network of interrelated elements (e.g., the number of Eclipse plug-ins and their dependencies between them can be used to assess the ecosystem's interrelatedness).

Assessing the quality of OSS ecosystems is of vital importance because quality assurance is a way to prevent bad decisions, avoid problems, and it allows to verify the compliance with the requirements and the business goals. It can also be used for quality systematic monitoring to provide feedback and execute preventive actions. For example, before deciding to integrate a project into an established OSS ecosystem it is crucial to perform a good quality assessment to avoid problems such as inactive user communities, low level of community cohesion, or even synergetic evolution problems, i.e., lack of collaboration between the key developers.

One way to ensure that the quality assessment has covered the most important characteristics of the ecosystem is to use a quality model, *"the set of characteristics and the relationships between them which provide the basis for specifying quality requirements and evaluating quality"* [3]. Unfortunately, currently there is not any quality model for OSS ecosystems available in the literature, except from some measures distributed among many papers.

To fill this gap, in this paper we present QuESo, a quality model for the quality assessment of OSS ecosystems. To obtain this quality model we used design science methodology [4], first, we searched in the literature for all available measures related to OSS ecosystems, second, we designed the quality model using both a bottom-up strategy by classifying the measures found, and a top-down strategy by analysing the relationships in the quality characteristics that can be assessed by the measures (e.g., to assess the community activeness we can count the number of changes in the source repository or the number of messages in the mailing lists in a recent period of time), and finally, we maded a preliminary solution evaluation.

The rest of the paper is structured as follows: in Sect. 2 we review the related work; in Sect. 3 we explain the research methodology; in Sect. 4 we explain the QuESo quality model; in Sect. 5 we provide examples of real measures and their meaning; in Sect. 6 we provide an initial validation of the model; in Sect. 7 we discuss some observations made in this work; and finally, in Sect. 8 we provide the conclusions and the future work.

2   Related Work

When talking about quality models in the software domain it is inevitable to mention the ISO quality model [5]. This quality model targets the quality of a software product, from three perspectives: internal, external, and quality of use. The specific quality characteristics of the ISO quality model do not cover the important dimensions of OSS ecosystems such as the ones related to the community or the ones related to the *health* of the ecosystem.

The QualOSS quality model [6] gives a good representation for one of the three dimensions covered by QuESo, the OSS community. However we had to extend it with new characteristics that are relevant in the context of OSS ecosystems (see Sect. 4.2).

As we will explain in Sect. 3, we have found many papers that, although do not provide a quality model, they propose a good set of measures to evaluate some aspects of OSS ecosystems. We would like to mention the works that provided the most interesting measures.

- Hartigh et al. [7] developed a concrete measure tool for evaluating business ecosystems based on the classification made by Iansiti and Levien [8]. They conceptualized the business ecosystem health as financial health and network health based on a set of eight measures.
- Mens and Goeminne. [9] provided a set of measures (e.g., number of commits, total bugs, mailing list), by studying the developer community, including the way developers work, cooperate, communicate and share information.
- Neu et al. [10] presented a web application for ecosystem analysis by means of interactive visualizations. The authors used the application to analysis the *GNOME* ecosystem study case.
- Kilamo et al. [11] studied the problem of building open source communities for industrial software that was originally developed as closed source.

Finally we remark the existence of two other secondary studies about software ecosystems [12,13], but in both cases the studies did not have a research question about quality metrics or quality assessment for software ecosystems. Also, it is worth mentioning that as a way to complete our SLR we included the results of these two studies to our SLR (see Sect. 3.1).

3   Research Methodology

We structure our research in terms of design science since it involves creating new artefacts and acquiring new knowledge. Our research methodology follows the engineering cycle as described by [4]. We have performed a first engineering cycle that includes steps for (1) problem investigation, (2) solution design and (3) a preliminary solution evaluation. In the rest of these sections we describe the strategies followed in each step.

3.1   Problem Investigation: Systematic Literature Review

Our problem investigation step was devoted to search in the literature for all available measures related to OSS ecosystems and establish criteria to judge wich measures to consider for developing QuESo. A Systematic Literature Review (SLR) is a method to identify, evaluate, and interpret the available research relevant to a particular topic, research question, or phenomenon of interest [14].

The literature review protocol is part of a wider SLR that we are conducting with the goal of identifying the primary studies related to OSS ecosystems. A more detailed explanation of the protocol can be found in Franco-Bedoya et al. [15].

The research question that addresses the measures and indicators related to the ecosystem quality is: *What measures or attributes are defined to assess or evaluate open source software ecosystems?*

We defined a search string based on keywords derived from all the SLR research questions: *"(OSS OR FOSS OR FLOSS OR Open Source OR Free Software OR Libre Software) AND ecosystem"*.

The search strategy used was a combination of sources: digital libraries, manual searches, the inclusion of specific papers from the two secondary studies mentioned in Sect. 2 and the chapters in a recently published book about software ecosystems [16].

As a result of the SLR, 53 primary studies were selected, from them we identified 17 related to the identification of measures to evaluate the quality of OSS ecosystems. Figure 1 illustrates the SLR selection process.

Once we had collected the measures from the selected papers, we used the following criteria from Hartigh et al. (2013) and Neu et al. [7, 10] to include them in QuESo:

1. *User-friendly and operationalizable:* measures should be logical, easy to use and operationalizable into a measurable entity.
2. *Non-redundant:* when we identified similar measures we selected only one of them, but we kept all the sources for traceability.

After excluding non-operationalizable and merging the similar measures with the previous criteria, we finally selected 68 different measures for the QuESo quality model (note that some of the measures are used to assess more than one characteristic of the quality model).

3.2   Solution Design: Quality Model Construction

There exist several proposals for quality model construction that focus on software quality. Most of them follow top-down strategies [17, 18]. In short, they take as a basis a reference quality model such as the ISO quality model [5], take their quality characteristics as departing point and refine them till they end up with a hierarchy with specific measures at its lower level. Remarkably, the proposal in Radulovic and Garcia-Castro [19] is mainly bottom-up oriented, i.e., it takes a set of measures as departing point to build the model. For our purposes, a

Fig. 1. Selection of primary studies.

bottom-up approach is the most adequate because: (1) a well-established refer-ence quality model (or even, in its defect, a complete and systematic body of knowledge) for software ecosystems is still missing [20], and (2) there already exist a myriad of specific measures that can be applied to OSS ecosystems and that have been identified in our SLR. Furthermore, although it focuses on the construction of software quality models, we can easily use it to the construction of a quality model for OSS ecosystems.

Radulovic and Garcia-Castro [19] proposal has a clearly defined sequence of steps:

1. To identify basic measures.
2. To identify derived measures.
3. To identify quality measures (by aggregation of basic and derived measures).
4. To identify relationships between measures.
5. To specify relationships between measures.
6. To define domain-specific quality sub-characteristics.
7. To align quality sub-characteristics with a quality model.

Note that the alignment in the seventh step partly implies top-down rea-soning. Quality sub-characteristics that have been previously defined are related to others already specified in the existing model. If needed, some new quality sub-characteristics can be specified, or existing ones can be modified or excluded.

We have followed all the steps of the proposal. In particular, for steps 1 and 2, devoted to identify measures, we have based our work on the SLR described in Sect. 3.1. The application of step 7 requires the use of a reference quality model. Since, to our knowledge, a quality model for the whole scope of OSS ecosystems is still missing, we have decided to use QualOSS [6] which measures the per-formance of open source communities. Clearly, new quality sub-characteristics

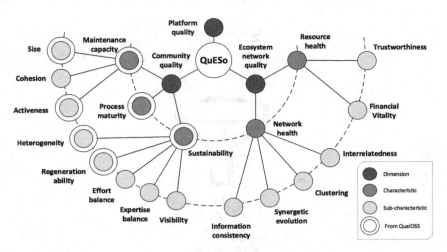

Fig. 2. QuESo quality model.

emerging from measures related to the ecosystem considered as a whole will have to be specified, since they are not addressed by QualOSS.

3.3   Solution Evaluation

As a first step for the solution evaluation we have validated the feasibility of obtaining the measures included in our QuESo quality model and, consequently, the feasibility of evaluating the characteristics and subcharacteristics proposed in QuESo. We have done this by taking the ecosystem around GNOME projects as a case study and have analyzed the literature related to the GNOME ecosystem to extract for which measures there are available values documented in the literature. The rest of details of the evaluation process are described in Sect. 6.

4   QuESo Quality Model

In this section we describe the QuESo quality model obtained as a result of the application of the procedure described in Sect. 3.2. The model is composed of two types of interrelated elements: quality characteristics and measures. Quality characteristics correspond to the attributes of an open source software ecosystem that are considered relevant for evaluation. The quality characteristics are organized in a hierarchy of levels that is described in the rest of this section. For the lack of space, in the tables presented in this paper we have omitted the descriptions. The whole set of measures with their definitions is available in the Appendix A. Also, note that we opted to keep the measure names that appear in the primary studies, even that in some cases the name given is not the most appropriate, we discuss about this topic in Sect. 7.

The quality characteristics in QuESo have been organized in three dimensions: (1) those that relate to the *platform* around which the ecosystem is built, (2) those that relate to the *community* (or set of communities) of the ecosystem and (3) those that are related to the *ecosystem as a network* of elements, such as projects or companies (see Fig. 2).

4.1   Platform-Related Quality Characteristics

Platform-related quality characteristics consist of the set of attributes that are relevant for the evaluation of the software platform.

As a result of our SLR, we have observed that the literature do not provide measures for evaluating open source platform-related quality characteristics. This fact may indicate that there are not significant differential issues for open source software quality with respect to generic software quality that motivates the need of specific measures.

Then, similarly as done in the QualOSS model, since a mature proposal such as ISO 25000-SQuaRE [5] focuses on generic software quality, QuESo adopts directly the characteristics and sub-characteristics proposed by ISO 25000-SQuaRE and this part of the quality model is omitted in the paper.

4.2   Community-Related Quality Characteristics

Following the procedure described in Sect. 3.2, the QuESo proposal for community-related quality characteristics is based both on the set of measures identified in our SLR and on the QualOSS quality model [6] (see Fig. 2).

QualOSS specifies three community characteristics, namely, *maintenance capacity, sustainability* and *process maturity.*

Maintenance Capacity. Soto et al. define *maintenance capacity* as the ability of a community to provide the resources necessary for maintaining its products and mention that aspects relevant to it are the number of contributors to a project and the amount of time they contribute to the development effort. In order to align maintenance capacity with our identified measures it is refined in three sub-characteristics: *size, cohesion* and *activeness.* The *size* of the community influences its maintenance capacity and can be evaluated by measures such as *number of core developers* and *number of committers.* The ability of the community to collaborate defined by its *cohesion* is also relevant. A measure that can be used to evaluate cohesion is the *ecosystem connectedness* in the community social network. Finally, the *activeness* of the community can be evaluated by measures such as *bug tracking activity* and *number of commits.* We have identified 26 measures that can be used to measure the maintenance capacity (see Table 1).

Sustainability. *Sustainability* is the likelihood that a community remains able to maintain the products it develops over an extended period of time. According to Soto et al. it is affected by *heterogeneity* and *regeneration ability* and, as a result of our measure analysis, we have specified additional sub-characteristics besides them: *effort balance, expertise balance* and *visibility.*

The *heterogeneity* of a community contributes to its sustainability. For instance, if a community is mainly composed of employees of a particular

Table 1. List of measures for *maintenance capacity*.

Subcharacteristic	Measure
Size	Number of contributors
Size	Number of members
Size	Number of authors
Size	Number of bug fixers
Size	Number of committers
Size	Number of core developers
Size	Number of nodes and edges
Cohesion	Betweenness centrality
Cohesion	Cluster of collaborating developers
Cohesion	Ecosystem connectedness
Cohesion	Outdegree of keystone actors
Activeness	Bug tracking activity
Activeness	Buildup of assets
Activeness	Community effort
Activeness	Date of last commit
Activeness	Files changed
Activeness	Files per version
Activeness	Lines added
Activeness	Lines changed
Activeness	Lines removed
Activeness	Mailing list
Activeness	Number of commits
Activeness	Contributor commit rate
Activeness	Developer activity diagrams
Activeness	Temporal community effort
Activeness	Number of event people

company, there is the risk of the company cutting its financial support. *Heterogeneity* can be evaluated by measures such as *geographical distribution* of community members.

Regeneration ability also enhances sustainability since a community that has been able to grow in the past increases its chances of not declining in the future. A measure that we have identified for it is for instance, *new members* which counts the number of new members of the community at any point of time.

The *effort balance* is relevant for sustainability i.e., if most of the contribution effort comes from one or a small number of members of the community and it is not uniformly distributed, then its continuity is highly dependent on that small set of members. On the other hand, a balanced effort distribution among all members facilitates its continuity over time. Some measures for effort balance are: *number of developer projects* and *number of developer releases*.

Table 2. List of measures for *sustainability*.

Subcharacteristic	Measure
Heterogeneity	Geographical distribution
Regeneration ability	Temporal community effort
Regeneration ability	New members
Effort balance	Contributor commit rate
Effort balance	Developer activity diagrams
Effort balance	Maximum number of commits of a developer
Effort balance	Member effort
Effort balance	Member activity rate
Effort balance	Number of activity communities
Effort balance	Number of developer releases
Effort balance	Number of developer projects
Effort balance	Project developer experience
Effort balance	Temporal community effort
Effort balance	Total effort of members
Expertise balance	Expertise view contributor
Expertise balance	Principal member activity
Expertise balance	Relation between categorical event and developer participation
Visibility	Number of event people
Visibility	Amount of inquires or feature requests
Visibility	Job advertisements
Visibility	Number of downloads
Visibility	Number of mailing list users
Visibility	Number of passive user
Visibility	Number of readers
Visibility	Number of scientific publications
Visibility	Social media hits
Visibility	Visibility
Visibility	Web page requests

In a similar way, the *expertise balance* among most members of a community is again a way to guarantee its sustainability. A community highly dependent on the expertise of one or a few members suffers from a risky situation. A measure for this is, for instance, *expertise view contributor* which calculates a contributor expertise based on the number and type of files he changed within a month.

The *visibility* of a community gives it the capacity of attracting people to contribute and support it if needed. Examples of measures identified for visibility are: *number of downloads, social media hits* and *web page requests*.

QuESo has 28 measures that can be used to measure the sustainability (see Table 2).

Process Maturity. *Process maturity* is the ability of a developer community to consistently achieve development-related goals by following established processes. It can be assessed for specific software development tasks with the answers of questions such as: *is there a documented process for the task?* [6]. Apparently, this characteristic requires qualitative assessment more than quantitative measures. This is consistent with the results of our SLR since we have not identified measures devoted to evaluate process maturity aspects. The absence of measures for process maturity hampers the application of the bottom-up process to further refine this characteristic.

4.3   Ecosystem Network Quality Characteristics

Since QualOSS does not address the network-related quality, this part of QuESo is exclusively based on the analysis of measures identified in our SLR.

QuESo proposes two ecosystem network-related characteristics: *resource health* and *network health*. In this paper we take as definition for *health* applied to software ecosystems: *longevity and a propensity for growth* [21,22].

Resource Health. *Resource health* facilitates the combination of value activities from multiple actors to obtain value-creating end products [23]. It is related to the financial health concept defined by Hartigh et al. [7]: *"The financial health is a long-term financially based reflection of a partner's strength of management and of its competences to exploit opportunities that arise within the ecosystem and is directly related to the capability of an ecosystem to face and survive disruptions"*. In the OSS ecosystem case this means that there is a set of partners or actors functioning as a unit and interacting among them. Their relationships are frequently operated through the exchange of information and resources. Two sub-characteristics, particularly relevant to resource health, are the *financial vitality* and the *trustworthiness* of the ecosystem.

The *financial vitality* is the viability and the ability to expand (i.e., robustness, ability to increase size and strength) of the ecosystem [24]. Two examples of financial measures that evaluate it are *liquidity* and *solvency*. They can be obtained directly, e.g., using balance sheet data of partners, but also indirectly, through the network relations.

Trustworthiness is the ability to establish a trusted partnership of shared responsibility in building an overall open source ecosystem [25]. Operational financial measures obtained from bankruptcy models (e.g., *Z-score* and *Zeta model*) are adequate to measure it because they take short-term and long-term survival into account [7].

QuESo has 5 measures that can be used to measure the resource health (see Table 3).

Network Health. Hartigh et al. [7] define *network health* as a representation of how well partners are connected in the ecosystem and the impact that each partner has in its local network. Healthy ecosystems show many relations and subsystems of different types of elements that are intensely related [26]. Furthermore, in a healthy OSS ecosystem network, these relations are mutualistic [27].

Table 3. List of measures for *resource health.*

Subcharacteristic	Measure
Trustworthiness	Zeta model
Trustworthiness	Z-score
Financial vitality	Liquidity
Financial vitality	Solvency
Financial vitality	Network resources

Van der Linden et al. [28] proposed to evaluate the network health of an OSS ecosystem before its adoption. To align network health with the identified measures we have refined it into four sub-characteristics: *interrelatedness, clustering, synergetic evolution* and *information consistency.*

Interrelatedness is the ability of the nodes of an OSS ecosystem to establish connections between them. It can be evaluated by measures such as *centrality* i.e., the number of network relations of a node, and *project activity diagrams* that allows to obtain the kind of project evolution.

Clustering is the capacity of the species (or nodes) in the entire ecosystem to be classified around its projects. It also enables small OSS projects to come together as a large social network with a critical mass [29]. Basic measures as *number community projects, number of files* and *variety in products* can be used to identify clusters using social network analysis techniques [30].

Synergetic evolution is the ability of the subsystems that constitute the whole ecosystem to form a dynamic and stable space-time structure [24,31]. Measures such as *ecosystem entropy* and *ecosystem reciprocity* can be used to evaluate synergetic evolution. The *ecosystem entropy* measure is based on the definition of software system entropy from Jacobson [32] who states that it is a measure for the disorder that always increases when a system is modified. *Ecosystem reciprocity* measures direct and active collaboration between the company and its customers in creating value propositions (e.g., through collaboration with key developers in an OSS community and other companies within the ecosystem) [33].

Information consistency is the consistency of the core information elements across the breadth of an ecosystem. The *code vocabulary map* measure evaluates this sub-characteristic. It consists of a summary of terms used in the source code that can be used to obtain a general overview of the domain language of the project's network.

QuESo has 15 measures that can measure the network health (see Table 4).

5 Examples of Measures

In this section we provide several examples extracted from the papers selected in the SLR. In particular we have selected the examples that belong to the *GNOME* software ecosystem. Our intention is to clarify the type of measures that are mentioned in this paper with examples.

In the following we present the selected *GNOME* examples of measure values organized by the characteristics of the QuESo quality model. We omit *process maturity* because we have not found quantitative measures to evaluate it (see explanation in Sect. 4.2). We also omit *resource health* measures because examples for them are not reported in the SLR papers for the *GNOME* ecosystem.

- The *maintenance capacity* can be evaluated from the *number of authors* measure which gives the amount of people that change files in a project. According to Goeminne and Mens [34] data, for the *GNOME* ecosystem there have been 3.500 different people having contributed at least once to at least one of the *GNOME* projects between 1997 and 2012. The *number of commits* measure is also relevant. Each commit corresponds to the action of making a set of changes permanent. According to Jergensen and Sarma [35] Jergensen and Sarma (2011) approximately 480.000 commits were made in *GNOME* from 1997 to 2007.
- A measure for *sustainability* is the *member activity rate* which gives a value between 0 and 1 that helps to analyse the effort balance, i.e., a zero value indicates a uniform distribution of the work, which means that each person has the same activity rate while a value of 1 means that a single person carries out all the work. The *member activity rate* for the *GNOME Evince* project has had a value between 0,7 and 0,8 from 1999 to 2009 according to Mens and Goeminne [34].
- The *network health* of an ecosystem can be evaluated by measures such as *number community projects* and *number of active projects*. For the *GNOME* ecosystem, there were more than 1.300 projects between 1997 and 2012 and more than 25 % of them had been active for more than six and a half years. At the lower side of the spectrum, more than 25 % of all projects had been active less than one year [36]. Another measure for network health is the *contributor activity graph*. According to Neu et al. [10], one of the contributors of the *GNOME* ecosystem has been working in 499 projects and has more than 15.000 changes between 1998 and 2011.

6   Validation: GNOME Case

In this section we present an early version of our quality model validation. The goal of this validation is to provide evidence of the feasibility to obtain the measures, and consequently, the feasibility to evaluate the corresponding characteristics and sub characteristics proposed in QuESo. We hope to validate this feasibility using the QuESo measures identified in the literature related to the *GNOME* ecosystem

6.1   Quality Model Validation

The validation of a quality model is very important and very difficult activity [37]. It is not practically possible to specify or measure all subcharacteristics

Table 4. List of measures for *network health.*

Subcharacteristic	Measure
Interrelatedness	Contributor activity graph
Interrelatedness	Project activity diagrams
Interrelatedness	Networks node connection
Interrelatedness	Ecosystem connectedness
Interrelatedness	Ecosystem cohesion
Interrelatedness	Centrality
Interrelatedness	Variety of partners
Clustering	Variety in products
Clustering	Number community projects
Clustering	Number of active projects
Clustering	Number of files
Synergetic evolution	Distribution over the species
Synergetic evolution	Ecosystem entropy
Synergetic evolution	Ecosystem reciprocity
Information consistency	Code vocabulary map

for all parts of a OSS ecosystem. It also requires long period of time. Similarly it is not usually practical to specify or measure quality in use for all possible stakeholders scenarios [5]. The model should be tailored before use to identify those characteristics and subcharacteristics that are most important, and the different types of measure depending on the stakeholder goals and also to provide some evidence of the feasibility to obtain these measures, as mentioned in [21], one of the most habitual problems is the *absence of data* to calculate the measures. However, in order to gain confidence in the quality of the work, an initial feasibility and availability validation of the QuESo measures will be done.

6.2 GNOME Ecosystem Case

In this section we present an early version of our quality model validation. The goal of this validation is to provide evidence of the feasibility to obtain the measures, and consequently, the feasibility to evaluate the corresponding characteristics and sub characteristics proposed in QuESo. We hope to validate this feasibility using the QuESo measures identified in the literature related to the *GNOME* ecosystem.

We divided the process in two phases, similar to Samoladas [38]: the identification of the literature related to *GNOME* ecosystem and the specification of the QuESO measures that are available for the *GNOME* ecosystem.

In the first phase, we have identified several papers that have measures for analysing the *GNOME* ecosystem. In the second phase the selected works were analysed as follows: first the measures with available values were extracted,

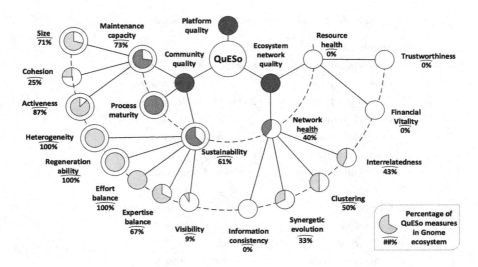

Fig. 3. *GNOME* ecosystem evaluation with QuESo.

secondly the measures were classified according to the QuESo measure classification, and finally analysed the situation for each quality aspects of QuESo.

Figure 3 shows the QuESo graphical model with the percentage of measures found in the literature for each quality aspect and Table 5 shows the number of measures found for each subcharacteristisc. In the Appendix B we show a detailed table with the *GNOME* measures and the papers associated. The column source of this table lists the papers with values for each measure. The *community quality* dimension has measures associated with each subcharacteristic, and some of them have values for all the associated measures. However, in the case of the *ecosystem network quality* dimension we have not found values for the measures related to *resource health*, and only the 40 % of measures of *network health* have values.

6.3   Observations

From the results shown in Fig. 3 and Table 5 we made some observations:

- There are many works with measure values for the community while there are few works with measure values related to the ecosystem network.
- The papers found do not cover the whole set measures in the QuESo quality model.

The first observation is also mentioned by other authors, for example, Jansen et al. [21] wrote that there is little literature that studied OSS from an ecosystem perspective, while Manikas et al. [39] wrote that most of the works studied OSS from a project or community perspective.

For the second observation, we cannot state that there is full availability of measure values, however it worth to mention that in this case we limited

Table 5. List of measures by QuESo subcharacteristic.

Sub-characteristic	Number of measures
Size	5
Cohesion	1
Activeness	13
Heterogeneity	1
Regeneration ability	2
Effort balance	11
Expertice Balance	2
Visibility	1
Information consistency	0
Synergetic evolution	1
Clustering	2
Interrelatedness	3
Trustworthiness	0
Financial vitality	0

the sources to the ones published in the literature. Other methods can include direct access to the *GNOME* data sources (e.g., the number of files, number of downloads, web page request, and code vocabulary map). Other measures such as z-score, liquidity, and solvency can be obtained using surveys or public data.

7   Discussion

Some observations were made during the design of this quality model. In the following, the most interesting ones are discussed:

- *Completeness:* since we followed a mainly bottom-up strategy, the completeness of the quality model depends on how complete the set of measures found in the literature is. In this sense, we would like to remark that our quality model may be not complete by one or more of the following reasons: there may be some papers with relevant measures not included in the SLR because they were not present in digital libraries or because our search string did not find them; another reason could be that some important measures are not yet reported in the literature. In this work, our intention was not to invent new measures but to organize the existing ones into a quality model.
- *Quantitative vs. Qualitative:* the measures found in the literature are mostly quantitative, but a quality assessment may also include qualitative evaluations. For example, we commented in Sect. 4.2 the lack of measures for process maturity because in this case the assessment needs to be done with qualitative evaluations of the community. Since we have focused on quantitative measures, there may be other characteristics of the quality model that require or that may be complemented with qualitative evaluations.

- *Unbalanced Distribution of Measures:* just by looking into the measure tables, it is easy to observe that the amount of measures for some characteristics is high (e.g., *activeness* with 17 measures, *visibility* with 11 measures) while for other is very low (e.g., *heterogeneity* with 1 measure, *information consistency* with 1 measure). This unbalanced situation could be an indicator that more research is needed for the characteristics with a low amount of measures.
- *Measure Names:* we have named the measures included in the QuESo quality model with the same names they are referred to in the SLR papers from where they were extracted. The reason for this is to improve traceability. However, some of those measure names might be ambiguous or misleading because it is not evident from them how the measure is evaluated (e.g., *project activity diagrams*). To improve measure understandability we have listed their definitions in the Appendix A.
- *Assesment Process:* It is worth mentioning that to perform a complete quality assessment of a software ecosystem we first would need to define the assessment process which is out of the scope of this paper. The *quality assessment process* will have to deal with, e.g., How are the values of each measure interpreted (i.e., defining what are the good and the bad values)?; How can the measures be merged to provide the assessment for a particular sub-characteristic of the quality model?; or What are the principles to perform the assessment with missing, incorrect, and/or inconsistent measure data? We are will provide the answer to these and other questions as part of our future work in this topic.

8   Conclusions

In this paper we have presented QuESo, a quality model for assessing the quality of OSS ecosystems. This quality model has been constructed following a bottom-up strategy that consisted in searching the available measures for OSS ecosystems in the literature and then organize them into several quality characteristics. The presented quality model covers three aspects of OSS ecosystems: the platform, the community, and the ecosystem network; which altogether are a good representation of the most important aspects of an OSS ecosystem.

This quality model can be used as a starting point for the quality assessment of an OSS ecosystem, and it is in our plans for the future work to define a complete quality assessment process (as described in Sect. 5) and to apply it in a real quality assessment. As consequence new measures may be needed for the assessment, but this is the best way to improve, and complete the quality model, and a way to prove its capabilities in quality assessment.

Acknowledgements. This work is a result of the RISCOSS project, funded by the EC 7th Framework Programme FP7/2007–2013 under the agreement number 318249. We would also like to thank Carme Quer for her assistance and the contribution of EOSSAC project, founded by the Ministry of Economy and Competitiveness of the Spanish government (TIN2013-44641-P) is also acknowledged.

Appendix A: Measure Definitions

Amount of Inquires or Feature Requests. Number of inquire or feedbacks received for the OSS community. Contributions could be corrective, adaptive, perfective or preventive. R8.

Betweenness Centrality. Reflects the number of shortest paths that pass through a specific node. R1.

Bug tracking Activity. Number of comments created in project bug tracker and total number of actions in the bug tracker. R2, R3, R6, R8, R15.

Buildup of Assets. Total factor productivity over time. Can be measured using individual company data. R4.

Centrality. Number of relations clique memberships. Number of individual network relations of a partner. The more central partner is the most persistent. When the partners are in clique or cluster, its persistence is considered high. Because is regarded as a secure environment. R1, R4, R6, R7.

Cluster of Collaborating Developers. The nodes are developers and the edges between them represent projects on which they collaborated. They both make modifications to the project for at least a certain number of times. R9, R10.

Code Vocabulary Map. Summary of terms used in the source code of the project. The vocabulary map is a tool for the developer who wants to obtain a general overview of the domain language of a project. R9.

Community Effort. The combined effort of all members belonging to community. R3.

Contributor Activity Graph. The contributor distribution at ecosystem level. R12.

Contributor Commit Rate. Average between first and last commit. R12.

Date of Last Commit. Date of last commit of a project/community. R11.

Developer Activity Diagrams. Give an overview of the contributors daily activity within an ecosystem. R10, R12.

Distribution over the Species. Variety measure for niche creation factor. The equality of the division of partners over the species. E.g., the distribution between numbers of resellers, number of system integrators, numbers of OEM's. R4, R11.

Ecosystem Cohesion. Number of relations present in a subgroup/maximum possible of relation among all the nodes in the sub-group. R4.

Ecosystem Connectedness. Number of relations as a proportion of the theoretically maximum number of relations in all ecosystem. Is a metric of connectedness. Is a property that keeps communities structure safe from risks, guaranteeing their well-being and health. R4.

Ecosystem Entropy. The second law of thermodynamics, in principle, states that a closed system's disorder cannot be reduced, it can only remain unchanged or increase. A measure of this disorder is entropy. This law also seems plausible for software systems; as a system is modified, its disorder, or entropy, always increases. Can be viewed as being similar to the measurement of the existence of order or disorder among the participating software components, software products, or software organizations. R17.

Expertise View Contributor. Visualization about a contributor expertise based on file extensions (number and type of files changed within a month). R12.

Files Changed. Number of files that has been changed. R12.

Files per Version. Number of files per version. R6, R11, R12.

Geographical Distribution. Geographical distribution of community members. R2.

Job Advertisements. Number of job advertisements on the project/community. R8.

Lines Added. Lines added. R7, R12.

Lines Changed. Lines changed. R12.

Lines Removed. Lines removed. R12.

Liquidity. Provide an indication whether a partner is able to meet its short-term obligations. Can be measured with: financial status of a partner; counting the number of new members in a business ecosystem. R4.

Mailing List. Number of messages posted to project mailing lists and the number of responses obtained from those messages. R1, R2, R6, R11, R15.

Maximum Number of Commits of a Developer. The size and density of a contributor in a project. R3, R12.

Member Activity Rate. Activity rate 1 means that a single person carries out all the work. R11.

Member Effort. The effort of member m in community c. R3, R10, R11.

Network Resources. Measure for delivery innovations factor of productivity. They can be measured directly, e.g., using balance of partners, but also indirectly, through the network relations. R4.

Networks Node Connection. Connections between central and non-central species or partners. R4.

New Members. Counting the number of new members at any point in time. R4.

Number of Active Projects. Number of active projects. R3, R10.

Number of Authors. Number of authors for projects. Author can change files in a project. R3, R11.

Number of Bug Fixers. Number bug fixers in the community. R8.

Number Committers. Number of committers per project. R3, R9, R11.

Number of Activity Communities. The number of activity communities in which member m is involved. R3, R7.

Number of Commits. Total number of commits containing source code, documentation, and translation. Average number of commits per week (project/community). R3, R6, R9, R10, R11, R12, R14, R15.

Number of Community Project. Number of projects built on top of the platform of a community. R3, R8.

Number of Contributors. Total of contributors per project. R3, R8, R12.

Number of Core Developers. Core developer contribute most of the code and oversee the design and evolution. of the project. R6, R10.

Number of Developer Releases. Number of releases that a developer has been active on a project. R6.

Number of Developer Projects. Number of projects of a developer. R12.

Number of Downloads. Number of downloads from the official community portal or mirrors. R7, R8.

Number of Event People. The number of people participating in project events and meetings gives direct information on the activity in the community. R8.

Number of Files. Files during projects life. R14, R11.

Number of Mailing List Users. Number of users subscribed to the project mailing list. R2, R6, R8, R11.

Number of Members. The number of activity members involved in community c. R3, R5, R6, R16.

Number of Nodes and Edge. Number of nodes and edges. R1.

Number of Passive User. Passive users in the community. R8.

Number of Readers. Number of readers in the community. R8.

Number of Scientific Publications. Number of scientific publications mentioning the community. R8.

Outdegree of Keystone Actors. Is defined as someone who has a lot of developers he works with and also plays a large role in the software ecosystem. R7

Principal Member Activity. The principal activity of a member m for a given time t. Community c for which m carried out the most effort. R3, R10, R11.

Project Activity Diagrams. Allow identify the project evolution comparing six metrics; calculating the contributors involvement distribution. R2, R12.

Project Developer Experience. Total number of releases in which the developer was active. R6.

Reciprocity of the Ecosystem. *(definition not provided)*. R7.

Relation between Categorical Event and Developer Participation. Relation between categorical event and developer participation. R15.

Social Media Hits. Number of hits the project gets in the social media. R7, R8.

Solvency. Value creation measure for niche creation. Can be measured by standard metrics such as revenue share or profit share of newly introduced products or technologies. An alternative is to look at the build-up of partner equity. R4.

Temporal Community Effort. The combined effort of all members belonging to community c during time period t. R3.

Total Effort of Members. Total effort done by a particular community member m in a set of communities C. R3.

Variety in Products. Offered by the partner depends on alliances with other partners. Euclidean distances towards the overall mean of the business ecosystem can be used to measured most of these variety of scores. R4, R13.

Variety of Partners. Covariance with market indicates the variety of different partners a partner has. R4.

Visibility. Tell us something about the centrality of a partner in the market. Popularity of the partner R4.

Web Page Requests. Total request to OSS community web page. R8.

Zeta Model. Bankruptcy classification score model. R4.

Z-score. Bankruptcy model to test the creditworthiness and solvency of partners. R4.

Appendix B: QuESo Measures in *GNOME* Ecosystem

Measure	Sources
Bug tracking activity	R2, R3, R6, R11
Centrality	R6
Cluster of collaborating developers	R10
Community effort	R3
Contributor activity graph	R12
Contributor commit rate	R12
Date of last commit	R11
Developer activity diagrams	R10, R12
Distribution over the species	R11
Expertise view contributor	R12
Files changed	R12
Files per version	R6, R11, R12
Geographical distribution	R2
Lines added	R12
Lines changed	R12
Lines removed	R12
Mailing list	R2, R6, R11
Maximum Number of commits of a developer	R3, R12
Member effort	R10
Members activity rate	R11
New members	R6
Number community projects	R3
Number of active projects	R3, R10
Number of activity communities	R3, R7
Number of authors	R3, R11
Number of commiters	R3, R11
Number of commits	R3, R6, R10, R12
Number of contributors	R3, R12
Number of core developers	R6, R10
Number of developer projects	R12
Number of developer releases	R6
Number of mailing list users	R2, R6, R11
Number of members	R3, R6
Principal member activity	R3
Project activity diagrams	R2, R12
Project developer experience	R6
Temporal community effort	R3
Total effort of members	R3

References

1. Jansen, S., Cusumano, M.: Defining software ecosystems: a survey of software platforms and business network governance. [20], pp. 13–28
2. Lungu, M., Malnati, J., Lanza, M.: Visualizing gnome with the small project observatory. In: Proceedings of the 6th MSR, IEEE. pp. 103–106 (2009)
3. ISO/IEC 9126: Product quality - Part 1: Quality model (2001)
4. Wieringa, R.: Design science as nested problem solving. In: Proceedings of the 4th International Conference on Design Science Research in Information Systems and Technology, pp. 8:1–8:12. ACM, New York, NY, USA (2009)
5. ISO/IEC 25000: Systems and software engineering - Systems and software Quality Requirements and Evaluation (SQuaRE) - Guide to SQuaRE (2014)
6. Soto, M., Ciolkowski, M.: The QualOSS open source assessment model measuring performance of open source communities. In: Proceedings of the 3rd ESEM. pp. 498–501 (2009)
7. Hartigh, E., Visscher, W., Tol, M., Salas, A.J.: Measuring the health of a business ecosystem. [20], pp. 221–245
8. Iansiti, M., Levien, R.: Keystones and dominators: framing operating and technology strategy in a business ecosystem. Technical report, Harvard Business School (2004)
9. Mens, T., Goeminne, M.: Analysing the evolution of social aspects of open source software ecosystems. In: Proceedings of the 3rd IWSECO. pp. 1–14 (2011)
10. Neu, S., Lanza, M., Hattori, L., D'Ambros, M.: Telling stories about GNOME with complicity. In: Proceedings of the 6th VISSOFT, pp. 1–8 (2011)
11. Kilamo, T., Hammouda, I., Mikkonen, T., Aaltonen, T.: From proprietary to open source - growing an open source ecosystem. J. Syst. Softw. **85**, 1467–1478 (2012)
12. Manikas, K., Hansen, K.M.: Software ecosystems a systematic literature review. J. Syst. Softw. **86**, 1294–1306 (2013)
13. Barbosa, O., Alves, C.: A systematic mapping study on software ecosystems. In: Proceedings of the 3rd IWSECO, pp. 15–26 (2011)
14. Kitchenham, B., Charters, S.: Guidelines for performing systematic literature reviews in software engineering version 2.3. Technical report, Keele University EBSE (2007)
15. Franco-Bedoya, O., Ameller, D., Costal, D., Franch, X.: Protocol for a systematic literature review on open source-software ecosystems. Technical report, Universitat Politcnica de Catalunya (2014). Available on www.essi.upc.edu/~gessi/papers/queso-slrprotocol.pdf
16. Jansen, S., van Capelleveen, G.: Quality review and approval methods for extensions in software ecosystems. [20], pp. 187–217
17. Franch, X., Carvallo, J.P.: Using quality models in software package selection. IEEE Softw. **20**, 34–41 (2003)
18. Behkamal, B., Kahani, M., Akbari, M.K.: Customizing ISO 9126 quality model for evaluation of B2B applications. Inf. Softw. Technol. **51**, 599–609 (2009)
19. Radulovic, F., Garcia-Castro, R.: Extending software quality models - a sample in the domain of semantic technologies. In: Proceedings of the 23rd SEKE, pp. 25–30 (2011)
20. Jansen, S., Brinkkemper, S., Cusumano, M.: Software Ecosystems: Analyzing and Managing Business Networks in the Software Industry. Edward Elgar Publishing, Northampton (2013)

21. Jansen, S.: Measuring the health of open source software ecosystems: beyond the scope of project health. Inf. Softw. Technol. **56**, 1508–1519 (2014)
22. Lucassen, G., Rooij, K., Jansen, S.: Ecosystem health of cloud PaaS providers. In: Proceedings of the 4th ICSOB, pp. 183–194 (2013)
23. Anderson, J.C., Narus, J.A., Narayandas, D.: Business Market Management: Understanding, Creating, and Delivering Value, 3rd edn. Prentice Hall, Upper Saddle River (2009)
24. Li, X., Jie, X., Li, Q., Zhang, Q.: Research on the evaluation of business ecosystem health. In: Proceedings of the 6th ICMSEM, pp. 1009–1020. Springer (2013)
25. Agerfalk, P.J., Fitzgerald, B.: Outsourcing to an unknown workforce: exploring opensourcing as a global sourcing strategy. Mis Quartely **32**, 385–409 (2008)
26. Gamalielsson, J., Lundell, B., Lings, B.: The Nagios community: an extended quantitative analysis. In: Proceedings of the 6th OSS, pp. 85–96. Springer (2010)
27. Lundell, B., Forssten, B.: Exploring health within OSS ecosystems. In: Proceedings of the 1st OSCOMM. pp. 1–5 (2009)
28. van der Linden, F., Lundell, B., Marttiin, P.: Commodification of industrial software: a case for open source. IEEE Softw. **26**, 77–83 (2009)
29. Scacchi, W.: Free/open source software development: recent research results and emerging opportunities. In: Proceedings of the 6th ESEC-FSE, pp. 459–468 (2007)
30. Lungu, M., Lanza, M., Gîrba, T., Robbes, R.: The small project observatory: visualizing software ecosystems. Sci. Comput. Prog. **75**, 264–275 (2010)
31. Haken, H.: Naturwissenschaften. Synergetics **67**, 121–128 (1980)
32. Jacobson, I.: Object-Oriented Software Engineering: A Use Case Driven Approach. Addison Wesley, Redwood City (2004)
33. Glott, R., Haaland, K., Bannier, S.: D3.1 Draft Business Model Risk Requirements Report (2013) Deliverable of the RISCOSS FP7 project (grant 318249)
34. Goeminne, M., Claes, M., Mens, T.: A historical dataset for the gnome ecosystem. In: Proceedings of the 10th Working Conference on Mining Software Repositories. MSR 2013, pp. 225–228. ACM (2013)
35. Jergensen, C., Sarma, A.: The onion patch: migration in open source ecosystems. In: Proceedings of the 19th SIGSOFT and 13th ESEC/FSE, pp. 70–80. ACM (2011)
36. Goeminne, M., Mens, T.: Analyzing ecosystems for open source software developer communities. [20], pp. 247–275
37. von Wangenheim, C., Hauck, J., Zoucas, A., Salviano, C., McCaffery, F., Shull, F.: Creating software process capability/maturity models. IEEE Softw. **27**, 92–94 (2010)
38. Samoladas, I., Gousios, G., Spinellis, D., Stamelos, I.: The SQO-OSS quality model: measurement based open source software evaluation. In: Russo, B., Damiani, E., Hissam, S., Lundell, B., Succi, G. (eds.) Open Source Development, Communities and Quality. The International Federation for Information Processing, vol. 275, pp. 237–248. Springer, US (2008)
39. Manikas, K., Hansen, K.M.: Reviewing the health of software ecosystems-a conceptual framework proposal. In: Proceedings of the International Workshop on Software Ecosystems, pp. 33–44. Citeseer (2013)

SLR References

R1. Gamalielsson, J., Lundell, B., and Lings, B. (2010). The Nagios community: An extended quantitative analysis. In *Proceedings of the 6th OSS*, pages 85–96. Springer.

R2. Goeminne, M. and Mens, T. (2010). A framework for analysing and visualising open source software ecosystems. In *Proceedings of IWPSE-EVOL*, pages 42–47.

R3. Goeminne, M. and Mens, T. (2013). *Software Ecosystems: Analyzing and Managing Business Networks in the Software Industry*, chapter Analyzing ecosystems for open source software developer communities, pages 247–275. In [20].

R4. Hartigh, E., Visscher, W., Tol, M., and Salas, A. J. (2013). *Software Ecosystems: Analyzing and Managing Business Networks in the Software Industry*, chapter Measuring the health of a business ecosystem, pages 221–245. In [20].

R5. Jansen, S., Souer, J., Luinenburg, L., and Brinkkemper, S. (2012). Shades of gray: Opening up a software producing organization with the open software enterprise model. *Journal of Systems and Software*, 85(7):1495–1510.

R6. Jergensen, C. and Sarma, A. (2011). The onion patch: migration in open source ecosystems. In *Proceedings of the 19th ACM-SIGSOFT*, pages 70–80.

R7. Kabbedijk, J. and Jansen, S. (2011). Steering insight: An exploration of the ruby software ecosystem. In *Proceedings of the 2nd ICSOB*, pages 44–55. Springer.

R8. Kilamo, T., Hammouda, I., Mikkonen, T., and Aaltonen, T. (2012). From proprietary to open source - Growing an open source ecosystem. *Journal of Systems and Software*, 85(7):1467–1478.

R9. Lungu, M., Lanza, M., Gîrba, T., and Robbes, R. (2010). The Small Project Observatory: Visualizing software ecosystems. *Science of Computer Programming*, 75(4):264–275.

R10. Lungu, M., Malnati, J., and Lanza, M. (2009). Visualizing gnome with the small project observatory. In *Proceedings of the 6th MSR*, pages 103–106. IEEE.

R11. Mens, T. and Goeminne, M. (2011). Analysing Evolution of Social Aspects of Open Source Software Ecosystems. In *Proceedings of the 3rd IWSECO*, pages 1–14.

R12. Neu, S., Lanza, M., Hattori, L., and D'Ambros, M. (2011). Telling stories about GNOME with Complicity. In *Proceedings of the 6th VISSOFT*, pages 1–8.

R13. Scacchi, W. and Alspaugh, T. A. (2012). Understanding the role of licenses and evolution in open architecture software ecosystems. *Journal of Systems and Software*, 85(7):1479–1494.

R14. Shao, J., Kuk, G., Anand, S., Morley, J. G., Jackson, M. J., and Mitchell, T. (2012). Mapping Collaboration in Open Source Geospatial Ecosystem. *Transactions in GIS*, 16(4):581–597.

R15. Ververs, E., van Bommel, R., and Jansen, S. (2011). Influences on developer participation in the Debian software ecosystem. In *Proceedings of the MEDES*, pages 89–93. ACM.

R16. Weiss, M. (2011). Economics of collectives. In *Proceedings of the 15th SPLC*, pages 39:1–39:8. ACM.

R17. Yu, L., Cawley, J., and Ramaswamy, S. (2012). Entropy-Based Study of Components in Open-Source Software Ecosystems. *INFOCOMP Journal of Computer Science*, 11(1):22–31.

Definition of Software Quality Evaluation and Measurement Plans: A Reported Experience Inside the Audio-Visual Preservation Context

Isabella Biscoglio[✉] and Eda Marchetti

Institute of Information Science and Technologies "Alessandro Faedo",
National Research Council, Pisa, Italy
{isabella.biscoglio,eda.marchetti}@isti.cnr.it

Abstract. The digital preservation want to guarantee accessible and usable over time digital audio-visual media content, regardless of the challenges of media failure and technological change. For this aim, the current technologies for digital audio-visual media preservation deal with complex technological, organizational, economic and rights-related issues: ensuring the development and use of high-quality software could be a key factor for their success. The paper reports an experience matured inside the Presto4U project concerning the requirements elicitation corresponding of some functional and non-functional requirements. These have been mapped on some characteristics and sub-characteristics of a quality model and a customized software measurement plans has been implemented. An example of the quality evaluation plans application is also reported.

Keywords: Software quality · Requirements elicitation · Digital audio-visual media preservation · Measurement

1 Introduction

Over the last fifteen years the dynamic continuously evolving nature of the IT industry concerning audio-video media and technologies has produced the important issues of the long-term preservation of digital audio-visual media. This research field is becoming more and more complex due to the vast range of topics it includes: like for instance technological, organizational, economic and rights-related issues. Although good solutions are emerging it remains very difficult for the great majority of media owners to gain access to advanced audio-visual preservation technologies. Major problems are connected with the short technology cycles and lifetimes which causes a rapid product decay and technological obsolescence. These issues have an impact on digital material preservation in terms of source and process of preservation.

In this context one of the currently on-going European project targeting the topic of audiovisual preservation is Presto4U project - European Technology for Digital Audiovisual Media Preservation [32]. Inside the Presto4U project the identification of a quality evaluation process, able to guarantee the development and use of high-quality software both by technology and service providers as well as media owners, has been

© Springer International Publishing Switzerland 2015
A. Holzinger et al. (Eds.): ICSOFT 2014, CCIS 555, pp. 63–80, 2015.
DOI: 10.1007/978-3-319-25579-8_4

adopted and promoted as a key solutions for solving audiovisual media preservation issues. Thus a crucial work of the project, and of this paper, is the identification of a quality evaluation plan for the Communities of Practice (CoPs), i.e. the principal group of actors of audiovisual media preservation (users, technology vendors and service providers), able to satisfy the specific requirements identified during the project life-time. Indeed these plans will be useful to achieving the established quality level and to make easy the technology transfer of research results.

On the other hand the software quality and its evaluation have been discussed for several years and from different points of view [30]. Also in the context of standard-ization, quality is very well defined and many international standards have been published about software processes and products quality [13, 15, 19, 20, 22]. However to the best of our knowledge none of the available quality standards and/or best practices has been currently specialized and adapted for the specific digital audio-visual preservation context. All these documents and sources of information constitute a very interesting base for the digital preservation context, as models, characteristics, mea-sures and methods that they present can be considered or readapted for preservation purposes. Thus audio-visual technologies could be evaluated on the basis of software quality standards and the results could suggest important decisions about their adoption or improvement. Nevertheless, for this aim it is necessary a preliminary activity of preservation requirement elicitation and a successive mapping of these preservation requirements on the characteristics and sub-characteristics of a quality model on which these requirements impact. Only later an evaluation process could be implementable.

Continuing the work initiated in [4, 5], this paper presents the procedural steps followed from requirements elicitation to the definition of a specific quality model and the relative customized software measurement plans. With respect to specific quality issues for the digital collections, following activities are carried out: the definition of a software product quality model customized for audio-visual collection tools; the definition of two high-level quality evaluation plans; the specification of customized software measure-ment plans on the basis of international standards on software products quality.

The paper is organized as in the following: the Sect. 2 presents the motivation of this work. The Sect. 3 introduces the topic of software quality and an overview about the international standards for software quality. In Sect. 4, the quality evaluation procedure and the adopted quality models are presented. In Sect. 5, the explorative case study is shown, and an example of product evaluation provided. Discussion and conclusion close the paper.

2 Motivation

The decay and the technological obsolescence of the software products that are used in digital material preservation context represent a serious problem in terms of sources and process of preservation, content management, digital archiving, etc. As above introduced, ensuring use of high-quality software by the help of international standards, can limit these risks and promote the adoption of good practices.

In the digital preservation context, two models are currently used as a reference. One is the Open Archival Information System (OAIS) [14]. This model concerns technical aspects of digital object's life cycle, as ingest, archival storage, data management and access, and it also recommends metadata issues. It mainly targets the preservation aspects regarding terminology and archival concepts or different long-term preservation strategies and techniques. However it does not deal with quality aspects of the software. The other is the non-functional requirements (NFR) Framework [7] which is focused on the elicitation requirement activity. This framework is mainly based on a graph of interconnected goals each one representing an NFR for the system under development. This paper does not rely on [7, 14], because the first does not deal with quality aspects of the software and the latter requires for its application a background of technical knowledge that many involved (Presto4U) stakeholders do not have.

The paper target instead the standards family ISO/IEC 25000, 2005 [22], which is focused on software quality evaluation models. Models, characteristics, measures and methods proposed in these standards have been specialized or readapted for audio-visual preservation purposes. However as discussed in [31] these standards only provide a conceptual framework, and not a ready-to-use solutions usable in every context. The necessity of adaptation and revision becomes a pressing exigency, mainly when the considered systems or products do not perfectly fit with the characteristics and peculiarities of classical software engineering.

Besides, even when the standards are very comprehensive and specific, they still show some common weaknesses, which could have an important impact on applicability of the standards themselves [1, 2, 29, 33] such as:

- the terminology: it could be not fully aligned with the classic measurement terminology in software engineering;
- the metrics identification: the metrics provided by the various standard could not be properly aligned;
- the results analysis: not all the standards propose the same ranking for the considered metrics. Thus possible conversions or alignment of various ranking considered should be defined;
- the same reference scale: wherever possible for the same ranking the same reference scale should be adopted so make easier finals quality assessment value.
- the extension of the characteristics: each quality standards should try to include or extend the characteristics already defined in different available standards so to have a more uniform and complete coverage of quality requirements.

According to [6, 8] the risk of failure for the measurement programs could be: a misunderstanding of what is to be measured, why and how it is to be measured; an inadequate data collection; a wrong interpretations of data; the lack of trained and expert resources required to dedicate to measurement; the expensive costs for measurement programs; the incorrect mapping of organization goals with appropriate measures.

The criticalities underlined in the various quality evaluation procedures in many cases make very difficult the adoption of the standards into the products development. In spite of the limits of international standards applicability, considering the quality as a limited number of independent characteristics [15] allows to evaluate the most interesting for each CoPs characteristics and quality levels ("internal", "external" and "in-use").

The ambitions of this paper are to overcome some of the above-mentioned weaknesses considering the specific context of the audio-visual preservation by and to define the of audio-video preservation needs and related requirements so to enhance the quality evaluation procedure and the adoption of the international standards.

3 Background

In the field of software engineering, the evaluation of software product quality is vital to both acquisition and development of software that meets quality requirements. In the following, some of the most important international standards will be presented; preliminary some specific terms will be shown then detail about software quality are highlighted. In particular: *software quality* "the totality of features and characteristics of a software product that bear on its ability to satisfy stated or implied needs" [13]; *software quality characteristics* "a set of attributes of a software product by which its quality is described and evaluated. A software quality characteristic may be refined into multiple levels of sub-characteristics" [13]; *Software quality metric* "a quantitative scale and method, which can be used to determine the value a feature takes for a specific software product" [13].

About software quality, the standardization bodies that have mostly published are:

- ISO (International Organization for Standardization).
- IEC (International Electrotechnical Commission).
- IEEE (Institute for Electrical and Electronic Engineers).

The IEC cooperates closely with ISO and IEEE, and the standards developed jointly with ISO carry the acronym of both organizations.

Considering the ISO and IEC, two of the most important joint standards developed for the software quality evaluation have been: the ISO/IEC 9126 "Software engineering - Product Quality" with its four versions [15–18]. The principal merit of ISO/IEC 9126 standard can be found in its attempt to reduce the product quality concept to a limited number of independent characteristics and to have developed the notion of various levels of qualities ("internal", "external" and "in-use"). Nevertheless, it was not successful in providing meaningful, quantitatively expressed (or measurable) indicators associated to quality characteristics [34].

The standards [13, 19] are converged into ISO/IEC 25000, SQuaRE [22] which represents families of standards and constitutes the result of an effort to harmonize previous standards in order to establish criteria for the specification of software products quality requirements, their measurement and evaluation. The general objective for SQuaRE is to respond to the evolving needs of users (those who develop and those who acquire software products) through an improved and unified set of normative documents covering three different and complementary quality processes: requirements specification, measurement and evaluation.

Other standards involved in the quality assessment are: ISO/IEC 15939 standard [21], that defines a measurement process applicable to system and software engineering and management disciplines, the ISO/IEC/IEEE 12207 standard [27] which focuses on the processes in the life cycle of a software product or service and the ISO/IEC/IEEE

15288 [28], which targets the processes in the life cycle of a system. Finally there is ISO/IEC 15504 [20], which deals with process assessment and its implementations in terms of guidelines and tools.

The IEEE standards encompass software and systems lifecycles, from concept and development to delivery and maintenance. Also the reuse of software components is included. The most important are: the standard IEEE 830 [9], which focus on content and characteristics of a Software Requirements Specification, the standard IEEE 1012 [10], which defines the Verification & Validation (V&V) processes in terms of specific activities and includes [27] and IEEE 1074 [11] which defines the process activities mandatory for the development and maintenance of software.

4 Quality Evaluation Procedure

In this section the experience matured inside the Presto4U project for the definition of the software quality evaluation procedure is reported. In tune with the nature of the project and its particular interests, each CoP worked for producing a customized set of preservation needs to be given to software quality expert evaluators. According to a bottom-up approach, in order to ensure that the products meet user and customer needs, various stakeholders, chosen among the project partners, have been involved for producing a software *quality model customized* for digital collections. In particular the aspects considered during the requirements elicitation activity have been:

1. the definition of the project *scope:* digital audio-visual preservation;
2. the definition of the project *purpose:* the project aims to develop a body of knowledge on the status of digital preservation practice (problems and needs), to map preservation needs in quality characteristics, to evaluate the used tools, to identify useful research results and to promote their adoption and implementation;
3. the definition of the different *products* that could be considered as a target for the quality evaluation procedure. In the audiovisual preservation context, they can be either tools for mapping between metadata formats and standards or for archiving and restoring of audiovisual files, or for automatic extracting and enriching of metadata of audiovisual contents, or for evaluating the quality of the various contents (like images and sounds).

On the basis of these elements and the availability of the involved stakeholders, the first steps of a quality evaluation process have been performed and the most important quality aspects in the digital audio-visual preservation context have been highlighted.

Successively, on the bases of the set of audio-visual preservation needs of each CoP, a list of functional and non-functional requirements expressed in natural language has been defined. These requirements have been mapped on some characteristics and sub-characteristics of the quality model defined from an original software product quality model according to [23] so that two *high-level quality evaluation plans* (one for functional requirements and one for non- functional requirements) have been defined. Then according to [25] the identified subsets of software product characteristics have been associated to quality measures and measurement functions and two *customized software measurement plans* have been defined. Finally the evaluation stringency has been selected as opportune test strategies to be applied and test results to be achieved.

The target of the evaluation procedure considered is therefore to identify for each CoP the most important issues that could be responsible of the preservation quality level. Without the pretense to define general results, in the following sections further details about the steps useful for producing the *high level software product quality evaluation plans* and the *customized software product measurement plans* are presented.

Inside a complete software product quality evaluation process, the high level software product quality evaluation plans constitute an outcome of the first phase of the process, called "establish the evaluation requirements", and an input of the second phase called "specify the evaluation" which produces in turn as outcome the customized software measurement plans. On the basis of these last plans the software quality of the storage tools used inside the Presto4U project will be subsequently measured. However, phases that follow the "specify the evaluation" in product quality evaluation process [26], i.e. "designing the evaluation and "executing the evaluation" are out of the scope of this paper. In the following sections further detail of the phase of the evaluation procedure considered are provided.

4.1   Establishing the Evaluation Requirements

Inspired by [26] and by the software product quality evaluation process that it contains, the activity of "establishing the evaluation" requirements included the following steps:

1. *Establishing the Purpose of the Evaluation:* As a purpose of the project was evaluating the used tools in order to identify useful research that could promote their adoption, purpose of the evaluation is reconsidering the acceptability of these products.
2. *Obtaining the Software Product Quality Requirements:* In order to ensure that the products meet user and customer needs, *stakeholders* were detected for collecting information and a *quality model* was defined as reference. In the Presto4U evaluation process stakeholders were identified among the staff of the CoPs. By interviews and questionnaires, a list of audio-visual preservation needs came to light. In particular, for overcoming initial differences between basic terminologies (software engineering vs audio-video preservation), a shared and informal glossary has been preliminary defined preliminary. For confidential reasons this glossary cannot be included in this paper. On the basis of detected preservation needs, a list of audio-visual preservation requirements has been defined using as quality model the *product quality model* reported in [23].
3. *Identify Product Parts to be Included in the Evaluation:* Inside the audio-visual preservation environment different products could be considered as a target for the quality evaluation: such as tools for archiving and restoring of audiovisual files, for evaluating the quality of the various contents (like images and sounds) and so on. Besides, each product can have specific preservation quality requirements due to the target usage or its different nature (product purchased, in a development stage, fully

developed, etc.) or the hardware, software and network environment in which the product will be used. The types of identified products are tools that perform different quality aspects like for instance the quality of the content ("are the images good and the sound clean?"), the validity of the files ("are they adherent to the file standards and correctly playable?"). The parts of tools that could response to these questions are these parts to be included in the evaluation.

4. *Define the Stringency of the Evaluation in order to Provide Confidence to it:* As the evaluation stringency should be related to a set of characteristics and sub-characteristics that establish the expected evaluation levels, the detected quality requirements have been mapped on the characteristics and sub-characteristics of the detected quality model, which is the product quality model of [23].

The mapping of the preservation requirements into the quality model constitutes a preliminary high level software product quality evaluation plan. Subsequently to quality evaluation plan development, in the phase called "specify the evaluation", the evaluation measures to be applied, the decision criteria to be defined and the evaluation results to be achieved have been detailed.

4.2 Specify the Evaluation

In [24, 25] the measures applicable for the evaluation of each characteristic and sub-characteristic are provided. Besides these two standards contain common and essential to measurement terms with their definitions like *Measure (noun),* i.e. the variable to which a value is assigned as the result of measurement and *Measurement,* i.e. the set of operations having the object of determining a value of a measure;

Inside the Presto4U project during the "specify the evaluation" stage the identified characteristics and sub-characteristics have been associated with measures, measurement functions, test strategies and expected test result. In particular the steps implemented have been the following [26]:

1. *Selecting Metrics:* The definition of the quality characteristics into sub-characteristics does not allow their direct measurement, therefore metrics useful to software development have to be defined. Every quantifiable internal attribute of software and every quantifiable external attribute of the software interacting with its environment that correlates with a characteristic can be established as a *metric.* Metrics can differ depending on the CoP exigencies, environment and the phases of the development process in which they are used. Metrics used in the development process should be correlated to the user perspective metrics, because the metrics from the user's view are crucial.

2. *Defining Decision Criteria for Quality Measures:* Usually decision criteria are numerical thresholds useful to determine the need for action or the degree of confidence of a certain result. These have to be defined according with quality requirements and corresponding evaluation criteria. Benchmarks, statistical control limits, historical data could be used as a reference.

3. *Establishing Decision Criteria for Evaluation:* To assess the quality of the product, the results of the evaluation of the different characteristics need to be summarised.

A procedure with separate criteria for each involved characteristics should be considered. The procedure could be provided in terms of individual sub-characteristics, or a weighted combination of sub-characteristics. The procedure can include other aspects such as time and cost that contribute to the assessment of quality of a software product in a particular environment.

On the basis of the customized quality model and the evaluation and measurement plans, the software quality of the digital collection tools used inside the Presto4U project will be subsequently evaluated. However this last activity is out of the scope of this paper.

5   Explorative Case Study

In this section an experiment of software quality evaluation, for digital collection in the audio-video preservation environment is reported. The experiment has been developed thanks to the collaboration with TATE Gallery as partner representative of the Video Art, Art Museums and Galleries CoP [35]. Therefore, in the case study, the considered stakeholders have been identified among the staff of TATE Gallery.

As reported in the Sect. 4.1 the "establishing the evaluation requirements" is a preliminary activity of the evaluation process. To derive the *high level software product quality evaluation plans* the following steps have been defined:

1. *Definition of Preservation Needs:* by interviews and questionnaires, a list of preservation needs should be generated.
2. *Identification of Preservation Requirements:* through an iterative refinement process the preservation requirements should be identified from the declared needs. In particular on a list of functional and non-functional requirements expressed in natural language has been defined.
3. *Definition of the Preservation Quality Plan:* the preservation requirements should be mapped in some characteristics and sub-characteristics of the product quality model. As result two high level software product quality evaluation plans (one for functional and one for non-functional requirements) have been defined.

Considering instead the second phase called "specify the evaluation" to derive the *customized software measurement plans* two the following steps have been defined:

1. *Selecting Metrics and their Decision Criteria:* For each sub-characteristic identified in the high level software product quality evaluation plans the most suitable metric is selected according to the digital collection exigencies. Moreover the measured value of each sub-characteristic has been mapped on the customized scale decided in agreement of the degrees of satisfaction of the digital collection requirements.
2. *Establishing Criteria for Evaluation:* For each characteristics identified in the high level software product quality evaluation plans the assessment results has been summarized in terms of a weighted combination of sub-characteristics.

In the rest of this section further details of the implementation of these steps in the considered case study are provided.

5.1   Preservation Needs

In the considered case study the identified preservation needs considered study have been specified for the digital video art collections software tools. The list provided here below is just a meaningful extract of the overall set of collected. The list has been then elaborated to derive the set of preservation requirements as detailed in the next section.

1. *The software should perform the functions of data ingest, archival storage and migrating digital file to new formats or carriers when necessary.*
2. *The software should be modified without any impact on existing quality.*
3. *The software should be interoperable with TATE Gallery collection management system.*
4. *All copies must be recorded as components on the collection management system (TMS) and the purpose and status of a particular copy must also be recorded.*
5. *Any access to the file is restricted.*
6. *Location information must be accurate and kept up to date and record the presence of a digital file.*
7. *Ingest and storage activities must not compromise the video quality of the video material.*
8. *The original video quality must be preserved.*
9. *Preservation actions and decisions must be documented and transparent. Every action or modification on the media files must be recorded and traced.*
10. *Looking, controlling and operating on the system content.*
11. *The software should be able to be transferred in different broadcast environments and to be adaptable to their specific exigencies.*

5.2   Preservation Requirements

Usually the requirements can be written either in natural language or in semi-formal language (with graphical notations, precise syntax and a non-rigorous semantic) or in formal language (mathematics-based language with syntax and semantics formally defined). Among them, the first is the most common and easy way to express software requirements despite the ambiguity risk [3]. Expressed in natural language requirements can be easy communicated and discussed among various technical and no-technical stakeholders, before being used in the subsequent product development phases. In this case study, natural language requirements have been necessary for the discussions among project partners that operate in different from software engineering fields, therefore from the previous list of preservation needs, a list of requirements has been refined.

- Req. 1: The software has to perform all the functionalities that it is developed for.
- Req. 2: The software should let the possibility to integrate/correct/modify user-specific features or components without any impact on existing product quality.
- Req. 3: The tool should be interoperable with different collection management systems and should let the possibility to import data from different format.

- Req. 3.1: The tool should import material in both 25 Hz and 29.97 Hz formats.
- Req. 3.2: The tool should input/output different file formats like for instance: AVI, FLV, MOV, MPEG-1, MPEG-2, MPEG-4, SWF, WMV for video collection
- Req. 4: The software should track all copies and record the status of each copy.
- Req. 5: Any access to the file is restricted.
- Req. 6: Location information must be accurate and traceable.
- Req. 6.1: The tool should store different information about a file such as: Object No, Title, Artist, Dims, Comp No, Comp Name, Comp Desc, Media Fmt, Duration, Video Std, Aspect Ratio, When Made?, Where made?, Provenance, TiBM label, Current Location, Video Res., Colour, Audio, Details of Master, Misc, Author.
- Req. 7: During its activity, the software should not allow the alteration of the ingested material video quality.
- Req. 7.1: The system should include a quality control flags, monitor the level of errors, and support corrections when occurred.
- Req. 8: Preservation actions and decisions can be proven to have taken place and cannot be repudiated later.
- Req. 9: Every action or modification on the files must be recorded and traced.
- Req. 10: The software should let easy control and operate on the content.
- Req. 11: The software should be adapted for different, evolving, operational or usage environments.

5.3 Definition of the Evaluation Plans

The last step for the definition of the high level quality evaluation plans (one for functional requirements and one for non-functional requirements) includes the classification of the main just above-cited requirements into functional or non-functional and their mapping into the characteristics and sub-characteristics of the adopted quality model [23]. In particular for the non-functional requirements a more detailed refinements have been required in order to avoiding generic and non-quantifiable terms that can generate ambiguities and misunderstandings [3, 9]. Here below a possible mapping between requirements and definitions of the sub-characteristics are reported.

Req. 1 – *The software has to perform all the functionalities that it is developed for.*

Classification: functional
Characteristic: functional suitability
Sub-characteristic: functional completeness - Degree to which the set of functions covers all the specified tasks and user objectives.

Req. 2 – *The software should let the possibility to integrate/correct/modify user-specific features or components without any impact on existing product quality.*

Classification: non-functional
Characteristic: maintainability
Sub-characteristic: modifiability - Degree to which a product or system can be effectively and efficiently modified without introducing defects or degrading existing product quality.

Req. 3 – *The tool should be interoperable with different collection management systems and should let the possibility to import data from different format.*

Classification: non-functional
Characteristic: compatibility
Sub-characteristic: interoperability - degree to which two or more systems, products or components can exchange information and use the information that has been exchanged.

Req. 4 – *The software should track all copies and record the purpose or status of each copy.*

Classification: non-functional
Characteristic: reliability
Sub-characteristic: availability - degree to which a system, product or component is operational and accessible when required for use.

Req. 5 – *Any access to the file is restricted.*

Classification: non-functional
Characteristic: security
Sub-characteristic: confidentiality - degree to which a product or system ensures that data are accessible only to those authorized to have access.

Req. 6 – *Location information must be accurate and traceable.*

Classification: non-functional
Characteristic: security
Sub-characteristic: authenticity - degree to which the identity of a subject or resource can be proved to be the one claimed.

Req. 7 – *During its activity, the software should not allow the alteration of the ingested material video quality.*

Classification: non-functional
Characteristic: usability
Sub-characteristic: user error protection – degree to which a system protects users against making errors.

Req. 8 – *Preservation actions and decisions can be proven to have taken place and cannot be repudiated later.*

Classification: non-functional
Characteristic: security
Sub-characteristic: non-repudiation - degree to which actions or events can be proven to have taken place, so that the events or actions cannot be repudiated later.

Req. 9 – *Every action or modification on the media files must be recorded and traced.*

Classification: non-functional
Characteristic: security

Sub-characteristic: accountability - degree to which the actions of an entity can be traced uniquely to the entity.

Req. 10 – *The software should let easy control and operate on the content.*

Classification: non-functional
Characteristic: usability
Sub-characteristic: operability - degree to which a product or system has attributes that make it easy to operate and control.

Req. 11 – *The software should be adapted for different, evolving, operational or usage environments.*

Classification: non-functional
Characteristic: portability
Sub-characteristic: adaptability - degree to which a product or system can effectively and efficiently be adapted for different or evolving hardware, software or other operational or usage environments.

Considering in particular the functional requirements Req. 1, according to the suggestions of the involved stakeholders, a level of need has been associated to each of the functionality. The levels of need have been classified as follows: *Essential* - Must have; *Conditional* - Could deal also without, but it would be better to have; *Optimal* - May be appreciated in some cases, but in most cases it doesn't make the difference.

In Table 1 an extract of the final high level quality evaluation plan for the functional requirement Req. 1 is presented. In particular in the first two columns a more detailed specification of the needs and the relative functionalities respectively is provided; while in the third column the level of need associated to each functionality is specified. As evidenced by the forth column all the functional requirements of the considered case study have been associated to Functional Suitability characteristic and to Functional completeness sub-characteristic.

Table 1. High level quality evaluation plan for functional requirements.

Needs	Functionalities	Level of needs	Characteristics and sub-characteristics
GUI Ingestion	The tool shall make GUI ingestion	Essential	Functional suitability -
Preservation of original content properties	The tool shall preserve the properties of the audio-visual media original content	Essential	*functional completeness*
Extension with add-ons and plugins	The tool should allow extension with add-ons and plugins	Conditional	
Populate and draw data and statistics from collection management systems	The tool may populate and draw data and statistics from collection management systems	Optimal	

In Table 2 an extract of the final high level quality evaluation plan for the non-functional requirements is presented.

Table 2. High level software product quality plan for non-functional requirements.

Product quality model		Requirements
Characteristics	Sub-characteristics	
Compatibility	Interoperability	REQ. 3
Usability	Operability	REQ. 10
	User error protection	REQ. 7
Reliability	Availability	REQ. 4
Security	Confidentiality	REQ. 5
	Non-repudiation	REQ. 8
	Accountability	REQ. 9
	Authenticity	REQ. 6
Maintainability	Modifiability	REQ. 2
Portability	Adaptability	REQ. 11

These two plans have been successively refined in the next steps of the quality evaluation process with techniques, measures to be applied, decision criteria to be defined and evaluation results to be achieved for better specifying the evaluation. However in spite of their high level detail, they are just an example of quality evaluation process refinement on only few of the possible characteristics and sub-characteristics of the quality model. The refinement highlights the most important quality aspects in the specific context of digital video art collections, which are mainly related to security.

5.4 Definition of the Measurement Plans

During the phase called "specify the evaluation" two customized software quality measurement plans (for functional and non-functional requirements respectively) have been defined following the steps defined in Sect. 4.2. In particular for each identified characteristic and sub-characteristic, measure, measurement function, test strategy and expected test result have been detected and adapted to the preservation context in order to reduce the cost and effort due to generic quality evaluations.

The detected measures have been chosen as it was supposed a possible relation between their corresponding characteristics and the sub-characteristics and the digital preservation needs inside PRESTO4U. In this case study the presence of this relation is deduced in collaboration with domain experts.

In Table 3 the customized software quality measurement plan for functional requirements is presented. In particular for the associated measure (Functional implementation coverage forth column) the measurement function refined for this case study is reported in the fifth column. The refinement has been done in order to take in consideration the level of need (see Sect. 5.3) expressed for the digital collection tools. As a consequence also the Test Strategy and the Test Results has been redefined accordingly (sixth and seventh column respectively).

Table 3. Measurement plan for functional requirements.

Reqs	Product Quality Model		Measure	Measurement Function	Test Strategy	Test Results
	Charats	Sub-Charats				
REQ.1	Functional suitability	Functional completeness	Functional implementation coverage	$X=(X1+X2*0.5+X3*0.25)/1.75$ with $X1=1 - (A / B)$ A= Number of missing or unsatisfying essential functions B= Number of mandatory functions essential in the evaluation $X2= 1 - (C / D)$ C= Number of missing or unsatisfying conditional functions assessed in the evaluation D= Number of conditional functions $X3= 1- (E / F)$ E= Number of missing or unsatisfying optional functions assessed in the evaluation F= Number of optional functions	Each function is evaluated as essential, conditional or optional. The presence/absence of each function in the tool is checked. This does not include the evaluation of the goodness of the function implementation.	Closer to 1 value is better

Table 4. Measurement plan for non-functional requirements.

Reqs	Product Quality Model		Measure	Measurement Function	Test Strategy	Test Results
	Charats	Sub-Charats				
REQ.3	Compatibility	Interoperability	Input/out data formats	$X = A / B$ A = number of data formats regarded by the tool B = total number of data formats to be exchanged (total number of data formats listed as software requirements).	Counting how many of the data format listed are regarded in the tool and adding those not included	Closer to 1 value is better
REQ.10	Usability	Operability	Message clarity	$X = A / B$ A = number of messages that are understood easily(without ambiguity) B = total number of implemented messages (without ambiguity)	Evaluating how easily can messages from a system be understood	Closer to 1 value is better
REQ.7		User error protection	Avoidance of incorrect operation	$X = A / B$ A = number of functions implemented to avoid critical or serious malfunctions being caused by incorrect operation B = total number of incorrect operation patterns	Counting how many functions have incorrect operation avoidance capability	Closer to 1 value is better
REQ.4	Reliability	Availability	Mean down time	$X = A / B$ A= Total down time B= Number of observed breakdowns	Calculating the average time during the system is not operational and accessible when a failure occurs before gradual start up	(from 0 to infinite). The longer is better
REQ.5	Security	Confidentiality	Data encryption	$X = A/B$ A = number of data items correctly encrypted/decrypted B = number of data items to be required encryption/decryption.	Calculating how correctly is the encryption/decryption of data items implemented according to stated in the requirement specification	Closer to 1 value is better
REQ.8		Non-repudiation	utilization of digital signature	$X = A/B$ A = number of events processed using digital signature B = number of events requiring non- repudiation property.	Calculating what proportion of events requiring non-repudiation are processed using digital signature	Closer to 1 value is better
REQ.9		Accountability	Access auditability	$X = A/B$ A = number of accesses to system and data recorded in the system log B = number of accesses actually occurred.	Calculating how complete is the audit trail concerning the user access to the system and data	Closer to 1 value is better
REQ.6		Authenticity	Authentication methods	A = number of provided authentication methods (e.g, ID/password or IC card)	Evaluating how well does the system authenticate the identity of a subject or resource	(from 0 to infinite). The longer is better
REQ.2	Maintainability	Modifiability	Modification success rate	$X = 1 - B/A$ A = number of troubles within a certain period before modification B = number of troubles in the same period after modification	Calculating to what extent can software system be operated without failures after the modification	Closer to 1 value is better
REQ.11	Portability	Adaptability	System software environmental adaptability	$X = 1- A/B$ A= Number of operational functions of which tasks were not completed or were not enough resulted to meet adequate level during testing B= Total number of functions which were tested in different software environment.	Calculating if the software system is capable enough to adapt itself to different system software environment.	Closer to 1 value is better

Finally in Table 4 the customized software quality measurement plan for non-functional requirements is presented. In particular in the fourth column the measure selected for each sub-characteristic is reported. In the fifth column the redefined measurement function is provided. As for the previous plan this has been performed in collaboration with domain experts and in order to take in consideration the peculiarities of the preservation environment. As a consequence also the test results have been redefined accordingly.

5.5 Example of Product Evaluation

On the basis of the customized quality model and the evaluation and measurement plans, the software quality of the digital collection tools used inside the Presto4U project will be assessed. This stage is currently an ongoing step of the project and just preliminary and partial results are available. For confidentiality reasons these data are not provide here, however for aim of completeness two examples of measurement relative to some specific sub-characteristics are presented in the following of this section.

The first example concern the evaluation of an hypothetical tool for digital collection, called TOOL1, according to the functionalities it implements. In particular TOO1 is supposed to provide the following set of functionalities: (i) GUI ingestion; (ii) preservation of the audio-visual media original content, (iii) population and draw data and statistics from collection management. For the evaluation of TOOL1, the high level quality evaluation plan of Table 1 and the relative measurement plan of Table 3 are used as reference model.

Thus the measurement function associated to the Functional Completeness sub-characteristic $(X = (X1 + X2*0.5 + X3*0.25)/1.75)$ is applied and the test results for TOOL1 computed. In this case $X1 = 1-(0 /2) = 1$ because both of the two essential functions are implemented; $X2 = 1-(1 /1) = 0$ because the unique conditional functions is not implemented; $X3 = 1-(0 /1) = 1$ because the unique optional functions is implemented. The final value for the Functional Completeness of TOOL1 is $(1 + 0*0.5 + 1*0.25)/1.75 = 1,25/1.75 = 0.714$ that is quite close to the optimal value 1.

The second example concern the evaluation of the TOOL1 consider its degree of interoperability. In particular TOO1 is supposed to provide the following set of file formats for video collection: MPEG-1, MPEG-2, MPEG-4. For the evaluation of TOOL1, the high level quality evaluation plan of Table 2 and the relative measurement plan of Table 4 are used as reference model.

Thus the measurement function associated to the Interoperability sub-characteristic $(X = A/B)$ is applied and the test results for TOOL1 computed. In this case value $A = 3$ because the number of data formats included in TOOL1 is 3 (MPEG-1, MPEG-2, MPEG-4); value $B = 8$ because the total number of data formats listed in the software requirements Req 3.2 is 8 (AVI, FLV, MOV, MPEG-1, MPEG-2, MPEG-4, SWF, WMV). Thus the final value for the Interoperability sub-characteristic of TOOL1 is $3/8 = 1.25/1.75 = 0.375$ that is far from the optimal value 1.

6 Discussion and Conclusion

The paper present an experiment of the definition of software quality evaluation and measurement plans for digital collection tool. In particular, revising and expanding work done in [4, 5] high-level quality evaluation plans for functional and non-functional requirements have been introduced together with their respective measurement plans. This experiment has included the refinement and the specialization of the measures proposed in the international standards according to specific digital collection preservation requirements so to overcome some of weaknesses of the standard applicability and to reduce the cost and effort that would have been spent if more generic quality evaluations were adopted.

In this paper, the experience matured inside the digital preservation environment stops at this phase, that is named as *specifying the evaluation* in [26]. Even if preliminary the obtained results highlighted important quality aspects and criticalities in the software quality evaluation process. In particular most of the problems rose in the alignment of the classical terminology of the software engineering context with the one that is specific for the preservation environment. Thus a shared and informal glossary has been preliminary defined so to avoiding possible misunderstandings. Moreover, this experience highlighted the necessity of the definition of two quality evaluation plans customized according to specific needs to be considered and specific characteristics to be measured. Indeed the list of characteristics and sub-characteristics provided in the standards do not completely reflect the specific exigencies of the particular environments as, for example, the preservation environment. In line with one of the research results about the applicability of the standards, it is opportune underlining also the necessity of the specialization of the measurement plans by the introduction or refinement of specific measurement functions able to take in consideration the organizational limits and constraints.

The procedure customized for the audio-visual preservation has been positively accepted inside the Presto4U project that, for the first time, faces the problems of the applicability of international standards for software quality assessment. Different stakeholders have considered the proposed procedure, the encountered problems and the practical proposed solutions a good reference to replicate the experience in software engineering contexts different from audio-visual preservation one.

On the basis of the customized evaluation and measurement plans, the software quality of the digital collection tools used inside the Presto4U project are currently under evaluation. Even if still very preliminary and partial the obtained results confirmed the usefulness of the proposed approach and constitute a valid basis for preservation tool selection both for domain experts and standard user facing for the first time the problem of digital collection.

Acknowledgements. This work has been partially funded by the EC FP7 Presto4U Project No. 600845. The authors would like to thank Mario Fusani for the interesting and useful discussions.

References

1. Abran, A., Al-Qutaish, R.E., Cuadrado-Gallego, J.: Analysis of the ISO 9126 on software product quality evaluation from the metrology and ISO 15939 perspectives. WSEAS Trans. Comput. **5**(11), 2778–2786 (2006)
2. Azuma, M.: The impact of ICT evolution and application explosion on software quality: a solution by ISO/IEC 250nn square series of standards. In: WoSQ 2011, pp. 1–2. ACM, New York, NY, USA (2011)
3. Berry, D.M., Kamsties, E., Krieger, M.M.: From contract drafting to software specification: linguistic sources of ambiguity. Technical report, University of Waterloo (2003)
4. Biscoglio, I., Marchetti, E.: A case of adoption of 25000 standards family - establishing evaluation requirements in the audio-visual preservation context. In: ICSOFT-EA 2014, pp. 222–233. Vienna, Austria (2014)
5. Biscoglio, I., Marchetti, E.: An experiment of software quality evaluation in the audio-visual media preservation context. In: QUATIC 2014 to appear. Guimarães, Portugal (2014)
6. Bundschuh, M., Dekkers, C.: The Measurement Compendium: Estimating and Benchmarking Success with Functional Size Measurement. Springer, Heidelberg (2008)
7. Chung, L., Nixon, J.M.B., Yu, A.: Non-functional Requirements in Software Engineering. Springer, Reading (2000)
8. Gopal, A., Krishnan, M.S., Mukhopadhyay, T., Goldenson, D.R.: Measurement programs in software development: determinants of success. IEEE Trans. Softw. Eng. **28**(9), 863–875 (2002)
9. IEEE 830: Recommended practice for software requirements specifications (1998)
10. IEEE 1012: System and software verification and validation (2004)
11. IEEE 1074: IEEE standard for developing software life cycle processes (2006)
12. ISO 9000-3: Quality management and quality assurance standards – Part 3: guidelines for the application of ISO 9001 to the development, supply and maintenance of software (2001)
13. ISO 9126: Information technology, software product evaluation, quality characteristics and guidelines for their use (1991)
14. ISO 14721: Space data and information transfer systems – open archival information system (OAIS) – reference model (2012)
15. ISO/IEC 9126 – 1: Software engineering - product quality part 1: quality mode (2001)
16. ISO/IEC 9126 – 2: Software engineering - product quality part 2: external metrics (2001)
17. ISO/IEC 9126 – 3: Software engineering - product quality part 3: internal metrics (2001)
18. ISO/IEC 9126 – 4: Software engineering - product quality part 4: quality in use metrics (2001)
19. ISO/IEC 14598 (parts 1 to 6): Software engineering — software product evaluation (1998)
20. ISO/IEC 15504: Information technology — process assessment (2004)
21. ISO/IEC 15939: Systems and software engineering – measurement process (2007)
22. ISO/IEC FDIS 25000: Systems and software engineering — Systems and software quality requirements and evaluation (SQuaRE) (2005)
23. ISO/IEC FDIS 25010: Systems and software engineering — (SQuaRE) — system and software quality models (2011)
24. ISO/IEC 25022: Systems and software engineering - SQuaRE – measurement of quality in use (2012)
25. ISO/IEC 25023: Systems and software engineering - SQuaRE – measurement of system and software product quality (2012)
26. ISO/IEC 25040: Systems and software engineering - SQuaRE – evaluation process (2010)

27. ISO/IEC/IEEE 12207: Systems and software engineering — software life cycle processes (2008)
28. ISO/IEC/IEEE 15288: Systems and software engineering — system life cycle processes (2008)
29. Olsina, L., Lew, P., Dieser, A., Rivera, B.: Updating quality models for evaluating new generation web applications. J. Web Eng. **11**, 209–246 (2012)
30. Pfleeger, S.L.: Software Engineering. Theory and Practice, 4th edn. Prentice Hall, Englewood Cliffs (2009)
31. Polillo, R.: A core quality model for web applications. J. Web Eng. **11**, 181–208 (2012)
32. Presto4U project. www.prestocentre.org/4u
33. Al-Quataish, R.E.: An investigation of the weaknesses of the ISO 9126 international standard. In: International Conference on Computer and Electrical Engineering, IEEE, pp. 275–279 (2009)
34. Software Engineering Institute: the international process research consortium: a process research framework, pp. 20–28 (December 2006)
35. TATE Gallery. www.tate.org.uk/

Context and Data Management for Multitenant Enterprise Applications in SaaS Environments: A Middleware Approach

Chun-Feng Liao$^{(\boxtimes)}$, Kung Chen, and Jiu-Jye Chen

Department of Computer Science, National Chengchi University, Taipei, Taiwan
{cfliao,chenk,100971009}@nccu.edu.tw

Abstract. Software as a service (SaaS) is a promising service model of cloud computing. Its key characteristic is the ability for clients to use a software application on a pay-as-you-go subscription basis. To be economically sustainable, a SaaS application must be multitenant. However, it is generally agreed that designing a multitenant enterprise application in SaaS environments is a non-trival task. In this work, we propose an integrated service middleware that addresses cross-cutting concerns when developing and deploying multitenant enterprise SaaS applications. To verify the feasibility of our approach, a sample SaaS application have been implemented on the proposed middleware. Also, two tenant-specific virtual applications are constructed to demonstrate multi-tenancy. Finally, a series of performance evaluations are conducted to assess the overheads of making an enterprise application multitenant enabled.

Keywords: Multitenancy · Schema-mapping · Universal table · SaaS

1 Introduction

Recently, a considerable number of studies have been made on Cloud Computing, which is defined by NIST (National Institute of Standards and Technology) as a computing capability that provides on-demand self-service, broad network access, resource pooling, rapid elasticity, and measured service [1]. The NIST definition also identifies three popular service model in a cloud environment, namely, Infrastructure as Service (IaaS), Platform as Service (PaaS), and Software as a Service (SaaS). Among the service models in cloud computing, SaaS (Software as a Service) is reported to be the most competitive [2]. Its central defining characteristic is the ability for clients to use a software application on a pay-as-you-go subscription basis. However, to be economically sustainable, a SaaS application must leverage resource sharing to a great extent by accommodating different clients (or called tenants) of the application while making it appear to each that they have the application all to themselves. In other words, a SaaS application must be a multitenant application [3].

Despite the benefits and popularity of multitenant SaaS applications, the approach for implementing such applications is still not well-studied and

© Springer International Publishing Switzerland 2015
A. Holzinger et al. (Eds.): ICSOFT 2014, CCIS 555, pp. 81–96, 2015.
DOI: 10.1007/978-3-319-25579-8_5

documented [4]. Technically speaking, SaaS-level multi-tenancy employs a single application instance to serve multiple tenants. In other word, tenants of a SaaS application are oblivious to the fact that the resources (e.g. CPU time, network bandwidth, and data storage) are shared among tenants. For instance, a SaaS application must implement affinity (how tasks are transparently distributed), persistence (how data are transparently distributed and managed), performance isolation, QoS differentiation, and tenant-specific customization [5]. These issues are relatively hard to tackle and require higher expertise.

Several cross-cutting concerns need to be addressed when implementing a multitenant SaaS application, which can be into two layers, namely, the application layer and the data layer. The core issue in the application layer is how to devise a transparent way to store and to propagate the tenant-specific information (or called tenant contexts). Typically, enterprise applications tend to store tenant contexts in a platform-dependent session implementation. However, if the tenant contexts are stored in this way, then in order to propagating tenant contexts into a business method, either the method signature or the body of the business method must be modified to access the platform-specific session implementation. Both of these approaches involve significant modification of code and made business methods being tightly coupled on platform-specific API.

In addition, traditional "sticky session" [6] handling mechanisms are also platform-specific and require careful configuration in a clustered environment. As nodes in the cloud environment is usually virtualized, heterogeneous and elastic, it is even harder to devise a platform independent approach for handling sticky sessions. A more transparent way to store and propagate tenant context is thus apparently required.

Meanwhile, although it is generally agreed that the multitenant data layer is one of the most important concerns [7], there is also little investigation on data layer concerns in a multitenant application. There are two inter-related issues to be addressed in this layer: schema layout management and tenant-specific schema customization. In the design space of the multitenant schema layout management strategy, various alternative approaches form a continuum between the isolated data style and the shared data style [3]. As pointed out by Aulbach et al., the shared data style provides very good consolidation but lacks schema extensibility [8]. Many shared data style assumes that either each tenant has a dedicated set of tables and have the same schema or all tenants are consolidated in one set of tables but share an identical schema. Among commonly used schema-mapping techniques, Universal Table seems to be a promising shared data style since it is possible to preserve extensibility at the same time. Essentially, a Universal Table is a generic structure that has virtually no schema attached to it. Although it is commonly held that Universal Table layout would incur a large amount of performance overhead, it is the approach adopted by SalesForce.com, which is a successful SaaS vendor best known for its CRM service that supports more than 55,000 tenants [9]. However, it is not clear how the Froce.com SaaS applications leased by tenants transparently transform the query statements for the logical schema to the ones for the physical schema.

As the above-mentioned design issues, application layer or data layer, are cross-cutting concerns of a multitenant application, they should be modularized so that developers are able to implement, deploy, and integrate to such customizations to the applications with minimal additional programming and configuration efforts. A general approach is to devise a middleware-level facility that supports transparently tenant context management, automatic mapping of multiple single-tenant logical schemas to one multitenant physical schema in the database, and flexible customization of tenant-specific logical schemas. Hence, we propose a service middleware that addresses these issues.

Specifically, our objective is to design a middleware that provides: (1) a platform independent tenant context management service that stores and propagates tenant contexts based on the thread-specific storage pattern [10]; (2) a data service that implements multitenant Universal Table schema layout; (3) a multitenant ORM (object-relational mapping) customization service that enables the customization of tenant-specific domain objects and their mappings to the underlying schema layout. On top of this middleware, we construct a simple SaaS application, ShoppingForce.com, to demonstrate the feasibility of our approach. Finally, we also present results of the performance assessments of this work.

2   Related Work

It is commonly agreed that resource sharing is the key to yield cost benefits in a cloud environment. An emerging approach to support resource sharing is the concept of Multitenancy, which employs a single application instance to serve multiple tenants. The design issues of multitenant enterprise applications fall into two groups: the application layer and the data layer. In the application layer, several challenges arise when transforming these applications into multitenant ones: (1) how to obtain tenant-specific information (or called tenant contexts), (2) where to store the tenant contexts, and (3) how to propagate tenant contexts among components [11]. Several approaches have been proposed to deal with the first issues mentioned above, including intercepting filters [12], aspects [13], or contexts [14]. What seems to be lacking, however, is an appropriate mechanism for storing and propagating of tenant contexts.

In the data layer, Pereira and Chiueh mentioned the concepts of a multitenant query rewriting engine in the future work section [15]. Li proposes a heuristic-based query rewriting mechanism for transforming queries to the logical schema to HBase, which is an implementation of BigTable [16]. Aulbach et al. survey several schema-mapping techniques, including Universal Table [8]. The data architecture used by Force.com [9] falls into the category of Universal Table, which is the foundation of our data layer design.

Several attempts have been made to provide a common platform for multitenant enterprise applications. However, the objectives of these attempts either focus on isolation issues [17], administration issues [18], or only provide conceptual discussion [19]. This paper concentrates the issue of tenant context and data management and realize our approach as a service middleware.

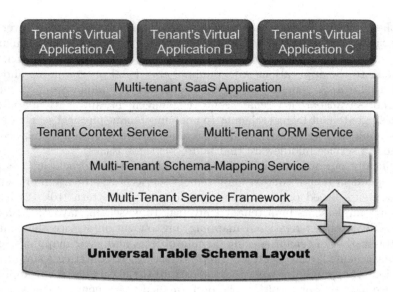

Fig. 1. Overall architecture of the proposed service middleware.

3   Middleware Design

In this section, we shall present the design of the three core services of the proposed middleware. As depicted in Fig. 1, the three core services are the Tenant
Context Service, the multitenant ORM Service, and the multitenant Schema-
Mapping Service. A multitenant SaaS application, which is able to host several
tenant-specific virtual applications, can be built on top of the proposed middleware. The detailed mechanisms of the three core services will be introduced in
the following sub-sections.

3.1   Tenant Context Management Service

A key characteristic of a multitenant SaaS application is that it must provide
tenant-specific user interfaces, business logics and data to a certain extent. To
realize tenant-specific customization of an application, some artifacts, usually
called isolation points, have to be isolated for different tenants [12]. To implement tenant-specific customization, program logics in the isolation points must
have access to tenant contexts. Therefore, it is important to find a way for storing
and propagating tenant contexts among the isolation points spreading in a multitenant SaaS application. If the clients of a SaaS application are Web-based,
then a common approach is to store tenant contexts in a platform-dependent
HTTP session implementation. Essentially, an HTTP session is an abstraction
of a shared storage which is accessible through a specific sequence of user-system
interactions. For instance, the shopping cart in an e-commerce web site is usually
stored in an HTTP session.

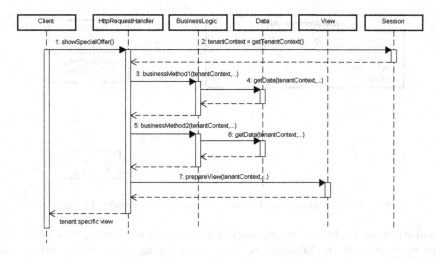

Fig. 2. In traditional HTTP Session approach, all method signatures throughout the call sequences have to be modified.

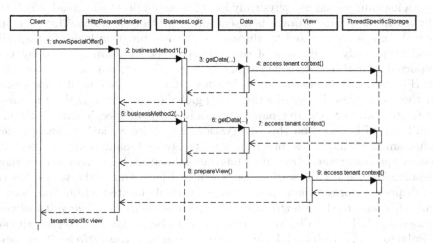

Fig. 3. In the tenant specific storage approach, only isolation points are modified.

However, the above-mentioned approach leads to several problems. First, the approach is not applicable to non-web-based clients. Second, if not carefully designed, the HTTP session can be unstable and brittle due to the sticky session problem, proxy farm problem, or net quasar problem [20]. Most importantly, the multitenant processing logic will be "polluted" by platform-specifics of the underlying HTTP implementation. Taking Java-based Web application as an example, the multitenant processing logic must use a Servlet API to access tenant contexts, causing the logic being dependent on the Servlet API. Moreover, the method signatures for user interfaces, business logics and data access have to be modified to propagate tenant contexts (see Fig. 2). To minimize the efforts

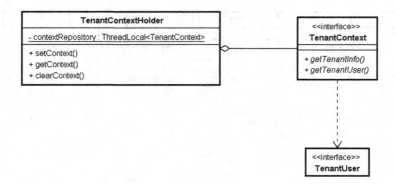

Fig. 4. Managing tenant context from thread-specific storage

of migrating an single-tenant application into multitenant ones, it is preferable to avoid significant modification of code or being tightly coupled with some platform specific API.

Thread-specific storage is a design pattern that allows multiple threads to access a logically global but physically local for each individual thread [10]. Internally, a thread-specific storage is essentially a globally accessible list of maps, where the maps are indexed by thread IDs. Hence, program logics in a specific thread t can only access one of the map, that is, the map indexed by t. It is reported that thread-specific storage is more efficient, reusable and portable [10]. However, if it is not carefully designed, it can lead to an obscure system structure because of the use of a (logically) global object. As a result, it is important to store and propagate tenant contexts in a thread-specific storage through an uniform API. Based on this observation, we devise a platform independent mechanism that allows the program logic to access tenant contexts, stored in a tenant-specific storage, from user interfaces, business logics and data without depending on the HTTP session, as shown in Fig. 3. Currently, we realize the thread-specific storage via a static member variable located within the *Tenant-ContextHolder* called *contextRepository*, which is realized by *ThreadLocal* class provided by JDK (see Fig. 4). Tenant contexts belonging to different threads are isolated by *ThreadLocal*. In other words, although *contextRepository* seems to be global to the system, when a thread accesses it by calling the *getContext* method, only the tenant context specific to the calling thread is returned.

3.2   Multitenant Schema-Mapping Service

This section describes the design of the proposed Universal-Table-based multitenant schema-mapping service. Before examining the detailed mechanisms, it is helpful to introduce the overall data architecture and design issues of Universal Table. Essentially, Universal Table is a generic storage consisting of a GUID (Global Unique Identifier), a tenant ID, and a fixed number of generic data columns (i.e. the *Data* Table in Fig. 5). The metadata of logical tables (objects), logical columns (fields), logical relationship, logical primary keys, and

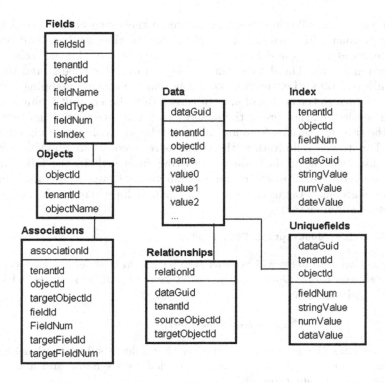

Fig. 5. The data architecture of Universal table schema-mapping.

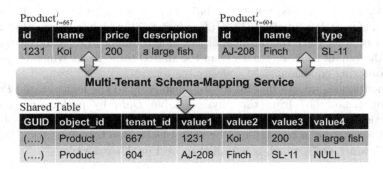

Fig. 6. Example of Universal table schema-mapping.

logical index information of records are stored in *Objects, Fields, Relationships, Uniquefields,* and *Index,* respectively (see Fig. 5). In the sequel, we follow the convention in [9] and use the term objects and tables as well as fields and columns interchangeably.

Consider a hypothetical e-commerce SaaS application, ShoppingForce.com, that enables its tenants to sell products and to process orders on-line. Since different tenants have their own unique needs in describing their products,

ShoppingForce.com allows its tenants to create their own customized schemas for their products. Figure 6 illustrates the scenario. Here we have two product tables (i.e. $Product_{t=667}^{l}$ and $Product_{t=604}^{l}$, where l denotes "logical" schema and t denotes tenant id). The data in the two logical tables will be stored together into a universal table (i.e. the *Shared* Table) via the schema mapping service.

We now turn to the design of our Universal-Table-based multitenant schema-mapping service. At the core of the service is a set of query rewriting rules that specify the transformations from logical queries to physical queries via relational algebra. Due to space limitation, the reader is referred to our previous work for detailed specification of those query rewriting rules [21]. In the following, we sketch the overall query rewriting mechanism via an example of transforming a projection statement. Let us assume that a tenant, whose id is 667, has submitted a projection statement:

```
SELECT price, description FROM Product.
```

This projection statement will be rewritten to a form that selects physical fields from the shared table, *Data*. Firstly, the statement will be represented by the following algebraic form:

$$\bar{\pi}_{<price,description>}[667](Product),$$

where $\bar{\pi}$ denotes the projection operation that selects subscripted fields, e.g., *price, description*, from a logical table specified by its name and a tenant id annotation, e.g., *Product* and 667.

Secondly, we look up the *objectId* from the *Objects* table via the logical table name, (*Product*), and the tenant id, 667. This is specified by using the object name transformation function $\xi^{object}(Product, 667)$, which is assumed to return 1 in this example. With the physical object id and tenant id, we can select all the rows of the tenant's *Product* data from the shared table *Data*, which is specified by the following equation.

As mentioned, we can find all records belonging to the logical table *Product* owned by tenant 667 from the physical table *Data* by performing a physical selection statement filtered by *tenantId* and *objectId*. The value of physical field *objectId* can be obtained by the object name transformation function $\xi^{object}(Product, 667)$, which is assumed to be 1 in this example:

$$\sigma_{objectId=1 \wedge tenantId=667}(Data). \tag{1}$$

Thirdly, given the *objectId*, we may obtain the mapping between logical field names and physical field names using the *Fields* table. We specify the mapping via the field name transformation function $\xi^{field}(Product, n_f, 667)$, where the logical field names *id, name, price,* and *description* are obtained by substituting n_f by *value1, value2, value3,* and *value4*, respectively. As a result, the logical table *Product* can be reconstructed by appending a rename operation, ρ, and a projection operation in front of the expression in (1):

$$7t(Product) = \rho_{(id,name,price,description)} \tag{2}$$
$$\pi_{<value1,value2,value3,value4>}$$
$$\sigma_{objectId=1 \wedge tenantId=667}(Data).$$

Note that the projection operation $\pi_{<value1,value2,value3,value4>}$ is required since the *Data* table has additional fields to keep track of metadata of a record such as *GUID*, *objectId* and *tenantId* fields of the *Data* table, as depicted in Fig. 6.

Now that we have reconstructed the logical table *Product* from *Data*, we can apply arbitrary query operations to it:

$$\pi_{<price,description>}[667](Product) =$$
$$\pi_{<price,description>}$$
$$\rho_{(id,name,price,description)} \tag{3}$$
$$\pi_{<value1,value2,value3,value4>}$$
$$\sigma_{objectId=1 \wedge tenantId=667}(Data).$$

Then, the physical form of the tenant-aware logical projection statement can be derived as follows:

```
SELECT price, description FROM (
    SELECT  value1 AS id, value2 AS name,
            value3 AS price, value4 AS description
    FROM Data
    WHERE objectId=1 AND tenantId=667 ).
```

Finally, it is important to point out that the rewriting rules are realized in *MultiTenantDataServiceFacade*, as shown in Fig. 9, which is the facade for the adapters to the ORM framework. This design made the implementation of rewriting rules easier to be integrated with the ORM framework, which will be explained in detail in the next section.

3.3 Multitenant Object-Relational Mapping Service

Because of the difficulties arising from object-relational impedance mismatch [22], contemporary enterprise applications typically access database through an Object-Relational Mapping (ORM) framework. However, the SQL rewriting mechanisms introduced in the previous section do not deal with the interoperability issues with ORM. Hence, in this section, we propose an transparent approach for integrating SQL rewriting mechanisms into an ORM framework.

Generally speaking, the first step of ORM design is to define the mappings between object fields and database fields. Such mappings are usually specified by the annotations in the source code. To be consistent with the annotation-based convention, we use the annotation *@MultiTenantCapable* to indicate that the annotated object is going to be mapped to a multitenant database. For instance, to annotate the *Product* to be multitenant capable, the only additional effort is to add an *@MultiTenantCapable* annotation, as shown below:

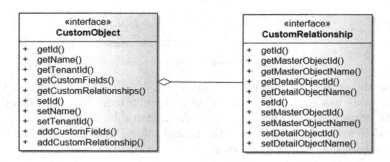

Fig. 7. The structure of CustomObject and CustomRelationShip.

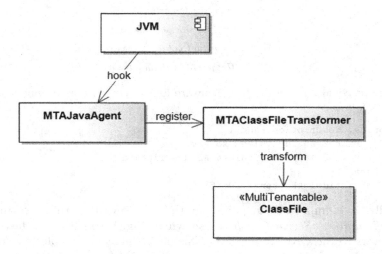

Fig. 8. The design of runtime bytecode transformation mechanism.

```
@MultiTenantCapable
Public class Product {...}.
```

Except the annotation, no additional modification is required from the developer's point of view.

We are now ready to introduce the underlying techniques of the proposed approach. In order to map user-customized domain objects into Universal Table schema layout, metadata information such as class name, field name and relationship has to be extracted and then attached to the mapping object. As depicted in Fig. 7, we defined two general interface, namely, *CustomObject*, *CustomField* and *CustomRelationship*, to store the metadata information mentioned above. At runtime, the system periodically checks any newly added user-customized domain objects. If the annotation *@MultiTenantCapable* is observed, then the annotated object will be enhanced to implement the *CustomObject* and related interfaces on the fly by a bytecode rewriting mechanism to be sketched below. In particular, the implementation of the mappings between user-customized domain

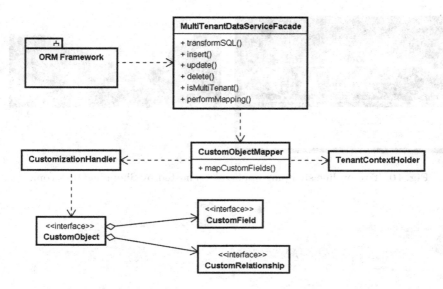

Fig. 9. The overall design of multitenant ORM.

objects and the underlying schema layout is dynamically generated and injected into the bytecode of these objects.

Figure 9 displays the overall structure of how the proposed mechanism adapts to an existing ORM framework. There is a class called *MultiTenantServiceFacade* that serves as a unified entry point so that the proposed mechanism is more portable to different ORM frameworks. The SQL rewriting rules presented in the previous section in are implemented in the insert, update, delete methods of *MultiTenantServiceFacade*. The object-relational mapping tasks are delegated to *CustomObjectMapper*, which uses *CustomizationHandler* to interact with user-customized domain objects. It is worth mentioning that, due to the use of thread specific storage pattern, *CustomObjectMapper* and *CustomizationHandler* are able to obtain the reference to tenant contexts in situ without any parameter passing.

Currently, we implement the proposed design based on JavaAgent [23], as the bytecode transformation tool and DataNucleus's JDO [24] implementation, as the underlying ORM framework. DataNucleus [25] is designed based on OSGi platform [26] so that our extension can be easily integrated into it as a bundle. As shown in Fig. 8, the main transforming logic is implemented in a specific class called *MTAClassFileTransformer* which is initialized by JavaAgent and is hooked in JVM. Before the annotated classes are loaded, JVM will delegate to *MTAClassFileTransformer* so that it has a chance to modify the bytecode.

4   Implementation

We studied the feasibility of the proposed middleware by implementing a Java-based prototype. To verify the prototype, we also implemented a simple SaaS

Fig. 10. Two on-line shopping applications hosted by ShoppingForce.com.

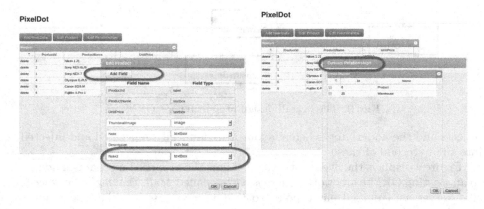

Fig. 11. The object customization and relationship customization pages in Shopping-Force.com.

application called ShoppingForce.com on top of the middleware. The SaaS application is able to access the underlying tenant context management, ORM, and schame-mapping services.

In the application layer, we realize the thread-specific storage via a static member variable, which is realized by the *ThreadLocal* class provided by JDK. Tenant contexts belonging to different threads are isolated by *ThreadLocal*. In other words, although thread-specific storage seems to be global to the system, when a thread accesses it by calling the *getContext* method, only the tenant context that is specific to the calling thread is returned. In the data layer, to access the physical schema, the application uses JDOQL (JDO Database Query Language) [24] and manipulates JDO API. Then, The JDOQL is translated internally to SQL statements and then used as the inputs of the proposed rewriting schemes.

To create a virtual application, the tenant applies for an account on-line and a tenant profile is then generated accordingly. We have created two different on-line shopping applications hosted on ShoppingForce.com. Sometimes, a tenant needs to modify default virtual schema such as adding tenant-specific columns.

In such case, ShoppingForce.com provides a set of schema customization pages which can be accessed from the account management page, as shown in Fig. 11.

5 Experiments

To test the performance of the tenant-aware schema layout management service in the data layer, we conducted experiments in a stand-alone switched network. In the network, the test client and the test server are deployed on two separate PCs with Intel Core i7 3.4-GHz processor with 4G bytes memory. For the test client, we use Apache JMeter 2.9 [27], a well-known open source and general-purpose performance measurement platform, which can be used to simulate arbitrary load types on the server or network to test overall performance under different load types. The service middleware and the database is deployed on the test server, where the database is MySQL Community Server 5.7 with InnoDB engine running on Ubuntu Linux 12.04.

For the experiments, we set up a imaginary scenario, in which there are 100 tenants and each tenant stores 100,000 records in both a Universal Table implementation and a Private Table implementation. In the Universal Table implementation, there are respectively 10 million, 10 million, and 5 million records stored in the *Indexes*, *UniqueFields*, and *Relationships* table. For each tests, based on the above scenario settings, several concurrent threads that issue query requests to the service middleware. After a request is finished, the JMeter platform gathers the responded results and reports the turnaround time. We performed experiments for Selection, Projection, and Join statements of Private Table and Universal Table implementations, respectively. When performing the tests, built-in cache mechanism of query processer is turned off to better reflect the actual overheads induced by the transformed SQL.

A summary of experimental results for Private Table and Universal Table is shown in Table 1. Compared to the Private Table implementation, which serves as a baseline, there is a great performance penalty for "multitenant-ifying" the database. The main reason is that schema-mapping involves overheads of additional database access since all meta information of logical-physical mapping has to be stored in physical storage. However, we believe that the overhead is acceptable for most enterprise SaaS applications because the worst turnaround time of query operations is still less than 20 ms. Moreover, the performance

Table 1. Average turnaround time of queries on private table and Universal table schema layouts (in milliseconds).

Operation type	Private table (Baseline)	Universal table (SQL)	Universal table (ORM)
Select	0.4469	5.1793	14.0067
Insert	1.3823	13.7154	14.4246
Delete	0.5264	10.2565	16.0911
Update	0.5238	9.1029	15.3657

can be improved significantly if the built-in cache mechanism of query processor is turned on. It is also worthy to point out that the turnaround time for ORM implementation is a bit slower than the direct SQL implementation. This result reflects the trade-offs between code maintainability (via the use of ORM framework) and performance.

6   Conclusions

In this article, we report the design of a multitenant-enabled middleware for supporting the development and deployment of enterprise multitenant SaaS applications. The proposed service middleware addresses three essential design aspects, namely, tenant context storage and propagation, schema-mapping, and the integration of ORM framework, of enterprise SaaS applications. We have also presented a prototype implementation of the proposed approach and conducted performance evaluations to assess the overheads. In addition, a sample multitenant SaaS application, the ShoppingForce.com and two tenant-specific virtual applications are also constructed to demonstrate the feasibility of the service middleware. Further research is required to investigate approaches for enhancing the security aspect of the proposed middleware. Specifically, multitenancy promotes resource sharing, which unavoidably trades a certain amount of security for the lower service costs. Fortunately, security issues caused by resource sharing can be significantly reduced if the multitenant SaaS application is deployed on a middleware platform that employs advanced access control and program monitoring mechanisms for intercepting unauthorized accesses to a shared resource. Hence, we shall look into those mechanisms and investigate how to leverage them to prevent unauthorized data accesses, such as checking tenant ID's. On a different front, we are going to explore more transparent ways, such as aspect-oriented programming or dependency injection, to help developers transform a single tenant enterprise application into a multitenant one based on the proposed service middleware with less efforts.

Acknowledgements. This work is sponsored by Ministry of Science and Technology, Taiwan, under grant 103-2221-E-004-005, 103-2221-E-004-018, and 103-2218-E-004-001.

References

1. Mell, P., Grance, T.: The NIST Definition of Cloud Computing, 2nd edn, pp. 800–145. NIST Special Publication (2011)
2. Momm, C., Krebs, R.: A qualitative discussion of different approaches for implementing multi-tenant saas offerings. In: Proceedings of Software Engineering 2011, Workshop (2011)
3. Chong, F., Carroro, G.: Architecture strategies for catching the long tail (2011). http://msdn.microsoft.com/en-us/library/aa479069.aspx

4. Koziolek, H.: The sposad architectural style for multi-tenant software applications. In: Proceedings of the 9th Working IEEE/IFIP Conferences on Software Architecture (2012)
5. Krebs, R., Momm, C., Konev, S.: Architectural concerns in multi-tenant saas applications. In: Proceedings of the International Conference on Cloud Computing and Service Science (CLOSER12) (2012)
6. Galchev, G., Fleischer, C., Luik, O., Kilian, F., Stanev, G.: Session handling based on shared session information, US Patent App. 11/322,596 (2007)
7. Fang, S., Tong, Q.: A comparison of multi-tenant data storage solutions for software-as-a-service. In: Proceedings of the 6th International Conference on Computer Science and Education (ICCSE 2011) (2011)
8. Aulbach, S., Grust, T., Jacobs, D., Kemper, A., Rittinger, J.: Multi-tenant databases for software as a service: schema-mapping techniques. In: Proceedings of the 2008 ACM SIGMOD International Conference on Management of Data (2008)
9. Weissman, C.D., Bobrowski, S.: The design of the force.com multitenant internet application development platform. In: Proceedings of the 2009 ACM SIGMOD International Conference on Management of Data (2009)
10. Schmidt, D.C., Stal, M., Rohnert, H., Buschmann, F.: Pattern-Oriented Software Architecture, Patterns for Concurrent and Networked Objects, vol. 2. Wiley, New York (1996)
11. Bezemer, C.P., Zaidman, A.: Challenges of reengineering into multi-tenant saas applications. Delft University of Technology, Technical report TUD-SERG-2010-012 (2010)
12. Cai, H., Wang, N., Zhou, M.J.: A transparent approach of enabling saas multitenancy in the cloud. In: Proceedings of IEEE World Congress on Services (2010)
13. Wang, H., Zheng, Z.: Software architecture driven configurability of multi-tenant SaaS application. In: Wang, F.L., Gong, Z., Luo, X., Lei, J. (eds.) Web Information Systems and Mining. LNCS, vol. 6318, pp. 418–424. Springer, Heidelberg (2010)
14. Truyen, E., Cardozo, N., Walraven, S., Vallejos, J., Bainomugisha, E., Gunther, S., D'Hondt, T., Joosen, W.: Context-oriented programming for customizable SaaS applications. In: Proceedings of ACM Symposium on Applied Computing (2012)
15. Pereira, J., Chiueh, T.C.: SQL Rewriting Engine and its Applications, Technical report. Stony Brook University (2007)
16. Li, C.: Transforming relational database into hbase: a case study. In: 2010 IEEE International Conference on Software Engineering and Service Sciences (ICSESS). IEEE (2010)
17. Azeez, A., Perera, S., Gamage, D., Linton, R., Siriwardana, P., Leelaratne, D., Weerawarana, S., Fremantle, P.: Multi-tenant soa middleware for cloud computing. In: 2010 IEEE 3rd International Conference on Cloud Computing (Cloud). IEEE (2010)
18. Strauch, S., Andrikopoulos, V., Sáez, S.G., Leymann, F., Muhler, D.: Enabling tenant-aware administration and management for jbi environments. In: 2012 5th IEEE International Conference on Service-Oriented Computing and Applications (SOCA). IEEE (2012)
19. Shimamura, H., Soejima, K., Kuroda, T., Nishimura, S.: Realization of the high-density SaaS infrastructure with a fine-grained multitenant framework. NEC Tech. J. 5, 132–136 (2010)
20. Joines, S., Willenborg, R., Hygn, K.: Performance Analysis for Java Web Sites. Addison-Wesley Professional (2003)

21. Liao, C.F., Chen, K., Chen, J.J.: Toward a tenant-aware query rewriting engine for universal table schema-mapping. In: 2012 IEEE 4th International Conference on Cloud Computing Technology and Science (CloudCom) (2012)

22. Ambler, S.: Agile Database Techniques: Effective Strategies for the Agile Software Developer. Wiley (2003)

23. Aarniala, J.: Instrumenting java bytecode. In: Seminar Work for the Compiler-scourse, Department of Computer Science, University of Helsinki, Finland (2005)

24. Russell, C.: Java Data Objects 2.0. JSR 243 Specification (2010)

25. Miller, F., Vandome, A., John, M.: DataNucleus. VDM Publishing, Saarbrucken (2010)

26. Hall, R., Pauls, K., McCulloch, S.: OSGi in Action: Creating Modular Applications in Java. Manning Publications Company, Greenwich (2011)

27. Halili, E.H.: Apache Jmeter: A Practical Beginner's Guide to Automated Testing and Performance Measurement for your Websites. Packt Publishing, Birmingham (2008)

The Fixed-Price Contract: A Challenge for the Software Development Project

Cornelia Gaebert[✉]

Research Group on Strategic Information Management,
European Research Center for Information Systems, University of Muenster,
Leonardo Campus 11, 48149 Muenster, Germany
cornelia.gaebert@uni-muenster.de,
cornelia.gaebert@indal.de

Abstract. Describing the software development project between customer and supplier at the contracting level as interaction of the involved organizations in terms of game theory, we can show that the parties are in a dilemma situation regarding the effort for closing the gaps of incomplete requirement specifications. Incomplete, ambiguous, and changing requirements are the number one reason for failure of software development projects. Customer and supplier have to interchange information for closing requirement gaps. However, gathering and interchanging information generates undesirable costs. The most commonly used contract model is a fixed-price contract. Under this condition, the supplier is forced to cooperate, whereas the customer prefers to defect regarding closing requirement gaps. In support of our theoretical argument, we carried out an empirical investigation. We derive suggestions for improving the fixed-price contract design of software development projects as well as for the cooperation behavior during the project.

Keywords: Software development project · Outsourcing · Failure · Information asymmetry · Dilemma structures · Incomplete contract

1 Introduction

Despite project management improvements and professionalization of the software development process, the number of failing software development projects has remained high for decades [7, 28].

Organizations expect to mitigate this risk by outsourcing [5]. They expect that the supplier take the risk for the project failing when working under autonomy. The customer considers the supplier responsible for budget, time, and quality.

Researchers in the field of software project management and software engineering have focused their studies on the project's internal problems, even when external suppliers carry out the projects [1, 22]. Moreover, they provide recommendations for practical action straight from the success factors derived from reasons of failure (see also [9]). They consider the qualifications of all stakeholders as well as the continuous improvement of project management [4], such as the change from structured to agile project management [32].

© Springer International Publishing Switzerland 2015
A. Holzinger et al. (Eds.): ICSOFT 2014, CCIS 555, pp. 97–112, 2015.
DOI: 10.1007/978-3-319-25579-8_6

This paper shifts the spotlight on the relationship between customer and supplier. We argue for describing the software development project at the contracting level, as a cooperation of two parties: the one that needs a software system to meet their individual requirements, and the one that has the ability to produce the software system. We call the first party the *customer,* and the second the *supplier.* First, both parties pursue economic targets.

The aim of this paper is to show that a formal description of the cooperation between the supplier and customer of a software development project will open new perspectives for understanding the failure of these projects. We provide a theoretical rationale for the failure of software development projects. Therefore, we introduce and justify a model of the software development project as a two-party interaction game, in which the delivery of information is the crucial element in each interaction. Using this approach, it will be possible to analyze contractual situations for software projects with respect to risks of failure. We will show how the structure of this interaction results in a high risk of failure for such projects. Nonetheless, from our model we can derive some suggestions for the contract design of software development projects and for the cooperation behavior during the project.

We base our argument on the number one reason for failure, incomplete, ambiguous, and changing requirements [7, 18, 19, 27, 28]. In this paper, we call this deficit *requirement gaps.* As we will show in Sect. 2.1, this is inherent in the setting of a software development project. Therefore, the customer and supplier need to interact with each other to establish clear requirements, explain changes, and exchange information over time. In Sect. 2.2, we briefly show the possible behavior of the actors in this situation. Regarding the delivery of needed information, the parties are in a situation called the *prisoner's dilemma.* Therefore, we introduce in Sect. 2.3 the prisoner's dilemma as a formal description [30]. Section 2.4 describes the software development projects in terms of game theory. We must ultimately expect that when both parties defect from cooperation, the project tends to fail. Finally, we show in Sect. 2.5, that even under the mostly agreeable fixed-price contract [23], the customer want to save costs. However, the customer will be dissatisfied with the quality of the developed software. Consequently, the contract is unable to fulfill its function and the project tends to fail.

In Sect. 3, we support this theoretical argumentation using a two-step empirical investigation. First, we interviewed experts, both customers and suppliers, using a formal questionnaire. Second, we conducted in-depth expert interviews. The empirical results show the relevance of these concepts for the understanding of problems in software development projects.

Finally, in Sect. 4 we summarize these suggestions and describe some directions for further research, starting with this model.

2 The Project as a Two Party Game

Researchers in the field of software project management focus primarily on the control of decisions and activities of the acting participants and stakeholders within the development organization [16, 24]. They often describe them as rational agents having goals and making decisions for the cooperation with other actors, with the purpose of achieving a maximum of benefit [6, 31]. However, as shown by Tollefsen [29], we can also consider organizations like companies or public authorities as rational agents who have their own goals and make rational decisions for reaching these goals.

At the organizational level, regarding a software development project, we can define two kinds of actors: First, there are organizations acting as the customer; and second are the organizations acting as the supplier. The customer has business goals that result in requirements for a software system, which are described in a requirement specification document. The supplier has the ability to develop an information system that meets those requirements. Therefore, the customer and supplier sign a contract to carry out a software development project.

2.1 System-Inherent Causes for Incomplete Requirement Specifications

In an ideal world, the requirement specification is complete, unambiguous, and clear. In such a world, the supplier has calculated all efforts for the implementation of the requirements before signing the contract. Based on the specification, the designers and developers will implement the needed system. No communication and no interaction between the parties will be necessary during the project.

Unfortunately, requirements are not complete and unambiguous. As shown in research literature [18, 19], and as stated by all experts in our empirical survey (see Sect. 3), gaps exist in the requirements specifications. Researchers and practitioners have exerted a lot of effort in developing methods for producing better specifications without gaps, misunderstandings, and unclear descriptions.

Nevertheless, as we will argue in the following, there are system-inherent causes for the gaps in requirement specifications.

First, software requirement specifications contain knowledge in a strict sense only about the past and the present. For instance, the customer knows problems that exist with the currently used system, the present market situation, and business cases. About the future, there are only assumptions. In particular, how the new system will change the business processes is not a matter of fact, but a matter of expectation and anticipation.

Second, the requirement engineer can only document consciously available knowledge, and to some extent subconsciously available knowledge. However, in all business processes, relevant conditions and information exist that no one knows about [15]. The customer has knowledge primarily regarding the business for which the software system is needed. In contrast, the supplier has knowledge regarding technical issues, like the properties of used frameworks and development techniques. Furthermore, on the supplier's side, experiences from other projects regarding user acceptance and performance problems exist. This knowledge is also relevant for the development of a software system, but in the moment of documenting the requirements it is not available.

Third, the software development project needs time. The customer and the supplier interact and exchange information during the project's development. As their settings change, new requirements may arise.

Consequently, we have to accept the fact, that requirement specifications will contain gaps also in the future, and even if research in requirement engineering finds new and better methods.

2.2 Possible Choices of Rational Actors

As we have shown, the customer and the supplier must sign the contract based on an incomplete requirement specification. Closing the gaps is part of each software development project, and there is no way to avoid this situation. The question arises, how a rational actor will behave in this situation.

Both actors have the choice to participate in the closing of specification gaps, or to avoid these efforts and to demand this effort from the other party. Therefore, we have to analyze four cases.

(1) The customer tries to avoid effort, whereas the supplier exerts effort in closing the gaps. The customer may argue that the supplier should calculate these efforts during the calculation of the projects costs. Furthermore, the supplier has seen the specification before signing the contract and has committed to implement the needed system, if necessary by detailing the requirements. In such cases, customers will argue that there are no real gaps in the requirements but there are some details left to be defined during the system design phase. Thus, the supplier is responsible for specifying these details. The customer will avoid delivering resources for clarification. The supplier must specify assumptions and define suggestions, and the customer is free to accept or to reject them.
The result is an enormous effort on the supplier's side, whereas the customer will save on costs and will get the needed system with little effort on their own part.

(2) The reverse situation is also possible. The supplier can avoid exerting effort in closing the gaps and can demand all information needed from the customer. If the supplier finds a specification gap during the design and the implementation of the system, he will ask the customer for clarification and deny sending their own experts or making his own suggestions based on experiences from other projects. In this case, there will be high costs on the customer's side, whereas the supplier incurs no extra costs for closing the gaps. Furthermore, the supplier has the ability to initiate change requests to get extra payments.

(3) It is possible, that both parties avoid any effort in closing the requirement gaps. The supplier may implement the system without asking the customer if there is a problem with the specification. Alternatively, if the supplier asks, he can be satisfied with any answer from the customer and does not reflect it on own experiences. The customer may also avoid effort for clarification. Both sides may see the other side as being responsible for closing the gaps and may ignore arising problems. The result of this behavior is that both sides save efforts during the project, but in the end, the system does not meet the real business requirements of the customer. The project is highly risky, and if it fails, the customer will not pay the price for the development. Therefore, in such a case, both parties will probably lose their investments.

(4) Finally, both parties may cooperate, sending their experts and delivering all information and experiences for finding the right solution in the case of requirement gaps. The efforts on both sides then are high; however, the project can finish with a system that meets the requirements.

Clearly, the fourth case is the best way to finish a project successfully. However, in reality, both the customer and the supplier have to save costs by avoiding extra effort. Therefore, it is not self-evident that the parties cooperate as described in this scenario.

For some time *game theory* has described the structure of the situation as prisoner's dilemma [30]. In recent years, the prisoner's dilemma has already been used in the analysis of dilemma structures between developers within software development projects [13, 31]. We will use this model as an analytical tool for understanding the situation of the projects' parties. First, we will introduce the original picture, giving the model its name. Then we will apply it to the project situation.

2.3 The Prisoner's Dilemma

In the prisoner's dilemma, a prosecutor questions two prisoners individually. Both prisoners (player) can deny the alleged offense (cooperate with each other), and both result in an imprisonment of 5 years. However, each of them can also admit and incriminate the other (defect). If only one of them admits, he or she gets the acquittal (leniency) and the other gets 20 years of imprisonment. If both confess, each receives 10 years of imprisonment. Although it would be best for both prisoners, if they denied the offense, they will both confess because of the incentive conditions of the situation. The special situation in capturing the dilemma situation is that both actors miss the potential gains from cooperation just because they follow their own incentives and thus act rationally.

Figure 1 depicts the situation and the preferences of the prisoners in a schematic way. We enter the payoff for each player in four quadrants: A, B, C, and D. We enter the results of player X in the lower-left corner of each quadrant, and we list the payoffs of player Y in the upper-right corner. The arrows in the figure mark the advantage calculi. The horizontal arrows describe the tendency of Y; the vertical arrows describe the tendency of X.

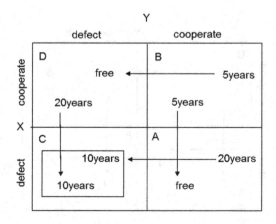

Fig. 1. Prisoner's dilemma.

For X and Y, defecting is the dominant strategy, which they will choose. Both prisoners make their rational decisions independently from the other, knowing the possible choices that the other may make. If the other cooperates, for each prisoner it would be best to defect, because he will be free. If the other one defects, for each it is also the better choice to defect. Consequently, both prisoners will defect and will get a bad result. If both decide to cooperate, the result would be much better.

The frame in the lower-left quadrant C shows the (Nash) equilibrium, the result that rational actors will get in a prisoner's dilemma situation.

2.4   The Customer and the Supplier in a Dilemma Situation

Now, for applying the prisoner's dilemma to the software development project, we identify the player Y with the customer and player X with the supplier. If the customer defects and the supplier cooperate, the latter will close all specification gaps at his own cost, and the customer will get the best result (case 1 in Sect. 2.2, quadrant D in Fig. 1). In contrast, if the supplier defects by avoiding the needed effort, and the customer works hard to close all gaps, it will be the best for the supplier (case 2, quadrant A in Fig. 1). If both parties cooperate, both incur some costs, but they get the best system as the result of the project (case 4, quadrant B in Fig. 1). Finally, if neither the customer nor the supplier work on closing the gaps, they will exert less effort, but the result is a bad system that does not meet the requirements (case 3, quadrant C in Fig. 1).

If both the supplier and the customer in a software development project act as rational actors, they both must avoid any effort in closing gaps in the requirement specification – the result will be a bad system.

Please note, only the order of evaluation is in this situation crucial for the result, not the concrete rating level [2]. Therefore, we can translate the payoff to simple numerical amounts for the better representation of the problem structure of the dilemma situation in the form of a prisoner's dilemma [3]. Figure 2 depicts the four cases in four fields.

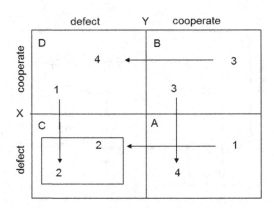

Fig. 2. The prisoner's dilemma of the software development project in normal form with payoffs.

The supplier (player X) gets in quadrant A a result of 4 (only the customer closes gaps). In quadrant B, both get a payoff of 3 (both close gaps), and in C a payoff of 2 (nobody closes gaps). In the D quadrant, the supplier realized his worst result of 1 (only the supplier closes gaps). The customer (player Y) obtains in quadrant D his best result with the payment of 4. The customer achieves his worst result in quadrant A with a payoff of 1. Divergent preferences determine the order of evaluation of possible results: For the supplier, it is A > B > C > D and for the customer it is D > B > C > A. The payoff matrix of the one is therefore the transposed payoff matrix of the other.

The rational actors achieve the dominant result because there is no effective behavior binding, i.e. the supplier and the customer are in a so-called institutional vacuum [3]. If the supplier and the customer want to escape this dilemma, they must prevent the institutional vacuum so that they are no longer in a dilemma structure. They can achieve this only through collective self-commitment to cooperation, through simultaneous abandonment of the solutions in the quadrants A and D. Both can improve their payoff only in this way. They must find rules that reward cooperation and punish defection to guarantee effective behavior binding. Following the cooperation agreement must be the rational choice for the actors. Each actor will decide this way, only if the achieved result is better for him than the solution without agreement. The agreement must eliminate the conflict. It causes the actors no longer to operate independently [11]. The players cooperate only if they know the alternative solutions and if they are sure how the other one will act [8].

If a negative sanction is established for both players in the case of defection, the possible payoffs change (Fig. 3). The preferences are changing, and so the order of evaluation of the results changes. Cooperation will be the dominant strategy. The enticing thing about this situation is that no actor cares how the other player is set. The individual gets, in any case, a payoff of 3 if he cooperates. The actors found a new opportunity space by way of rules. These rules change the incentives so that the actors can still defect, but they do not want to defect. It is not about improving the game, but about playing another game.

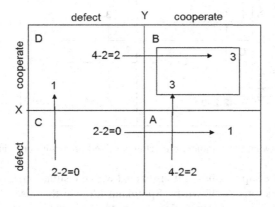

Fig. 3. Negative sanction for both.

2.5   Rational Behavior in Dilemma Situations

As empirical studies show, contractual arrangements between both parties vary between fixed-price and time-and-material contracts [10, 14]. Fixed-price contracts consist as the name suggests of a fixed-price for the developed software. In the case of a time-and-material contract, the customer pays for a specified amount per hour. Sometimes, the two contract types are combined, such as a fixed-price for the initial development and time-and-material for its enhancement.

With a time-and-material contract, neither the customer nor the supplier has incentives to avoid efforts in closing the requirement gaps. This contract type eliminates this conflict as long as the customer is willing to pay. However, fixed-price contracts dominate the contract types. Under the conditions of a fixed-price contract, the customer in particular has the chance to exert pressure on the supplier by threatening to reject the system and to deny paying the agreed-upon price. Some authors explicitly demand to control the suppliers' work in detail [24].

Because of the sanction for the supplier in such a contract situation, the order of evaluation for the supplier changes (Fig. 4). The preferences of the supplier switch from defecting to cooperating. The customer receives the penalty as a bonus, so his preference does not change. His payoff for defection is always higher than his cooperation payoff. The balance adjusts itself in quadrant D, where the customer achieves his best result. The inescapable conclusion of this finding is that the customer will not want to cooperate in closing the gaps because, no matter how the supplier chooses, he always achieves his best result with defection. He just needs to ensure that he collects the penalty from the supplier in the case that the supplier has not demonstrably fulfilled the contract. The actors will not achieve the equilibrium solution in quadrant B.

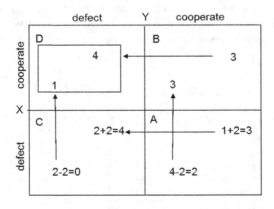

Fig. 4. The software development project under fixed-price with one-sided sanctions.

Nevertheless, the supplier has options to deal with the situation, and he must do this, if he is a rational actor. As shown by Spremann [26], in the case of asymmetrically distributed information, there are options for hidden actions. In software projects, the supplier has the chance to save effort on quality issues as performance, maintainability, reliability, and other quality attributes. Problems from this behavior will appear after finishing the project, and due to the fact, that there are many possible causes for problems, the supplier may deny the responsibility for these problems. Therefore, also the customer should have an interest in finding a contract design as described in Fig. 3.

Is it possible in a software development project as under investigation of this study to implement negative sanctions in the case of defection for both parties? It is not difficult to implement sanctions regarding the supplier. If the supplier does not meet the milestones, or if the quality of the software system is bad, it is possible for the customer to deduct a penalty from the agreed price.

On the other side, a sanction for the customer would mean that he has to pay a higher price. This would escape the fixed-price condition, so it does not seem possible to implement such a sanction.

3   Empirical Support of the Theoretical Argument

We support our theoretical findings with an empirical survey. First, it is essential that the supplier get mostly a fixed-price for the software system. If the customer would pay an effort-based price for all of the work done by the supplier, no dilemma situation would arise. Second, do the customer and supplier agree that there are gaps in the requirement specifications delivered by the customer by signing the contract? Third, is there a potential conflict resulting from this situation? Do both parties quite agree that there is conflict? To support the practical relevance of these assumptions, we carried out an empirical investigation.

For this empirical part of our study, we conducted a two-step evaluation. First, we developed a questionnaire in the form of a standardized online survey as a special kind of standardized survey [17]. Next, we conducted personal interviews to deepen our understanding of the results from the questionnaire. The period of the evaluation was one year.

For the questionnaire, we chose the standardized online survey to give the respondents an opportunity to reflect and to question their own companies [25]. The format of the online survey itself was legitimate because the interviewees were an IT-savvy group. Open answers supplemented the closed questions to not be too restrictive and to gather the covered information [20]. In the following, we will analyze and interpret the results descriptively.

We interviewed experienced project participants on both sides (customer and supplier). The questionnaire had to take the management perspective as well as the view of the project management into account. Because it is not possible to address trivially the population of all manufacturers and customers of custom software, and because questioning the population about any associated unacceptably high cost is not realistic, we chose a smaller population. Therefore, we could not achieve complete representativeness [25]. For practical reasons, we addressed the 45 members of a network of IT companies in Germany. Fifty additional addressees were available from other contacts. To expand the circle of respondents and to amplify the customer side, we used contacts in social networks such as Facebook (approximately 30), Xing (approximately 20), and Twitter (approximately 50). This ensured that the respondents had experience in different contexts of possible projects. Of the 200 addressees who were requested to participate in the survey, 29 actually completed the questionnaire (14 suppliers, 5 customers, 9 suppliers and customers (both), and one other).

An independent survey that evaluated the willingness to participate in the survey suggested a conscientious answering of the questions. A total of 48.3 % of the respondents indicated that they belong to management and that they have responsibility for the contracts; 27.6 % are project managers; 6.9 % are employees at the working level; and 17.2 % perform other activities, such as consulting. 89.7 % of the respondents had 10 or more years of experience with software development projects. The participants represented a broad range of sizes of projects with regard to the duration and number of employees.

For the exemplary and in-depth interviews, we conducted semi-structured expert interviews. We questioned, on the one side, a consultant with experience in software projects for approximately 15 years. He supports big companies in defining and organizing the contractual issues of software projects. On the other side, we spoke with a supplier with experience in software projects for approximately 20 years. He is an owner of a software development company with 10 programmers. Considering the sensitivity of failure research and the resulting difficulty in gaining access to project details, this methodology was most appropriate. The incomplete script of the semi-structured interview format left room for improvising questions [21]. The first interview lasted approximately 3 h; the second lasted 1.5 h. We made extensive notes during the interviews, which we evaluated afterward through a qualitative content analysis. Because we demanded appointed circumstances and facts, we avoided free interpretation problems [12].

3.1 Results from the Online Survey

The survey showed that the proportion of fixed-price contracts for software development projects is extremely high (Fig. 5). Taking into account that even the so-called agile fixed-price, time-and-material (T&M) price with ceiling ultimately determines the maximum total budget for the consumer, the proportion of this type of contract is a total of more than three quarters of the software development projects. A manager on the side of the supplier added in free text: "Even if it is charged at T&M, the expectation of the customer is the compliance with the budget /value of the order."

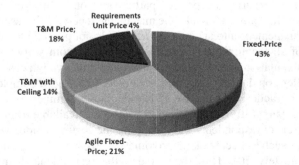

Fig. 5. Proportion of different types of contracts on software development projects.

On the bottom line, the T&M price with ceiling and the agile fixed-price mean the implementation of the requirements at fixed cost. Often the ceiling does not differ significantly from the calculated expense. An agile fixed-price, however, allows one to the implementation of requirements when new requirements emerge. Then, these new requirements can replace earlier ones. However, such contractual subtleties relate only to new requirements. A third party (judge) can evaluate them. Nevertheless, this rarely helps in cases of closing the requirement gaps. Rather, closing gaps only makes unconscious knowledge aware. For the customer, it appeared typically obvious, whereas it was unknown to the supplier and vice versa. Filling the gaps makes it known explicitly.

The customers predominantly determine the contract model (Fig. 6). Although 80 % of the customers indicate that they at least often determine the contract model, suppliers say quite the opposite. Two-thirds of them admit that they have little or no influence on the contract model. One comment from a project leader on the supplier side is: "I do not understand the question. The contract model is in all cases defined by the customer." Thus, customers clearly choose the contract design.

Fig. 6. Answer to the question "Do you determine the contract model?".

Customers and suppliers have different views on emerging problems inside a fixed-price project, like when an imbalance occurs in terms of time, cost, and quality (Fig. 7).

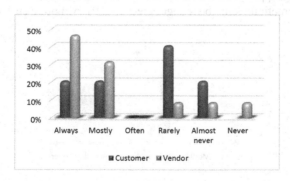

Fig. 7. Is an imbalance of time, cost, or quality in the project under fixed-price problematic?

Although 77 % of the suppliers consider such a situation always or usually as problematic, 60 % of the customers believe that this is rarely or almost never a problem for them.

Against this background, it is important to consider how the contract reflects gaps in the requirement specifications and how the signed contract supports the project itself.

After all, such gaps lead to increased interaction. Most respondents stated for the vast number of projects (Fig. 8) that such gaps exist.

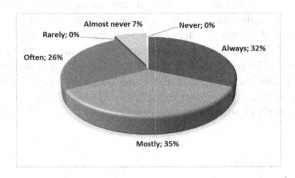

Fig. 8. Frequency of requirement gaps.

Almost a third of the respondents said that such gaps "always" happen; 93 % say that this case occurs at least often. However, a fixed-price contract hardly takes this sufficiently into account. For suppliers to do this seems hardly to be possible, as the notes to the relevant questions show. They try to work with a kind of overhead calculation but requirement gaps "are rarely sufficiently taken into account."

However, contracts widely do not reflect this fact. On the question, whether contractors continuously update the contract during the project, 81 % of participants responded that this rarely or never happens.

Customers and suppliers have a different perspective regarding whether gaps leading to unforeseen interaction would be renegotiated (Fig. 9). Although customers are of the

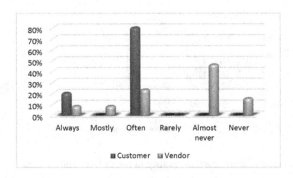

Fig. 9. Renegotiate customer and supplier requirement gaps.

opinion that this would always or at least often happen, 61 % of the suppliers believe that there are never or almost never renegotiations.

Two-thirds of all respondents say that gaps in the requirement specifications always or almost always lead to unplanned discussions. The contract usually does not take into account the extra costs, which interactions trigger.

3.2 Results from Interviews

We documented the interviews in a structured way with references to each question and to the paragraph of the answer. In the following, we give a short overview of the results. In brackets, we note the reference to the minutes of the interviews. For example, (S Q3A2) references the supplier interview, question 3, answer paragraph 2.

Both interview partners said that the mostly preferred contract model is the fixed-price contract, especially if the requirements are documented and if they seem to be clear (C Q3A1, S Q5A2). This is because of the customer's restriction in having a limited budget and that customers must calculate the expected benefits against the costs beforehand (C Q16A1, (S Q6A1).

Nevertheless, because "it is very seldom that the requirements are specified in a formal way" (C Q10A1), it is almost impossible to calculate the real costs. In addition, the supplier stated: "The problem does not come from the fixed-price itself, but from unclear, incomplete, or changing requirements. And the problem is that the customer is not willing to change the price if he changes the requirements" (S Q6A3).

The interviews supported the finding from the online survey, that the customers mostly dominate the contract design (S Q5A2, C Q3A1). Nevertheless, both interview partners gave hints, that obligations for a cooperating behavior of the customer are possible in practice (C Q14A4, S Q11A6).

Because the requirement specifications were so important, we asked our interview partners to explain the reasons for the gaps, the possibilities for dealing with these gaps, as well as the consequences. Both sides cited the reasons as being "special" or "exceptional use cases" that the experts were not aware of during the requirements analysis or were too difficult to model (C Q11A1; C Q11A4; S Q10A1). Furthermore, the facts were "obvious" (C Q11A3) or "self-evident" (S Q10A1) to the business experts, so they did not speak about them. Nonfunctional requirements were often unknown to the users (S Q10A1).

Both interview partners showed a high degree of uncertainty regarding the behavior, intentions, and skills of the other side. Customers try to get certainty beforehand from information like "descriptions of credential projects, facts about the know-how of their staff, information about the methods in designing and processing a software project" (C Q7A1). With "governance structures for the project" (C Q5A1) the customer hopes to "get at early phases of the project a good feeling of the progress and the quality of the vendor's work" (C Q6A1). However, uncertainty remains high: "Nearly nobody can distinguish the clever, good one from the slow and poor one. And if the vendor mentions that there are unforeseeable problems, you don't know if he is right or he is not professional enough for doing his job" (C Q16A1).

Regarding the same issue, the interview partner from the supplier side said, "a new management, problems in his market, new relevant law, and maybe, the customer does not need the software anymore or the costs will be higher than the effects. Then, maybe, the customer's management tries to cancel the project" (S Q11A5).

On the customer side, the strategy is to handle all problems in a formal way and to avoid all discussions regarding effort in narrowing the gaps in the requirements (C Q11A5; C Q15A1). In contrast, the supplier obviously has strategies of its own, knowing that the customer cannot see all that the supplier is doing (S Q12A1).

4   Conclusions

The objective of this paper was to describe the software development project as an interaction between two organizations, both acting as rational agents, both having economic targets. We have shown that these actors are in a dilemma situation, known from game theory as the prisoner's dilemma. In such a situation, the individual rational behavior of both actors leads to a result that does not satisfy either parties—neither the customer nor the supplier.

The root cause of this situation is the incompleteness of the requirement specifications. As theoretical and empirical investigations show, a specification without gaps is not possible. Therefore, the parties must cooperate when closing the gaps. Nonetheless, particularly under the most widely used fixed-price contract, both parties must avoid efforts in this cooperation.

Certainly, our investigation is not representative. However, our aim was to support our theoretical findings. As our survey shows, the customer often dominates the contractual regulations. In this situation, the customer can avoid the effort in closing the requirement gaps, whereas the supplier is forced to cooperate. As a rational agent, the supplier will use information asymmetries to save effort by hidden actions. This results in a poorly developed software system. Based on our two-party model, future research can analyze the dependencies of asymmetrically distributed information and software quality.

Using the game theory, we can describe the problem, but we can also show the way out. We can derive from the model the suggestion to connect defection with a sanction, and therefore change the situation. Defining the obligations for closing the requirement gaps for both the customer and the supplier within the contract can serve as such a sanction. We suggest that customers and suppliers agree on clear and tangible obligations for the customer regarding the cooperation for filling the gaps in requirement specifications. These contractual obligations should contain information on the necessary staff and the time required. Then, if the customer fails to meet these obligations, the parties may agree on a bonus for the supplier to be offset with possible penalties. In further research, we can include the theory of incomplete contracts.

Furthermore, we can use the results from research about the prisoner's dilemma [2]. If both parties are willing and able to cooperate, then it can be rational to start interactions with cooperation. In this way, both sides need a system to recognize and measure the behavior of the other party. Because experience is a prerequisite for trust, further research should examine whether the methods and concepts in the software development project are suitable for the formation of experience. We can derive such concepts from approaches of economic theories using the theoretical descriptions of customer and supplier as rational agents.

References

1. Al-Ahmad, W., Al-Fagih, K., Khanfar, K., Alsamara, K., Abuleil, S., Abu-Salem, H.: A taxonomy of an IT project failure: root causes. Int. Manag. Rev. **5**(1), 93–104 (2009)
2. Axelrod, R.: Die Evolution der Kooperation, Studienausgabe (7nd edn), München (2009)
3. Beckmann, M., Pies, I.: Freiheit durch Bindung - Zur ökonomischen Logik von Verhaltenskodizes, Diskussionspapier Nr. 2006-9, Lehrstuhl für Wirtschaftsethik der Martin-Luther-Universität Halle (2006)
4. Buhl, H.U., Meier, M.C.: Die Verantwortung der Wirtschaftsinformatik bei IT-Großprojekten. Wirtschaftsinformatik **2**, 59–62 (2011)
5. Chua, C.E.H., Lim, W.-K., Soh, C., Sia, S.K.: Client strategies in vendor transition: a threat balancing perspective. J. Strateg. Inf. Syst. **21**(1), 72–83 (2012)
6. Cockburn, A.: The end of software engineering and the start of economic-cooperative gaming. ComSIS **1**(1), 1–32 (2004)
7. El Emam, K., Koru, A.G.: A replicated survey of IT software project failures. IEEE Softw. **25**(5), 84–90 (2008)
8. Davis, L.H.: Prisoners, paradox, and rationality. Paradoxes of rationality and cooperation. In: Campell, R., Sowden, L. (eds.) Prisoner's Dilemma and Newcomb's Problem, pp. 46–59. UBC Press, Vancouver (1985). Reprint of American Philosophical Quarterly 14, 4, 1977, 319–327
9. Dwivedi, Y.K., Ravichandran, K., Williams, M.D., Miller, S., Lal, B., Antony, G.V., Kartik, M.: IS/IT project failures: a review of the extant literature for deriving a taxonomy of failure factors. In: Dwivedi, Y.K., Henriksen, H.Z., Wastell, D., De', R. (eds.) TDIT 2013. IFIP AICT, vol. 402, pp. 73–88. Springer, Heidelberg (2013)
10. Fink, L., Lichtenstein, Y., Wyss, S.: Ex post adaptations and hybrid contracts in software development services. Appl. Econ. **45**(32), 4533–4544 (2013)
11. Gauthier, D.: Maximization constrained: the rationality of cooperation. Paradoxes of rationality and cooperation. In: Campell, R., Sowden, L. (eds.) Prisoner's Dilemma and Newcomb's Problem, pp. 75–93. UBC Press, Vancouver (1985)
12. Gläser, J., Laudel, G.: Experteninterviews und qualitative Inhaltsanalyse, 4th edn. VS Verlag, Wiesbaden (2010)
13. Hazzan, O., Dubinsky, Y.: Social perspective of software development methods: the case of the prisoner dilemma and extreme programming. In: Baumeister, H., Marchesi, M., Holcombe, M. (eds.) XP 2005. LNCS, vol. 3556, pp. 74–81. Springer, Heidelberg (2005)
14. Kalnins, A., Mayer, K.J.: Relationships and hybrid contracts: an analysis of contract choice in information technology. J. Law Econ. Organ. **20**(1), 207–229 (2004)
15. Kano, N., Seraku, N., Takahashi, F., Tsuji, S.: Attractive quality and must be quality. Qual. J. Japan. Soc. Qual. Control **14**(2), 39–44 (1984)
16. Keil, M., Smith, H.J., Pawlowski, S., Jin, L.: 'Why didn't somebody tell me?': Climate, information asymmetry, and bad news about troubled projects. SIGMIS Database **35**(2), 65–84 (2004)
17. Klammer, B.: Empirische Sozialforschung. Eine Einführung für Kommunikationswissenschaftler und Journalisten. Utb, Konstanz (2005)
18. Liu, J.Y.-C., Chen, H.-G., Chen, C.C., Sheu, T.S.: Relationships among interpersonal conflict, requirements uncertainty, and software project performance (2011)
19. McGee, S., Greer, D.: Towards an understanding of the causes and effects of software requirements change: two case studies. Requirement Eng. **17**, 133–155 (2012)
20. Mayer, H.: Interview und schriftliche Befragung. Entwicklung, Durchführung und Auswertung. Oldenbourg Wissenschaftsverlag, München (2012)

21. Myers, M.D., Newman, M.: The qualitative interview in IS research: examining the craft. Inf. Organ. **17**(1), 2–26 (2007)
22. Natovich, J.: Vendor related risks in IT development: a chronology of an outsourced project failure. Technol. Anal. Strateg. Manag. **15**(4), 409–419 (2003)
23. Oestereich, B.: Der agile Festpreis und andere Preis- und Vertragsmodelle. Objekt-Spektrum **01**(2006), 29–33 (2006)
24. Rustagi, S., King, W.R., Kirsch, L.J.: Predictors of formal control usage in IT outsourcing partnerships. Inf. Syst. Res. **19**(2), 126–143 (2008)
25. Schnell, R., Hill, P., Esser, E.: Methoden der Sozialforschung, 9th edn. Oldenbourg Wissenschaftsverlag, München (2011)
26. Spremann, K.: Asymmetrische Information. ZfB **60**(5/6), 561–586 (1990)
27. Standish Group 1995: CHAOS Report. http://www.projectsmart.co.uk/docs/chaos-report.pdf. Accessed 21 June 2011
28. Standish Group, 2010. CHAOS MANIFESTO, The Laws of Chaos and the CHAOS 100 Best PM Practices. https://secure.standishgroup.com/reports/reports.php#reports. Accessed 26 June 2011
29. Tollefsen, D.: Organizations as true believers. J. Soc. Philos. **33**(3), 395–410 (2002)
30. Tucker, A.W.: Biographie, prisoner's dilemma (1950). http://www.princeton.edu/pr/news/95/q1/0126tucker.html
31. Yilmaz, M., O'Connor, R.V., Collins, J.: Improving software development process through economic mechanism design communications. Comput. Inf. Sci. **99**, 177–188 (2010)
32. Zannier, C., Maurer, F.: Comparing decision making in agile and non-agile software organizations. In: Damiani, E., Concas, G., Scotto, M., Succi, G. (eds.) XP 2007. LNCS, vol. 4536, pp. 1–8. Springer, Heidelberg (2007)

Model Transformation by Example Driven ATL Transformation Rules Development Using Model Differences

Joseba A. Agirre[✉], Goiuria Sagardui, and Leire Etxeberria

Mondragon Unibertsitatea, MGEP, Mondragon, Spain
{jaagirre,gsagardui,letxeberria}@mondragon.edu

Abstract. The use of Model Driven Development (MDD) approach is increasing in industry. MDD approach raises the level of abstraction using models as main artifacts of software engineering processes. The development of model transformations is a critical step in MDD. Tasks for defining, specifying and maintaining model transformation rules can be complex in MDD. Model Transformation By Example (MTBE) approaches have been proposed to ease the development process of transformation rules. Starting from pairs of example models the transformation rules are derived semi-automatically.

The aim of our approach is to derive the adaptation operations that must be implemented in a legacy model transformation to fulfill a new transformation requirement. An MTBE approach and a tool to develop and evolve ATL transformation rules have been developed. Our approach derives the transformations operations automatically using execution traceability data and models differences. The developed MTBE approach can be applied to evolve legacy model transformations. The tool can be used with endogenous and exogenous model to model transformations. The approach has been validated with several model transformations and the results have been collected. A real case study is introduced to demonstrate the usefulness of the tool.

Keywords: Model driven development · Model transformation development · Model transformation by example · Model transformation execution trace · Model differences

1 Introduction

Model transformations are fundamental in Model Driven Development (MDD). A model transformation takes input models conforming to the source metamodel and produces output models conforming to the target meta-model. To express meta-models and models several tool exist, for example the popular Eclipse Modeling Framework (EMF). On MDD, a model transformation is specified through a set of transformation rules, usually using transformation languages such as Atlas Transformation Language (ATL) [1], QVT [2] or EPSILON [3]. There are two kinds of model transformations: endogenous and exogenous [4]. *Endogenous transformations* are transformations between models expressed with the same meta-model. *Exogenous transformations* are transformations between models expressed using different meta-models. Tasks for

© Springer International Publishing Switzerland 2015
A. Holzinger et al. (Eds.): ICSOFT 2014, CCIS 555, pp. 113–130, 2015.
DOI: 10.1007/978-3-319-25579-8_7

defining, specifying and maintaining transformation rules are usually complex and critical in MDD.

In order to facilitate the development of transformations rules reuse mechanisms [5], reusable transformation design patterns [6] and refactoring operations [7] have been described. Model Transformation By Example (MTBE) [8] approaches have been proposed to ease the development process of transformation rules. By-example approaches define transformations using examples models. In MTBE starting from pairs of example input/output models the transformation rules are derived. Different MTBE approaches exists [9]. MTBE approaches for model transformation are classified in two types (I) demonstration based and (II) correspondences based. *Model transformation by demonstration* (MTBD) [10] specifies the desired transformation using modifications performed on example models. *MTBE based on correspondences* uses pairs of input/output models and a mapping data between them to derive the transformation rules. MTBE approaches allow specifying the model transformation using models, which is very intuitive. Transformation rules are generated semi-automatically so the model transformation development process is improved. Examples models can also be used to test the implemented transformations [9].

Evolving legacy model transformations is a complex task. The aim of the approach is to reduce maintenance efforts when modifications are required in a model transformation. Our approach is focused on generating semi-automatically transformation rules from pairs of example input/output models and transformation rules execution traces (see Fig. 1). The main characteristic of the approach is that it can be used to evolve legacy model transformations. Models differences, obtained after modifying a source model and a target model, are the core of the approach. Concretely the expected output model and the present produced output model, when transformation is executed, are compared. And adaptations of the transformation implementation are derived.

In this paper, we present a JAVA & EMF tool (TransEvol) for semi-automatic derivation of ATL model to model transformations to fulfill a new transformation

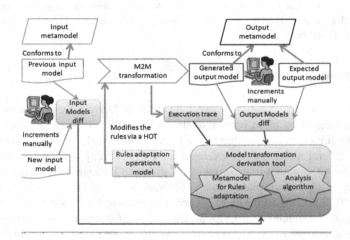

Fig. 1. Approach for automatic model transformation analysis to derive adaptation operations.

requirement. This paper provides the following contributions to the study of MTBE (I) MTBE approach based on model differences for exogenous and endogenous model transformations, (II) a MTBE approach applicable to ATL legacy model transformations and (III) Validation of the usefulness of the approach in a real legacy model transformation using a tool that we have developed.

In the following sections we detail the solution which guides the implementation of model transformations. First, in Sect. 2, the legacy model transformation example that motivated the need for automating the evolution of transformation rules is presented. Section 3 describes the MTBE approach used for the model transformation development. The fourth resumes the results of applying the approach on the motivating example. Then in Sect. 5 a brief description of the related work is presented. Finally in Sect. 6 the conclusions and future work are resumed.

2 Legacy Model Transformation Example

In [11] a MDD code generation system is presented. The MDD system generates ANSI-C code from component-based SW architectures, previously designed in UML. The MDD system generates the C code in two steps. As in Model Driven Architecture (MDA) [12] platform independent models (PIM) are transformed into platform specific models (PSM), and finally the PSM is transformed in code. In our case study, UML designs are transformed to intermediate models representing ANSI-C code through a model to model (M2M) transformation. SIMPLEC [13] metamodel is used to represent a subset of ANSI-C. The exogenous M2M transformation is implemented using ATL transformation language. Once the SIMPLEC models are obtained, a model to text (M2T) transformation is applied to SIMPLEC models to generate ANSI-C code. XPAND2 based templates are used to generate the output source code. Figure 2 resumes the example MDD code generation system.

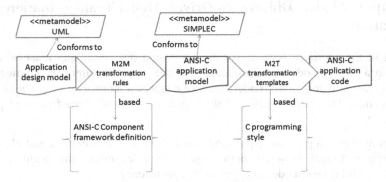

Fig. 2. UML to C MDD code generation system.

The M2M transformation is composed by 8 ATL modules with 73 transformation rules and 44 helper functions. The M2T transformation has 31 templates to generate the ANSI-C code from SIMPLE-C models. Originally, the MDD system of the case study did not offer concurrency characteristics at the design model and at the generated code. At one point, to add concurrency capabilities was required. This kind of situation is defined as abstraction evolution [14]. In abstraction evolution new domain concepts must be added to the MDD system, so several artifacts of the MDD system are affected. In this case, the source metamodel (UML) does not support the abstractions required to offer concurrency, so it is necessary to extend the metamodel or to add a new metamodel.

The UML MARTE (Modeling and Analysis of Real-Time and Embedded Systems) [15] profile was selected to add concurrency concepts in the design models. MARTE profile is an UML extension that provides support for specification, design, and verification of real time and embedded systems in UML. Due to the division of the generation in two stages the M2T transformation and the SIMPLEC metamodel did not require any change. Obviously, the source metamodel extension implies a co-evolution of the M2M transformation. The only documentation available about the M2M transformation was a few input models, so an exhaustive navigation was required to adapt manually the complex M2M transformation.

Our approach is based on defining the desired transformation by editing a previous input model and demonstrating the changes in transformations that lead to a target model. To relate the differences to a legacy model transformation an execution trace data is required. Combining the example models data with the transformation execution trace data the adaptation operations that must be implemented in the legacy model transformations are derived automatically (see Fig. 1). This way the development time is reduced and the probability to incur in errors is reduced. A JAVA & EMF tool has been developed to deduce automatically the adaptation operations on ATL transformation rules. The tool implements an algorithm to derive adaptation operations using model differences and execution trace data. A metamodel to express adaptation operations on transformation rules has been defined.

3   Outputs Models Differences Driven Model Transformation Analysis

The aim of the approach is to derive the adaptation operations that must be implemented in a legacy model transformation to fulfill a new requirement. Starting from pairs of example input/output models the tool deduces a number of adaptations in the transformation. The transformation analysis process consists of the following phases (see Fig. 1):

1. Adapt manually a previous input model to add the new requirement and obtain the differential model between both models (For example, the addition of a UML MARTE task model to express the concurrency).
2. Adapt manually a previous output model to add the requirement and obtain the differential model between the both models (For example, adding SIMPLEC elements that represent the implementation of the designed task model).
3. Obtain the traceability between the previous design model, the generated output model and the transformation rules. ATL2Trace [30] Higher Order Transformation

(HOT) is applied to the transformation under development to obtain the execution trace.

4. Deduce the adaptations to be made in the transformation rules to fulfill the new
5. transformation requirement using TransEvol.
6. Execute a higher order transformation to semi-automatically adapt the transformation rules.
7. Manually finish the transformation rules implementation.
8. Validate the transformation implementation using the manually generated input and output model.

Figures 3, 4 and 5 show an example of the artifacts that take part in the analysis process. Some details of the case study have been omitted in the interest of improving the understandability. First, the input model is modified manually to add a task model with three periodic tasks to the example design (see Fig. 3). To specify the model transformation the output model must be modified to integrate the SIMPLEC elements that correspond to the designed task model. Three new methods are added to the output model (see Fig. 4). Using this information, the approach detects a one-to-one mapping and a new matched rule must be generated. To bind the new output elements with its container element a binding statement also must be created in the rule that generates the container. Figure 5 lists the resulting transformation rules.

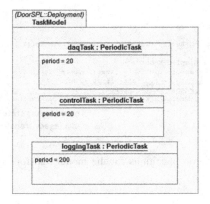

Fig. 3. The task model aggregated to the example design model.

The transformation rules analysis tool, TransEvol, relates EMFDiff [16] differences types of the output models to adaptation operations to apply on the model transformation. The tool implements an algorithm that derives adaptation operations from the difference model between a model generated by the M2M transformation (GOm, Generated output model) and an expected output model (EOm)). This difference model is called Output models differential ($\Delta Om = EOm - GOm$) and is generated using EMFCompare [17] and conforms to EMFDiff metamodel. The EMFDiff metamodel types used to analyze the model transformation are: addition of an element (*ModelElementChangeLeft*), removal of an element (*ModelElementChangeRight*),

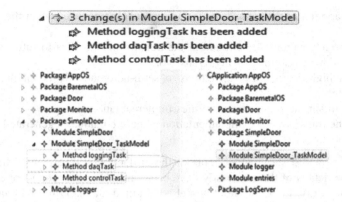

Fig. 4. The output model differences due to the task model.

```
rule PeriodicTask2Method {                    new matched rule
    from
        i: Uml!InstanceSpecification
    to
        m : SimpleC!Method(
            name <- i.name
            ,code <- thisModule.periodicTaskCode(i)
        )
}

rule ComponentTaskModelInterface(
    from
        r: Uml!Realization ( r.supplierIsTaskModel() )
    to
        m : SimpleC!Module(
            name <- r.client->first().name+'_TaskModel'
            ,path <- r.client->first().name
            ,methods <-  r.getPeriodicTasks()
            ,externals <- r.client->first().getKomponentModule()
        )
                                          new binding statememt
}                                         in a legacy transformation
                                          rule
```

Fig. 5. The required adaptation operations for the model transformation to integrate the task model concepts.

change of an element container (*MoveModelElement*), addition of an attribute (*AttributeChangeLeftTarget*), addition of a reference (*ReferenceChangeLeftTarget*), modification of a reference (*UpdateReference*) and modification of an attribute (*UpdateAttribute*). The EMFDiff differences offer basically the data of the new element, the deleted or updated element, the element affected by the change and the container of the new element.

3.1   Specifying Adaptation Operation for the Transformation Rules

TransEvol tool uses a metamodel called MMRuleAdaptation (Fig. 6) to express the required adaptation operations for the transformation rules. The transformation rules are subject to the following refinement modifications: *addRule, splitRule, deleteRule, deleteOutputPatternElement, deleteBinding, addInputPatternElement addOutputPatternElement, addBinding, moveOutputPatternElement, moveBinding, updateBinding, UpdateFilter* and *UpdateSource.* After the analysis, the tool generates a model expressing the required adaptation. Any modification operation is defined as an AdaptationTarget. Each adaptation target has a set of adaptation operations. Each adaptation operation requires different information to specify the modification, see Table 1. The metamodel uses ATL metamodel elements to express the data related to each modification operation. Table 1 collects the data required to express each adaptation operation.

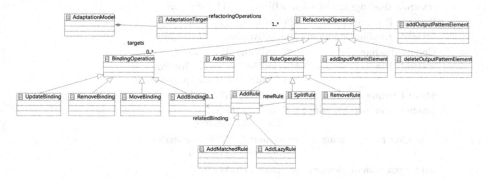

Fig. 6. MMRuleAdaptation metamodel.

3.2 Relationship Between EMFDiff Difference Types and Adaptation Operations

The tool relates EMFDiff differences types of the output models with adaptation operations. Table 2 resumes the relation between EMFDiff types and adaptation operations. Not always the same difference type instance is related to the same adaptation operation.

The algorithm first takes a difference element of the ΔOm and decides which kind of difference is:

1. Addition of output model elements
2. Removal of an output model element
3. Change of an element container
4. Addition and modification of attributes
5. Addition and modification of references

Once the type of the difference is decided, the algorithm must deduce the modification that must be applied to the model transformation. Depending on the scenario of the model transformation the adaptation operation for an output EMFDiff difference type may be slightly different. For example when some elements are added to the output model ($\Delta Om > 0$) a matched rule, a lazy rule or an output pattern element must

Table 1. MMAdapatationRule metamodel's adaptation operations.

Adaptation operation	Required data
Add Rule	newRule*: ATL!Rule* relatedBinding: *MMRuleAdaptation!AddBinding*
Add MatchedRule (extends addRule)	newRule*: ATL!Rule* relatedBinding: *MMRuleAdaptation!AddBinding*
Add LazyRule (extends addRule)	newRule*: ATL!Rule* relatedBinding : *MMRuleAdaptation!AddBinding*
Split Rule	affectedRule: *ATL!Rule* newRule: *MMRuleAdaptation!AddRule*
Add Binding (extends BindingOperation)	affectedRule: *ATL!Rule* newBinding : *ATL!Binding*
Remove Binding (extends BindingOperation)	affectedRule: *ATL!Rule* affectedBinding: *ATL!Binding*
Update Binding (extends BindingOperation)	affectedRule: *ATL!Rule* affectedBinding: *ATL!Binding* newValue:OCL!OclExpression
Move Binding (extends BindingOperation)	affectedRule: *ATL!Rule* toRule: *ATL!Rule* binding: *ATL!Binding*
Add filter to input pattern	newFilter: *OCL!OclExpression* affectedRule: *ATL!Rule*
Add input pattern element	affectedRule: *ATL!Rule* *newInput:ATL!InputPatternElement*
Add output pattern elemen	affectedRule: *ATL!Rule* *outputPattern: ATL!OutputPatternElement*
Delete out pattern element	affectedRule: *ATL!Rule* *outputPattern: ATL!OutputPatternElement*

be added, and also a binding must be created to associate the new element with a previously created model element. The addition of an output model element can be due to a one-to-one mapping, one-to-many mapping (different output elements types), one-to-many mapping (same output elements type) or many-to-many mapping. Depending on the scenario of the element addition the adaptation operations vary. To select the scenario the tool uses the ΔOm, ΔIm, ΔImc and ΔOmc models data.

Addition of Elements: One-to-One Mapping Scenario. The conditions to detect a one-to-one mapping scenario are: (I) The number of *ModelElementChangeLeft* in the ΔIm and the ΔOm is equal to 1, (II) the metamodel class coverage increment for the input and output metamodel must be 1. This scenario requires a new matched rule. The adaptation operation of adding a new matched rule is compound by a new rule and a binding. The data required to define the new matched rule is the Input Pattern element, the output pattern element and the rule name. The input pattern element is the type of any of the added element of the ΔIm model. The output pattern element is the type of one of the added element of the ΔOm. The rule name is the concatenation of both types. To create the binding that relates the new target element to its container the rule that

Table 2. Relationship between EMFDiff metamodel types and adaptation operations for model transformations.

EMFDiff difference type	EMFDiff type description	Adaptation operations
ModelElement ChangeLeft	Addition of an element	Add matched rule and add binding
		Add lazy rule and add binding
ModelElement ChangeRight	Removal of an element	Add filter
		Remove rule
MoveModelElement	Change of container	Split rule and modify binding
		Move binding
ReferenceChange LeftTarget	Addition of a reference	Add binding
UpdateReference	Update of a reference value	Update binding
		Add input pattern
AttributeChange LeftTarget	Addition of an attribute value	AddBinding
UpdateAttribute	Modification of an attribute value	Add binding
		Update binding
		Add input pattern

created the container element must be searched. To search the rule that creates the container the execution traceability data is used. Once the affected rule is founded the binding statement is established.

Addition of Elements: One-to-Many Mapping Scenario. The second kind of scenario is related to one-to-many mappings. This kind of scenarios requires the creation of a new output pattern element or a new lazy rule. If different types of target elements are created new output pattern elements are added to a rule. If instances of the same type are created for an input element type lazy rules are required. The transformation examples can be specified differently, Table 3 resumes one-to-many scenarios that the algorithm detects.

Addition of Elements: Many-to-Many Mapping Scenario. Many-to-many scenario is defined when a set of elements are added and both ΔImc and ΔOmc are higher than one. Two strategies can apply to this scenario. The first strategy is to specify the transformation example with a set of one-to-many mapping examples, where ΔImc is equal to 1 in each step. When ΔImc is greater than 1 the algorithm must align input elements with output elements using the similarity of its properties values. In those cases false positives adaptation operations can be deduced. For those cases a warning message is used. That way the transformation rules developers can analyze the adaptation operation model proposal and change it manually.

Removal of an Output Model Element. Two removal scenarios are detected by the algorithm. A matched rule is removed when $\Delta Omc = -1$. The other scenario occurs when $\Delta Omc = 0$ and some *ModelElementChangeRight* appears (see Table 4). This scenario requires a filtering operation in the input pattern element. In both cases the

Table 3. One-to-many mapping scenarios.

Previous transformation	Desired transformation	Scenario data	Adaptation operation
		$\Delta Im = 0$ $\Delta Om = N$ $\Delta Imc = 0$ $\Delta Omc = 1$	Add output pattern element
		$\Delta Im < \Delta Om$ $\Delta Imc = 1$ $\Delta Omc = N$	Add matched rule with multiple output pattern elements
		$\Delta Im < \Delta Om$ $\Delta Imc = 1$ $\Delta Omc = N$	Add matched Rule with multiple output pattern elements
		$\Delta Im < \Delta Om$ $\Delta Imc = 1$ $\Delta Omc = 1$	Add matched rule Add Lazy rule
		$\Delta Im < \Delta Om$ $\Delta Imc = 0$ $\Delta Omc = 0$	Add Lazy rule

Legend:
Arrow: Transformation
Geometric shapes (left side of the arrow): Elements of the input model
Geometric shapes (right side of the arrow): Elements of the Output model

Table 4. Removing output elements.

Previous transformation	Expected transformation

Legend:
Arrow: Transformation
Geometric shapes (left side of the arrow): Elements of the input model
Geometric shapes (right side of the arrow): Elements of the Output model

affected rule is founded searching in the execution trace the rule that generates the removed elements.

Change of an Element Container. Sometimes without any modification in the input models ($\Delta Imc = 1$ and $\Delta Im = 0$) the model transformation evolves and requires to change the instance of the container of an output element or even the container type. Both scenarios are detected by the algorithm. The first scenario involves a split rule operation. To split the affected rule a copy of the rule is done but filtering is added to the input pattern and a binding must be modified. When the type of the container changes a binding must be deleted in the rule that created the previous container and a binding must be added in the rule that created the desired container. To search those affected rules the execution trace of the previously executed transformation is used.

Addition and Modification of Attributes or References. The operations related to these scenarios are modification of a binding or an addition of a binding. In these cases, the execution trace is used to search the affected rule. The information of the output elements that have the difference (*Updateattribute, UpdateReference, ReferenceChangeLeftElement* and *AttributeChangeLeftElement*) is used to search the affected rule in the traceability data and to define the binding statement.

The Algorithm: Summary. Using the differences models and the traceability information the analysis of the transformation can be done. The difference model is based on model elements and not on metamodel elements, so several differences may be referred to the same change to be made in the transformation rules. We therefore must filter the adaptation operations to obtain the final adaptation operation model. Figure 7 represents a simplification of the algorithm.

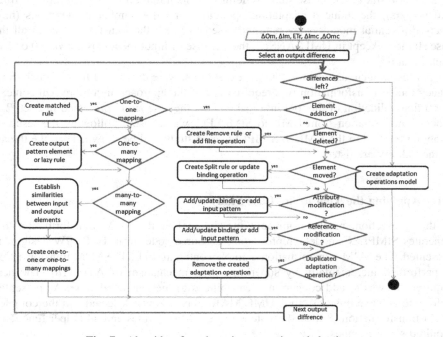

Fig. 7. Algorithm for adaptation operations deduction.

4   Implementing the Adaptation Operations

Once the adaptation operations model is generated the last step is to implement and validate the adaptation operations applied to the transformation rules. A HOT has been implemented to perform automatically the adaptation operations on the ATL module. The HOT takes as input the ATL module and the adaptation model. Despite the tool can detect the listed operations actually the HOT only implements *addRule*, *addBinding*, *splitRrule* and *addFilter*. The operations that are not executed by the HOT must be implemented manually. Once the transformation rules are adapted the new input model and the desired output models are used to validate the implementation of the transformation rule.

5   Validation of the Approach

During the development of the tool 8 small model transformations were used to validate the detection and generation of the different adaptation operations. Those examples are toy examples taken from the ATL Zoo. Two of them were endogenous transformations and others were exogenous. The used endogenous transformations were model refinements: the flattening of state machines and the introduction of the bridge design pattern on UML class diagrams. The Table 5 resumes the results obtained in each case study. Each case study is defined by its initial dimension (number of rules and helpers), the induced adaptation operations and the number of iterations (how many differential models were required) used to finish the transformation. In all the case studies, except in UML2ANSIC, the increase of input meta-classes were 0 or 1 in each iteration.

All the exogenous transformations, except one, were developed from scratch. So a legacy model transformation was required to test the approach in a more real context. For a first validation of the tool in a real context the case study presented in Sect. 2, a model transformation from UML to SIMPLEC, was chosen. Following the result of applying the tool to the UML to SIMPLEC case study will be shown. Then the threats to the validity are listed.

5.1   Applying the Tool to the Case Study

In this subsection, results from applying the tool to the M2M transformation that generates SIMPLEC models, representing C source code, from UML SW designs, is presented. The M2M transformation is implemented in ATL. The M2M transformation is performed incrementally by superimposition mechanism of ATL [18]. The new requirement was to add concurrency capabilities to the generated code. As presented before, to achieve this objective, UML MARTE profile was selected and the complex M2M transformation (8 files, 40 matched rules, 30 lazy rules and 44 helper functions) required some changes.

To apply the tool a previously used UML design was selected: a UML design of an automatic door controller without concurrency. The M2M transformation was executed

Table 5. Case studies results.

Model transformation	Type	Dimension	Derived adaptation operations	Number of iterations
UML to ANSI-C	Exogenous	40 matched rules 30 lazy rules 33 helper	3 add matched rules (with its bindings) 1 add lazy rule (with its bindings) 4 add bindings	2
StateMachine to flattened	Endogenous	7 matched rules	2 add filter to input pattern (negative condition) 1 split rule (with its filter pattern) 2 update binding 2 add lazy rules(with its bindings) 1 add binding	4
ListMetamodel Refactoring	Exogenous	0	2 add matched rule	2
Bridge pattern	Endogenous	8 matched rules	1 split rule (with add filter) 1 update binding	1
Families to person	Exogenous	0	1 add matched rule 1 split rule 1 add filter	3
Tree to Node	Exogenous	0	2 add matched rules 1 add filter to input pattern	1
TreeToList	Exogenous	0	2 add matched rules 1 add filter to input pattern	3
Port example	Exogenous	0	2 add matched rules 1 split rule (with the filters)	3
Side effect example	Exogenous	0	1 addition input pattern 3 add matches rules (with the bindings)	4

to generate the output model. Also the transformation execution trace model was generated. To start with the analysis, using UML MARTE a task model was added to the automatic door controller design. The API selected to express concurrency was a bare-metal API similar to FreeRTOS API. On the next step, the expected target output model with concurrency was created changing manually the generated output model. Finally, the difference models between the original and the incremented models were generated using EMFCompare Tool. A total of 13 differences were detected between the input models and 12 differences were detected on the output models.

Instead of specifying all the differences in one step the transformation example was divided in two steps. (I) the platform provider, the concurrency API, was specified as MARTE describes, (II) the task model was designed and each task was related to its behavior.

In the first step, the concurrency API model (two functions: *addTask* and *schedule*) was defined using MARTE stereotypes in the design model and a header with the API definition was added to the output model. The scenario was: $\Delta Imc = 3$, $\Delta Omc = 0$, $\Delta Im = 4$ and $\Delta Om = 3$. Three one-to-one mappings were detected, so three matched rules were deduced in this step: (I) the generation of the header of the API model (II) the *addTask* function and (III) the *schedule* function.

The second step requires the creation of the task model. And also the assignment of the behavior to each task. In this case the scenario was: $\Delta Imc = 3$, $\Delta Omc = 0$, $\Delta Im = 10$ and $\Delta Om = 10$. Seven of the ΔOm differences were *ReferenceChangeLeftTarget* type. The remaining three differences were addition of output elements. The adaptation operations deduced were four *addBinding* operations, that affected legacy transformation rules, and *two addMatchedRule* due to two one-to-many mappings detected. The models and the result corresponding to the task model can be seen in Figs. 3, 4, and 5.

When the tool derives add rule operations also a binding statement to attach the new elements with the container is derived. In those cases, the binding statement expression is implemented by a helper function. The tool generates the helper header definition and the call statement. The algorithm of the helper functions is completed manually.

The final model transformation implementation was validated applying the transformation to the new design model and comparing the new generated model with the expected model. All the deduced adaptation operations were correct. To apply the tool it is enough knowing the changes that are necessary in the M2M transformation input and output models. Previous knowledge of the model transformation implementation is not required, so the time required to adapt the M2M transformation is reduced.

5.2 Threats to Validity

The proposed case study is a real system and thus do not consider a certain number of factors that could affect the validation of the method:

- *Correctness:* Although initial case study show promising results, as all the transformation rules have been correctly identified, algorithm should be proved in more complex and different examples to improve the coverage of the validation.
- *Scalability:* The selected case study has legacy transformations (8 files, 40 matches rules, 30 lazy rules and 44 helper functions) and we deployed 13 differences in input models and 12 differences in output models. Although the case study is a real system, validation with bigger case studies is required.
- *Negative Construction:* the algorithm supports the remove matched rule operation and the add filter operation. In this real case study there are not negative constructions. However, the negative constructions have been proved with toy examples during the development of the tool.
- *Many to Many Mappings:* In the case study there are not many to many mappings. At present the tool can detect many to many mappings. However some ambiguities occurs generating the adaptation operations using the tool. To deal with many to

many mappings the transformation must be specified with a set of one to many mapping examples.

6 Related Work

The presented approach is highly related to MTBE. There are previous MTBE approaches which already deal with automatic generation of model transformations starting from pairs of example models. Most of the approaches are based on formal mapping to derive the transformations [19]. Reference [20] approach uses correspondence model between input and output model to generate ATL transformation rules. Instead offering a mapping model [21] annotates with extra information the source metamodel and the target metamodel to derive the required ATL transformation rules. Our approach also creates ATL transformation rules but a mapping between the desired input and output model or extra information besides the models differentials is not required.

In [22] a genetic programming based approach to derive model transformation rules (implemented with JESS) from input/output models is presented. This approach does not require fine-grained transformation traces. But due to the nature of the search algorithm the approach cannot be used to evolve a legacy model to model transformation. Something similar occurs with [23] where a heuristic algorithm is used to generate a new transformed model by similarity with other transformation example models. This approach is a self-tuning transformation so it cannot be used with legacy model transformations.

MTBD are based on defining the desired transformation by editing a source model and demonstrating the changes that evolve to a target model. Most of the MTBD are used on endogenous model transformation [24] not as MTBE based on correspondences, which can be used with exogenous transformations. Reference [25] presents a MTBD approach that can be applied to exogenous model transformation. This approach uses a state-based comparison to determine the executed modification operations after modeling the desired transformation. Using an incremental approach, in each step using a small transformation rule demonstration, internal templates representing the transformation rules are created. Once all the steps are done the templates are transformed to ATL transformation rules. This approach offers an interactive step where the developer can annotate the templates prior to generate the ATL rules to add information about the matching strategies. Because the approach uses templates created by transformation rules demonstrations it is not easy to apply this approach to legacy model transformations. Negative application conditions as well as many-to-one attribute correspondences are not considered. Our approach derives the transformations operations automatically using execution traceability data and models differences. This way the approach can be used to evolve legacy model transformations.

Most example-based approaches are constructive, that is, the new information always imply adding new elements to the artifact (a transformation in this case). Deleting is more complex. The presented approach can deal with negative constructions.

Metamodel and transformation co-evolution solution also exists. In [26] input metamodel differences are used to derive the evolution on the transformation rules. In [27] weaving between metamodels and transformation rules is used to analyze the impact on the transformation rules due to input metamodel evolution. These works only derives the modification on the transformation rules when regular metamodel evolution, as attribute modification or metaclass rename, occurs. When new elements on the input metamodel appear, the approach cannot derive the transformation rules.

Most of the MTBE cannot be applied to legacy model transformations. The main contribution of our MTBE approach is that it can be applied to evolve ATL legacy model transformations. Our approach can be applied to both exogenous and endogenous model transformations. We also have validated our approach in a real case study.

7   Conclusions and Future Work

An MTBE approach and a tool to evolve ATL transformation have been presented. A metamodel for expressing adaptation operations for transformation rules and the algorithm to derive the adaptation operations for M2M transformations have been described. The tool has been used successfully for adapting exogenous legacy model transformations to new transformation requirements. The tool generates semi-automatically adaptation operations for ATL transformation rules. The helpers used in the binding statements are only defined and called. The implementation of the helper functions must be done manually. The algorithm used to derive adaptation operation and the metamodel used to express the operations can be used to express operations for transformation languages such as QVT or EPSILON. The tool may require some changes to work with other transformation languages execution traces and also a new HOT, must be implemented for each transformation language.

The algorithm can detect one-to-one, one-to-many and many to many mappings. Negative construction examples are also detected. Actually the derivation of many to many and many to one mapping requires manual intervention. The tool uses output models differentials and execution trace data. In [28] the same data is used to locate the implementation errors in transformation rules implemented with EPSILON. The tool can be used with that orientation but must be analyzed how.

Once the functionality of the tool has been tested with small examples and a medium real legacy system, more validation on scalability and correctness are required. Currently, we are working on the definition of a methodology for the specification of correct example models. In short-term the tool is going to be used in a legacy model transformation to aggregate some security requirements to the output models as in [29].

Acknowledgements. This work has been developed in the DA2SEC project and UE2014-12 AURE project context funded by the Department of Education, Universities and Research of the Basque Government. The work has been developed by the embedded system group supported by the Department of Education, Universities and Research of the Basque Government.

References

1. Jouault, F., Allilaire, F., Bézivin, J., Kurtev, I.: ATL: a model transformation tool. Sci. Comput. Program. **72**(1–2), 31–39 (2008)
2. Object Management Group (OMG): Meta Object Facility (MOF) 2.0 Query/View/ Transformation (QVT) Specification, version 1.1 (2011)
3. Kolovos, D.S., Paige, R.F., Polack, F.A.C.: The epsilon transformation language. In: Gray, J., Vallecillo, A., Pierantonio, A. (eds.) ICMT 2008. LNCS, vol. 5063, pp. 46–60. Springer, Heidelberg (2008)
4. Mens, T., Van Gorp, P.: A taxonomy of model transformation. Electron. Notes Theor. Comput. Sci. **152**, 125–142 (2006)
5. Wimmer, M., Kappel, G., Kusel, A., Retschitzegger, W., Schönböck, J., Schwinger, W.: Fact or fiction – reuse in rule-based model-to-model transformation languages. In: Hu, Z., de Lara, J. (eds.) ICMT 2012. LNCS, vol. 7307, pp. 280–295. Springer, Heidelberg (2012)
6. Iacob, M.E., Steen, M.W., Heerink, L.: Reusable model transformation patterns. In: 2008 12th Enterprise Distributed Object Computing Conference Workshops, pp. 1–10. IEEE (2008)
7. Wimmer, M., Perez, S.M., Jouault, F., Cabot, J.: A catalogue of refactorings for model-to-model transformations. J. Object Technol. **11**(2), 21–40 (2012)
8. Varró, D.: Model transformation by example. In: Whittle, J., Reggio, G., Harel, D., Wang, J. (eds.) MoDELS 2006. LNCS, vol. 4199, pp. 410–424. Springer, Heidelberg (2006)
9. Kappel, G., Langer, P., Wimmer, M., Retschitzegger, W., Schwinger, W.: Model transformation by-example: a survey of the first wave. In: Düsterhöft, A., Klettke, M., Schewe, K.-D. (eds.) Conceptual Modelling and Its Theoretical Foundations. LNCS, vol. 7260, pp. 197–215. Springer, Heidelberg (2012)
10. White, J., Gray, J., Sun, Y.: Model transformation by demonstration. In: Selic, B., Schürr, A. (eds.) MODELS 2009. LNCS, vol. 5795, pp. 712–726. Springer, Heidelberg (2009)
11. Agirre, J., Sagardui, G., Etxeberria, L.: A flexible model driven software development process for component based embedded control systems. In: III Jornadas de Computación Empotradas JCE, SARTECO (2012)
12. Mellor, S.J.: MDA Distilled: Principles of Model-Driven Architecture. Addison-Wesley Professional, Boston (2004)
13. Agirre J., Sagardui, G., Etxeberria, L.: Plataforma DSDM para la Generación de Software Basado en Componentes en Entornos Empotrados. In: JISBD, pp. 7–15 (2010)
14. Van Deursen, A., Visser, E., Warmer, J.: Model-driven software evolution: A research agenda. In: Proceedings of International Workshop on Model-Driven Software Evolution (MoDSE), ECSMR 2007 (2007)
15. Object Management Group (OMG): Modeling and analysis of real-time and embedded systems (MARTE), version 1.0 (2009). http://www.omg.org/spec/MARTE/1.0/
16. Toulmé, A.: Presentation of EMF compare utility. In: Eclipse Modeling Symposium (2006)
17. Brun, C., Pierantonio, A.: Model differences in the Eclipse modelling framework. In: EJIP (2008)
18. Wagelaar, D., Van Der Straeten, R., Deridder, D.: Module superimposition: a composition technique for rule-based model transformation languages. Softw. Syst. Model. **9**(3), 285–309 (2009)
19. Balogh, Z., Varró, D.: Model transformation by example using inductive logic programming. Softw. Syst. Model. **8**(3), 347–364 (2009)

20. Strommer, M., Wimmer, M.: A framework for model transformation by-example: Concepts and tool support. In: Paige, R.F., Meyer, B. (eds.) Objects, Components, Models and Patterns. LNBIP, vol. 11, pp. 372–391. Springer, Heidelberg (2008)
21. García-Magariño, I., Gómez-Sanz, J.J., Fuentes-Fernández, R.: Model transformation by-example: an algorithm for generating many-to-many transformation rules in several model transformation languages. In: Paige, R.F. (ed.) ICMT 2009. LNCS, vol. 5563, pp. 52–66. Springer, Heidelberg (2009)
22. Faunes, M., Sahraoui, H., Boukadoum, M.: Genetic-programming approach to learn model transformation rules from examples. In: Kappel, G., Duddy, K. (eds.) ICMB 2013. LNCS, vol. 7909, pp. 17–32. Springer, Heidelberg (2013)
23. Kessentini, M., Sahraoui, H., Boukadoum, M., Omar, O.B.: Search-based model transformation by example. Softw. Syst. Model. 11(2), 209–226 (2012)
24. Sun, Y., Gray, J.: End-user support for debugging demonstration-based model transformation execution. In: Van Gorp, P., Ritter, T., Rose, L.M. (eds.) ECMFA 2013. LNCS, vol. 7949, pp. 86–100. Springer, Heidelberg (2013)
25. Wimmer, M., Langer, P., Kappel, G.: Model-to-model transformations by demonstration. In: Gogolla, M., Tratt, L. (eds.) ICMT 2010. LNCS, vol. 6142, pp. 153–167. Springer, Heidelberg (2010)
26. Levy, F., Muniz, P.: Applying MTBE manually: a method and an example. In: MDEBE@MoDELS (2013)
27. Iovino, L., Pierantonio, A., Malavolta, I.: On the impact significance of metamodel evolution in MDE. J. Object Technol. 11(3), 31–33 (2012)
28. Matragkas, N., Kolovos, D., Paige, R., Zolotas, A.: A traceability-driven approach to model transformation testing. In: AMT@MoDELS (2013)
29. Sun, Y., Gray, J., Delamare, R., Baudry, B., White, J.: Automating the maintenance of nonfunctional system properties using demonstration-based model transformation. J. Softw. Evol. Process 25(12), 1335–1356 (2013)
30. Joault, F.: Loosely coupled traceability for ATL. In: Proceedings of the European Conference on Model Driven Architecture Workshop on Traceability, ECMDA (2005)

Mining Web Server Logs for Creating Workload Models

Fredrik Abbors$^{(\boxtimes)}$, Dragos Truscan, and Tanwir Ahmad

Åbo Akademi University, Joukahaisenkatu 3-5 A, Turku, Finland
{fredrik.abbors,dragos.truscan,tanwir.ahmad}@abo.fi

Abstract. We present a tool-supported approach where we used data mining techniques for automatically inferring workload models from historical web access log data. The workload models are represented as Probabilistic Timed Automata (PTA) and describe how users interact with the system. Via their stochastic nature, PTAs have more advantages over traditional approaches which simply playback scripted or pre-recorded traces: they are easier to create and maintain and achieve higher coverage of the tested application. The purpose of these models is to mimic real-user behavior as closely as possible when generating load. To show the validity and applicability of our proposed approach, we present a few experiments. The results show, that the workload models automatically derived from web server logs are able to generate similar load with the one applied by real-users on the system and that they can be used as the starting point for performance testing process.

Keywords: Workload model generation · Log file analysis · Performance testing · Probabilistic timed automata

1 Introduction

The primary idea in performance testing is to establish how well a system performs in terms of responsiveness, stability, resource utilization, etc., under a given synthetic workload. The synthetic workload is usually generated from some kind of workload profile either on-the-fly or pre-generated. However, Ferrari states that synthetic workload should mimic the expected workload as closely as possible [1], otherwise it is not possible to draw any reliable conclusions from the results. This means that if load is generated from a workload model, then the model must represent the real-world user behavior as closely as possible. In addition, Jain points out that one of the most common mistakes in load testing is the use of unrepresentative load [2].

There already exists a broad range of well established web analytics software both as open source (Analog, AWStats, Webalyzer), proprietary (Sawmill, NetInsight, Urchin), as well as web hosted ones (Google Analytics, Analyzer, Insight). All these tools have different pricing models and range from free up to several hundred euros per month. These tools provide all kinds of information

© Springer International Publishing Switzerland 2015
A. Holzinger et al. (Eds.): ICSOFT 2014, CCIS 555, pp. 131–150, 2015.
DOI: 10.1007/978-3-319-25579-8_8

regarding the user clients, different statistics, daily number of visitors, average site hits, etc. Some tools can even visualize navigation paths that visitors take on the site. However, this usually requires a high-priced premium subscription. What the above tools do not provide is a deeper classification of the users or even a artefact that can directly be used for load testing. Such an artefact, based on real user data, would be the ideal source for generating synthetic load in a performance testing environment. Instead, the performance tester have to interpret the provided information and build his own artefact, from where load is generated. Automatically creating this artefact would also significantly speed up the performance testing process by removing the need of manual labour, and thus saving time and money.

This paper investigates an approach for automatically creating workload models from web server log data. More specifically, we are targeting HTTP-based systems with *RESTful* [3] interfaces. The proposed approach uses the K-means algorithm to classify users into groups based on the requested resources and, subsequently, a probabilistic workload model is automatically built for each group.

The presented approach and its tool support integrate with our performance testing process using the *MBPeT* [4] tool. The MBPeT tool generates load in real-time by executing the workload models in parallel. The parallel execution is meant to simulate the concurrent nature of normal web requests coming from real-world users. The tool itself has a distributed master/slave architecture which makes it suitable for cloud environments. However, the approach proposed in this paper can be used independently for analyzing and classifying the usage of a web site.

The rest of the paper is structured as follow: In Sect. 2, we give an overview of the related work. In Sect. 3, we present our performance testing process and tool chain in which we integrate our approach. Section 4 describes the approach, whereas, in Sect. 5, we present tool support. Section 6 shows our approach applied on a real-world example. In Sect. 7, we demonstrate the validity of our work with several experiments. Finally, in Sect. 8, we present conclusions and discuss future work.

2   Related Work

Load testing is still often done manually by specifying load scripts that describe the user behavior in terms of a subprogram [5,6]. The subprogram is then run for each virtual user, possibly with the data being pre-generated or randomly generated. With regard to the data, these types of approaches exhibit a certain degree of randomization. However, the behavior of each virtual user is mainly a repetition of pre-defined traces. Most of these approaches are prone to errors due to much manual work and lack of abstraction that stochastic models offer. However, the question: "How to create a realistic stochastic performance model?" remains.

There exists a plethora of tools on the market that can analyze HTTP-based logs and provide the user with statistical information and graphs regarding the system. Some tools might even offer the user with common and reoccurring patterns. However, to the best of our knowledge, there is no web analytics software that will create a stochastic model from log data.

Kathuria et al. proposed an approach for clustering users into groups based on the intent of the web query or the search string [7]. The authors divide the user intent into three categories: navigational, informational, and transactional. The proposed approach clusters web queries into one of the three categories based on a K-means algorithm. Our approach differs from this one in the sense that we cluster the users by their behavior by looking at the request pattern and accessed resources, whereas in their approach, the authors cluster users based on the intent or meaning behind the web query.

Vaarandi [8] proposes a *Simple Logfile Clustering Tool* consequently called *SLCT*. SLCT uses a clustering algorithm that detects frequent patterns in system event logs. The event logs typically contain log data in various formats from a wide range of devices, such as printers, scanners, routers, etc. The tool automatically detects common patterns in the structure of the event log. The approach is using data mining and clustering techniques to detect normal and anomalous log file lines. The approach is different from ours in the sense that we assume that the logging format is known and we build a stochastic model that can be used for performance testing from common patterns found in the log.

Shi [9] presents an approach for clustering user interest in web pages using the K-means algorithm. The author uses fuzzy linguistic variables to describe the time duration that users spend on web pages. The final user classification is then done using the K-means algorithm based on the time the users spend on each page. This research is different from ours in the sense that we are not classifying users based on the amount of time they spend on a web page but rather on their access pattern.

The solutions proposed by Mannila et al. [10] and Ma and Hellerstein [11] are targeted towards discovering temporal patterns from event logs using data mining techniques and various association rules. Both approaches assume a common logging format. Although association rules algorithms are powerful in detecting temporal associations between events, they do not focus on user classification and workload modeling for performance testing.

Another approach is presented by Anastasiou and Knottenbelt [12]. Here, the authors propose a tool, *PEPPERCORN*, that will infer a performance model from a set of log files containing raw location tracking traces. From the data, the tool will automatically create a Petri Net Performance Model (PNPM). The resulting PNPM is used to make an analysis of the system performance, identify bottlenecks, and to compute end-to-end response times by simulating the model. The approach differs from our in the sense that it operates on different structured data and that the resulting Petri Net model is used for making a performance analysis of the system and not for load generation. In addition, we construct probabilistic time automata from which we later on generate synthetic load.

Lutteroth and Weber describe a performance testing process similar to ours [13]. Load is generated from a stochastic model represented by a form chart. The main differences between their and our approach is that we use different type

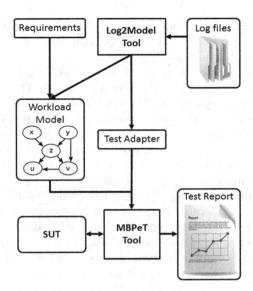

Fig. 1. Performance testing process.

of models and that we automatically infer our models from log data while they create the models manually. In addition, due to their nature, form chart models are less scalable compared to PTAs.

3   Process and Tool Chain

The work presented in this paper connects to our previous model-based performance testing process using the MBPeT tool (see Fig. 1). MBPeT is a performance testing tool which generates load by simulating several workload models concurrently to get a synthetic semi-random workload mix. The tool generates the load in a distributed fashion and applies it in real-time to the system under test (SUT), while measuring several key performance indicators, such as response time, throughput, error rate, etc. At the end of the test session, a detailed test report is provided.

MBPeT requires *workload models* and a *test adapter* as an input to generate load, as follows:

3.1   Workload Models

Traditionally, performance testing starts first with identifying key performance scenarios, based on the idea that certain scenarios are more frequent than others or certain scenarios impact more on the performance of the system than other scenarios. A performance scenario is a sequence of actions performed by an identified group of users [14]. However, this has traditionally been a manual step in the performance testing process. Typically, the identified scenarios are put

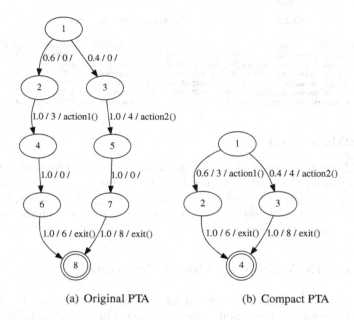

(a) Original PTA   (b) Compact PTA

Fig. 2. Example of a probabilistic timed automata.

together in a model or subprogram and later executed to produce load that is sent to the system.

In our approach, we use *probabilistic timed automata* (PTA) [15] to model the likelyhood of user actions. The PTA consists of a set of *locations* interconnected to each other via a set of *edges*. A PTA also includes the notion of time and probabilities (see Fig. 2(a)). Edges are labeled with different values: *probability value*, *think time*, and *action*. The *probability value* represents the likelihood of that particular edge being taken based on a probability mass function. The *think time* describes the amount of time that a user thinks or waits between two consecutive actions. An *action* is a request or a set of requests that the user sends to the system. Executing an action means making a probabilistic choice, waiting for the specified think time, and executing the actual action. In order to reduce complexity of the PTA, we use a compact notation where the probability value, think time, and action are modeled on the same edge (see Fig. 2(b)). Previously, the model was created manually from the performance requirements of the system and based on an estimated user behavior.

3.2 Test Adapter

MBPeT tool utilizes a test adapter to translate abstract actions found in a workload model into concrete actions understandable by the SUT. For example, in case of a web application, a *browse* action would have to be translated into a HTTP *GET* request. Usually the test adapter is implemented manually. For each action in the model the corresponding lines of code (e.g., in order to send a HTTP request to the SUT) have to be written.

Table 1. Requests to be structured in a tree.

Client IP-address	User-Identifier	User Id	Date	Method	Resource	Protocol	Status Code	Size of Object
87.153.57.43	example.site.com	bob	[20/Aug/2013:14:22:35 -0500]	GET	/browse	HTTP/1.0	200	855
87.153.57.43	example.site.com	bob	[20/Aug/2013:14:23:42 -0500]	GET	/basket/book/add	HTTP/1.0	200	685
87.153.57.43	example.site.com	bob	[20/Aug/2013:14:23:58 -0500]	GET	/basket/book/delete	HTTP/1.0	200	936
136.242.54.78	example.site.com	alice	[21/Aug/2013:23:44:45 -0700]	GET	/browse"	HTTP/1.0	200	855
136.242.54.78	example.site.com	alice	[21/Aug/2013:23:46:27 -0700]	GET	/basket/phone/add	HTTP/1.0	200	685
136.242.54.78	example.site.com	alice	[21/Aug/2013:23:57:02 -0700]	GET	/basket/view.html	HTTP/1.0	200	1772

3.3   Log2Model Tool

The Log2Model tool proposed in this work, is used as an alternative for automatically creating the workload models and the test adapter required by the MBPeT tool. Basically, the tool analyses historic usage of a web application or web service by mining its web server log files. The algorithm behind Log2Model will be discussed in the following section.

4   Automatic Workload Model Creation

In this section, we describe the method for automatically creating the workload model from log data and we discuss relevant aspects in more detail. The starting point of our approach is a web server log provided by web servers such as Apache or Microsoft Server. A typical format for a server log is shown in Table 1. The log is processed in several steps and a workload model is produced.

4.1   Parsing

The log file is parsed line by line using a pattern that matches the logging format. In our approach, a new virtual user is created when a new client IP-address[1] is encountered in the log. For each request made to the sever, the requested resource is stored in a list associated with a virtual user. The date and time information of the request together with the time difference to the previous request is also stored. The latter is what we denote as *think time* between two requests. For example, consider the requests in Table 1. The information would result in two new virtual users (Alice and Bob) being created. Bob made a request for a document while Alice made requests for two different pictures. The time between Alice's two requests was 34 s. This is what we note as *think time* between two requests. Please note, that it is impossible to know what the think time was before the first request, since we have no information about what Alice did before then. This will be important later on when we divide requests into different sessions.

Parsing the log file also entails ignoring irrelevant data. This could be e.g., lines that start with a pound sign ("#") or some other unwanted characters. This usually indicate that the line is to be interpreted as a comment and not as a log

---

[1] Our approach uses IP-addresses for user classification since the UserId is only available for authenticated users and usually not present in the log.

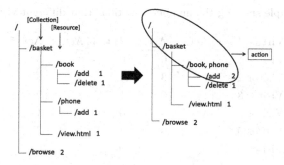

Fig. 3. Example of request tree reduction.

entry. It is not uncommon to encounter requests made by autonomous machines, also referred to as bots. These types of requests are identified and removed from the log into a separate list. The commonly known bots are specified in a whitelist that can be updated by the user. Requests from bots are detected in two ways. Firstly, by looking at the resource that has been requested. Some bots usually request a specific resource, namely *robots.txt*. This file contains information of what the bots should not index on the site. Secondly, we can refer bots from the user agent that made the request. It is not uncommon that the name of the user agent contains the word bot e.g., *Googlebot* or *Bingbot*.

4.2   Pre-processing

From the previous step, we obtain a list of virtual users and for each virtual user a list of requests made from the same client IP-address. In the pre-processing phase, these lists of requests are split up into shorter lists called *sessions*. A session is a sequence of requests made to the web server which represent the user activity in a certain time interval. It is not always trivial to say when one session ends and another begins, since the time interval varies from session to session. Traditionally, a session ends when a certain period of inactivity is detected, (e.g., 30 min). Hence, we define a session *timeout value* which is used to split the list of requests of a given user into sessions. In other words, we are searching for a time gap between two successive requests from the same virtual user that is greater than the specified timeout value. When a gap is found, the request trace is split, and a new session is started.

4.3   Building a Request Tree

Visitors interact with web sites by carrying out *actions*. Actions can be seen as abstract transactions or templates that fit many different requests. These requests can be quite similar in structure, yet not identical to each other. For example, consider a normal web shop where users add products to the basket. Adding two different products to the basket will result in two different web requests even though the action is the same. In this step, we group similar requests into actions.

Table 2. Example showing the number of actions that different visitors perform.

Virtual User	Act. 1	Act. 2	Act. 3	Act. 4	Act. 5
Visitor 1	2	0	0	3	3
Visitor 2	0	3	4	3	3
Visitor 3	1	0	1	8	9
Visitor 4	4	6	0	0	1
Visitor 5	0	0	4	8	7
Visitor 6	5	2	0	7	0

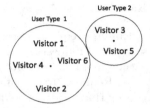

Fig. 4. K-means clustering on data from Table 2.

To achieve this, we first put the requests into a tree structure. For example, consider the example in Table 1. We split the string of the requested resource by the "/" separator and structure it into a tree. Figure 3-left shows how the requests in Table 1 would be structured. We always keep count of how many times we end up in a leaf node. For each new log line, we try to fit the request into the tree, otherwise a new branch is created.

After parsing a large log file, we obtain a large tree that might be difficult to manage. However, the tree can be reduced into a smaller tree by grouping together nodes. The algorithm is recursive and nodes at the same level in the tree are grouped together if they share joint sub-nodes. Figure 3-right shows how a tree can be reduced into a smaller tree. Once the request tree has been reduced as much as possible, every path in the reduced tree, that reaches a leaf node, is then considered as an *action* that can be executed against the system.

Consider the second request made by both Bob and Alice in Table 1. These two requests are basically the same type of request. They both request a resource from the same collection. This is similar to a *REST* interface where one uses *collections* and *resources*. It would seem obvious that these two requests are the result of the same action, only that the user requested different resources. Hence, by grouping together requests of the same type to the same resources, the tree can be reduced to a smaller tree. Similar requests are grouped into an *action*.

Requests in the tree can also be joined by manually inspecting the tree and grouping nodes that are a result of the same action. If a node in the path has more than one parameter, (e.g., it is a result of grouping two resources) that part of the request can be parameterized. For example, the request "/basket/book,phone/add" is a parameterized action where either *book* or *phone* should be used when sending the actual request to the system.

Table 3. Example showing different clustering parameters.

Virtual User	#Get	#Post	ATT	ASL	ARS
Visitor 1	25	3	44	653	696
Visitor 2	17	0	25	277	1353
Visitor 3	31	3	54	1904	473
Visitor 4	19	1	23	444	943

4.4   User Classification

Before we start constructing a workload model representing the user behavior, we cluster different virtual users into groups according to their behavior. By user behavior we mean a behavioral pattern that a group of web site visitors have in common. A *User Type* can be seen as a group abstracting several visitors of a web site.

To group visitors based on the actions they perform we use the K-means algorithm [16]. Table 2 shows the properties used for clustering. The properties are the *actions* obtained from the reduced request tree and the numbers represent the number of times a visitor has performed that action. The only input in this step is the number of desired clusters which has to be specified a priori. Figure 4 show how the different visitors in Table 2 would be clustered into groups (or *User Types*) using the K-means algorithm.

K-means clustering is an old method that involves assigning data points to k different clusters so that it minimizes the total squared distance between each point and its closest cluster center. One of the most widely used algorithms is simply referred to as "K-means" and it is a well documented algorithm that have several proposed optimization to it.

Our approach also allows us to cluster virtual users based on other characteristics. Table 3 shows an example using different clustering parameters, such as the total number of GET requests sent to the system (*#Get*) the total number of POST requests sent to the system (*#Post*), the Average Think Time (*ATT*), the Average Session Length (*ASL*), and Average Response Size (*ARS*).

This method, however, gives different clustering results compared to the previous method and can be used as a complement if the first method gives unsatisfactory results.

4.5   Removing Infrequent Sessions

Before we start building the workload model for each selected cluster, we filter out low frequency sessions. If we would include all possible sessions in the final workload model it would become too cluttered, difficult to understand, and it would include actions which do not contribute significantly to the load due to their low frequency rate.

Removing sessions that have low frequency is achieved by sorting sessions in descending order according to their execution rate. We filter out low frequent

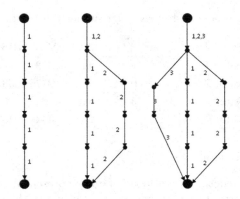

Fig. 5. Model built in a step-wise manner.

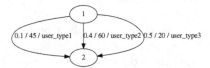

Fig. 6. Root model describing different user types their waiting times and probability.

sessions according to a Pareto probability density function [17] by cutting off the tail beneath a certain threshold value. The threshold value is given as a percentage value. That means that sessions below the threshold are simply ignored and treated as irrelevant. The threshold value can however be adjusted on-the-fly to include more or fewer sessions in the workload model.

4.6   Building the Workload Model

The workload models that we create describe the common behavior of all virtual users belonging to the same cluster. We say that the model describes the behavior of a particular *User Type*. Creating the model for a particular user type is a step-wise process where we overlap sessions of all visitors belonging to the same cluster.

Session by session we gradually build a model, while reusing existing nodes in the model as much as possible. At each step, we note the number of times an edge has been traversed, the action, and the think time value. We use this information to calculate the probability and average think time of each edge in the model.

Figure 5 depicts how the workload model is gradually built. One session at a time is included in the workload model. An edge represents an action being sent to the system. The numbers associated to the edges represent session IDs. Each node represents a place, where the visitor waits before sending the next action. One by one we include all the session belonging to the same cluster, while reusing existing nodes as much as possible. Identical sessions will be laid on top of each

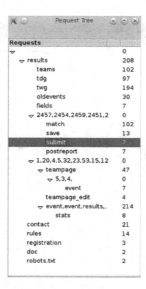

Fig. 7. Example of the request tree.

other and at each step, we note the number of times an edge has been traversed, the action, and the think time value. We use this information to calculate the probability and average think time of each edge.

We calculate the probability for an action as the ratio of a particular action to all the actions going out from a node. In a similar way, we calculate the think time of an action by computing the average of all think time values of an action.

In order to guarantee that the workload generated from the workload model matches the workload present in the log file, we calculate the user arrival rate. This information together with the distribution between user types is described in a higher level model called the *root model*. Figure 6 depicts such a model.

The labels on the edges are separated by a "/" and refer to the *probability*, *waiting time*, and *user type*, respectively. The probability value describes the distribution between different user types. The waiting time describes the average waiting time between sessions. The user type value simply denotes what workload model to execute. To calculate the waiting time of a user type, we first have to study the waiting time between different sessions of a particular user. We then calculate the user waiting time by computing an average time between sessions for every user belonging to a cluster.

5   Tool Support

Tool support for our approach was implemented using the Python [18] programming language. To increase the performance of the tool and make use of as many processor cores as possible for the most computation intensive tasks, we made use of Python's multiprocessing library.

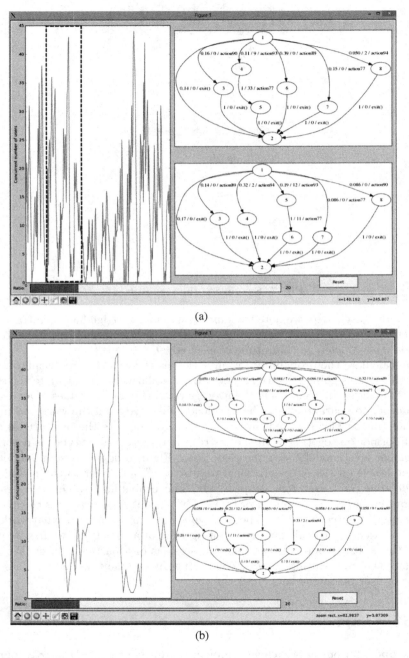

Fig. 8. Log2Model tool screenshots showing two workload models and the corresponding ramp (a) and refined workload models and the corresponding ramp based on the zoom box (b).

Our tool has a set of pre-defined patterns for common logging formats that are typically used in modern web servers (e.g., Apache and Microsoft Server). However, if the pattern of the log file is not automatically recognized (e.g., due to a custom logging format) the user can manually specify a logging pattern via a regular expression. Once the log is parsed, the data is stored into a database. This way we avoid having to re-parse large log files from one experiment to another.

Before parsing a log file, the tool prompts the user for a session time out value and the number of user clusters. This information, however, has to be provided a priori. Once the file has been parsed and the reduced request tree has been built, the user has a chance to manually inspect the tree. Requests can be grouped manually by dragging one node on top of the other. Figure 7 shows an example of such a request tree.

When the workload models have been built for each cluster they are presented to the user. Figure 8(a) shows an example where 2 clusters have been used. The left pane shows the number of concurrent users detected throughout the logging period. The slider bar at the bottom of the figure can be used to adjust the threshold value, which determines how many sessions to include in the model. A higher threshold value usually means more sessions are included in the model, leading to a more complex model. By zooming in on specific regions of interest in the left pane, new models that correspond to the selected region are automatically generated and updated in the GUI. Figure 8(b) shows two new clusters and a new ramp function that corresponds to the data in the selected region in Fig. 8(a).

When saving the model, the tool will create two additional artefacts: a ramp function and the test adapter code. The ramp is exported as a data set of (time, numeber_of_users) pairs, which can be either directly used by the MBPeT tool or can be used for further analysis and processing, for instance selecting only a part of it, or applying different smoothing spline regressions depending on the needs of the tester.

The test adapter will contain a code skeleton implementing, in a parametrized form, mappings of the actions in the workload models to HTTP requests. For compatibility with the MBPeT tool, the adapter code is currently exported to Python code using the standard Python libraries for HTTP communication, but it can be easily customized for other programming languages or libraries.

6   Example

In this section, we apply our approach to a web log file containing real-users data. The web site[2] used in this example maintains scores of football games played in the football league called *pubiliiga*. It also stores information about where and when the games are played, rules, teams, etc. The web site has been created using the Django framework [19] and runs on top of an Apache web server.

---

[2] www.pubiliiga.fi.

6.1   Parsing and Filtering

The log that we used was 323 MB in size and contained roughly 1.3 million lines of log data. The web site was visited by 20,000 unique users that resulted in 365,000 page views between April 25th of 2009 and August 23rd of 2013. However, most of the users only visited the web site once or twice and there were only about 2,000 frequent users that regularly visited the web site. Also, since the web site is updated frequently on the same platform on which it is running, the log contained a significant amount of data from erroneous requests made by the simple method of trail and error during development. All erroneous requests and requests made from known robots were filtered out. The results that we are going to show in this section are generated from a selected section of the log data containing a mere 30,000 lines of log data, generated by 1092 unique users.

6.2   Processing the Data

We used a session timeout value of 60 min to determine where to split the list of requests into sessions. In this experiment, we clustered users into two different groups. The total time to process the data was around 10 seconds. The computer was equipped with a 8 core Intel i7 2.93 GHz processor and had 16 GB of memory.

Table 4 shows a summary of the execution time for different steps of the algorithm for different log sizes. The final step, building the workload model, was purposely left out since it varies considerably depending on the chosen number of clusters and threshold value.

6.3   Building the Workload Models

Figures 9 and 10 shows the constructed workload models for one of the clusters. A total of 985 virtual users were grouped into this cluster. Figure 9 shows the workload model when using a threshold value of 0.5, which means that 50 percent of the traces are included in the model, starting from the highest frequency ones. However, the model is too complicated to be used for analysis or load generation, and some of the sessions are rarely executed due to a very low probability.

Table 4. Table showing execution times for different log sizes in terms of lines of log entries.

Phase	30.000	50.000	100.000	200.000	400.000
Parsing	6 s	10 s	22 s	50 s	2 min
Pre-processing	4 s	9 s	10 s	21 s	31 s
Request tree reduction	0.3 s	0.3 s	0.8 s	2 s	5 s
Clustering	0.08 s	0.08 s	0.4 s	5 s	60 s
Total	10.38 s	19.38 s	33.2 s	1 min 18 s	3 min 36 s

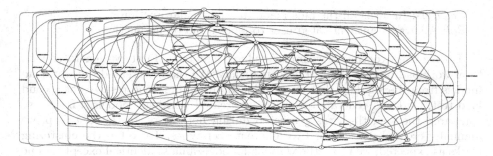

Fig. 9. Workload model for cluster 1, (threshold = 50 %).

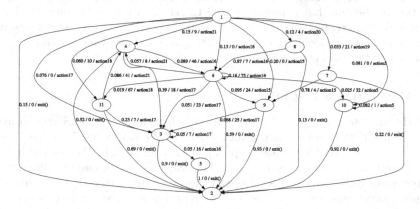

Fig. 10. Workload model for cluster 1, (threshold = 30 %).

Figure 10 shows the workload model with a threshold value of 0.3. Here we can see that the model is much more readable and we can actually start to make sense of the navigational patterns in the workload model. For confidentiality reasons the actual request types have been left of and replaced by abstract types. The workload models created for the second cluster looked almost the same. Creating the models took approximately 2 s. However, the execution times may hugely vary depending on the selected threshold value.

7   Validation

In this section, we demonstrate the validity of our approach on an auctioning web service, generically called YAAS (Yet Another Auction Site). The YAAS web service was developed as a university stand-alone project. The web service has a *RESTful* interface and has 5 simple actions:

- *Browse*: Returns all active auctions.
- *Search*: Returns auctions that matches the search query.
- *Get_Auction*: Returns information about a particular auction.

- *Get_Bids*: Returns all the bids made to a particular auction.
- *Bid*: Allows an authenticated user to place a bid on an auction.

During this experiment we preformed two load tests. First, we generated load from workload models that we built manually. We then re-created the workload models from the log data that was produced during first load test. In the second load test, load was generated from the re-created workload models. Finally, we compared the load that was generated during both tests. In the first step, we manually created models for two different user types. To test if the clustering works as expected, we made the workload models almost identical except for one request. One user type is doing distinctively a browse request while the other user type is always doing a search request. Figure 12(a) depicts the model for *user type 1*, the one that is performing distinctively a browse request. A similar model was also created for *user type 2*. If the algorithm can cluster users into different groups when only one action distinguishes them, then we consider the clustering to be good enough.

7.1   Generating a Log File

Once the models were built, they were used to load test the YAAS system using our in-house performance testing tool *MBPeT*. We simulated 10 virtual users (60 % user type 1 and 40 % user type 2) in parallel for 2 h. We set the virtual users to wait 20 s between each session. This value is later going to influence the timeout value during pre-processing phase. From the produced log file, containing roughly 10,000 lines, we re-created the original models as accurately as possible. We point out that the original model is of a probabilistic nature, which means that distinctly different traces with different lengths can be generated from a fairly simple model. For example, the shortest session had only 1 action, while the longest session had 22 actions. Also, we do not have exact control over how many times each trace is executed by a user.

7.2   Recreating the Models

To make sure that we split the sessions in a similar way we used a timeout value of 20 s. No other delay between the requests was that large. We also clustered

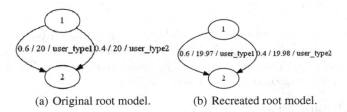

(a) Original root model.   (b) Recreated root model.

Fig. 11. Root models.

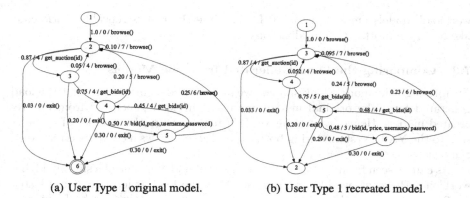

(a) User Type 1 original model.   (b) User Type 1 recreated model.

Fig. 12. Original vs. Recreated user profiles.

Table 5. Comparison between the two test runs.

Request	Load Test 1	Load Test 2
Search(string)	1263	1294
Browse()	1895	1942
Get_Auction(id)	2762	2821
Get_bids(id)	2697	2625
Bid(id, price, username, password)	1288	1265
Total	9903	9947
Request Rate	1.37 req/sec	1.38 req/sec

the data into 2 user types. Each user type is later going to be represented with a separate workload model. In this experiment we did not filter out any user sessions, hence we used a threshold value of 1.0, meaning all traces found in the log were used to recreate the models. Figure 12(a) shows the original workload model while Fig. 12(b) shows the re-constructed workload model for *User Type 1*. A similar model was also created for *User Type 2*. As one can see, the only difference from the original model is the probability values on the edges. However close, the probability values in the original models do not match exactly those in the generated workload models. This is due to the fact that we use a stochastic model for generating the load and we do not have an exact control of what traces are generated. Figure 11(a) shows original root model while Fig. 11(a) shows the re-created root model. From the figures we can see that the probability values of the re-created root model match that of the original root model (60 % and 40 %) and that the waiting time is close to 20 s (19.97 and 19.98).

Due to space limitation we only show a comparison of the original versus recreated user profiles for one of the two user types. A similar result was obtained for the second type as well.

The test adapter generated to support the above workload models was around 250 LOC. The actual number of LOC used to implement the 5 actions in the workload models amounted to 130 LOC, while the rest is reusable static code like library imports and initializations.

7.3   Comparing the Load Generated from the Models

Even though the models look similar, we also wanted to make sure that the load generated from the original models matched the load generated from our re-created models. Hence, we let the MBPeT tool measure the number of requests sent to the YAAS system during both steps. Table 5 shows a comparison between the test runs.

As can be seen from the table, the re-created model produced a slightly higher workload. However, we like to point out that the load generation phase lasted for 2 h and we see a difference of 44 requests. This is backed up by looking at the measured request rate. Load test 1 generated 1.37 req/sec, while load test 2 is virtually identical with 1.38 req/sec.

8   Conclusions

In this paper, we have presented a tool-supported approach for creating performance models from historical log data. The models are of a stochastic nature and specify the probabilistic distribution of actions that are executed against the system.

The approach is automated, hence reducing the effort necessary to create workload models for performance testing. In contrast, Cai et al. [20] report that they spent around 18 h to manually create a test plan and the JMeter scripts for the reference Java PetStore application [21].

The experiments presented in this paper have shown that the approach can adequately create workload models from log files and that they mimic the real user behavior when used for load testing. Further, the models themselves give insight in how users behave. This information can be valuable for optimizing functions in the system and enforcing certain navigational patterns on the web site.

Future work will targeted towards handling larger amount of log data. Currently the tool is not optimized enough to operate efficiently on large data amounts. Another improvement is automatic session detection. Currently the tool follows a pre-defined timeout value for detecting sessions. Automatic session detection could suggest different timeout values for different users, hence, improving on the overall quality of the recreated model. Currently, we are only clustering users according to accessed resources. In the future, we would like to extend the K-means clustering algorithm to cluster based on other relevant factors like: request method, size of resource, user request rate, etc. This clustering method could suggest models that, when executed, exercise the workload patterns on the system, thus, potentially finding "hidden" bottlenecks. Further, an interesting experiment would be to analyze only failed or dropped requests. This way one could for instance study the details of how a DoS-attack was carried out and what pages were hit during the attack.

Acknowledgements. Our sincerest gratitude go to the owners of www.pubilliiga.fi for letting us use their data in our experiments.

References

1. Ferrari, D.: On the foundations of artificial workload design. In: Proceedings of the 1984 ACM SIGMETRICS Conference on Measurement and Modeling of Computer Systems, SIGMETRICS 1984, pp. 8–14. ACM, New York (1984)
2. Al-Jaar, R.: Book review: The art of computer systems performance analysis: Techniques for experimental design, measurement, simulation, and modeling by raj jain (John Wiley & Sons). SIGMETRICS Perform. Eval. Rev. **19**, 5–11 (1991)
3. Richardson, L., Ruby, S.: Restful web services, 1st edn. O'Reilly, Sebastopol (2007)
4. Abbors, F., Ahmad, T., Truscan, D., Porres, I.: MBPeT: a model-based performance testing tool. In: 2012 Fourth International Conference on Advances in System Testing and Validation Lifecycle (2012)
5. Rudolf, A., Pirker, R.: E-business testing: user perceptions and performance issues. In: Proceedings of the First Asia-Pacific Conference on Quality Software (APAQS 2000), pp. 315–323. IEEE Computer Society, Washington, DC (2000)
6. Subraya, B.M., Subrahmanya, S.V.: Object driven performance testing in web applications. In: Proceedings of the First Asia-Pacific Conference on Quality Software (APAQS 2000), pp. 17–26. IEEE Computer Society (2000)
7. Kathuria, A., Jansen, B.J., Hafernik, C.T., Spink, A.: Classifying the user intent of web queries using k-means clustering. In: Internet Research. Number 5, pp. 563–581. Emerald Group Publishing (2010)
8. Vaarandi, R.: A data clustering algorithm for mining patterns from event logs. In: Proceedings of the 3rd IEEE Workshop on IP Operations and Management (IPOM 2003), pp. 119–126. IEEE (2003)
9. Shi, P.: An efficient approach for clustering web access patterns from web logs. International Journal of Advanced Science and Technology 5, 1–14 (2009). SERSC
10. Mannila, H., Toivonen, H., Inkeri Verkamo, A.: Discovery of frequent episodes in event sequences. Data Min. Knowl. Discov. **1**, 259–289 (1997)
11. Ma, S., Hellerstein, J.L.: Mining partially periodic event patterns with unknown periods. In: Proceedings of the 17th International Conference on Data Engineering, pp. 205–214. IEEE Computer Society, Washington, DC (2001)
12. Anastasiou, N., Knottenbelt, W.: PEPERCORN: inferring performance models from location tracking data. In: Joshi, K., Siegle, M., Stoelinga, M., D'Argenio, P.R. (eds.) QEST 2013. LNCS, vol. 8054, pp. 169–172. Springer, Heidelberg (2013)
13. Lutteroth, C., Weber, G.: Modeling a realistic workload for performance testing. In: 12th International Conference on Enterprise Distributed Object Computing, pp. 149–158. IEEE Computer Society (2008)
14. Petriu, D.C., Shen, H.: Applying the UML Performance Profile: Graph Grammar-based Derivation of LQN Models from UML Specifications, pp. 159–177. Springer-Verlag (2002)
15. Jurdziński, M., Kwiatkowska, M., Norman, G., Trivedi, A.: Concavely-priced probabilistic timed automata. In: Bravetti, M., Zavattaro, G. (eds.) CONCUR 2009. LNCS, vol. 5710, pp. 415–430. Springer, Heidelberg (2009)
16. MacQueen, J.B.: Some methods for classification and analysis of multivariate observations. In: Proceedings of 5-th Berkeley Symposium on Mathematical Statistics and Probability. Number 1, pp. 281–297. University of California Press, Berkeley (1967)

17. Arnold, B.: Pareto and generalized pareto distributions. In: Chotikapanich, D. (ed.) Modeling Income Distributions and Lorenz Curves. vol. 5, Economic Studies in Equality, Social Exclusion and Well-Being, pp. 119–145. Springer, New York (2008)
18. Python: Python programming language. http://www.python.org/. Accessed 30 December 2014
19. Python: Django Framework. https://www.djangoproject.com/. Accessed 30 December 2014
20. Cai, Y., Grundy, J., Hosking, J.: Synthesizing client load models for performance engineering via web crawling. In: Proceedings of the Twenty-Second IEEE/ACM International Conference on Automated Software Engineering, ASE 2007, pp. 353–362. ACM (2007)
21. Oracle: Java Pet Store 2.0 reference application (2014). http://www.oracle.com/technetwork/java/index-136650.html. Accessed 30 December 2014

New Flexible Architectures for Reconfigurable Wireless Sensor Networks

Hanen Grichi[✉], Olfa Mosbahi, and Mohamed Khalgui

National Institute of Applied Science and Technology,
University of Carthage, Tunis, Tunisia
hanen.grichi@gmail.com
http://www.insat.rnu.tn

Abstract. This chapter deals with reconfigurable wireless sensor networks (to be named by *RWSN*). A *RWSN* is composed of distributed autonomous nodes that execute programs (reconfigurable software tasks) and control local sensors to monitor physical or environmental conditions. We propose three reconfiguration forms to be executed in our *RWSN*: (i) hardware reconfiguration allowing the activation/deactivation of nodes, (ii) software reconfiguration allowing the addition/ removal/ update of tasks and (iii) protocol reconfiguration allowing the modification of routing protocols between nodes. We propose, in this chapter, a zone-based multi-agent architecture for *RWSN* to optimize the distributed reconfigurations. Each agent of this architecture is modeled by nested state machines in order to control the problem complexity. The chapter's contribution is applied to a case study that we simulate with WSNet (Wireless Sensor Network simulator) [5] to show the originality of this new architecture.

Keywords: Wireless sensor network · Reconguration · Multi-agent architecture · Nested state machine · Simulation

1 Introduction

Wireless Sensor Networks (to be named *WSN*) become today an important established technology for a large number of applications (pollution prevention [1], agriculture [4], military, structures and buildings health, etc.). *WSNs* usually consist of many small devices called sensor nodes. Each node is able to allow local control processing and communications with remote nodes under real-time and energy constraints. Wireless Sensor Networks can be homogeneous (sensor nodes are of the same nature) or heterogeneous (with different types of nodes) [12]. We are interested in this chapter in homogeneous *WSN*. Several related works [6] describe the wireless sensor network (*WSN*) as a system of spatially distributed sensor nodes that collect important information in the target environment. Each sensor node has limited computation capacity, local memory, power supply [15] and communication link. Each directed link connects two neighboring nodes

© Springer International Publishing Switzerland 2015
A. Holzinger et al. (Eds.): ICSOFT 2014, CCIS 555, pp. 151–169, 2015.
DOI: 10.1007/978-3-319-25579-8_9

through a network [7]. The most generic model for a *WSN* is based on the data gathering [11] and communication capabilities of sensors.

Nowadays, *WSN* migrate to an auto-programming technology which is based on intelligent sensor networking infrastructures [1]. The system can change its behavior at run-time, it is what we call a reconfigurable system. Two reconfiguration policies could be identified: static (offline: by stopping the *WSN* to make required modifications and restart it) or dynamic (online: by changing the network structures during its execution) [12]. In the second case, we have also two kinds of reconfiguration: manual (executed by users) and automatic (executed by agents). The researchers define the *RWSN* (Reconfigurable *WSN*) as an adaptive *WSN*. The reconfiguration can also add/remove one/more physical elements of the network by activating/deactivating them. The reconfiguration touches first the material (allowing the activation/deactivation of nodes), second the software (allowing the reconfiguration of tasks) and third the communication protocols (allowing the adaptation of routing protocols between nodes). Many projects deal with *RWSN* such as *WASAN* [9], *ReWINS* [8], *TWIST* project [3], but they cover one or two reconfiguration types (hardware, software or protocol) and not mix all of them.

Our problem consists in the application of these three reconfiguration types: what is the gain that we can get by using any hardware reconfiguration, or software reconfiguration or also the protocol reconfiguration? If we reduce the communication by applying reconfiguration scenarios, can we win in terms of energy? We try in this chapter to answer these questions by defining three forms of reconfiguration for low power *RWSNs*. We define a new zone-based multi-agent architecture for *RWSN* where a communication protocol is well-defined for useful distributed reconfigurations. We decompose the *RWSN* to a set of zones where each one gathers a number of nodes. The radius of each zone is a parameter to be defined by users according to several characteristics of the followed technology. We define a Controller Agent (*CrA*) that handles the reconfiguration strategies of the whole network, and assign a Zone Agent for each zone (*ZA*) to control the local reconfiguration scenarios. Each node of a particular zone is controlled by a Slave Agent (*SA*) that monitors the local reconfiguration scenarios inside the node. This original multi-agent architecture combines all possible reconfiguration forms to be adapted for the environment where we minimize the energy consumption. This adaptive architecture is modeled by nested state machines in order to control the specification complexity. With our solution, we gain in terms of energy to be consumed by each node and the number of exchanged messages between nodes in the network. This architecture supports the delegation between agents and controls the complexity by providing hierarchical structure of *RWSN*. We apply and simulate the chapter's contribution to a case study to be assumed as a running example, and compare our results to some related works in order to show the originality of this architecture.

The chapter is organized as follows: after introduction and background, Sect. 3 presents our position between related works. Section 4 proposes a new definition of *RWSN* to be explained on a case study. The multi-agent architecture of the *RWSN* is proposed in Sect. 5. Section 6 presents the coordination protocol between different agents. The simulation and evaluation of our contribution is provided in Sect. 7 before concluding the chapter in Sect. 8.

2   Background

We briefly present the formalism of finite state machines to be used in the following for the modelling of *RWSN*. Finite State Machine (*FSM*) is an abstract machine that can be in one of finite number of states. It changes the behavior from a state to another by firing a transition in response to a particular event. A *FSM* is an efficient way to specify constraints of the overall behavior of a system [14]. A classic form of a *FSM* is a direct graph with the following elements: $G=(Q, \Sigma, Z, \delta, q_0, F)$ where: (a) **Vertices Q** is a finite set of states $(Q_1, Q_2, ..., Q_i)$ such that each state (Q_i) models a system's behavior at an instant t, (b) **Input symbols** Σ is a finite collection of input symbols or designators. This part of graph represents the finite set of initial states, (c) **Output symbols Z** is a finite collection of output symbols or designators. This part of graph represents the final state of the system, (d) **Edges** δ represents transitions from one state to another as caused by input symbols, (e) **S**tart state q_0 is the start state $q_0 \in Q$, (f) **Accepting state(s) F**: $F \in Q$ is the set of accepting states. We define Nested State Machines as a set of *FSM* such that a state of one corresponds to another machine. This solution is useful for the modeling of a complex system where the information should be modeled on different hierarchical levels in order to control the complexity.

3   State of the Art

In the present day, several researches deal with *RWSN* where a reconfiguration can be applied in three levels: hardware, software and data routing. **Hardware reconfigurations** are defined in [2] by adding *FPGA*-based intelligent modules to nodes. In [9], the wireless autonomous sensor and networks of actors (*WASAN*) define **hardware reconfigurations** as dynamic operations that model platforms of evaluation and assistance. To model well the **protocol reconfiguration**, the existence of reconfigurable interfaces is essential; Harish Ramamurthy in [8] presents the *ReWINS* project (Reconfigurable Wireless Interface for Networking), to manage the reconfigurability thanks to a 'Central Control Unit'. The Reconfigurable Wireless Sensor Network for Structural Health Monitoring [13], is also another project of *RWSN*. This proposition has the possibility to reconfigure the parameters of the monitoring application (**software reconfiguration**), depending on the needs of the end-user operating at the sink node. To optimize the radio transmission of data and avoid interferences (**protocol reconfiguration**), each sink node establishes a reserved communication link with each of the sensor nodes. In [3], the *TWIST* project (a scalable and flexible tested architecture for indoor deployment of wireless sensor networks) defines two reconfiguration forms: **software/ hardware**. This project uses the

USB infrastructure for the **hardware reconfiguration** and the software one is controlled by a set of interfaces to be implemented on a station.

We note that all related works do not address all possible reconfiguration forms together that the current chapter deals with. We propose a new zone-based multi-agent architecture for *RWSN*. Our proposition is original and different from all others since we treat all reconfiguration forms, control the complexity of modeling by using nested state machines and optimize the energy consumption as well as the exchanged messages between nodes thanks to the zone-based solution.

4   Contribution: New Solutions for *RWSN*

We present in this section, our new solutions for *RWSN*. We present our new definition of the reconfigurable wireless sensor network.

4.1   *RWSN*: Definition

We define a reconfiguration scenario as any response to a request in order to adapt the system to its environment and to improve also its performance. We consider three kinds of reconfigurations: (i) software reconfiguration allowing the addition/removal and update of Os-tasks or data, (ii) hardware reconfiguration allowing the activation/deactivation of sensor nodes, (iii) protocol reconfiguration allowing the optimization/degradation of the protocol (e.g. addition/removal/update of messages to be exchanged between nodes as well as their routing paths). We denote in the following by a *RWSN*, a reconfigurable *WSN* that automatically modifies its software and/or hardware architecture and/or inter-nodes communication protocol. Contrary to all related works, a *RWSN* is defined as a dynamic reconfigurable *WSN*, that automatically modifies at run time the architecture as well as structure of the network. This modification can touch the material (e.g. sensors), the software (e.g. OS tasks) and the data routing. Note that the *TWIST* project [3] does not address the protocol reconfiguration. The *ReWINS* project [8] does not suppose the reconfiguration of WSN as a dynamic and automatic reconfiguration. In the current chapter, we extend all related works and address all possible reconfiguration forms that can be applied at run time on *RWSN*.

4.2   *RWSN*: New Architecture

We give in the following some definitions that will be used in the following.

- *RWSN*: a set of Nbz zones and S stations. A station controls the whole network, whereas each zone is composed of n nodes such that each node gathers m hardware detectors to be controlled by software tasks. Note that a communication protocol is applied between nodes of a same or of different zones. We define Nbz = number of the zones in *WSN* and Zi as the zone number i of the network.

– *RWSN* zone: a geographical space to be defined by all the points included in the area of this zone. This zone is fixed by a radius to be defined by the *RWSN* designer.
– *RWSN* station: a supervisor in a *RWSN* to be characterized by: (i) A memory, that should be bigger than a node memory, (ii) A bandwidth, that represents the velocity of data transmission with nodes.
– Reconfigurable node: a device to be composed with others. It runs under energy, real-time and functional constraints. A node is characterized by: (i) An identifier *(ID)* which is unique in the zone, (ii) a set of m detectors DTi $(i = 1,2,...,m)$ where each sensor is modeled by two variables: the state $(Sd$: active or not), and the value to be detected (Vd), (iii) a power unit represented by two batteries (we denote by $PwBi(t)$ the current value of battery's charge and $PwBiMax$ the maximum load), (iv) the router (R) that supports the communications with other nodes.
– Reconfigurable sensor: a detector that consumes energy to provide required services for the node. We suppose that it is controlled by a unique OS-Task.
– Reconfigurable protocol: a protocol that supports the communication between nodes. We assume it as reconfigurable since we suppose that messages can be added or removed at run-time. Table 1 describes the parameters of a routing table in each node in order to characterize each communication between them.

Table 1. Node routing table parameters.

ID	Node Identifier
ID_{Zone}	Zone Identifier
ID_{Dest}	Final Destination Node Identifier
ID_{Next}	Next Node Identifier in communication path (neighbor)
Time	Execution time for communication by a node

4.3   Reconfiguration Forms

We have three forms of reconfigurations:

– **Software Reconfiguration.** Modifies the behaviors of nodes at run time. The modification is made on the software architecture by: (i) adding (or removing) OS-tasks to be executed in nodes, (ii) modifying their scheduling, (iii) modifying the used data by tasks.
– **Hardware Reconfiguration.** This kind of reconfiguration consists of: (i) activation/deactivation of detectors, (ii) activation/deactivation of nodes. The deactivation of all detectors in a node implies its deactivation. In fact, activating only one detector in a node results in its activation.
– **Protocol Reconfiguration.** Consists in modifying the data routing when software and hardware reconfigurations are applied at run-time.

4.4   Case Study

We propose as a running example, a *RWSN* to be denoted by *Sys*. It is composed of 3 zones *(Z1, Z2, Z3)* where each one Z_i is composed of three nodes. These three zones are supervised by a station *(S)*. Each node $Nz_j, (j=1..9)$ is characterized by two detectors, two batteries and a router *(R_j)*. Each detector DT_m, *(m =1 or 2)* can detect the temperature (to be denoted by DT_1) and the humidity of the environment (to be denoted by DT_2). It is characterized by a state *(Sd*: {activate= 1, deactivate= 0}), and the detected value *(Vd)*. The two batteries are denoted by B_k (k = 1 or 2). Each battery B_k is characterized by a current value of load *(PwB_{k,j})* and a value of maximum load *(PwBMax_{k,j})*. We suppose initially, that Nz_5 executes only DT_1.

Software Reconfiguration. We define the following three tasks $\{T1, T2, T3\}$: (i) *T1*: controls the temperature and detects signal when it is higher than 45°. (ii) *T2*: reduces the threshold from 45° to 30°. This task can be used for any detection of fire. (iii) *T3*: controls the humidity of the environment. We define 3 software reconfigurations: $\{SR1, SR2, SR3\}$. (a) *SR1*: a reconfiguration that allows the addition of *(T1)* to each node in a summer day; (b) *SR2*: is applied to each summer night to remove the task *(T1)* and to add *(T2)*. (c) *SR3*: updates the threshold to be taken by *(T3)*.

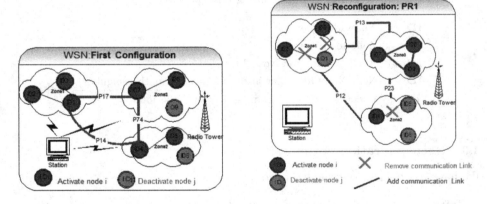

Fig. 1. First and second reconfiguration of WSN.

Hardware Reconfiguration. In order to minimize the dissipated energy, we apply hardware reconfigurations $\{HR1, HR2, HR3\}$ on 3 sensor nodes *(Nz1* from *Z1*, *Nz5* from *Z2*, *Nz9* from *Z3)* (i) *HR1*: deactivates *Nz1* from *Z1* by deactivating $(DT_1(1)$ of *Nz1* and $DT_2(1)$ of *Nz1)*, (ii) *HR2*: deactivates $DT_1(5)$ for the node *Nz5*, (iii) *HR3*: activates *Nz9* from *Z3* by activating $DT_2(9)$ of *Nz9*. The hardware reconfiguration, in this case, can change the routing information between nodes. The link of communication between *Nz1* and its neighbors is cut (the same case as *Nz5*). By using *HR3*, *(Nz9)* can be connected to its neighbors (see the modification in Fig. 1).

Protocol Reconfiguration. If we apply *HR1, HR2* and *HR3* (deactivation of *Nz1, Nz5* and activation of *Nz9*), the routing tables of *(Nz1, Nz5, Nz9)* will be changed from first routing table parameters to the second one. In this case the protocol reconfiguration eliminates 3 communication links between nodes (*Nz1, Nz5*), and adds 2 other links to (*Nz9*).

	Nz1	Nz5	Nz9
State	Activate	Activate	Deactivate
ID	ID1	ID5	ID9
ID$_{Zone}$	Z1	Z2	Z3
ID$_{Dest}$	ID7	ID1	
ID$_{Next}$	ID2, ID3	ID4	
Time	0.02s	0.01s	

First routing table parameters

	Nz1	Nz5	Nz9
State	Deactivate	Deactivate	Activate
ID	ID1	ID5	ID9
ID$_{Zone}$	Z1	Z2	Z3
ID$_{Dest}$	ID7	ID9	ID2
ID$_{Next}$	ID2 Or ID3	ID4	ID7 Or ID8
Time			0.02s

Second routing table parameters

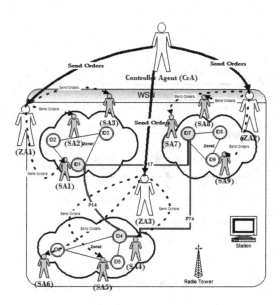

Fig. 2. Multi-Agent architecture for RWSN.

5 New Multi-agent Architecture for (*RWSN*)

We present in this section, our new multi-agent architecture for *RWSN*. We present the formalization and the modeling of our multi agent architecture.

5.1 Motivation

To handle all cited forms, we propose a multi-agent architecture for RWSN. This architecture is composed of a Controller Agent (*CrA*) that controls the whole architecture, a Zone Agent (ZA) to be affected to each zone in order to control its nodes, and a Slave Agent (SA) that controls each node of any zone. All these agents handle the different reconfiguration forms that we described above. In order to control the complexity, each agent has a hierarchical architecture to be modeled by Nested State Machines. We show in Fig. 2 this new multi-agent architecture of $RWSN$. We model the multi-agent architecture for RWSN as a system to be composed by one CrA, a set of (ZA) and a set of (SA): Sys={CrA, φZA, φSA}; φZA= set of all Zone Agents; φSA = set of all Slave Agents; In one Zone = {ZA, φSA}.

5.2   Formalization of *RWSN*

In this section, we present the formalization of the proposed RWSN. We start with the controller Agent logic.

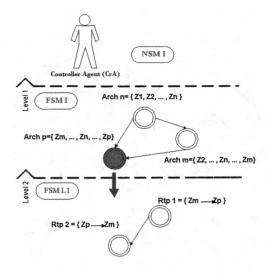

Fig. 3. Controller agent architecture (Color figure online).

Controller Agent (CrA) Logic. For the modeling of this agent, we propose two levels: (i) **First Reconfiguration Level: CrA Architecture:** The (CrA) defines in this level the set of active and deactive zones under well-defined conditions at a particular time. This level will be modeled latter with the State Machine ($FSM\ I$). (ii) **Second Reconfiguration Level: CrA Data Flows:** This level describes the different flows of data to be exchanged between the active zones that we define in level 1. For each state of ($FSM\ I$) that models level 1, we define in the current second level a particular state machine that defines all the possible data flows. A state of this State Machine defines a particular reconfiguration scenario that changes the routing policy software between zones. In Fig. 3, the red state of ($FSM\ I$) defines a subset of active zones and corresponds to the state machine (*FSM I.1*) in level 2. The state *Rtp 1* represents a first routing solution between these zones and *Rtp 2* represents another routing solution.

Zone Agent (*ZA*) Logic. We propose four levels for this agent: (i) **first reconfiguration level: *ZA* Architecture:** we describe in this level the different active and deactive nodes under well-defined conditions at a particular time. This level is characterized by a superset of nodes such that any reconfiguration scenario corresponds to the activation of a subset, (ii) **second reconfiguration level: *ZA*Data Flows/ Detectors:** the second level of the Zone Agent (*ZA*) defines the set of detectors that should be active in each node under well-defined conditions at a particular time. This second level defines also the different data flows that can be followed to exchange data between the active nodes of the zone. The activation of detectors as well as the definition of reconfiguration data flows belong to the same level since they are depending in logic, (iii) **third reconfiguration level: *ZA* Scheduling:** this level defines the different reconfigurable scheduling of OS-tasks that control active detectors in active nodes under well-defined condition at a particular time, (iv) **fourth reconfiguration level: *ZA* Data value:** This level defines the different values and structure of data to be used by the OS-tasks of active nodes under well-defined conditions at a particular time.

To handle the complexity of the problem, we use nested state machines to model the Zone Agent.

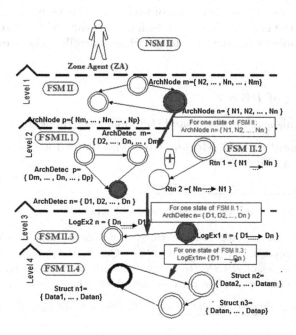

Fig. 4. Zone agent architecture.

In Fig. 4, the red state *ArchNode* n defines the different active nodes of a zone at a particular time t under well-defined conditions, this state corresponds to two state machines *FSM II.1* and *FSM II.2* in level 2. *FSM II.1* defines in this zone all possible activations of detectors. *FSM II.2* represents the different routing solutions between active nodes in this zone. The red state *ArchDetect* n defines under well-defined conditions the different detectors which should be active in active nodes of the zone. *Rtn 1* defines a particular solution to exchange data between active nodes in a zone. Two states of these state machines of level 2 define a particular state machine in level 3 where a state defines a particular scheduling of active tasks. The red state *LogEx1* n defines the execution logic of tasks and defines a new state machine *FSM II.4* in level 4. Each state in *FSM II.4* defines particular values and structures of data to be used by actives tasks. Thanks to this solution we can cover all possible reconfiguration forms while controlling the complexity of the problem.

Slave Agent (SA) Logic. This agent executes the reconfiguration strategies to be defined by CrA and ZA.

Note Finally that to gain in terms of energy for example, each Zone Agent (ZA) controls at run-time the load in the batteries of each slave before applying required reconfiguration scenarios that can possibly remove tasks or also deactivate nodes in order to preserve power as much as possible. We note also that we are interested in the architecture of $RWSN$ without detailing the technical solutions to add/remove tasks or activate/deactivate nodes. We are not interested also in the real-time scheduling of tasks that will be in another work. The contribution of the current chapter is dealing with the architecture of $RWSN$ to address all possible reconfiguration forms while controlling the complexity of the problem.

5.3   Modeling of $RWSN$

We present in this section, the nested state machines modeling the agents.

Controller Agent (CrA) Model. We model the two levels of (CrA) by the following state machines.

-First modeling level: CrA Architecture:

$$GC_1 = (Qc, \delta c, qc_0) \text{ where:}$$

(a) **Vertices Qc**: set of states such that each state corresponds to active zones at a particular time $(Qc_1, Qc_2, ..., Qc_i)$. We denote by $Qc_i = (MN_1, MN_2, ..., MN_n)$ the set of active master nodes of $RWSN$, (b) **Edges** δc: activation or deactivation of master nodes, (c) **Start state** qc_0: a first architecture which defines the default active zones.

-Second modeling level: CrA Data flows: For each state $Qc_i \in Qc$ in GC1, we define:

$$GC_2 = (Qp, \delta p, qp_0) \text{ where:}$$

(a) **Vertices Qp**: set of states where each one represents a particular routing solution between active zones ($Qp_{i1}, Qp_{i2}, ..., Qp_{ij}$). (b) **Edges** δp: the modification of data flows between active zones. (c) **Start state qp$_0$**: the data flows between the default active zones.

Zone Agent (ZA) Model. We define in the following the nested state machines of each (ZA).

-First modeling level: ZA Architecture:

$$GD_1 = (Qd, \delta d, qd_0) \text{ where:}$$

(a)**Vertices Qd**: set of states such that each one represents a subset of active nodes in a zone, $Qd_i = (N_1, N_2, ..., N_i)$, (c)**Edges** δd: activation/deactivation of nodes in a zone, (d)**Start state** qd_0: default list of nodes in a zone.

-Second modeling level: ZA Data flows/detectors: For each state Qd_i of GD_1, we define two state machines GN_2 and GN'_2:

$$GN_2 = (Qn, \delta n, qn_0) \text{ where:}$$

(a)**Vertices Qn**: set of states where each one represents a particular routing solution between active nodes of a zone, (b)**Edges** δn: modification of data flows between active nodes, (c)**Start state qn$_0$**: data flows between default active nodes Qn_{i1}.

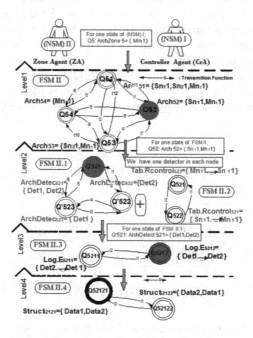

Fig. 5. Running example for ZA modeling.

$$GN'_2 = (Qn', \delta n', qn'_0,)\text{ where:}$$

(a)**Vertices Qn'**: set of states such that each one represents detectors to be active at a particular time, $(Qn'_{i1}, Qn'_{i2}, ..., Qn'_{ij})$. We can define $Qn'_{ij}=(Detc_1, Detc_2, ..., Detc_n)$ as a set of active detectors, (b)**Edges** $\delta n'$: activation/deactivation of detectors, (c)**Start state qn$_0$'**: the default list of detectors in a node: Qn'_{i1}.

-Third modeling level: *ZA* Scheduling: For each state Qn_{ij} in GN_2 and Qn'_{ij} in GN'_2, we define:

$$GE_3 = (Qe, \delta e, qe_0)\text{ where:}$$

(a)**Vertices Qe**: set of states such that each one represents the scheduling of OS-tasks implementing active nodes in a zone, $(Q_{ij1}, Q_{ij2}, ..., Q_{ijk})$, (b)**Edges** δe: modification of the execution sense of detectors by respecting the dependence of the latter, (c)**Start state qe$_0$**: the default scheduling of OS-tasks Qe_{ij1}

-Fourth modeling level: *ZA* Data value: For each state Qe_{ijk} in GE_3, we define:

$$GS_4 = (Qs, \delta s, qs_0)\text{ where:}$$

(a)**Vertices Qs**: set of states where each state represents data structures and values to be used by active tasks, $(Q_{ijk1}, Q_{ijk2}, ..., Q_{ijkl})$, (b)**Edges** δs: modification of data structure or values, (c)**Start state qs$_0$**: the default data structures Q_{ijk1}.

The Fig. 5 defines the nested state machines that model *ZA1* of *Z1*. *FSM II* is a state machine that defines all possible activations of nodes in the zone, the red state Q52 corresponds to two state machines *FSM II.1* and *FSM II.2* in level 2. Q_{521} represents a particular data flow between active nodes in a zone. Q_{521} is a set of active detectors in a node. Both of the two states correspond to a particular state machine in level 3. Q_{5212} represents a particular scheduling of OS-tasks that control active detectors in level 2. Q_{5212} corresponds to particular data structures *FSM II.4* in level 4, Q_{52121} corresponds to a particular data structures and values to be used by active nodes in this zone *Zone1*.

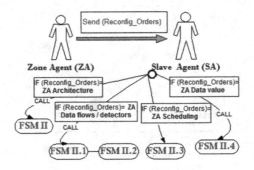

Fig. 6. Running example for SA modeling.

Slave Agent Modeling (*SA*). This agent executes directly the orders of the corresponding (*ZA*). Figure 6 shows the reaction of a slave agent in Zone1 when it receives an order from a corresponding Zone Agent.

6 Coordination Protocol Between Agents

We propose a communication protocol between the different agents (*CrA*, *ZA*, *SA*) of this architecture. It is based on the following operation: (i) *CrA Algorithm*: the operation that links *CrA* to any *ZA*. (ii) *ZA Algorithm*: the operation between any *ZA* and any corresponding *SA*. (iii) *Oper 1*: an operation allowing the activation/deactivation of nodes in a zone. (iv) *Oper2*: an operation allowing a modification of data flows in a zone (v) *Oper3*: an operation allowing the activation/deactivation of detectors in a node. (vi) *Oper4*: an operation allowing the modification of scheduling in a zone and (vii) *Oper5*: an operation allowing the modification of data structures or values in a zone.

CrA Algorithm: to apply a reconfiguration, *CrA* sends to any *ZA* an array containing the list of desired active zones with the new flow of data to be exchanged between them.

Algorithm 1. CrA Algorithm.

Z Zone; newArray(tabZoneActiv[nb]);   DS= Transm_Distance (threshold);
$D(CrA,j)= \alpha, j \neq CrA; (i,j)=\beta , j \neq i;$
REPEAT {*Send new vector(activ_zones) to neighbors zones:*
IF $D(CrA,j) \leq DS$; *Send (tabZoneActiv[nb], CrA, j);*
FOR EACH *dest j, find the next with dist_min to j;*
IF $D(i,j) \leq DS$; *Send(tabZoneActiv[nb], j, i); i+1; calculate(D(i,j));*}
UNTIL *D (i,j)= 0; source i = destination j;*
Send(ProtoCommunic (AC, ZoneDest1, ..., ZoneDestj));

ZA Algorithm: Step-By-Step: (ZA) sends to any (SA) a reconfiguration scenario.

Algorithm 2. ZA Algorithm.

We declare: VAR = orderReconfig(ZA, SA);
IF *(VAR =1) Send (ReconficArchitecNode(), ZA, SA);*
IF *(VAR =2) Send (ReconfProtoCommNod(), ZA, SA);*
IF *(VAR =3) Send (ReconfArchiDetectors(), ZA, SA);*
IF *(VAR =4) Send (ReconfLogicExecDetec(), ZA, SA);*
IF *(VAR =5) Send (ReconficStructData(), ZA, SA);*

IF *(VAR =1)* ⇒ *Execute Oper 1; We declare: Arch[] = new Array[nbNode]* ;
FOR EACH $Z_i \in setZone^i = \{Z_1, Z_2, ..., Z_i\}$;
FOR EACH $Nz_j(i)$ *Arch[] = ReconficArchitecNode()*
REPEAT IF *(PwB → 0) ; Sd(Nz$_j$(i))=0; Arch[IDj]=0;*
IF *Vd(Nzj(i))≥ threshold; Sd(Nzj(i))=1; Arch[IDj]=1; j=j+1;*
UNTIL *j= nbNode;* **RETURN** *Arch[]};*
IF *(VAR =2)* ⇒ *Execute Oper 2; ReconfProtoCommNodes(){*
IF *(N is an node address connected in zone) { Deliverdata (node, link); }*
ELSE IF *(The routing table contains a route for N) { Deliverdata (@nextnode, link); }*
ELSE IF *(There exists a default route) {(DefaultLink);}*
ELSE *{Send(error-message);} }*
IF *(VAR =3)* ⇒ *Execute Oper 3; ArchDetector[]= new Array[nbDetector]();*
FOR EACH $Nz_j(i)$ *ArchDetector[]= ReconfArchiDetectors();*
REPEAT IF *∀Sd(DT$_k$)=0; ArchDetector[ID$_k$]=0;*
IF *∃ Sd(DT$_k$)=0; ArchDetector[ID$_k$]=1;*
IF *Vd(DT$_k$) ≥ threshold;Sd(DT$_k$)=1 ; ArchDetector[ID$_k$]=1; k=k+1;j=j+1;* **UNTIL**
k= nbDetector; j= nbNode; **RETURN** *ArchDetector[];*
IF *(VAR =4)* ⇒ *Execute Oper 4; ActiDetec[]= new Array[nbActiDetec](); We declare:*
RandomStruct[] = new ActiDetec[](); RandomStruct[]= ReconfLogicExecDetec()
FOR *(k=0,k=j+1)* **REPEAT** *RandomStruct[k]= RANDOM (ActiDetec[i]);*
UNTIL *k= nbDetector;*
RETURN *RandomStruct[];*
IF *(VAR =5)* ⇒ *Execute Oper 5; We declare: DataStructure[]= new Array[nbData]();*
We declare: RandomStructure[] = new DataStructure[](); RandomStructure[]= Reconfic-
StructData()
FOR *(l=0,l=l+1)* **REPEAT** *RandomStructure[l]= RANDOM (DataStructure[l]);*
UNTIL *l= nbData;*
RETURN *RandomStructure[];*

7   Simulation and Evaluation

In order to show the benefits of our contribution, we apply a simulation of *RWSN*.
We start with a theoretical simulation before presenting a practical one (Fig. 7).

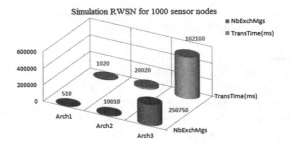

Fig. 7. Comparison between 3 architecture types: Arch 1, Arch 2, Arch 3.

7.1   Theoretical Simulation

We propose a system *(Sys 2)* to be composed of 10 zones *(Z1...Z10)*, each one is composed of 100 nodes: one master node *(Mni)* and 99 slaves *(Snj)*, and a station *(S)* to control the whole *RWSN*. Each node $Nz(j)$ in the same zone Zi is characterized by two sensors or detectors : DTn_j (n =1 or 2) to detect the temperature and the humidity of the environment. Each sensor node is equipped with a battery, thus the available energy is limited. Our system *(Sys)* is characterized as follows: (i) an omnidirectional antenna is installed in each sensor node and the transmission range is defined in 15m *(DS)*, (ii) the data are transmitted without any delay, (iii) the exchanged messages are with a constant size. To Apply the three forms of reconfiguration, we execute the following scenarios: (i) *(CrA)* sends the first reconfiguration to be applied: activation of all nodes (**Hardware reconfiguration**) and modification of temperature to be (45°) (**Software reconfiguration**), (ii) *(ZA)* of each zone receives this order and broadcasts it to each corresponding slave which applies this order, (iii) *(SA)* verifies the new routing table according to the recommendation of *ZA* (**Protocol reconfiguration**), (iv) All *(SA)* send the collected information in step by step to *(CrA)*. This scenario is described as follows:

Theoretical Simulation

10 zones; CrA; DS=15m;tabZoneActiv[10]=

Z1	Z2	Z3	Z4	Z5
Z6	Z7	Z8	Z9	Z10

tabDist[10]=

D1=D(CrA,Z1)=14m	D2=D(CrA,Z2)=13m
D3=D(CrA,Z3)=10m	D4=D(CrA,Z4)=14m
D5=D(CrA,Z5)=21m	D6=D(CrA,Z6)=26m
D7=D(CrA,Z7)=31m	D8=D(CrA,Z8)=34m
D9=D(CrA,Z9)=40m	D10=D(CrA,Z10)=42m

SEND STEP IF $Di \leq 15$, Di={1,...,10};
Send(tabZoneActiv[10], CrA, Z1); Send(tabZoneActiv[10], CrA, Z2); Send(tabZoneActiv[10], CrA, Z3);
Send(tabZoneActiv[10], CrA, Z4); Send(ProtoCommunic(CrA, Z1, Z2, Z3, Z4)); **END SEND STEP**
CALCUL $D(Zi,Zj)$; i={1,...,10}, j={5,...,10}; D(Zi,Zj)=Dj-Di; **IF** $D(Zi,Zj) \leq DS$; Send(tabZoneActiv[10], Zi, Zj);

D(Z1,Z5)=	D5-D1	21-14=7m
D(Z1,Z6)=	D6-D1	26-14=12m
D(Z1,Z7)=	D7-D1	31-14=17m
D(Z1,Z8)=	D8-D1	34-14=20m
D(Z1,Z9)=	D9-D1	40-14=26m
D(Z1,10)=	D10-D1	42-14=28m

Send(tabZoneActiv[10], Z1, Z5, Z6); Send(ProtoCommunic(Z1, Z5, Z6)); **CALCUL** $D(Zi,Zj)$; i={6,...,10},

	D(Z6,Z7)=	D7-D6	31-26=5m
j={7,...,10};	**D(Z6,Z8)=**	D8-D6	34-26=8m
	D(Z6,Z9)=	D9-D6	40-26=14m
	D(Z6,Z10)=	D10-D6	42-26=16m

Send(tabZoneActiv[10], Z6, Z7, Z8,Z9); Send(ProtoCommunic(Z6, Z7, Z8,Z9)); **CALCUL** $D(Z9,Z10)$;

D(Z9,Z10)=	D10-D9	40-42=2m

Send(tabZoneActiv[10], Z9, Z10); Send(ProtCommunic(Z9, Z10);
FOR EACH Z_i $\in$ setZone; (ZA) send to the (SA) an order of reconfig.
FOR EACH Nz_j(i); orderReconfig(ZA, SA) = 1; VAR =1 $\Rightarrow$ Send (ReconficArchitecNode(), ZA, SA); Arch[]= new Array[100]; Arch[] =ReconficArchitecNode()
REPEAT IF (PwB $\geq$ 0) ; Sd(Nz_j(i))=1; Arch[IDj]=1; j=j+1; **UNTIL** j= nbNode; **RETURN** Arch[]}; New-node-archit $\Rightarrow$ orderReconfig(ZA, SA) = 2; VAR =2 $\Rightarrow$ send (ReconfProtoCommNodes());
ReconfProtoCommNodes(){ **IF** (N an address of node connected in a zone Z_ { Deliverdata (Nz_j(i), link); **ELSE IF** ($\exists$ route $\in$ routing table); Deliverdata (Nz_j+1(i), link); send (DataStructure_j(i)[], CrA);}

To show the benefits of our contribution, we compare this work to the projects *TWIST* [3] and *ReWINS* [8]: (i) we compute the number of exchanged messages in our multi-agent architecture of RWSN (denoted by *Arch 1*) where 10 messages are exchanged between (CrA) and the 10 (ZA) agents. We suppose that we have 50 active nodes and 50 deactive ones per zone. In this case, 50 messages are exchanged between (ZA) and (SA). The number of exchanged messages: $NbExchMgs1 = 10+10*50=510$ messages. For the *TWIST* project [3], the authors use the notion of Super nodes, (denoted by *Arch 2*), which is similar to our Zone Agent but without a concept of active nodes. We have 10 messages to be exchanged between the station and super nodes (10 messages are equal to the number of super nodes) plus the messages to be exchanged between the super nodes and all others= $10*1000$. The number of exchanged messages is $NbExchMgs2= 10+10*1000=10010$ messages. For the project ReWINS [8], the authors do not consider an agent-based architecture. We denote this architecture by *Arch 3*, we have, 500 exchanged messages between the station and its nearly nodes plus the exchanged messages between the rest of the nodes. The number of exchanged messages is $NbExchMgs3 = \sum_{i=0}^{500} i = 250750$ messages. (ii) If we suppose that the time of transmission of any message is 2 ms, we can calculate the transmission time of all messages for these three solutions as follows.

Note that the minimization of exchanged messages between nodes reduces the total energy consumption in a RWSN. We can compute the complexity of our coordination protocol that we compare to related works [3,8]. Let n be the constant size of data to be exchanged between nodes, and N be the number of operations in the communication protocol (Oper 1, Oper 2, Oper 3, Oper 4, Oper 5), Nb(oppj) the number of sub-operations in the operation oppj, j=(A,..5), $Size(n)$: the algorithm size or the total number of sub-operations in the protocol. The complexity of our protocol is compared to related works [3,8] as follows: (a): For our architecture (*Arch 1*):

$$Size(n) = \sum_{j=1}^{5}(\sum_{i=0}^{n} nNb(oppj))=5(2n[\log_2 n]) = 10n[\log_2 n]$$ and the complexity is $O(10n[\log_2 n]) = O(n[\log_2 n])$. The $Size(n)$=recursive equation. (b): For TWIST [3] architecture (*Arch 2*), we have: $Size(n)= n(2n[\log_2 n]) = n^2[\log_2 n]$ and the complexity is $O(n2[\log_2 n])$. (c): For ReWINS [8] architecture (*Arch 3*), we have: $Size(n) = n^3$ and the complexity is $O(n^3)$.

7.2   Practical Simulation

We are interested in the exchange of signals between nodes when the temperature is between 30° and 50° ($30° \leq Temp \leq 50°$). Our major goal is to keep all nodes of the network on live as much as possible. We assume that if the number of dead nodes (node with battery charge = 0, $PwB=0$) reaches 30 % of the original number of nodes (in order of 300 nodes) then, the network collapses. We apply

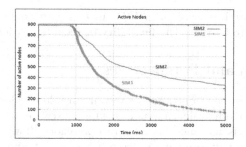

Fig. 8. Comparison between two simulation cases.

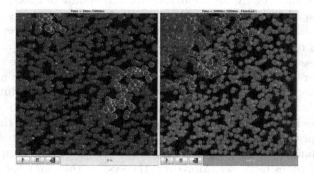

Fig. 9. The start and end of simulation.

our contribution to this case study by using WSNet (Wireless Sensor Network simulator) [5][1].

We assume two simulation strategies: (i) First case (*SIM1*): We suppose that we do not apply our contribution. Each node sends periodically the temperature information even it's higher than 50°), (ii) second case (*SIM2*): We apply our contribution by assuming that each node stops any emission of temperature information if it is higher than 50. Figure 8 shows the benefits of our contribution that we tested with WSNet.

We note that without the reconfiguration (*SIM1*), the network performance is low, since it collapses much faster than in (*SIM2*). Figure 9 presents additional results of our simulation by using WSNet. The red nodes are deactivated nodes (*PwB*=0), the brown area shows the high temperature zone, the nodes with a purple outline are active in the process of transmitting data and those in green are in their neighborhoods and participating in routing.

According to our theoretical and practical simulation, the advantages of the chapter's contribution :(i) a gain in transmission time of messages to be exchanged between nodes. This gain includes a decrease of transmission times, (ii) a gain in terms of energy since we gain in transmission of messages,

---

[1] We thank Ms. Zeineb Gueich for collaboration to prepare this experimentation.

(iii) a hierarchical architecture of *RWSN* in order to control the complexity of the problem and to increase the flexibility of reconfiguration.

8   Conclusions and Perspectives

This chapter proposes new solutions for reconfigurable wireless sensor networks to be composed of communicating nodes which execute reconfigurable tasks. The reconfiguration is assumed to be any operation allowing the adaptation of the network to its environment under different constraints. We define three forms of reconfigurations to increase the flexibility of the network: (i) software reconfiguration allowing the addition/removal and update of tasks, (ii) hardware reconfiguration allowing the activation/deactivation of sensor nodes or detectors, (iii) protocol reconfiguration allowing the modification of data flows. Nowadays, many projects deal with RWSN such as WASAN and TWIST [3]. Nevertheless no one addresses all these forms together. We propose a zone-based multi-agent architecture for *RWSN* where hierarchical agents are defined for a more flexibility of the network. We use nested state machines as a modeling solution to cover all these forms and control the complexity. A coordination protocol is defined between agents for their feasible coordination. We present in this chapter a theoretical and practical simulation that proves the chapter's contribution. The applicability bound of our proposed solution is the modelling complexity when the number of zones increases. Moreover, the system that we treat is real-time, but it is critical to meet all real-time constraints while handling different reconfiguration scenarios. The third applicability bound is the critical management of reconfiguration requests on the medium between the nodes especially when the number of zones increases.

We plan in the future work to verify functional and temporal properties for the formal validation of *RWSN*. The real-time scheduling in nodes as well as the functional safety will be possible future trends to be also followed. We can also,automate the decomposition of zones to gain in terms of transmission messages between nodes , in case of applying a reconfiguration scenario. A real industrial case study will be considered for more evaluations of our contribution.

References

1. Guptay, V., Kim, J., Pandya, A., Lakshmanan, K., Rajkumar, R., Tovary, E.: Nano-CF: a coordination framework for macro-programming in wireless sensor networks. In: Mesh and Ad Hoc Communications and Networks (SECON)(2011)
2. Bellis, S.J., Delaney, K., Barton, J., Razeeb, K.M.: Development of field programmable modular wireless sensor network nodes for ambient systems in Computer Communications, Special Issue on WSNs, pp. 1531–1544, August 2005
3. Handziski, V., Kopke, A., Willig, A., Wolisz, A.: TWIST: A Scalable and Reconfigurable Wireless Sensor Network Testbed for Indoor Deployments in Technical University Berlin, Telecommunication Networks Group, November 2005
4. Wang, F.: Case study: Using LabVIEW to Design a Greenhouse Remote Monitoring System, Northeast Agriculture University (2010)

5. Hamida, E.B., Santos, S.: WSNet : Simulation configuration Tutorial in ARES INRIA / CITI - INSA Lyon (2007)
6. Shwe, H.-Y., Wang, C., Chong, P.-H.J., Kumar, A.: Robust cubic-based 3-D localization for wireless sensor networks. Wireless Sens. Netw. J. 5(9), 169–179 (2013)
7. Chen, T.-S., Chang, C.-Y., Sheu, J.-P.: Efficient path-based multicast in wormhole-routed mesh networks. J. Sys. Archit. 46, 919–930 (2000)
8. Ramamurthy, H., Prabhu, B.S., Gadh, R.: Reconfigurable wireless interface for networking sensors (ReWINS). In: de Groot, S.H., Niemegeers, I.G.M.M. (eds.) PWC 2004. LNCS, vol. 3260, pp. 215–229. Springer, Heidelberg (2004)
9. Kindratenko, V., Pointer, D.: Mapping a sensor interface and a reconfigurable communication system to an FPGA core. Sens. Lett. 3, 174–178 (2005)
10. Chen, J., Zhang, L., Luo, J.: Reconfiguration cost analysis based on PetriNet for manufacturing system. J. Softw. Eng. Appl. 2, 361–369 (2009)
11. Xiong, J., Zhao, J., Chen, L.: Efficient data gathering in wireless sensor networks based on matrix completion and compressive sensing. IEEE Commun. Lett. 3, 1–3 (2013)
12. Saravanakumar, R., Susila, S.G., Li, J., Raja, J.: Energy efficient homogeneous and heterogeneous system for wireless sensor networks. Int. J. Comput. Appl. 17, 33–38 (2011)
13. Bocca, M., Cosar, E.I., Salminen, J., Eriksson, L.M.: A reconfigurable wireless sensor network for structural health monitoring. In: Structural Health Monitoring of Intelligent Infrastructure conference, July 2009
14. Samek, M.: Practical Statecharts in C/C++: Quantum Programming for Embedded Systems in CMP Books, imprint of CMP Media LLC (2003). ISBN 1-57820-110-1
15. Swamy, N.: Control Algorithms for Networked Control and Communication Systems, PhD thesis, Department of Electrical Engineering in the University of Texas at Arlington, Texas (2003)

A Measurement-Oriented Modelling Approach: Basic Concepts to Be Shared

Giulio D'Emilia[✉], Gaetanino Paolone, Emanuela Natale,
Antonella Gaspari, and Denis Del Villano

Department of Industrial and Information Engineering and of Economics,
University of L'Aquila, L'Aquila, Italy
{giulio.demilia,gaetanino.paolone,emanuela.natale}@univaq.it,
{antonella.gaspari,denis.delvillano}@graduate.univaq.it

Abstract. Measurements represent a fundamental component of Enterprise Information Systems and they play a key role in organizations. Their own languages, concepts and techniques, concerning how to approach and solve problems in industrial scenarios, inevitably characterize these two disciplines. The practical meaning of metrological concepts is often partially or completely misunderstood, in particular the extended uncertainty and the confidence level, which both can supply useful support in business activities. After explaining their physical meaning, in this paper the question being posed is how to get a methodology that allows to analyze, model and implement software subsystems able to render really usable information concerning measurements, keeping their informative peculiarities unchanged. The final goal of our research is to define a Use Case-based methodology for modeling the informative content of measurements and their usage, that starts from the business model of an enterprise and achieves a software model able to satisfy users' needs.

Keywords: Use case · Business modelling · System modelling · UML · Measurement · Uncertainty · Energy

1 Introduction

It is generally acknowledged that designing and developing software systems is becoming increasingly complex. Fortunately, there are methodologies and tools [1] to tackle this demanding and, sometimes critical, challenge. For example, the methodology proposed in [2–4] promotes the iterative and incremental development of complex software systems using a methodological framework that supports model-driven engineering. Such a methodology is inspired to the Rational Unified Process (RUP) [5] and it poses Use Cases (UC) at the center of the modelling [6].

Nowadays measurements, i.e. quantitative information from measured quantities, increasingly represent a fundamental component of Enterprise Information Systems (EIS) and they play a key role in organizations. While the automation of decision-making processes based on measurements appears to be a great opportunity, on the other hand difficulties are presumable. There is the possibility of having a large amount of data

© Springer International Publishing Switzerland 2015
A. Holzinger et al. (Eds.): ICSOFT 2014, CCIS 555, pp. 170–182, 2015.
DOI: 10.1007/978-3-319-25579-8_10

coming from measurements to be integrated into the Business Information System that have their primary language and who are not always well spread throughout all departments of the business organizations. Moreover, the source of information has an extremely wide variability in the measuring system implementing methods and in the quality of measurements. There are concepts related to the variability that may lead to content's smokiness but computerization may be a useful solution. Another difficulty is that the operating conditions can have, from one case to another, completely different characteristics and connotations. This is why the question we posed is how to get a methodology that allows us to analyze, model and implement software subsystems able to render really usable information concerning measurements, keeping their informative peculiarities unchanged. Please note that in literature there are very few examples that can support this [7]. Studies aiming to compare foundations of measurement theory to software measurement [8] do not appear, in fact, closer to these goals.

For an IT project to be successful, it must be as close as possible to business reality, in such a way that corporate users can find in the application [9] the same modus operandi of their own function: each actor plays a set of UCs within the organization and does so regardless of automation. Today, UCs are at the core of modelling and developing software applications [1, 10, 11]. The methodology appearing in [4] is an example of the proposal that gives the power to manage such a complexity through a layer of classes dedicated to UC automation. Their methodology examines the system behavioral aspects through a top-down process (such an approach is commonplace amidst software development methodologies), and then proceeds by means of stepwise refinements of the initial business model.

The final goal of our research is to define a methodological proposal for modeling the measurements and their usage that starts from the business model of an enterprise subsystem and achieves a software model able to satisfy the users' needs (i.e., that fully adheres to business processes). In line with this goal, the present contribution calls into question the convenience of using a top-down approach in business modeling, system modeling, design and implementation of a software system able to make the expected information available, going from the measurements to the management.

The next step (created with this paper) adapts the approach proposed in [2–4], transforming it in such a way that you can understand and design software application for the analysis of measurements starting from business system requirements. In summary, what we want to do is to extract UCs from the EIS and bring them into the computerized system (from Business Modeling to System Modeling) also in relation to the measurements to be carried out in any enterprise area, whether they are related to the production, power consumption and all other forms of detection.

The paper is organized as follows. Section 2 recalls essential elements of the methodology appeared in [2–4] needed for comprehending this work. Section 3 outlines essential characteristics of an EIS' subsystem dedicated to metering and its peculiarities in decision-making, regardless of the usage of computer. Section 4 starts the discussion about a possible transformation of the methodological process recalled in Sect. 2, which can lay a solid foundation for pursuing the aforementioned ultimate goal. Brief conclusions end the paper.

2 The Methodology

The methodology introduced in [2–4] allows to represent two models in detail: the business and the system model. Use case modeling and realization are the most important aspects of the methodology. The proposal is centered around four distinct layers (Fig. 1) with an iterative and incremental approach that leads to the realization of a Business Use Case (BUC) into the software application through stepwise refinements. The first two layers of UC analysis are placed in the business modeling context: their objective is to get a complete representation of the given business reality. The next two layers are rather placed in the system modeling context with the objective of representing the software system. More in detail, they illustrate that the first layer concerns an analysis of BUCs, which are then specialized by Business Use Case Realizations (BUCR) in the second layer. Afterwards, a trace operation is used to define the system UCs (third layer), which are then specialized by Use Case Realizations (UCR) (fourth layer). The latter ones can be implemented by Object Oriented classes.

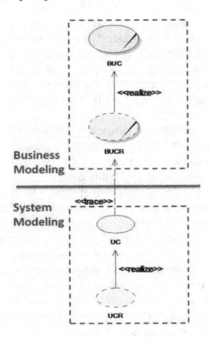

Fig. 1. A sketch of the methodological layers.

Next, we describe the methodology thoroughly with a brief example referring to a real-life document management project for a bank, where every layer contains a type of UML diagram. We will show that this example may be useful because whatever is being developed for a bank, that is to say a typical management case, can be applied to any industrial scenario. Figure 2 shows a fragment of the BUC diagram, placed in the first layer of Fig. 1.

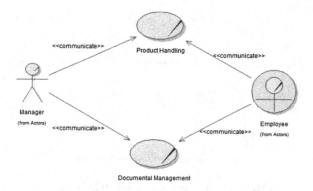

Fig. 2. The BUC diagram (1st layer).

The example shows how BUCs are used to express an actor/system interaction. For each BUC, we define the related BUCRs. Referring to the BUC Documental Management, Fig. 3 proposes six BUCRs.

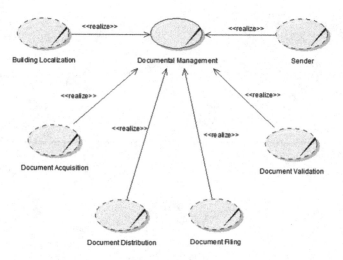

Fig. 3. The BUC *realize* diagram (2nd layer).

After the business modelling phase, we analyze the part of the system that will be automated. The trace operation can introduce many system UCs for a single BUCR. For example, in Documental Management, the document acquisition can be realized by the Bank, but by Suppliers as well (see Fig. 4). The output of the trace operation produces the system UCs in the third layer of Fig. 1.

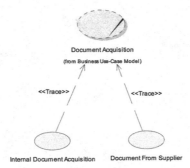

Fig. 4. The use case *trace* diagram (3rd layer).

In the last phase of the subsystem behavioral analysis, we must identify at least one system UCR for each system UC. In this phase we also introduce some technological UCRs, such as `LinkFile`. For the sake of brevity, we will not present an example of system UCR diagram, but it should be straightforward to understand that this operation introduces a further refinement of the subsystem.

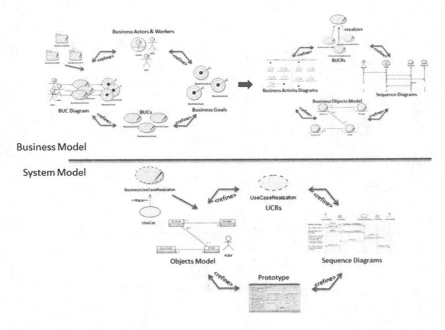

Fig. 5. Methodological overview.

The current methodology has a strong industrial impact because it has been repeatedly applied in real projects reaching good results and its adoption has brought benefits both in terms of the engineering aspects of design and development time [2]. Moreover, the methodology enables to build software systems with the help of a an existing

Java-based framework that implements a Java class for each UCR and allows to speed up the software development.

Figure 5 represents an overview of the methodology: it also shows the main involved artifacts. It is clear that, in conclusion, it is possible to reaffirm that the methodological process is UC-driven, since the UC artefact exists both in the business model and system model, although it is represented by different stereotypes, and is also exported to code.

3   The Measurement Viewpoint

Decision making requires both information and knowledge. Information (or its absence) is crucial to decision making [12]. In other circumstances the theory of measurement has already demonstrated to favor the ability to enter in the actual reality of the processes of interest [13]. Therefore, information deriving from measurement data may play a key role in business decision making. In business management, it is important that the decision is supported by appropriate tools, having the function to give the possibility to minimize the risk of errors so that the person can make complex decisions. In this sense, measurement uncertainty offers a considerable aid to quantify that risk, because it refers to the concept of the information reliability level (level of confidence).

3.1   Basis Concepts of the Measurement Theory

The measurement uncertainty is a parameter characterizing the dispersion of the values being attributed to a measurand, due to the random effect of many causes; three types of these are generally indicated, connected to the instrumentations and to the measurement method, to the operator and, finally, to the environment.

Some of these may be evaluated by a "type A" evaluation of measurement uncertainty from the statistical distribution of the quantity values from series of measurements and can be characterized by standard deviation. The other components, which can be evaluated by "type B" evaluation of measurement uncertainty, can also be characterized by standard deviation, evaluated by probability density functions based on experience or other information [14].

The measurement uncertainty reflects the unavoidable lack of exact knowledge of the value of the measurand, and a probability distribution over the set of possible values for the measurand is used to represent the information available on it. If the scenario of measurement is taken into account, the difference between the real operating situation and the ideal one means a random variability of measurements, even though the "true value" of quantity is set as constant. It must be pointed out that the "true value" of the quantity is a very satisfactory target to be pursued; knowing it means knowing everything about the phenomenon; therefore, if you know everything, nobody can contradict you, even though this is, obviously, impossible in a real condition.

In order to approach real situations, the answer to the question "what is the true value?" is given by the expanded uncertainty, that is the product of a standard measurement uncertainty by a coverage factor k. The coverage probability means the probability by which the true value of the measurand is contained in the uncertainty interval realized around the measurement. In most cases the probability distribution can be considered normal, and the coverage factor is set equal to 2 if a coverage probability of approximately 95 % is chosen. To obtain a better evaluation of the coverage factor associated to a specific coverage probability, especially when the number of measurements used for the uncertainty evaluation is low, a value taken from the Student distribution can be set [15].

The answer to the above question the measurements give is according this procedure; the "true value" is unknown but an interval could be shown where the "true value" is with a set coverage probability. Your decisions, your considerations have to be made thinking that every value of the interval is a possible "true value" with the given confidence level. Confidence level is a strategic parameter; increasing it means that all the possible value of the "true value" has been taken into account with a reduced risk of missing some one; the counter part of increasing confidence level and k for a set standard uncertainty is that we should be able to take decisions, to make actions effective with an enlarged set of possible values and this is, obviously, more difficult.

Optimizing the needed knowledge of the reality, standard uncertainty of measurements, and the risk of operating mistake, confidence level, can give a very useful contribution to the making of conscious decisions.

3.2 Measurements as a Tool for the Decision-Making

If the data are accurate, i.e. closer to the "true quantity value" of the measured quantity, they can be processed effectively creating an informative base with the following features:

- *shared*, i.e. integrated within business informative systems set in the specific industrial situation;
- *transparent*, i.e. objective and incontestable by the team members who participate in the decisional process;
- *significant*, i.e. consistent from the data quality viewpoint;
- *aware*, involving, in other words, an indication about the risk assumed by the decision maker, with reference to different alternative choices.

In that context, aiming at the fulfillment of these features, the attention must be paid to several challenging aspects for both information systems and metrology disciplines. Without limiting the general nature of the foregoing, an interesting area of use of a decision-making strategy based on measurement uncertainty of data coming from the field, is referred to an energy case of optimization. In particular, with reference to an industry operating in the aeronautical sector, simple measurements allowed us to validate a predictive model of energy consumption, to be used for the definition of a cost effective strategy for energy saving [16].

In this context, the decision-making strategy provides for the possibility of having a management tool that, for example, is able to return alternatively:

- the correspondence between a budget of improvement (I) and the target (t) that can be guaranteed, in front of a predetermined level of confidence (k) or risk deemed acceptable by the decision maker;

- the relation between a variable and adjustable improvement investment $\breve{I}$ and the probability $p(k')$ that a target set as t' is achieved.

In fact, in order to ensure, for the same investment I, and with a given level of confidence $p(k)$ to achieve a given objective t, it is necessary that the model gives the value $\bar{m}$ as a solution, which is related to the target of a quantity t exactly equal to the measurement uncertainty of the model, $U(m)$, according to the following logical implication:

$$p(t, I)\% = p(k) \rightarrow \bar{m} = t - U(\bar{m})$$

with:

$$U(\bar{m}) = k*u(\bar{m})$$

where:

$p(t, I)\%$: probability of reaching the target t, with the investment I;
n: degrees of freedom;
k, k': coverage factors (with $n = \infty$);
$p(k)$: probability (confidence level) associated with the model k coverage factor;
t, t': fixed or variable target depending on investment;
m: indication of the consumption model validated, i.e. provided of its uncertainty, $m = f(I)$;
$\bar{m}$: indication of the model that is in new condition after the fixed investment I;
$\bar{\bar{m}}$: indication of the model corresponding to the realization of the investment variable $\breve{I}$;
$u(m)$: standard uncertainty of the model;
$U(m)$: expanded uncertainty of the model.

Furthermore, it is possible to study the relationship, $p(k') = f'(\breve{I})$, between probability $p(k')$ to reach the target and the required investment $\breve{I}$. In fact, in front of an investment $\breve{I}$ the model will return an indication $m = f(I)$ corresponding to a reduction in consumption plausibly less ambitious (i.e. $\bar{\bar{m}} > \bar{m}$), being: $k' \neq k$.

4 The Approach We Look At

Designing a large enterprise software application is a complex and articulated process since it represents the company automation. The identification of the UCs appears particularly critical. It illustrates the interaction modes of the end-users with the system according to the usual business workflows. It is important to emphasize that the usage of a methodology, in the context of software engineering, has a fundamental importance for controlling the complexity of computerized solution.

As described in previous sections, measurements represent a key element in decision making. BUCs and BUCRs detection is a critical factor for the success of software applications which aim to be strategic for the business management and that are inspired by measurements. As a first step towards the definition of a methodology for the analysis and design of software for decision making that is based on measurements, we apply the methodology mentioned in Sect. 2 to a real case. The case study is referred to an energy case of optimization within an enterprise of avionic components: the main goal is to reach the energy consumption optimization.

In the proposed approach, the business modeling activity starts, in close collaboration with the enterprise top management, from the detection of Organization Units involved in the IT project and then proceeds discovering their Business Systems (BS) and their Business Goals (BG). Four BSs were detected and analyzed: in the example discussed hereinafter we focus on one of them, the BS `EnergyManagementArea`, involved in reaching the BG named `EnergyConsumptionEfficiency`.

Inside every BS we identify Business Actors, BUCs and BUCRs, using the construct BUC to represent a single interaction mode between actors and the system, and the construct BUCR to represent how business workers, business entities, and business events collaborate to perform a particular BUC [17].

After a thorough analysis of the Company, with particular attention to information flow inside the BS `EnergyManagementArea`, we identified several BUCs. In presenting our proposal, particularly interesting are the BUCs performed by the Business Worker Energy Manager, whose decisions are closely related to the measurements made on the field. Among those BUCs, (from the knowledge-intensive point of view) `ConsumptionTargetManagement` is the most complex, realized by 3 BUCRs (Fig. 6).

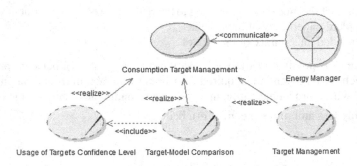

Fig. 6. Part of the case study BUC realize diagram.

To better understand the logic flow and document knowledge aspects involved in knowledge-intensive BUCRs, we widely use Business Activity Diagrams (BAD) (where a Business Activity (BA) denotes an elementary business operation or a knowledge-intensive task) and a strong narrative description. The ability of UML BADs to effectively describe complex business processes [18] allows us to depict the inference process that lets the Business Actor take a complex decision. A complex BA (that is an activity representing a number of intricate atomic tasks) may be depicted at different grain-size levels through the use of several BADs. For example, the BUCR `Target-Model Comparison` – representing the concepts expressed in Sect. 3 – was depicted using the BAD in Fig. 7 (which is only part of a larger diagram) and also widely documented through a narrative specification.

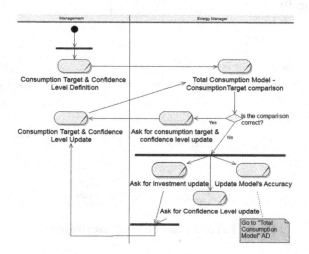

Fig. 7. Part of the case study BA diagram.

During the execution of the business modeling discipline, as provided for by theory, the main Business Entities (BE) (representing a significant and persistent piece of information that is manipulated by Business Actors and Business Workers [17]) were also identified and modelled.

Specific attention was paid to documenting classes of measurement-intensive business objects, i.e. those BEs strongly related to measurements. In their modeling, close attention was placed on maintaining the peculiarities of measurement unchanged and well-marked, in order to grant a key role in business decision making to information deriving from measurement data. Figure 8 shows a portion of the BEs diagram.

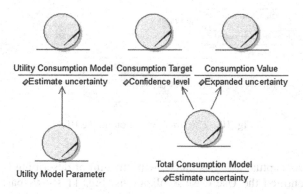

Fig. 8. The case study's business entities

After the Business Analysis, a *trace* operation was performed: according to the methodology, we identified the BUCRs to be computerized and we *traced* them into System UCs (Fig. 9).

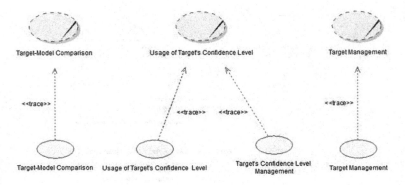

Fig. 9. Part of the case study UC trace diagram.

In the same manner and with the same aim, as provided for by the theory, a *trace* operation was performed only on the BEs needed for the system's computerization (Fig. 10).

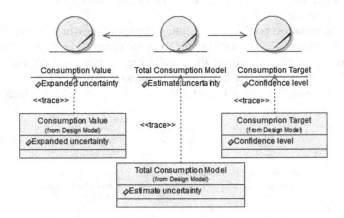

Fig. 10. The *trace* operation on the BEs.

During the conceptual analysis phase, with the aim of describing how each UC is realized, we identified the Use Case Realizations: Fig. 11 shows part of the *realize* diagram.

Fig. 11. An example of *realize* diagram.

Each UCR was also characterized and strongly supported in terms of one or more scenarios (usually represented by UML Sequence Diagrams or UML Activity Diagrams).

5 Conclusions

At the end of the case study's modelling process we believe the proposed approach produces a good representation of the EIS to be computerized, and a concrete image of subsystems to be automated. It is important to remark that we achieved this firm belief in close collaboration with several stakeholders involved in various aspects of the project, mainly measurements experts, decision makers, IT-business analysts and software engineers. Therefore, in our opinion, the usage of this methodological approach, broadly integrated with the usage of BADs (mainly to represents business decision-making patterns) allows to improve the quality of communications between the various stakeholders involved in modelling, and designing a measurement-intensive software system. Starting from the business modeling activity, the increase in the quality of information may help reaching a more effective system analysis and, at the end of the process, building a software system as close as possible to business reality and fully able to reveal its decision-making patterns.

Finally, we believe this approach may become a first step in reducing the informative gap (concerning the correct usage and interpretation of measurements) between business management, software engineers and measurement experts, giving some preliminary solutions deriving from the fact that in the best of our knowledge, measurements are not correctly used into automated decision making processes as often the typical concepts of measurement (uncertainty, level of confidence, …) are lost while being processed and made accessible to end-users. A change is needed in the usage of measurements in decision making processes modelling and computerization. The proposed top-down approach may be the first step in this change. Certainly, in order to completely clarify how measurements need to be correctly used and interpreted within an automated decision-making process, many aspects need to be studied more closely, with reference to the business modelling, to the type of approach (top-down, bottom-up, mixed), to the procedures of in field transfer of the results, etc.

References

1. Sukaviriya, N., Sinha, V., Mani, S.: Reflection of a year long model-driven business and UI modeling development project. In: Palanque, P., Gulliksen, J., Kotzé, P., Prates, R.O., Oestreicher, L., Gross, T., Winckler, M. (eds.) INTERACT 2009. LNCS, vol. 5727, pp. 749–762. Springer, Heidelberg (2009)
2. Paolone, G., Clementini, E., Liguori, G.: A methodology for building enterprise web 2.0 applications. In: The Modern Information Technology in the Innovation Processes of the Industrial Enterprises, Prague, Czech Republic, 12–14 November 2008
3. Paolone, G., Clementini, E., Liguori, G.: Design and development of web 2.0 applications. In: ITAIS 2008, Paris, France, 13–14 December 2008
4. Paolone, G., Clementini, E., Liguori, G., Cestra, G.: Web 2.0 applications: model-driven tools and design. In: ITAIS 2009, Costa Smeralda, Italy, 2–3 October 2009
5. Kruchten, P.: Rational Unified Process, An Introduction, 2nd edn. Addison Wesley, Boston (2003)
6. UML, Unified Modeling Language, version 2.4.1 (2012). http://www.uml.org/
7. Wen, B., Zhang, L.: Mapping enterprise process measure into information model. In: First International Workshop on Education and Computer Science, pp. 612–615 (2009)
8. Carbone, P., Buglione, L., Mari, L., Petri, D.: A comparison between foundations of metrology and software measurement. IEEE Trans. Instrum. Measur. **57**, 235–241 (2008)
9. Zhao, X., Zou, Y., Hawkins, J., Madapusi, B.: A business process driven approach for generating e-commerce user interfaces. In: Model Conference 2007, Nashville, TN, pp. 256–270, 30 September–5 October 2007
10. Zelinka, L., Vranić, V.: A configurable UML based use case modeling metamodel. In: First IEEE Eastern European Conference on the Engineering of Computer Based Systems (2009)
11. Duan, J.: An approach for modelling business application using refined use case. In: ISECS International Colloquium on Computing, Communication, Control, and Management (2009)
12. Beretta, F., De Carlo, F., Introna, V., Saccardi, D.: Progettare e gestire l'efficienza energetica. McGraw-Hill, New York (2012)
13. D'Emilia, G., Di Rosso, G., Gaspari, A., Massimo, A.: Metrological interpretation of a six sigma action for improving on line optical measurement of turbocharger dimensions in the automotive industry. Proc. Inst. Mech. Eng. D J. Autom. Eng. (2014)
14. ISO/IEC Guide 99:2007: International vocabulary of metrology - basic and general concepts and associated terms (VIM) (2007)
15. UNI CEI ENV 13005:2000: Guide to the expression of uncertainty in measurement (2000)
16. D'Emilia, G., Gaspari, A., Natale, E.: Uncertainty evaluation of energy flow in industrial applications as a key factor in setting improvement actions. Proposed for publication to Applied Energy (2014)
17. Johnston, S.: Rational UML profile for business modelling. IBM Rational (2004). www.ibm.com
18. Russell, N., van der Aalst, W.M.P., ter Hofstede, A.H.M., Wohed, P.: On the suitability of UML 2.0 activity diagrams for business process modeling. In: Stumptner, M., Hartmann, S., Kiyoki, Y. (eds.) 3rd Asia-Pacific Conference on Conceptual modeling. Conferences in Research and Practice in Information Technology, vol. 53 (2006)

Evolution of Feature-Oriented Software: How to Stay on Course and Avoid the Cliffs of Modularity Drift

Andrzej Olszak[✉], Sanja Lazarova-Molnar, and Bo Nørregaard Jørgensen

Centre for Energy Informatics, University of Southern Denmark, Odense, Denmark
{ao,slmo}@mmmi.sdu.dk, bnj@iti.sdu.dk

Abstract. With time software systems easily become obsolete if not updated to reflect the ever-changing needs of their users. This update process is far from trivial as each feature is not necessarily captured by a single module, but rather scattered across a number of different modules. The situation is further aggravated by the fact that a module can encompass a number of different features. Our goal is to measure and evaluate how easy it is to trace back and update a given piece of software based on its modularity. Modularity is known as the degree to which a system's components may be separated and recombined. The approach that we propose is based on the idea of using relative, as opposed to absolute, modularity metrics that measure the distance between the actual metric values for a given source code and their values achievable for the source code's ideally modularized counterpart. The approach, termed *modularization compass*, computes the modularity drift by optimizing the feature-oriented modularization of source code based on traceability links between features and source code. The optimized modularizations are created automatically by transforming the groupings of classes into packages, which is guided by a multi-objective grouping genetic algorithm. The proposed approach was evaluated by application to long-term release histories of three open-source Java applications.

Keywords: Software evolution · Feature-oriented modularization · Re-modularization · Software comprehension

1 Introduction

Software maintenance have always represented large and growing expense for organizations [1]. Incorporating changes requested by the users during software evolution is a non-trivial process because it requires deep understanding of the relations between software's problem domain and its solution domain [2]. Doing so is difficult because a problem domain is centered around user-observable units of functionality, i.e. so-called *features* [2, 3], whereas a solution domain is arranged around source-code units, known as modules, packages, classes, methods and instructions. Hence, modification of a feature in response to a particular change requested by users implies the ability to effectively map the feature to the concrete source-code units that need to be inspected, modified and tested. Furthermore, one needs to properly modularize the implementations of features into source-code modules to support software inspection and modification [4].

© Springer International Publishing Switzerland 2015
A. Holzinger et al. (Eds.): ICSOFT 2014, CCIS 555, pp. 183–201, 2015.
DOI: 10.1007/978-3-319-25579-8_11

Unfortunately, implementations of features are usually not explicitly represented into source-code modules in the organizations of software. Instead, an organization of software traditionally focuses on separating technical concerns such as model, view, controller or persistence into separate architectural layers, each represented by one or more source-code modules. As a result, implementations of features become *scattered* over multiple source-code modules and *tangled* with one another, as each feature typically crosscuts multiple architectural layers. These relations between feature specifications and source-code modules affect software evolution in several ways:

- *Scattering* denotes delocalization of implementation of a feature over several source-code units of an application [2] and corresponds to the software comprehension phenomenon of *delocalized plans* [5]. The presence of delocalized plans makes it difficult to identify relevant source-code units during change tasks [5, 6].
- *Tangling* of features denotes *interleaving* of implementations of multiple features within a single module of source code [7]. Such interleaving makes it difficult to understand how multiple features relate and how they reuse fragments of each others' implementations [8].

Apart from software comprehension, the mapping gap between features and source-code modules makes it very difficult to modify source code. Due to scattering, modification of one feature may require understanding and modification of several seemingly unrelated source-code modules. Due to tangling, a modification intended to affect only one feature may cause accidental change propagation to other features that happen to use the source-code module that is being modified.

Because of the evolutionary implications of scattering and tangling, it is important to keep track of the development of their values over subsequent evolutionary releases of software. The erosion of feature-oriented modularity, as indicated by the increasing scattering and tangling, has to be observed to provide a measure of the extent of development overhead that they may incur. Ultimately, such knowledge can be used to inform planning of feature-oriented remodularization efforts.

This paper proposes an approach termed *modularization compass* that quantifies the so-called drift of feature-oriented modularity in software. We define *drift in feature-oriented modularity* as the distance between the scattering and tangling metric values of the actual source code of a software release, and a counterpart that is ideally modularized with respect to the metrics of interest. The idealized counterparts are created through a remodularization process that optimizes the grouping of classes into packages according to feature-oriented criteria using a multi-objective grouping genetic algorithm. To compute the values of scattering and tangling our approach assumes availability of traceability links between features and source-code units, as obtainable from several existing feature-location approaches. Based on the measurements of scattering and tangling drifts, the modularization compass approach provides so-called *compass views* that depict evolution of the drift of the feature-oriented modularity over an application's lifetime.

This approach was implemented in the Java programming language and evaluated using long-term release histories of three open-source Java applications. There, the drift information from the modularization compass views was used to identify the development periods in which the potential benefits from restructuring the code would have been largest, and to determine whether this restructuring effort should have focused on reducing the scattering or the tangling of features. Apart from demonstrating the approach, a number of observations were made regarding the nature of drift of feature-oriented modularity.

The remaining part of the paper is structured as follows. Section 2 describes the state of the art of feature-oriented modularity. Section 3 presents the modularization compass approach. Section 4 evaluates the approach. Finally, Sect. 5 concludes the paper.

2   State of the Art

There exist several works that investigate the evolution of features and the modularity of their implementations over time.

Hsi and Potts [9] proposed to use three views: morphological, functional and object view to study the co-evolution of the representation of features in the user interface (UI), their textual specifications and their implementation in three releases of Microsoft's Word text processor. The presented qualitative analysis shows that the features providing the core functionality experience little change and tend to stabilize over time. This is because they tend to become more entangled with associations as new features are added. As a result, newer features are added on the periphery of the main functionality of the application in either small extensions or larger clumps.

Fischer and Gall [10] designed a visualization of feature co-evolution based on the logical coupling between source files created during adoption of change requests. This approach uncovers hidden dependencies among features and thereby identifies potential occurrences of architectural deterioration in directory structures of programs. The authors apply their approach to a four-year revision history of the Mozilla web browser to uncover unanticipated dependencies and co-evolution of features.

Hou and Wang [11] analyzed the evolution of features related to usability in the Eclipse IDE. This was done by both qualitative and quantitative manual analysis of change logs of the project. The authors identify the majority of changes as gradual refinements or incremental additions, accommodated by the project's architecture. Usability-related features are observed to be the largest component of work in the project, with a shift over time towards features concerned with integration and automation of other features. The observed incremental, rather than punctuated, growth of features of Eclipse is believed to be enabled by the stability of the architecture.

Greevy et al. [12] focused on qualitative assessment and visualization of evolutionary changes in implementations of features. Using the proposed visualization, the authors are able to reason about functional specialization of classes over time, extension of existing features with new classes and refactorings performed to features. The presented results depict an increase of feature count and addition of feature-specific classes over time.

In an earlier work, Olszak and Jørgensen [13] developed an approach to bi-directional remodularization of existing Java applications to improve the modularization of features in source code. Feature location was performed using an annotation-driven dynamic analysis mechanism, and new feature-oriented package structures were automatically created using a multi-objective genetic algorithm aiming at reducing scattering, tangling, coupling and increasing cohesion. The observed improvements suggested that the modularizations produced by this approach are good starting points when migrating applications to feature-oriented designs.

3   The Approach

Implementing a feature inherently requires a mixture of technically diverse classes. In particular, each non-trivial feature encompasses some forms of (1) interfacing classes that allow users to activate the feature and see the results of its execution, (2) logic and domain model classes that contain the essential processing algorithms, and (3) persistence classes that allow for storing and loading the results of a feature's execution. Hence, features can be viewed as implicit vertical slices that crosscut the common horizontal layers of an application's architecture. These implicit slices consist of graphs of collaborating classes that end up *scattered* and *tangled* within individual layers [14]. This is depicted in Fig. 1.

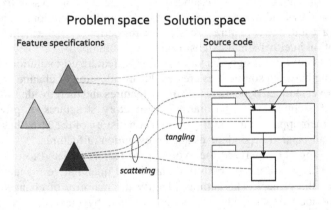

Fig. 1. Relations between feature specifications and units of source code.

Our approach quantifies these two facets of modularity of features using the following measures, based on formulations proposed by Brcina and Riebisch [15]:

- *Scattering of a feature is quantified* as the number of packages that contribute to implementing that feature. The average of these values, computed for all features in a system, is referred to as *FSCA*. The formulation of FSCA is described in detail in Sect. 4.3.
- *Tangling of a package is quantified* as the number of features that the package contributes to. The average of these values, computed for all packages in a system, is referred to as *FTANG*. The formulation of FTANG is described in detail in Sect. 4.3.

The extent to which scattering and tangling of features is minimized is a measure of how well features are modularized within source-code units. We refer to this as the *degree of feature-oriented modularity of software*.

In order to measure feature-oriented complexity of evolving features in terms of scattering and tangling, relations between the source-code units and individual features have to be identified. The process of identifying relations between source-code units and observable functionality of a system is known as *feature location* [16]. This work assumes that traceability links are readily available or are recovered for an application using one of the feature-location approaches available in the literature. In particular, for the evaluation purposes, Sect. 4 uses an existing feature-location approach based on source-code annotation and dynamic analysis.

3.1 Evolution of Feature-Oriented Modularity

The essence of how features of software applications evolve is well expressed by the laws of *continuing growth* and the law of *increasing complexity*, as formulated by Lehman [17]. According to the former, software applications need to expand and enhance their features over time in order to remain useful to their users. The latter postulates that these expansions will lead to increasing complexity of the source code, unless work is done to reduce it. One of the facets of the increasing complexity is the increasing complexity of how features are modularized in source code, as will be exemplified in the following.

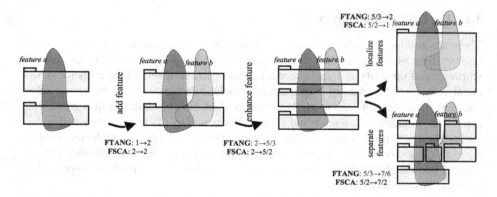

Fig. 2. Example impact of evolutionary changes on feature-oriented modularity.

The example application schematically depicted in Fig. 2 initially provides only one feature that is implemented by two layered modules. Hence, the initial average tangling FTANG in the application equals 1 (initially each module implements one feature), and the initial average scattering FSCA equals 2 (the feature is implemented by two modules).

The first change scenario depicts the effects of adding a new feature to the application without modifying the structure of the source code. Such a functional extension will naturally tend to increase the tangling of the application's modules, as a result of reusing parts of existing code among features. The second scenario shows the effects of enhancing one of the existing features. Because the enhancement is implemented as a new module in the application (a realistic example of doing so would be adding persistence capabilities), the scattering of the feature increases.

Thereafter, depicted are two possible contrasting scenarios of source-code restructurings undertaken to improve modularization of features. One of them is based on the merging of existing modules to minimize the scattering of features. As illustrated, this causes features to be more tangled with one another. The other restructuring reduces feature tangling by dividing existing modules along the boundaries of features. As a side effect, the scattering of features increases.

Based on this simple example, two important observations can be made:

Addition and enhancement of user functionality tends to increase tangling and scattering of features. Accordingly, difficulties of code comprehension and change propagation associated with these phenomena should be expected to increase as well.

Restructuring source code to minimize only one of the two properties of feature-oriented modularity (i.e. scattering or tangling) tends to degrade the other property. Hence, in order to achieve a simultaneous optimization of both conflicting criteria, a middle-ground restructuring needs to be devised. For the presented toy example, simple enumeration of all possible modularizations could achieve this. Enumeration, however, would certainly not be feasible for larger systems because the number of all possible distributions of N classes among M modules is equal to M^N.

3.2   The Drift of Modularity

There are multiple factors that have to be considered when planning a feature-oriented restructuring of an application. Fundamentally, undertaking a restructuring is only worthwhile if the costs of doing so are regained by lower development costs for subsequent releases. The costs of a restructuring include factors such as the actual effort required, the impact on time-to-market of the product, changes to design documentation, etc. On the benefits side, one should expect improvements of changeability and understandability of feature implementations during subsequent releases and hence a reduction of development costs. Unfortunately, estimating these benefits remains difficult without knowing how much the modularization of features can actually be improved by means of restructuring.

Hence, to make informed feature-oriented restructuring decisions, one should be able to foresee the consequences of performing a feature-oriented restructuring. In practice, this boils down to being able to foresee how much the current values of feature scattering and tangling can be reduced in course of restructurings.

Unfortunately, the achievable benefits of restructurings cannot be estimated by simply computing the distance between the current values of scattering and tangling metrics and their numerical minima. This is because the numerical minima of these and other metrics often do not correspond to realistic optimal modularizations of non-trivial applications, e.g. tangling equal to 1 requires no code sharing among features; scattering equal to 1 requires each feature to be fully contained in a single module; coupling equal to 0 requires no dependencies among modules, etc. The presence and the type of normalization factors embedded in each metric further complicate the situation.

To identify the maximum possible improvements of feature-oriented modularization, it is necessary to construct its optimized modularization, on which the reference scattering and tangling values can be measured. Assuming that doing so is possible with sufficient accuracy and in an automated manner (which assumption will be expanded in the next section), it would be possible to calculate the distance between the current values of scattering and tangling and their optimized values achievable, if the application is restructured according to feature-oriented criteria.

Based on this, we define the *drift of feature-oriented modularity* in an application as the distances between the absolute and the optimal values of the scattering, measured here using FSCA, and of tangling, measured here using FTANG.

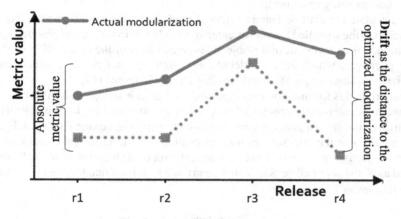

Fig. 3. Relativity of metric drift.

As schematically depicted in Fig. 3, the drift of feature-oriented modularity can be plotted over time for a given application to serve as a metaphorical *compass* that indicates how much the modularization of features diverges from the optimum with each subsequent release. Observing the drift trends can be used in several ways by developers to determine the need for initiating feature-oriented restructurings of the next releases of their applications.

The compass views of scattering and tangling drifts can be used to identify periods in which restructuring efforts would be most beneficial. Types of such periods include the ones in which the drift constitutes a large portion of the absolute metric value. An example of such a period is the release *r4* in Fig. 3, for which there is a large potential for reducing the absolute metric value by improving modularization of features. Moreover, in the release *r4* the drift increased significantly with relation to the previous release, and therefore restructuring could be considered in *r4* to prevent further divergence of the application's modularization from the optimum in the next release.

Moreover, by contrasting the drift plots for scattering and tangling, one can determine the character of restructuring most needed at a given point in time. For instance, large drift of scattering indicates a need for improving localization of individual features within modules, which may require reducing the overall number of modules. In contrast, large drift of tangling indicates a need for improving separation of features within modules, which may require increasing the overall number of modules.

3.3 Calculating Drift Using Optimization

Given the technical characteristics and automation potentials of existing methods for separating features [18], the modularization compass approach is based on regrouping classes in terms of packages to reduce scattering and tangling of features. While our purely class-based approach has limits in the level of feature separation that it can achieve, it has the important property of allowing complete automation of searching for desired feature-oriented package structures and subsequently establishing them in source code by using refactorings.

To calculate the drift of feature-oriented modularity, the modularization compass approach uses the so-called feature-oriented remodularization. *Feature-oriented remodularization* is the process of multi-objective optimization of the distribution of classes among packages, which aims at identifying Pareto-optimal package structures that minimize both scattering FSCA and tangling FTANG metrics [13].

In addition, this formulation encompasses two traditional object-oriented objectives that govern the inter- and intra-module dependencies among class, i.e. the objectives of maximizing cohesion in packages and minimizing coupling among packages. Formalized definitions of the four metrics used as evaluation criteria for the mentioned optimization objectives are listed in Fig. 4. There, the set of all features in an application is denoted as F, the set of all packages that contribute to at least one feature as P_F, and the set of all types as T.

$$FSCA(F) = \sum_{f \in F} \frac{|\{p \in P_F : f \rightsquigarrow p\}|}{|F|} \qquad \rightarrow min$$

$$FTANG(P_F) = \sum_{p \in P} \frac{|\{f \in F : f \rightsquigarrow p\}|}{|P_F|} \qquad \rightarrow min$$

$$PCOH(P) = \frac{\sum_{p \in P} pcoh(p,T)}{|P|}, \qquad \rightarrow max$$

$$pcoh(p,T) = \frac{\sum_{\substack{t1 \in T \\ t1 \Rightarrow p}} \sum_{\substack{t2 \in T \\ t2 \Rightarrow p}} |DD_{t1,t2} \cup DM_{t1,t2}|}{\sum_{\substack{t1 \in T \\ t1 \Rightarrow p}} \sum_{\substack{t2 \in T \\ t2 \Rightarrow p}} |MaxDD_{t1,t2} \cup MaxDM_{t1,t2}|}$$

$$PCOUP(P) = \sum_{\substack{p \in P \\ T \Rightarrow p}} pcoup(p,T), \qquad \rightarrow min$$

$$pcoup(p,T) = \sum_{\substack{t1 \in T \\ t1 \Rightarrow p}} \sum_{\substack{t2 \in T \\ t2 \nRightarrow p}} |DD_{t1,t2} \cup DM_{t1,t2}|$$

Fig. 4. Objectives for optimizing modularity of features.

The definitions of FSCA and FTANG correspond to the ones mentioned earlier and are simplified versions of the metrics proposed by Brcina and Riebisch [15] that are defined based on the $\rightsquigarrow$ (i.e. "implemented by") relation between features and packages. The reformulation made in this work removes the additional normalization factors and makes the metrics correspond directly to the numbers of features tangled in a package, and packages that a feature is scattered over. Doing so allows for easier interpretation of metric values, and is possible due to the modularity drift calculation being independent of metric normalization, as discussed earlier.

The cohesion metric PCOH is the package-level version of the RCI metric based on data-data (*DD*) and data-method (*DM*) relations proposed by Briand et al. [19]. In its essence, this metric computes for the set of packages P the average quotient of the actual number of intra-package static dependencies among classes and the maximum possible number of such dependencies. In turn, the package coupling metric PCOUP corresponds to a sum of the ACAIC, OCAIC, ACMIC, and OCMIC coupling measures, as defined by the same authors in [20], and thereby constitutes the sum of all inter-package static dependencies in an application.

The actual process of optimizing the application's modularity with respect to all the metrics is performed using a tailored formulation of a genetic algorithm that we refer to as *multi-objective grouping genetic algorithm* (MOGGA) [13]. The multi-objectivity is achieved by exploiting the notion of Pareto-optimality, whose efficiency in optimizing modularization of software systems according to multiple conflicting criteria was demonstrated by Harman and Tratt [21]. The grouping nature of the problem is exploited by using a set of tailored genetic operators based on the work of Seng et al. [22], who demonstrated their significant effect on improving the efficiency of traversing the search space of alternative modularizations. Hereby, MOGGA constitutes a composition of these two well-established approaches that is aims at leveraging their respective advantages.

In its essence, MOGGA evolves a population of individuals by means of *selection*, *reproduction* and *mutation* driven by the score of the individuals with respect to a fitness function. Each individual represents a particular distribution of classes among packages, expressed by an array of integers. Within this array, classes are represented by indexes in the arrays, and their assignment to packages is represented by the values of the corresponding array cells. The used representation scheme is exemplified in Fig. 5 using three classes and two packages.

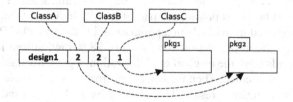

Fig. 5. The representation of grouping classes into packages.

MOGGA adapts two genetic operators that exploit the grouping-based nature of the remodularization problem. First, the crossover operator that forms two children from two parents is made to preserve packages as the building blocks of modularizations. The crossover operator makes individual modularizations exchange whole packages, rather than individual classes. The pairs of input individuals are chosen randomly, while prioritizing the individuals proportionally to their fitness. The usage of the crossover operator is schematically depicted in Fig. 6, where the complete package 2 from design1 is inserted into design2.

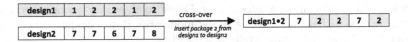

Fig. 6. The grouping crossover operator.

Secondly, a mutation operator is defined to randomly perform one of three actions: merge two packages with the smallest number of classes, split the largest package into two packages, and adopt an *orphan class* [23] being alone in a package into another package. Example application of the individual variants of this operator is depicted in Fig. 7.

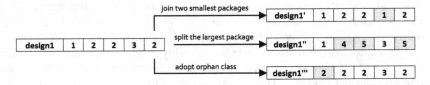

Fig. 7. The grouping mutation operator.

Evaluation of the fitness of the individual modularization alternatives is done by computing the four metrics of FSCA, FTANG, PCOH and PCOUP. Assigning the values of these metrics to each individual creates a basis for assessing and selecting the individuals representing the best modularizations of an application. In order to appropriately represent the regions of the four-dimensional search space that the individual modularizations in the population occupy, MOGGA adopts the concept of Pareto-optimality. Hence, the fitness of each individual becomes a tuple consisting of four independent metric values. Such a multi-modal fitness is used for comparing individuals based on the *Pareto-dominance* relation, which states that one out of two individuals is better than the other individual, if all of its fitness values are not worse, and at least one of the values is better. Thereby, it becomes possible to partially order individuals and to determine the set of non-dominated individuals in a population, i.e. the so-called Pareto-front.

Starting with an initial population consisting of 98 % randomized individuals and 2 % of the individuals from the original modularization, a predefined number of evolutionary iterations are executed. Then the last Pareto-front is used to select a single individual being the optimization result. This is done by ranking the individuals in the obtained four-dimensional Pareto-front with respect to each metric separately, and then choosing the individual that is ranked best on average. Please note that while this method is used here, existing literature defines a range of diverse methods for choosing a single solution out of a Pareto-front, e.g. [24, 25].

The final solution identified by MOGGA represents an optimized assignment of classes to a new set of packages. Proposed package structures can be then reviewed and flexibly adjusted by a developer in the provided UML-like visualization of the *Featureous Remodularization View* [26], as described in the following subsection.

3.4 Featureous Remodularization View

Featureous Remodularization View plugin supports developers in restructuring by allowing them to browse and adjust the automated remodularization results. The user interface of Featureous Remodularization View is centered on a graph-based representation of the package structure of an application. As shown in Fig. 8, this representation depicts packages as nodes and static dependencies among them as edges. The individual packages can be unfolded to reveal their enclosed classes and to refine the mapping of static dependencies accordingly. Furthermore, each class can be further unfolded to reveal a UML-like representation of its methods.

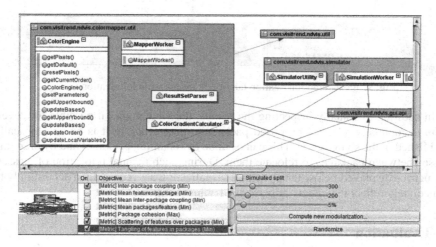

Fig. 8. Featureous remodularization view pre-remodularization tab.

The diagrammatic representation is used to visualize the package structures of both an original application through a *pre-remodularization* tab and of a remodularized application through a *post-remodularization* tab.

Apart from visual representation of package structure, the pre-remodularization tab allows for selection of optimization objectives and for configuration of the parameters of MOGGA. The user-configurable parameters are: (1) the number of iterations to be executed, (2) the size of evolved population and (3) the probability of mutation. Apart from the fours metrics used in this work, the view readily implements several other metrics that can be used as additional remodularization objectives in future studies.

After the remodularization process is invoked and finished, Featureous Remodularization View displays the result in a dedicated post-remodularization tab. As shown in Fig. 9, this view consists of the discussed diagrammatic visualization and a report window that summarizes the difference between the original and the remodularized application using a number of metrics.

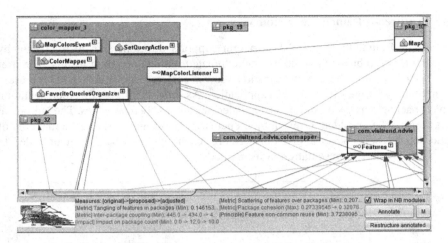

Fig. 9. Post-remodularization tab of featureous remodularization view.

In addition to visually inspecting the results, the view makes it possible for developers to manually adjust a proposed package structure before it is being physically established in the source code. This can be done by renaming packages and by dragging classes between packages to relocate them. During such manual relocation of classes, the metrics displayed below the structural visualization are recomputed accordingly to immediately reflect the effects of performed adjustments.

4   Evaluation

We have implemented the presented remodularization approach as part of the freely available Featureous tool for feature-oriented analysis of Java software [27]. The code transformations required for establishing the source-code modularizations were implemented using the Recoder code transformation library [28]. Furthermore, as will be discussed later, this evaluation relies on a dynamic feature-location approach provided by Featureous.

The goal of the study presented in this section is formulated as follows:

> *To evaluate whether drift-based metrics bring new insights into the evolution of feature-oriented modularity of applications, as compared to using their absolutes values.*

This is done by applying the approach to long-term release histories of three open-source Java applications that were chosen based on their size, maturity and availability of the historical revisions. The used applications are: *RText* – a text editor for programmers (17 releases spanning, 3 years) [29], *FreeMind* – a mind-mapping tool (13 releases, 5 years) [30] and *JHotDraw Pert* – a diagramming application being a showcase for the JHotDraw framework (11 releases, 8 years) [31].

4.1   Results of Feature Location

While the modularization compass approach does not impose any constraint on the feature-location approach to be used, we have chosen to use the dynamic feature-location approach provided by the Featureous tool. This feature-location approach identifies code units involved in implementing individual features by tracing the execution of an instrumented program during its interaction with a user. The tracing agent used for this purpose is guided by annotations that have to be placed by a programmer at appropriate starting methods of each feature. Apart from the use of annotations and user-driven feature triggering, this approach remains analogous to other dynamic approaches, such as software reconnaissance [16]. An extensive discussion of the conceptual and technical details of the used feature-location approach can be found in [13].

The most sensitive part to human interpretation was the one of recovery of feature specifications for each release of the three investigated applications. We have performed this recovery by inspecting the available user documentation and by listing the functionality exposed in the user interfaces of the applications. Table 1 lists the identified features and the releases in which they were added to the systems, if they were added during the investigated periods.

Table 1.   Investigated releases and their identified features.

Application releases	Identified features
RText Releases: 0.8.0; 0.8.1; 0.8.2; 0.8.3; 0.8.4; 0.8.5; 0.8.6; 0.8.7; 0.8.8; 0.8.9; 0.9.0; 0.9.2; 0.9.3; 0.9.4; 0.9.5; 0.9.7; 0.9.8	Display text, Document properties (0.9.0), Edit basic, Edit text, Exit program, Export document (0.8.7), Init program, Modify options, Customize text (0.9.0), Multiple documents, Navigate text, New document, Open document, Playback macro (0.9.0), Print document, Record macro, Save document, Show documentation, Source browser (added in 0.8.8 and removed in 0.9.0), Undo redo, Plugins (0.9.0)
FreeMind Releases: 0.0.2; 0.0.3; 0.1.0; 0.2.0; 0.3.0; 0.3.1; 0.4.0; 0.5.0; 0.6.0; 0.6.1; 0.6.5; 0.6.7; 0.7.1	Browse mode (0.3.0), Cloud node (0.7.1), Display map, Show documentation (0.2.0), Edit basic, Edit map, Evaluate (0.3.0), Exit program, Export map (0.5.0), File mode (0.1.0), Icons (0.6.7), Import/export branch (0.2.0), Init program, Link node (0.0.3), Modify edge, Modify node, Multiple maps (0.0.3), Multiple modes (0.1.0), Navigate map, New map, Open map, Print map (0.03), Save map, Zoom
JHotDraw Pert Releases: 5.2; 5.3; 5.4b1; 6.0b1; 7.0.7; 7.0.8; 7.0.9; 7.1; 7.2; 7.3; 7.3.1	Align, Dependency tool, Edit basic, Edit figure, Exit program, Export drawing (7.0.7), Group figures, Init program, Line tool (removed in 6.0b1), Modify figure, Multiple windows (7.0.7), New drawing, Open drawing, Order figures, Save as drawing, Selection tool, Snap to grid, Task tool, Text tool, Undo redo (5.3), Zoom (7.0.7)

4.2   Results of Feature Drift Measurement

In this evaluation, the drift of feature-oriented modularity was calculated by executing MOGGA on each release of the three applications. Based on observations from a series of pilot executions of MOGGA on target applications, we arrived at the following configuration of the algorithm that reduces the overall execution times while preserving high optimization level of the resulting modularizations. MOGGA was executed for a population of 300 individuals for 500 evolutionary iterations with mutation probability of 5 %. This configuration of the algorithm was applied to each release ten times to reduce the impact of non-determinism of genetic computation. The best of the solutions was used as a final result for each release. It is worth mentioning that while this config-uration of MOGGA was observed to produce Pareto-optimal solutions in acceptable timeframes for all investigated releases (i.e. in the order of magnitude of days), further adjustments to the algorithm parameters could lead to reducing these times even further.

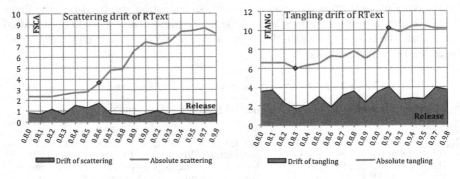

Fig. 10.   Drift measurements for releases of RText.

The results of measuring the drift of feature-oriented modularity using MOGGA are presented in the form of compass views in Fig. 10 for RText, in Fig. 11 for FreeMind, and in Fig. 12 for JHotDraw Pert. For each application, two plots are shown – one for evolution of scattering and one for evolution of tangling. In the plots, the absolute metric values are displayed as a line, whereas the calculated drift is displayed as an area at the bottom of the plots. This is aimed at simplifying the observation of development and relation of the drift to the absolute metric value.

The scattering drift plot for RText, shown in Fig. 10, can be divided into two distinct periods. The first period, ranging from release 0.8.0 to the 0.8.6, is a period of overall growth of the scattering drift. Despite the minor reductions observed in a few inter-mediate releases (i.e., 0.8.1, 0.8.3 and 0.8.5), the drift value doubled in this first period. This was also the period, in which the drift increased together with the absolute scattering and constituted on average 42 % of the scattering's value. During the second period, between releases 0.8.6 and 0.9.8, the drift was initially decreased, and thereafter main-tained a relatively constant level. Interestingly, this was achieved despite an over twofold increase in the absolute scattering of the application. This indicates that the modulari-zation decisions of the developers with respect to restraining features to a small number of packages were close to optimum in this period.

The tangling drift plot for RText, shown in Fig. 10, contains three interesting periods. Firstly, the period between the releases 0.8.0 and 0.8.3 is the period of sharp decreases of drift and absolute tangling and a decrease of the relative contribution of drift to the absolute tangling value. Secondly, between the releases 0.8.3 and 0.9.2, both the drift and the absolute tangling were increasing at a similar rate. Despite the overall growth, the drift appears here to be periodically reduced by the developers. Lastly, in the period 0.9.2 to 0.9.8 both the drift and the absolute tangling remain fairly constant. It is also this period, where the relative contribution of the drift is the lowest. However, it remains significantly higher than the relative contribution observed earlier of the scattering drift. Together, this data indicates that the features of RText were better localized than separated from one another in terms of packages.

The scattering drift plot for FreeMind, shown in Fig. 11, depicts several oscillations of the scattering drift over time. Initially, the oscillations are stronger but they eventually weaken over time. In comparison, the value of the absolute scattering of the application increases sharply between the releases 0.0.2 and 0.1.0, and thereafter remains approximately constant over the next 10 releases. This suggests that the application structure established at release 0.1.0 served well for the purpose of adding new features and extending the existing ones in a localized fashion.

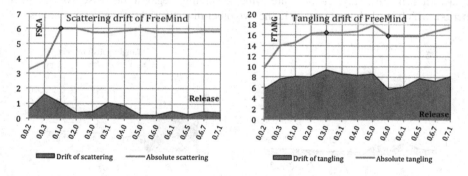

Fig. 11. Drift measurements for releases of FreeMind.

The tangling drift plot for FreeMind, shown in Fig. 11, can be divided into three periods: the period of increasing drift and increasing absolute tangling (0.0.2–0.3.0), the period of decreasing drift and stabilized absolute tangling (0.3.0–0.6.0), and the period of continued growth in both the drift and the absolute tangling. It can be seen that the overall changes of tangling drift and the absolute tangling reflect each other over time; only a minor difference in the growth rates can be observed, i.e. in the release 0.0.2 the drift constitutes 59 % of the absolute tangling value, whereas in release 0.7.1 it constitutes 47 % of the absolute tangling value. This high contribution indicates that FreeMind has a relatively high potential for improving the separation of features through source code restructuring. A potential trace of such efforts undertaken by the FreeMind developers is the transition from the release 0.5.0 to 0.6.0, where the drift of tangling was reduced by 34 %.

In both the scattering and tangling drift plots for JHotDraw Pert, shown in Fig. 12, it can be seen that the feature-oriented evolution of the application underwent a dramatic shift after release 6.0b1. Up till then, both the drifts and the absolute values of scattering and tangling were generally increasing. Starting from the release 7.0.7, these trends have changed. During the transition from 6.0b1 to 7.0.7, the drift of scattering was reduced almost completely, despite an increase in the absolute scattering, and both the drift and the absolute value of tangling were decreased significantly. Thereafter, both scattering and tangling drifts experienced only very small increases, whereas the absolute scattering value continued to rise and the absolute tangling value continued to slightly decrease.

It turns out that these observations find their reflection in the types of work on the application that the developers undertook in the period preceding the 7.0.7 release. The release notes from that period mention a large-scale architectural refactoring of the underlying JHotDraw framework. While it is difficult to tell whether improving the separation of individual features of Pert was among the intentions of these refactorings, it certainly became one of the results. Furthermore, the obtained reductions for both the drifts and the absolute value of scattering and tangling have shown to remain fairly stable after the source code refactoring – especially if compared to the rapid developments prior to the refactoring. Interestingly, the absolute value of tangling began to decrease over a longer period, which is a behavior unseen in the two other investigated software applications.

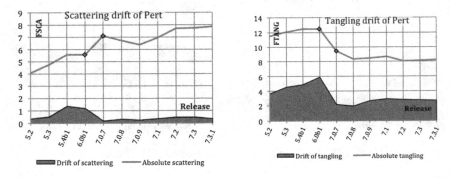

Fig. 12. Drift measurements for releases of JHotDraw Pert.

4.3 Discussion

The reported study applied the modularization compass approach to three real-world Java applications. The measured drift values were observed to evolve over the subsequent releases of the three applications in ways that were not trivially related to evolution of the absolute metric values. This indicates that for the study subjects, the drift measurements add a new type of information about the evolution of the applications' modularity over time.

The obtained drift measurements were used as an input to formulating a number of hypotheses about the reasons for the observed changes of the applications' feature-oriented modularity over time and a number of restructuring recommendations.

Overall, in all of the investigated applications the tangling drift constituted a significantly higher portion of FTANG than the scattering drift did for FSCA. This suggests that it is the separation of features from one another, rather than their confinement in few packages, that should be the primary restructuring goal for the three investigated applications. While at this point it is not possible to judge whether the insufficient separation of features is a common trait of layered object-oriented architectures, we see it as a viable hypothesis for further investigation.

Furthermore, periodical oscillations of the drift were observed in several cases that were not observed on the absolute metric values. This initial observation appears possibly be related to the observations of Anton and Potts [32] about the burst-like nature of adding new features. In a 50-year evolution of a telephone system, they observed new features to be introduced in discrete bursts, i.e. they exhibit punctuated rather than incremental or gradual evolution. These bursts were typically followed by periods of retrenchment that merged similar features and phased out older versions of new features. In our context, burst-like additions or enhancements of features could have resulted in rapid increases of drift, which were thereafter reduced during retrenchment periods.

5 Conclusions

The ability to change is both a blessing and a burden to software. On one hand, it allows systems to adapt to changing requirements imposed by users. On the other hand, changing existing source code is often difficult and the adoption of repetitive changes tends to erode the original structure of source code.

The work presented in this paper focused on the drift of feature-oriented modularity during the evolution of software applications. The proposed approach termed modularization compass measures this type of drift by comparing the original version of an application to its automatically remodularized counterpart. The remodularization process is performed by using a multi-objective grouping genetic algorithm that uses metrics of scattering, tangling, cohesion and coupling as the objectives for package structure optimization. The proposed package structures can be further reviewed and flexibly adjusted by a developer in the *Featureous Remodularization View*.

The approach was implemented in Java, and applied to three open-source Java applications. The obtained compass views showed significant differences between the evolution of absolute values of scattering and tangling and the evolution of their drifts. Based on the analysis of drifts over subsequent releases, we were able to identify when restructuring brings the largest improvement in feature modularity, and to determine that the restructuring effort for all three applications should focus on separating features from one another to reduce the significant drifts of their tangling.

Finally, the design and the evaluation of the approach resulted in several promising directions for future research and provided several preliminary observations about the general nature of evolution of software features.

References

1. Kemerer, C.F.: Software complexity and software maintenance: a survey of empirical research. Ann. Softw. Eng. **1**, 1–22 (1995)
2. Reid Turner, C., Fuggetta, A., Lavazza, L., Wolf, A.L.: A conceptual basis for feature engineering. J. Syst. Softw. **49**, 3–15 (1999)
3. Harrison, W., Box, P.: N degrees of separation: multi-dimensional separation of concerns. In: Proceedings of the 21st International Conference on Software Engineering (CSE 1999), pp. 10.00 (1999)
4. Parnas, D.L.: On the criteria to be used in decomposing systems into modules. Commun. ACM **15**, 1053–1058 (1972)
5. Letovsky, S.S.: Delocalized plans and program comprehension. Software, IEEE **3**, 41–49 (1986)
6. Eaddy, M., Zimmermann, T., Sherwood, K.D., Garg, V., Murphy, G.C., Nagappan, N., Aho, A.V.: Do crosscutting concerns cause defects? IEEE Trans. Software Eng. **34**, 497–515 (2008)
7. Rugaber, S., Stirewalt, K., Wills, L.M.: The interleaving problem in program understanding. In: Proceedings of 2nd Working Conference on Reverse Engineering, pp. 166–175. IEEE (1995)
8. Benestad, H.C., Anda, B., Arisholm, E.: Understanding cost drivers of software evolution: a quantitative and qualitative investigation of change effort in two evolving software systems. Empirical Softw. Eng. **15**, 166–203 (2010)
9. Hsi, I., Potts, C.: Studying the evolution and enhancement of software features. In: Proceedings of International Conference on Software Maintenance, pp. 143–151. IEEE, (2000)
10. Fischer, M., Gall, H.: Visualizing feature evolution of large-scale software based on problem and modification report data. J. Softw. Maintenance Evol. Res. Pract. **16**, 385–403 (2004)
11. Hou, D., Wang, Y.: An empirical analysis of the evolution of user-visible features in an integrated development environment. In: Proceedings of the 2009 Conference of the Center for Advanced Studies on Collaborative Research, pp. 122–135. IBM Corp. (2009)
12. Greevy, O., Ducasse, S., Girba, T.: Analyzing feature traces to incorporate the semantics of change in software evolution analysis. In: Proceedings of the 21st IEEE International Conference on Software Maintenance, ICSM 2005, pp. 347–356. IEEE (2005)
13. Olszak, A., Jørgensen, B.N.: Remodularizing Java programs for improved locality of feature implementations in source code. Sci. Comput. Program. **77**, 131–151 (2012)
14. van den Berg, K., Conejero, J.M., Hernández, J.: Analysis of crosscutting across software development phases based on traceability. In: Proceedings of the 2006 International Workshop on Early Aspects at ICSE, pp. 43–50. ACM (2006)
15. Brcina, R., Riebisch, M.: Architecting for evolvability by means of traceability and features. In: 23rd IEEE/ACM International Conference on Automated Software Engineering-Workshops, ASE Workshops 2008, pp. 72–81. IEEE (2008)
16. Wilde, N., Gomez, J.A., Gust, T., Strasburg, D.: Locating user functionality in old code. In: Proceedings Conference on Software Maintenance 1992, pp. 200–205. IEEE (1992)
17. Lehman, M.M.: Programs, life cycles, and laws of software evolution. Proc. IEEE **68**, 1060–1076 (1980)
18. Murphy, G.C., Lai, A., Walker, R.J., Robillard, M.P.: Separating features in source code: an exploratory study. In: Proceedings of the 23rd International Conference on Software Engineering, pp. 275–284. IEEE Computer Society (2001)

19. Briand, L.C., Daly, J.W., Wüst, J.: A unified framework for cohesion measurement in object-oriented systems. Empirical Softw. Eng. **3**, 65–117 (1998)
20. Briand, L.C., Daly, J.W., Wust, J.K.: A unified framework for coupling measurement in object-oriented systems. IEEE Trans. Software Eng. **25**, 91–121 (1999)
21. Harman, M., Tratt, L.: Pareto optimal search based refactoring at the design level. In: Proceedings of the 9th Annual Conference on Genetic and Evolutionary Computation, pp. 1106–1113. ACM (2007)
22. Seng, O., Bauer, M., Biehl, M., Pache, G.: Search-based improvement of subsystem decompositions. In: Proceedings of the 2005 Conference on Genetic and Evolutionary Computation, pp. 1045–1051. ACM (2005)
23. Tzerpos, V., Holt, R.C.: ACDC: an algorithm for comprehension-driven clustering. In: 2013 20th Working Conference on Reverse Engineering (WCRE), pp. 258–258. IEEE Computer Society (2000)
24. Rosenman, M., Gero, J.: Reducing the Pareto optimal set in multicriteria optimization (with applications to Pareto optimal dynamic programming). Engineering Optimization **8**, 189–206 (1985)
25. Chaudhari, P., Dharaskar, R., Thakare, V.: Computing the most significant solution from Pareto front obtained in multi-objective evolutionary. Int. J. Adv. Comput. Sci. Appl. (IJACSA) **1**, 63–68 (2010)
26. Olszak, A., Jørgensen, B.N.: Featureous: an integrated environment for feature-centric analysis and modification of object-oriented software. Int. J. Comput. Sci. Inf. Syst. **6**, 58–75 (2011)
27. http://featureous.org/
28. http://recoder.sourceforge.net/
29. http://fifesoft.com/rtext/
30. http://freemind.sourceforge.net/
31. http://www.jhotdraw.org/
32. Anton, A.I., Potts, C.: Functional paleontology: the evolution of user-visible system services. IEEE Trans. Software Eng. **29**, 151–166 (2003)

Can Organisational Theory and Multi-agent Systems Influence Next Generation Enterprise Modelling?

Balbir S. Barn[1(✉)], Tony Clark[1], and Vinay Kulkarni[2]

[1] Department of Computer Science, Middlesex University,
The Burroughs, London, U.K
{b.barn,t.n.clark}@mdx.ac.uk
[2] TRDDC, Tata Consultancy Services, Pune, India
vinay.vkulkarni@tcs.com

Abstract. This paper proposes that the current enterprise modelling approaches are overly reliant on the know how or tacit knowledge of enterprise architects for addressing organisational challenges such as business-IT alignment. Furthermore, current modelling languages only encourage linear thinking. By drawing upon existing research on (computational) organisation theory and multi-agent systems, we propose implementation requirements for a next generation enterprise modelling language that supports agent based simulation. The language is motivated by a detailed case study that illustrates the benefit of using simulation style languages.

Keywords: Organisation theory · Multi-agent systems · Actor theory · Enterprise modelling

1 Introduction

The modern enterprise is faced with the tricky challenge of responding to external drivers such as merger and acquisitions or potential new markets by adapting and managing internal change. Any change has to be managed with respect to business-IT alignment within the enterprise. Up to now, such a response has been dependent upon human expertise based on tacit knowledge and experience or "know how". Such a position is not sustainable with the rapid pace of change attributed to technology and globalization. This is confirmed with research that indicates that Strategic business-IT alignment has remained an ongoing concern for organisations [1] and researchers have addressed the importance of alignment and in particular the need for congruence between business strategy and IT strategy [2].

One specific approach that has been used to bear upon the problem of business alignment is the role of Enterprise Architecture (EA) [3]. However, the predominant theme has focused on developing enterprise models that are descriptive in nature and hence needing human expertise for their interpretation (see ([4,5])

© Springer International Publishing Switzerland 2015
A. Holzinger et al. (Eds.): ICSOFT 2014, CCIS 555, pp. 202–216, 2015.
DOI: 10.1007/978-3-319-25579-8_12

for two obvious examples). As a result, current approaches to Enterprise Modelling (EM) exhibit a high degree of latency in meeting key objectives such as alignment, adaptation *etc.* Thus EA in its current state does not readily lend itself to supporting the type of analysis that key decision makers typically utilize. Such stakeholders demand: ease of comprehension of the entire business so that decision-making can lead to efficient and effective change. In particular they require the ability to play out various what-if (*i.e.*, what will be the consequences of such and such action) and if-what (*i.e.*, what would have led to such and such situation) scenarios to arrive at the right response, establish feasibility of the response, and estimate a ROI of the response. Thus ways of simulating an enterprise are needed and currently EA modelling approaches do not readily support this requirement.

Away from the EA modelling community, organisational theory and in particular computational organisational theory manifested in technologies such as multi-agent systems provides an opportunity to re-purpose existing research outcomes to address the EA simulation and alignment conundrum. In doing so, this position paper proposes that next generation Enterprise modelling languages should draw upon concepts from organisational theory and multi-agent systems in order that appropriate machinery can be implemented to support the simulation requirement.

The remainder of this paper is structured as follows: Sect. 2 presents key concepts from organisational theory and multi-agent systems. Specifically it draws upon the established research relationship that exists between the two areas. Section 3 presents the main contribution of the paper and proposes a novel language based approach to enterprise modelling for simulation. The proposal draws upon components, goal modelling and agent technologies. This is illustrated by a detailed case study in Sect. 4. Section 5 discusses our plans for addressing the research challenges raised by the approach.

2   Organisational Theory and Multi-agent Systems

Our starting premise is the view that there is a pressing need for next generation EM languages to address the requirements described in Sect. 1 which can be broadly summarised as languages that: are machine manipulatable, support simulation through executability, and are model based. Such requirements raise two questions: What needs to be simulated? Secondly, what technologies can we deploy to support execution? In answering the first question we need to revert to organisational theory to understand the meaning of organisation and its constituting elements. Human organisations in particular have been the subject of detailed analysis from a range of disciplines including engineering, economics, psychology and sociology [6]. The resulting analysis of the literature for organisational theory leads to a persuasive argument for the use of agent technology, particularly multi-agent systems as candidate technology for supporting the simulation/executability requirements identified.

Ours is an organisational society such that organisations are the dominant characteristic of modern societies. One rationale for the existence of organisations posited by Carley and Gassser is that they exist to overcome the cognitive, physical, temporal and institutional limitations of individual agency [7]. While there are many ways in which these limitations can be overcome and the structure, form or architecture of an organisation contributes to such efforts, decades of research indicate that there is no optimal organisational design. Instead, the challenge morphs into one of adaptability and response to change. First, we present here, a necessarily brief overview of some of the key definitions and perspectives on organisations that underpin how we intend to articulate the concept of an organisation in the context of the model driven enterprise [8]. We first begin with a definition of the term organisation recognising that there are multiple definitions depending upon the perspective taken. The definition is reported from [9]:

> *organisations are social units (or human groupings) deliberately constructed and reconstructed to seek specific goals.*

We explore this definition further by considering how the study of organisations has generally investigated the constituent elements of an organisation and three dominant theoretical perspectives informing research. Leavitt identifies some core features of organisations [10]:

Social. Structure regularised aspects of relationships among participants in an organisation that may be both normative (embodying what ought to be) or factual order (actual structures).

Participants. Individuals who in return for a variety of inducements make contributions to the organisation. Participants may belong to more than one organisation.

Goals. An organisational goal is a desired state of affairs which the organisation attempts to realise. Goals are central to how an organisation functions and are often vague or very specific.

Technology. This is the means by which work is performed in an organisation. Technology can be interpreted as a manufacturing plant, the software systems enabling workers to perform work or even technical knowledge and skills of participants.

Environment. Organisations exist in a specific physical, socio-technical and cultural environment to which they must respond and adapt. All aspects of an organisation are influenced and contextualised by the environment. For example, software systems are purchased from external providers or developed by technicians trained in some other organisation.

These features are generic to organisations and can form the basis for extracting key concepts of an organisation. Carley [7] presents a similar set. Note that these features may vary in some way when viewed through a particular perspective or metaphor. The last century has seen three dominant perspectives (and overlaps) dominating research in organisation theory: organisations as Rational Systems; organisations as Natural Systems and organisations as Open Systems. A rational system perspective denotes a focus on efficiency and optimisation and ultimately presents a reductionist model. The open systems perspective is of most relevance to us as it ranges from a simple clockwork view (a dynamic system with pre-determined motions), cybernetic view (a system capable of self-regulation in terms of externally prescribed criterion such as a thermostat) to an open system (a system capable of self-maintenance based on throughputs of resources such as a living cell) [11].

These views are categorised by Gazendam [12] and conform to essentially two categories: Classical organisational theories and Systems theories. He suggests that classical theories have a strong correspondence to a machine metaphor where the organisation as a whole consists of agents performing tasks in fixed structures consisting of agent tasks, communication paths and spatio-temporal orderings. Systems theories on the other hand view the organisation comprising of sub-organisations fulfilling a specific function. Gazendam furthermore notes that: "System theories of organisation are relatively poor because they only pay attention to the system level, and remain rather abstract."

Theories based on the machine metaphor have formed the basis of research on (multi-) agent-based system in the late 1980 s and 1990s to study alternative viewpoints for describing organisations [13]. Here an *agent* is an autonomous and intelligent being such as a human or a simulator of a human realised by software (a computer agent) [12]. Systems that are comprised entirely of computer agents have been used as simulations of organisations and correspondingly offer interesting perspectives on the study of organisations. Multi-agent systems (MAS) and the associated Computational organisational Theory [7] provide the collective apparatus for investigation.

Computational organisational Theory (COT) aims to understand and model both human organisations and artificial organisations (multi-agent systems) that exhibit collective organisational properties such as the need to act collaboratively. Typical outputs of such research are the generation of new concepts and theories about organising and organisations. Historically many applications and models have been constructed but our review of the current enterprise modelling literature indicates that COT has not yet been applied to some of the tricky problems of enterprise modelling such as Business-IT alignment discussed in the introduction.

There are immediate information processing requirements that are deducible from the definition of organisation such as: information ubiquity, tasks, uncertainty distribution of organisational intelligence and necessity of communication through a model-based perspective. COT also suggests that: organisations are modelable, and so are manipulatable; are able to be designed to fit specific needs and there is an assumption that the costs of modelling and researching organisations in simulation mode rather than in vivo are lower [7].

Key characteristics of organisations such as that described by Leavitt and Carley emphasise structure and behaviour. Hoogendoorn et al. [14] propose these two aspects as necessary pre-requisites for modelling change when using MAS. In their proposal, organisations are described solely by the way groups and roles are arranged to form a whole. Related to this, Giorgini et al. use the i* framework [15] to define a series of architectural organisational styles which act as metaclasses and offer a set of design parameters for coordinating goals, actions and behavior and therefore govern how an organisation functions [16,17]. Our position contributes to enterprise modelling technologies by drawing upon research outputs from COT to meet the needs of an adaptive organisation located in a systematic understanding of socio-technical nature of an organisation [18].

If MAS and COT are an appropriate way forward, then there are additional requirements for methods that can support COT based approaches. Those tasked with modelling enterprises need guidance that: "allow the description of social structures, permit the use of tools to perform project management, and include IDE or CASE tools that facilitate the analysis and design of MASs [19]". Furthermore, all methodologies need to contain enough abstractions to model and support MASs, which are usually structured as societies of agents that play roles and exchange information following predefined protocols [20]. Isern et al. then go onto review a range of agent-oriented methodologies by evaluating their underlying meta models. Analysis of these meta models guides us toward the essential features of the language proposed in Sect. 3.

We have posited that current approaches to EM presents a linear form of enquiry requiring tacit knowledge based on an Architect's know how that prevents scaling up to rapidly address "what if" type of questions. Adopting technologies based on MAS requires robust models for representing the complexity and dynamic nature of organisations as they respond to external business drivers. In particular then MAS can be used to provide simulation models for exploration of complex environments. Simulation models can be explanatory models that can help identify kinds of behaviour expected under specific conditions or they can be predictive models that determine more precisely the kind of behaviour a system will display in the future [21].

Luck *et al.* propose a grouping of the agent-technologies, tools and techniques that can address these types of simulation for EM for theory building about an enterprise at three levels: organisational-level (focusing on larger aggregations of structures; Interaction-level (collaboration, communication and decision making between agents) and Agent-level (learning and reasoning [19]. Cross cutting concerns such as agent programming languages and methodologies (noted earlier) provide practical steps towards realisation of agent systems.

In the next section, we discuss how this partitioning has been used to influence our proposal.

3   Next Generation EM

We posit that any approach that is derived from ideas from the previous sections relies on being able to represent and process an organisation that is expressed in terms of a component-based abstraction. We envisage a product-line approach [22] whereby a suite of tools based on this abstraction is used to facilitate a collection of different organisation analysis and simulation activities. Each activity will constitute a domain, *e.g.*, cost analysis, resource analysis, mergers and acquisition, regulatory compliance. In principle, each new domain will require a new domain specific language to represent the concepts. How should such a proliferation of domains be accommodated by a single component abstraction?

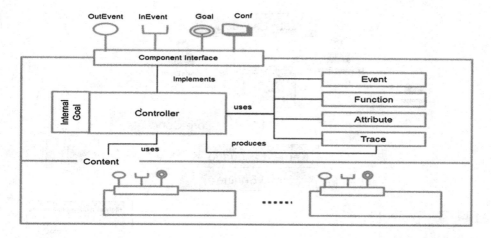

Fig. 1. Component abstraction (Core Concepts).

Our proposal is to construct an extensible kernel language called Enterprise Simulation Language (ESL), that is used as the target of translations from a range of domain specific languages (DSLs) that have been designed to support organisational analysis from a particular perspective. Each DSL supports an organisation analysis and simulation use-case. We then aim to construct a virtual machine for the kernel language so that it is executable. Model execution supports organisation simulation and some analysis use-cases. Links to external packages such as model-checkers will complete the analysis use-cases.

The use of a single kernel language provides a single focus of development effort and can help minimise the problem of point-to-point integration of analysis methods. Our hypothesis is that a small core collection of concepts, including *component, interface, goal, event, function* as shown in Fig. 1, are a suitable basis for most types of analysis and simulation use-case and therefore the kernel language will be defined in terms of these concepts.

Given its ability to accommodate multiple simulation and analysis use-cases, we envisage the language being the basis of a suite of organisational modelling, simulation and analysis tools, presented in the form of a single integrated extensible meta-tool EA Simulation Environment (*EASE-Y*) shown in Fig. 2. Since organisational information is likely to be very large (at least many tens of thousands of model elements) it is important the tool is implemented efficiently, is scalable, supports distributed concurrent development and is flexible in terms of its architecture. To this end we aim that the kernel language should be compiled to a machine language running on a dedicated kernel engine, the language integrates with standard repository technology, and can run equally well on single machines, networked machines and via the cloud.

Organisations consist of many autonomous components. Components are organised into dynamically changing hierarchical groups, operate concurrently, and manage goals that affect their behavior. We aim for the kernel language to reflect these features by having an operational semantics based on the Actor

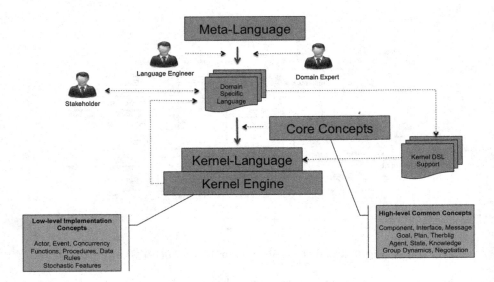

Fig. 2. The EASE-Y architecture.

Model of Computation (AMC) [23] and its relation to organisations, or iOrgs [24]. Actors have an address and manage an internal state that is private and cannot be shared with other actors in the system. Execution proceeds by sending asynchronous messages from a source actor to the address of a target actor. Synchronous messages can be achieved by sending an actor in an asynchronous message to which the result should be sent. Each message is handled in a separate execution thread associated with the target of the message and the message itself (collectively referred to as a task). During task-execution an actor may choose to change its state and behavior (becoming a new actor) that is immediately available to process the next message sent to the target address.

Our claim is that the AMC provides a suitable basis for execution and analysis of the concepts discussed in Sect. 2. Actors, sometimes individually and sometimes collectively, can be used to represent the features of a component. The rest of this section lists the key features that must be supported by the kernel language and how the actor approach can support them:

[**Adaptability**]. This is required because organisational components may change dynamically during a simulation. Resources, individuals, and even departments may move location, and have an affect on results. Furthermore, the behavior of a component may change over time as information changes within the system. An actor can, in principle, change behavior as a result of handling each message.

[**Modularity**]. Each part of an organisation is intended to perform a business function that can be expressed in terms of a collection of operations. The internal organisation in terms of people, IT systems and the implementation of various business processes is usually hidden. The AMC provides an interface of message handlers for each actor. Both the state and the implementation of the message interface are hidden from the outside. The specification of an actor in terms of its external interface can be expressed in terms of LTL formulas that constitute the external goal for a component.

[**Autonomy**]. A key feature of an organisation is that the behavior of each subcomponent is autonomous. A particular department is responsible for its own behavior and can generate output without the need for a stimulus. The AMC is highly concurrent with each actor being able to spawn multiple threads and over which other actors have no control (unless granted by the thread originator).

[**Distribution**]. An organisation may be distributed and this may be an important feature of its simulation. Furthermore, we have a requirement that the tooling for organisational analysis and simulation should support distributed concurrent development. The AMC associates actors with addresses to which messages are sent. Execution does not rely on the particular location of the actor (i.e. the mapping between the address and the actor behavior) that can be in the same address space, via a network connection or in the cloud.

[**Intent**]. In addition to autonomous behavior, an organisation component exhibits intent. This might take the form of an internal goal that guides the behavior of the component to ensure that it contributes to the overall mission of the organisation. Although actors do not directly provide support for such goals, we intend to use results from the field of Multi-Agent Systems [13] where support for goal-based reasoning is provided within each agent when determining how to handle messages.

[**Composition**]. An organisation is an assembly of components. As noted above, the topology of an organisation may be static or dynamic. Actors can be nested in more than one way. Actor behaviors are declared and new actors are dynamically created with an initial behavior (much like Java classes). The scope of actor behaviors can be nested to provide modularity. Adding a dynamically created actor to the state of a parent actor provides composition. Such actors can be sent as part of messages. If the source actor retains the address, then the communicated actor becomes shared between the source and the target of the message.

[**Extensibility**]. Our aim is to support a number of simulation and analysis use-cases. As such the kernel language will need to support a collection of independent domains. Whilst we expect the DSLs to target the kernel language it is likely that each domain will have its own fundamental concepts and actions (so-called Therbligs, [25]). We envisage such domain-specific features being defined in the kernel language and then pre-loaded to form an augmented target language for DSL translations.

[**Event-Driven**]. Organisational components cannot rely on when communications occur and where they originate. In addition, a component may simply cause an event to occur without knowing who will consume the event. This is to be contrasted with message-based communication where the target is always known to the source and where sometimes the message carries information about

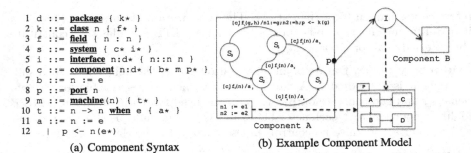

```
 1 d ::= package { k* }
 2 k ::= class n { f* }
 3 f ::= field { n : n }
 4 s ::= system { c* i* }
 5 i ::= interface n:d* { n::n n }
 6 c ::= component n:d* { b* m p* }
 7 b ::= n := e
 8 p ::= port n
 9 m ::= machine(n) { t* }
10 t ::= n -> n when e { a* }
11 a ::= n := e
12   | p <- n(e*)
```

(a) Component Syntax   (b) Example Component Model

Fig. 3. A component DSL.

Each component translates to a behaviour definition whose argument names are the component state variables. In addition the behaviour has a distinguished argument called state whose value is the current state of the component, and an argument for each port. The body of the behaviour is a sequence of rules generated from the component's machine. Each transition translates to a rule whose precondition checks the state and the transition guard, whose pattern corresponds to the interface operation, and whose command sends messages to a port before performing a **become** supplying the behaviour with the new state variable values. Each interface becomes a behaviour that maintains a list of actors to whom messages are broadcast.

(a) Translation Process

```
 1 let act I(actors) {
 2   add(a) -> become I(a:as);
 3   m      -> for a in as do send a(m)
 4 }
 5 let act A(state,p,n1,n2) {
 6   [c1 and state = s0]f1(g,h) -> {
 7     send p(k(g));
 8     become A(s1,p,g,h)
 9   }
10   ...
11 } in
12 let i = new I([]) in
13 let a = new A(s0,i,e1,e2) in
14 let b = new B(...) in
15 i.add(b)
```

(b) Example Translation

Fig. 4. Translation from DSL to ESL.

the source that becomes available to the target. The AMC is based on message passing where the source knows the address of the target. Given that the kernel language is the target of DSL transformations, support for event-based communication becomes an architectural issue where events are simply messages that are sent to an actor container that is responsible for delivering event-messages to dynamically changing collections of actors. Providing that the transformation establishes the correct assembly of actors and conforms to an appropriate message passing protocol then component events are supported without needing to make them an intrinsic part of the kernel.

Our current work on ESL has positioned ESL as a General Purpose Language (GPL) that is a kernel language for representing organisations. Organisations consist of many autonomous components, organised into dynamically changing hierarchical groups, operating concurrently, and managing goals that affect their behaviour. The details of the syntax and semantics of ESL are outside the scope of this paper. In summary, however, the syntax of the language comprises commands, expressions, patters and commands that are guarded by patterns and boolean expressions. The semantics of the language are based on the operational semantics of the AMC [23] and its relation to organisations, or iOrgs [24]. In essence, this becomes a series of object traces of both the system

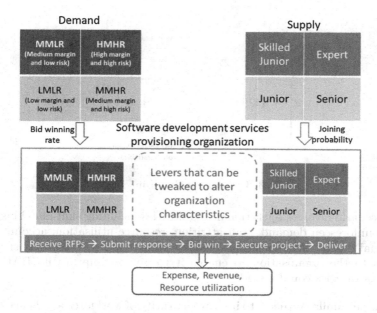

Fig. 5. Software provisioning organisation.

and individual actor traces. Currently, ESL is implemented in the programming language Racket.

For ESL to be effective at representing organisations, multiple DSLs that target ESL are necessary. A simplified example DSL is shown in Fig. 3(a) together with an example model in Fig. 3(b). Components communicate using messages whose types are defined by interfaces. The state of a component is defined by local variables and the behaviour by a state machine. All data is defined by class models.

An overview of the translation of model Fig. 3(b) to ESL shown in Fig. 4 where components and interfaces are translated to actors, messages and data is encoded as terms, and the state transition machine is encoded as guarded pattern-matching behaviour rules. Notice that ESL is more expressive than the DSL (actors are not static entities, unlike components, for example) although the latter lends itself to a familiar graphical syntax.

4   Case Study Illustration

How can ESL and DSLs be used together to carry out enterprise modelling activities? In this section, using a realistic case study we provide an illustrative example of how we envisage use of the ESL technology.

Consider an IT Services provider that delivers a range of service products such as development, maintenance and testing in response to requests for proposals. A project is resourced, executed using existing processes, and delivered to customers with resources being subsequently released. This business as usual

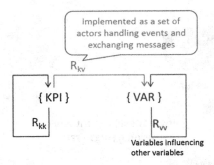

Fig. 6. Decision making using ESL.

(BAU) scenario involves operational complexities including skill-matching, dealing with unforeseen demand, staff attrition, resource utilisation, accounting for operational delays, while ensuring business targets are met. Various strategies are open to the organisation to enable it to aim to improve its BAU state. Example strategies could include:

- Increase in similar projects to improve maturity of workforce and hence quality and track record;
- Reduce project costs;
- Investment in training and productivity tools.

Each strategy however, has various scenarios as well as factors such as supply and demand that are dynamic and also dependent on the external business environment. A key requirement for management is know which strategy would be beneficial amongst the various alternatives and when to switch from one strategy to another so as to maintain or improve existing operating levels.

Figure 5 shows a software provisioning organisation operating in a static supply and demand context. It is measured on three metrics: revenue, expense and resource utilisation. Demand comprises of four kinds of software development projects: low margin low risk (LMLR), medium margin low risk (MMLR), medium margin high risk (MMHR) and high margin high risk (HMHR). The organisation bids for these projects and has different win-to-bid ratio for different kinds of projects.

A win-to-bid ratio signifies market perception of the ability to deliver a given kind of project on time and with the desired quality, and is largely determined by track record. Supply comprises four kinds of workforce resources: junior (J), skilled junior (SJ), senior (S) and expert (E), *e.g.*, execution of an HMHR project demands larger proportion of experts than, say, an LMLR project. SJ is a critical resource for all kinds of projects and hence is always in demand. Thus, the workforce composition J:SJ:S:E dictates what kind of projects can be delivered. Technology such as programmer productivity tools and automated testing can influence effectiveness at a price. A reserve of resources may be maintained in order to take advantage of opportunities as they arise.

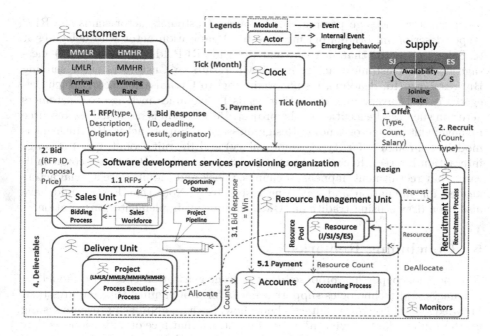

Fig. 7. Implementation architecture.

The organisation is faced with several business-critical decisions such as: Are resources optimally loaded or is there some slack? Will quoting a reduced price or delivery time be more effective at winning more bids? Will staff training or the use of productivity tools reduce delivery time? When would the benefits start outweighing the costs? What J:SJ:S:E configuration delivers optimal KPIs? What would be the impact of scarcity of experts on KPIs? What would be the result of focusing on high margin projects only?

Figure 6 shows a pictorial depiction of decision making in ESL. KPI denotes the set of observable variables indicative of system state or, in other words, goodness of the decision. VAR denotes the set of influencing variables having a control on the system state. Coherent influencing variables are grouped together into an Actor constituting its state. It is possible that an influencing variable may belong to more than one actor. As a result, state change of such variables needs to be propagated to other actors (having the variable as a constituent of its state) as well. This is implemented through message passing between the relevant set of actors. Value of a KPI is typically a function, not a mathematical formula though, of the values of its influencing variables which in turn may have a discrete value or a time-varying value distribution or a function over other influencing variables. These influences are implemented in terms of message passing between the relevant actors.

Figure 7 shows the organisation being modelled as a set of interacting actors namely, Customers, Supply, Organisation, Sales unit, Delivery unit, Resource management unit, Accounts and Recruitment unit. Actors interact with each other through message passing. For instance, Customers actor sends the RFP (type, description, originator) message to Organisation actor who delegates it to Sales unit actor that in turn send the Bid (RFP Id, proposal, price) message back to Customers actor. A bid win results in Customers actor sending Bid response (Id, deadline, result, originator) to Organisation actor which delegates it to Delivery unit actor that sends Deliverables message to Customers actor on successful execution of the project. Resignation is modelled as Resource management unit actor sending Resign message to Supply actor. Recruitment is modelled through Offer (type, count, salary) and Recruit (count, type) message interaction between Recruitment unit and Supply actors. Parameter count indicates that recruitment happens in chunks. Clock and Monitor are special actors needed for simulation and reporting respectively. Note that Fig. 7 could have also been drawn using traditional UML component implementation notation.

5   Concluding Remarks

This position paper has proposed that current generation enterprise modelling languages and technologies support a linear form of enquiry that requires tacit knowledge based on an Architect's know how. Such an approach prevents scaling up to rapidly address "what if" type of questions that face organisations as they seek to adapt to respond to ongoing change. At an abstract level, these types of requirements have been studied in other disciplines, including economics, political science, philosophy and linguistics leading to computation based organisational theories and technologies for describing agent interaction, communication and decision-making. For the kind of decision making problem illustrated in this paper, industry relies extensively on Excel. Such an approach typically represents the relationships between influencing factors or system variables in terms of static equations. The lack of support in expressing temporal aspects of an organisation (including the interference between variables with respect to time) limits the use of spreadsheets to being a data computation aid instead of data-driven decision making tool.

We have presented an argument that traces a route through (computational) organisation theory to propose that next generation enterprise modelling languages should address COT and multi-agent system approaches to provide a rich simulation platform that supports both explanatory models and predictive models for the "what if" question. In doing so, we recognise that there are open-ended research questions around methodology and proposed the simulation platform. We plan to validate our proposition in a number of ways. We are currently developing a collection of representative case studies based on real-world data in a laboratory setting. One case study illustrates how the proposed ideas and techniques can help data-driven decision making in an IT services providing organisation. Another case study will address merger and acquisition problem in wealth management domain. We intend to run co-design workshops with Business Management domain experts in order to evaluate their response to our proposals. We are currently extending μLEAP [26] to be the target kernel language. We have designed and implemented the kernel language meta-model as a prototype and intend to develop further versions as a virtual machine, possibly using multiple Java VMs as targets.

References

1. Luftman, J.: Assessing business-it alignment maturity. Strat. Inf. Technol. Gov. **4**, 99 (2004)
2. Chan, Y.E., Reich, B.H.: It alignment: what have we learned? J. Inf. Technol. **22**, 297–315 (2007)
3. Lankhorst, M.: Introduction to enterprise architecture. In: Lankhorst, M. (ed.) Modelling, Communication and Analysis. The Enterprise Engineering Series, pp. 1–10. Springer, Heidelberg (2005)
4. Veken, K.V.D.: Enterprise architecture modelling to support collaboration-the archimate language as a tool for communication (2013)
5. Zachman, J.A.: A framework for information systems architecture. IBM Sys. J **26**, 276–292 (1987)
6. Scott, W.R.: Organizations. Prentice-Hall, Englewood Cliffs (1992)
7. Carley, K.M., Gasser, L.: Computational organization theory, A modern approach to distributed artificial intelligence, Multiagent systems. MIT press, Cambridge (1999)
8. Clark, T., Kulkarni, V., Barn, B., France, R., Frank, U., Turk, D.: Towards the model driven organization. In: 2014 47th Hawaii International Conference on System Sciences (HICSS), pp. 4817–4826. IEEE (2014)
9. Parsons, T., Jones, I.: Structure and Process in Modern Societies, vol. 3. Free Press, New York (1960)
10. Leavitt, H.J.: Applied organization change in industry: structural, technical and human approaches. New Perspect. Organ. Res. **55**, 71 (1964)
11. Buckley, W.: Sociology and Modern Systems Theory. Prentice-Hall, Englewood Cliffs (1967)
12. Gazendam, H.W., Jorna, R.J., et al.: Theories about architecture and performance of multi-agent systems. University of Groningen (1998)
13. Wooldridge, M.: An Introduction to Multiagent Systems. Wiley, New york (2009)
14. Hoogendoorn, M., Jonker, C.M., Schut, M.C., Treur, J.: Modeling centralized organization of organizational change. Comput. Math. Organ. Theor. **13**, 147–184 (2007)
15. Yu, E.: Towards modelling and reasoning support for early-phase requirements engineering. In: Butterworth, R. (ed.) Proceedings of the Third IEEE International Symposium on Engineering, pp. 226–235. IEEE (1997)
16. Kolp, M., Giorgini, P., Mylopoulos, J.: Multi-agent architectures as organizational structures. Auton. Agents Multi Agent Sys. **13**, 3–25 (2006)
17. Argente, E., Julian, V., Botti, V.: Multi-agent system development based on organizations. Electron. Notes Theor. Comput. Sci. **150**, 55–71 (2006)
18. Bean, S.: Re-thinking enterprise architecture using systems and complexity approaches. J. Enterp. Archit. **6**, 7–13 (2010)
19. Luck, M., McBurney, P., Shehory, O., Willmott, S.: Agent technology: computing as interaction (a roadmap for agent based computing) (2005)
20. Isern, D., Sánchez, D., Moreno, A.: Organizational structures supported by agent-oriented methodologies. J. Sys. Softw. **84**, 169–184 (2011)

21. Siebers, P.O., Aickelin, U.: Introduction to multi-agent simulation. arXiv preprint (2008). arXiv:0803.3905
22. Reinhartz-Berger, I., Cohen, S., Bettin, J., Clark, T., Sturm, A.: Domain Engineering. Springer, Heidelberg (2013)
23. Hewitt, C.: Actor model of computation: scalable robust information systems. arXiv preprint (2010). arXiv:1008.1459
24. Hewitt, C.: Norms and commitment for iorgs (tm) information systems: Direct logic (tm) and participatory grounding checking. arXiv preprint (2009). arXiv:0906.2756
25. Stanton, N.A.: Hierarchical task analysis: developments, applications, and extensions. Appl. Ergon. **37**, 55–79 (2006)
26. Clark, T., Barn, B.S.: Outsourcing service provision through step-wise transformation. In: Proceedings of the 7th India Software Engineering Conference, ACM (2014)

Software Defect Prediction in Automotive and Telecom Domain: A Life-Cycle Approach

Rakesh Rana[1(✉)], Miroslaw Staron[1], Jörgen Hansson[2],
Martin Nilsson[3], and Wilhelm Meding[4]

[1] Computer Science and Engineering, Chalmers University of Gothenburg,
Gothenburg, Sweden
rakesh.rana@gu.se
[2] School of Informatics, University of Skövde, Skövde, Sweden
[3] Volvo Car Group, Gothenburg, Sweden
[4] Ericsson, Göteborg, Sweden

Abstract. Embedded software is playing an ever increasing role in providing functionality and user experience. At the same time, size and complexity of this software is also increasing which bring new challenges for ensuring quality and dependability. For developing high quality software with superior dependability characteristics requires an effective software development process with greater control. Methods of software defect predictions can help optimize the software verification and validation activities by providing useful information for test resource allocation and release planning decisions. We review the software development and testing process for two large companies from the automotive and telecom domain and map different defect prediction methods and their applicability to their lifecycle phases. Based on the overview and current trends we also identify possible directions for software defect prediction techniques and application in these domains.

Keywords: Defect prediction · Software life cycle · Automotive · Telecom · Test resource allocation · Release readiness

1 Introduction

Software today is an important part of telecom as well as automotive products. The demands for new products and functionalities in these domains keep pushing the size and complexity while also adding pressure to reduce cost and time to market. To meet the demands of high quality and reliability - significant effort is devoted on software V&V (Verification & Validation). Testing the software is an important part of software V&V used for ensuring correct functionality and reliability of software systems; but at the same time software testing is also a resource intensive activity accounting for up to 50 % of total software development costs [1] and even more for safety critical software systems.

Defects in software provide observable indicators to track the quality of software project/product under development. Different methods for analysis of software defect data have been developed and evaluated, these methods have also been used to provide

© Springer International Publishing Switzerland 2015
A. Holzinger et al. (Eds.): ICSOFT 2014, CCIS 555, pp. 217–232, 2015.
DOI: 10.1007/978-3-319-25579-8_13

range of benefits such as allowing early planning and allocation of resources to meet the desired goals of projects. Different methods of software defect analysis and predictions have different characteristics, they need variety of input data, are appropriate to be applied at specific levels and for certain applications. In this paper we summarize the state of the art methods for software defect predications. We place these methods on the software development life cycle of two companies from the telecom and automotive domain and map them to their appropriate level of granularity and application type.

We also contend for the position that with technology enabling collection and analysis of in-operations data efficiently in the automotive domain will enable software designers and developers to use this information to design more robust and user friendly features and functions.

This paper is the extended version of our previous work [2] where the focus of work was mapping software defect prediction techniques over the automotive software life cycle. In this paper we include another company from a different (telecom) domain. Software development within these two companies have large differences, thus in this paper we take a life cycle approach of applicability of software defect prediction techniques where software development process follows V-model (automotive domain) and for agile process (telecom domain).

2 Background and Related Work

2.1 Related Work

Expert opinions were used and their performance compared to other data based models in study by Staron and Meding [3] of defect data from the telecom domain where they found that simple statistical models based on moving averages provided better predictions for weekly defect inflow. Predictions by experts was also compared to predictions using software reliability growth models in the study by Almering et al. [4] reporting that SRGMs outperformed expert predictions who gave more conservative estimates.

Long term predictive power of SRGMs within the automotive domain was studied in authors earlier works [5, 6], demonstrating their usefulness in making defect and reliability predictions. Application of SRGMs for defect prediction has also been studied by Woods [7] on industrial data and different models performance compared in work by Pham [8].

Number of software metrics based on code characteristics such as size, complexity etc., and metrics based on changes to software artifacts during development have also been successfully used to classify defect prone software modules or estimate software defect densities. Khoshgoftaar and Allen [9] used logistic regression for classifying modules as fault-prone, while Menzies, Greenwald and Frank [10] used static code attributes to make defect prone forecasts. Methods that use code and change metrics as inputs and use machine learning methods for classification and forecasting have also been studied by Gondra [11] and Ceylan et al. [12].

Fenton and Neil [13] critique the use of statistical based software defect prediction models for their lack of causal link modelling and proposes use of Bayesian Belief

Networks (BBNs). Bayesian Nets have been used to show their applicability for defect forecasting at very early stages of software projects [14].

Our study complements earlier studies in defect predictions by illustrating when different methods of SDP are most appropriate over a software development life cycle. Based on the trends of software development and market demands, we also provide the road map of future for SDP within the automotive domain that can be helpful for effective application of these methods for making better predictions and thus enabling developing high quality and reliable software within this domain.

2.2   Software Development Life Cycle in Automotive Domain

Most automotive OEMs follow Model Driven Development (MDD) and since car/platform projects are often large and spread over several years, they are executed in number of iterations. In literature and development standards, software development life cycle in embedded and automotive domain has been illustrated as variants of iterative development based on spiral process model [15] and approaches based on V-model [16, 17].

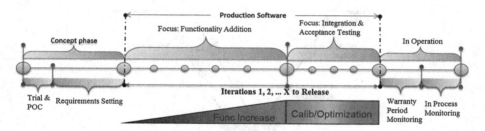

Fig. 1. Overview of software development lifecycle in the automotive domain.

The full EE (Electronics and Electrical System) development which constitutes the complete development of software and hardware (Electronic Control Units) in automotive domain, the different stages of process can be illustrated by Fig. 1, which are:

1. **Concept Phase:** Where a new functionality is designed and tested on prototypes and Proof of Concept (POC) is demonstrated.
2. **Production Software:** The main requirements (on vehicle level) are set for the upgrade (addition of new features in current system) and for the new functions approved for market introduction. Software and hardware intended to be included in production automobiles is developed in iterative manner following V-model or spiral development process.
   a. The first part of developing production software is dominated by the addition of the new functionality. While unit, integration and functional testing are part of each iteration during this phase as well, the focus is on addition of functionality as prescribed in the vehicle programme.
   b. In the second part of the production software development process, which is also carried out in number of iterations – the focus is shifted to integration and

acceptance testing. In this period, software and hardware performance is calibrated to match to the market demands.

3. **In Operation:** Once the new vehicle model is released into the market, the performance of software and hardware is monitored (through diagnostics) during its operation. The data collection on performance of software, hardware and vehicle is often higher within the warranty period than the latter phase where only essential data is collected and used for improving the future products.

The process followed at each iteration within the production software development can be described using a V-model (refer to Fig. 2). Essentially for each iteration first the requirements are set followed by System Design (functional design and system architecture). Following the system design ECU specifications are done which can also be referred as software design since software is usually designed for a specific ECUs and they are generally co-developed, optimized for particular functionality.

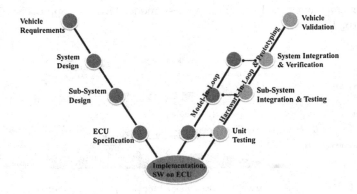

Fig. 2. Mapping automotive software life-cycle according to V-model.

Next comes the implementation where designed software is implemented or auto-generated from models. The code usually undergoes rigorous testing under simulated environment. The testing of software in simulated environment is termed Model-In-Loop testing. The software code is then integrated with the hardware/ECU and is tested in the Hardware-In-Loop testing (for all iterations) and testing within complete vehicle prototypes (for selected iterations). Major types of testing carried out to verify and validate the functionality include unit testing, sub-system integration and testing, system integration and testing, functional and acceptance testing.

2.3   Software Development Life Cycle in Telecom Domain

Ericsson develops large software products for mobile telecommunication networks. The software development process used in large part of the organization is based on the principles of agile and lean development, referred internally as Streamline development

(SD) [18]. In the process, cross functional teams are responsible for complete analysis, design, implementation, and testing of particular features of the product. The overview of the software development and testing process is presented in Fig. 3.

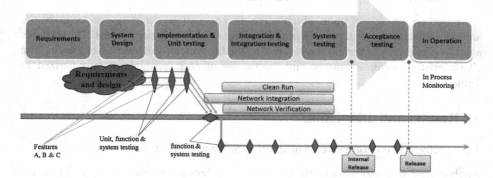

Fig. 3. Overview of software development lifecycle in the telecom domain.

The company has several large products for each of the product there is a main branch that is maintained at all times. A number of features agreed to be developed (marked with A, B and C in Fig. 3) are usually developed by separate teams after the requirements are set and system has been designed. The newly developed features undergo unit, function and system testing before being released into the main branch.

The main branch with added features is now branched out and subjected to function and system testing on regular basis. After the integration of new features into the network (network integration), this new version of software is also subjected to verification activities (Network Verification and Clean Run using specific test cases for new features). Network integration and verification is completed before the product is released internally. After the internal release, the product is subjected to further function and system testing before making the general release to customers.

The streamline development process followed in this company is aligned to the demands of market where new trends in the market require features to be developed and released in shorter intervals, still ensuring high quality.

2.4   Methods for Software Defect Predictions (SDP)

Early estimations of software defects can be used effectively to do better resource planning and allocations. Estimating and monitoring software defects further help to track the progress of given software project and improve release planning.

A number of methods have been used for predicting software defects, categorized as:

- Causal Models,
- Using Expert Opinions,

- Analogy Based Predictions,
- Constructive Quality Model,
- Correlation Based Models
- Capture/Recapture Models,
- Models based on Code and Change Metrics,
- Software Reliability Growth Models (SRGMs), etc.

Based on the type of input which is required by various categories of methods, the amount of data and sensitivity of methods to give stable predictions varies. The methods are thus useful only at certain stage(s) during the lifecycle of software development. The characteristics, main advantage and limitations of each method are summarized in Table 1.

3 Results and Discussion

3.1 Defects Prediction over Automotive Software Life Cycle

Applicability of various methods for software defect predictions over the life cycle phases of automotive software development is represented in Fig. 4. At the very beginning when new functionality has been tried and the concept has been shown to work, there is not much data available to used data heavy models. But it is possible to use expert opinions to make estimates of size, complexity and expected defect count/density for the proposed application. It is also possible to use expert opinions together with historical projects data using analogy based approach. The methods of defect prediction that can be applied at this stage are:

- Using Expert Opinions,
- Analogy Based Predictions

When the concept has been further tested, approved to go into production, requirements are defined. At this stage other properties such as size, design dependencies etc. are also made clear which allows for following methods for defect prediction:

- Causal Models,
- COnstructive QUALity MOdel (COQUALMO)

In the production phase, software is developed in an iterative manner. For each (internal) release, software from different sections (within OEM and software sourced from suppliers) is integrated followed by rigorous function and integration testing. With testing data at hand and possible access to source and evolution metrics, Models that need testing/code metrics data can be applied in this phase. Examples of such methods applicable during the iterative development/testing processes are:

- Software Reliability Growth Models (SRGM),
- Correlation Analysis,
- Capture/Recapture Analysis,
- Methods based on Code and Change Metrics

Table 1. Software defect prediction models, characteristics and applicability over SW life cycle.

Method	Input data required	Advantages and limitations
Causal models	Inputs about estimated size, complexity, qualitative inputs on planned testing and quality requirements	• Causal models biggest advantage is that they can be applied very early in the development process • Possible to analyse what-if scenarios to estimate output quality or level of testing needed to meet desired quality goals
Expert opinions	Domain experience (software development, testing and quality assessment)	• This is the quickest and most easy way to get the predictions (if experts are available) • Uncertainty of predictions is high and forecasts may be subjected to individual biases
Analogy based predictions	Project characteristics and observations from large number of historical projects	• Quick and easy to use, the current project is compared to previous project with most similar characteristics • Evolution of software process, development tool chain may lead to inapplicability or large prediction errors
Constructive quality model	Software size estimates, product, personal and project attributes; defect removal level	• Can be used to predict cost, schedule or the residual defect density of the software under development. • Needs large effort to calibrate the model.
Correlation analysis	Number of defects found in given iteration; size and test effort estimates can also be used in extended models	• This method needs little data input which is available after each iteration • The method provides easy to use rules that can be quickly applied • The model can also be used to identify modules that show higher/lower levels of defect density and thus allow early interventions
Capture/recapture analysis	Number of defects discovered in a given software artefact by independent defect detection activities, such as different code reviews	• This method can be applied at any level, file to product level (for higher levels representative sample of files/modules would be needed) • For code inspection/reviews, access to source code is needed

(Continued)

Table 1. (*Continued*)

Method	Input data required	Advantages and limitations
		• The method requires that two/more similar but independent resources are used for same software artefact, which requires additional resources
Regression models	Software code (or models) metrics as measure/proxies for different characteristics of software code/model; another input can be the change metrics	• Uses actual code/models characteristic metrics which means estimates are made based on data from actual software under development • Can only be applied when code/models are already implemented and access to the source code/model is available • The regression model relationship between input characteristics and output can be difficult to interpret – do not map causal relationship
Machine learning based models	Software code (or models) metrics as measure/proxies for different characteristics of software code/model; another input can be the change metrics	• Similar to regression models, these can be used for either classification (defective/not defective) or to estimate defect count/densities • Over time as more data is made available, the models improvise on their predictive accuracy by adjusting their value of parameters (learning by experience) • While some models as Decision Trees are easy to understand others may act like a black box (for example Artificial Neural Networks) where their internal working is not explicit.
Software reliability growth models	Defect inflow data of software under development (life cycle model) or software under testing.	• Can use defect inflow data to make defect predictions or forecast the reliability of software based system • Reliability growth models are also useful to assess the maturity/release readiness of software close to its release • These models need substantial data points to make precise and stable predictions

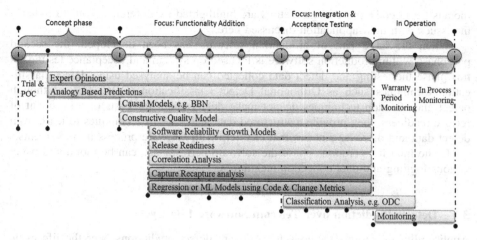

Fig. 4. Software defect prediction techniques mapped to automotive software development life cycle.

SRGMs do not need access to source code/model metrics data; these are black-box techniques that only use defect inflow data during development/testing to model the reliability of software systems. While these models can be applied when the software is under development/testing – they need substantial data points (defect inflow) to make stable predictions.

Correlation analysis models uses number of defects discovered in given iteration (and possibly more attributes) to predict number of defects for following iterations or total defect count for full project. Thus correlation based models can also be applied without the need for access to source code. For each iterative release, different methods can also be used to assess the release readiness of these internal releases.

Capture/Recapture techniques usually uses code inspection/reviews for defect predications, while methods based on code and change metrics require access to source code/functional models to measure characteristics such as size, complexity, dependencies etc., which are then used to make the defect proneness classification or forecasting of defect counts/densities. Thus methods based on code and change metrics and to large extent capture/recapture analysis can only be applied when access to source code/functional models is available.

Since large part of automotive software is often developed not by OEMs but their suppliers, access to source code may be an issue as most suppliers keep their source code un-accessible to OEMs. Thus applicability of methods that need access to source/software evolution metrics cannot be applied at all sections of automotive software development. Nonetheless these methods are applicable for application areas where software is developed in-house by the OEMs. Further since software development in automotive domain pre-dominantly uses MDD, functional/behavioural model metrics alternatives to code metrics may need to be used where their applicability and performance is currently not well documented. Thus in Fig. 4, defect prediction techniques using capture/recapture analysis, regression and machine learning based models using code and change metrics are highlighted by different colour to indicate the issues with their application discussed here.

When the large part of production software has been developed, the second part/phase within production software is focused on system and acceptance testing. In this phase the testing and defect data collected can be analysed using defect classification techniques such as Orthogonal Defect Classification (ODC) [19]. Although defect classification techniques do not make defect count forecasts or assessment of release readiness, they provide a structured data and analysis techniques to learn from defect data and discover patterns that can help with software process improvements.

In the final in-operations phase the software performance can be monitored using various logging and data collection techniques.

3.2 Defects Prediction over Telecom Software Life Cycle

Applicability of various methods for software defect predictions over the life cycle phases of software development in the telecom domain is represented in Fig. 5.

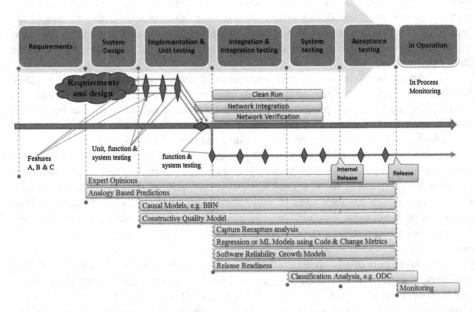

Fig. 5. Software defect prediction techniques mapped to streamline software development life cycle.

As described in Sect. 2.3, the software development process followed at the company (Ericsson) from the telecom domain is based on agile and lean principles and is referred to as streamline development [18]. The first important difference in this process compared to previous case of large EE platform projects in the automotive domain is the time-span; the life-cycle for selected features is in weeks which more or less correspond to one iteration in the automotive platform projects. Within these release cycles the different software defect prediction techniques are useful at different stages as:

- In the requirements phase, the requirements are specified and finalized for the features (A, B, C etc.) to be developed. Since not even requirements are fully specified yet, no techniques for software defect prediction can provide good estimates.
- Once the requirements have been defined and system is designed, expert based and analogy based predictions are useful. Expected defect count and defect proneness of given feature/project or modules can be predicted either based exclusively on the subjective experience of experts or it can be assisted with data and/or models from similar past projects.
- The following phase is marked by the development activity where software is usually hand coded (contrast to automotive domain where domain specific modelling languages such as Matlab/Simulink are common). With system design at hand and estimates on size and required functionality, causal models and constructive quality model can be sued in this phase for making defect predictions.
- After the implementation of feature(s) is mostly over, other techniques for software defect prediction can be used, there are:
  - Capture/recapture based models,
  - Regression and machine learning based models,
  - Software reliability growth models, and
  - Using methods for release readiness assessment.

Since coding in this domain is mostly done in-house the access to source code and software evolution/change metrics is not an issue. Thus techniques that require such data can be readily applied for defect predictions and release readiness assessment.

- After most of testing is over, defect classification techniques can help analyse the defect data to evaluate any process improvement potentials and undertake root cause analysis.
- The software is released internally after adequate function, system, and integration testing has been performed. The internal release is then subjected to rigorous acceptance testing before making it available for the customer.
- When in operation, useful log data is collected about the performance of system and any filed issues/reports are also collected and analysed.

3.3 Analysing Defects Data over Software Life Cycle

Another characteristic of defect analysis methods that is important for selecting the right technique for given purpose is at what level the technique/model can be applied. Based on the type of method and input data needed different models provide optimal results at different levels and their predictions can also be useful for various purposes.

Table 2 summarizes the levels and appropriate applications for each model type. The level of analysis can be done at:

- Product Level (PL),
- System Level (SL),
- Sub-System level (SSL),
- Functional Unit level (FU),
- MOdule (MO), or at the
- File Level (FL)

Table 2. Application level and useful purposes.

Model	Application level	Application area
Causal models	PL, SL, SSL	RPA, WIF
Expert opinions	PL, SL, SSL, FU	RPA, RRA, RCA, WIF
Analogy based predictions	PL, SL, SSL, FU	RPA, RRA
Constructive quality model	PL, SL, SSL, FU	RPA
Correlation analysis	SSL, FU, MO, FL	RRA, IDP, WIF
Capture/recapture analysis	All levels	RPA, RR, RCA, IDP
Regression models	SSL, FU, MO, FL	RRA, IDP, WIF
Machine learning based models	SSL, FU, MO, FL	RRA, IDP, WIF
SRGMs	PL, SL	RPA, RR, RCA

The applications where analysis of software defect data can be useful are:

- Resource Planning and Allocations (RPA),
- What-IF analysis (WIF),
- Release Readiness Assessment (RR),
- Root Cause Analysis (RCA), or for
- Identification of Defect Prone units (IDP)

4   Roadmap for Increasing Effectiveness of Software Defect Predictions

4.1   Using Field Data in the Automotive Domain

In the automotive software domain, the post release monitoring have been fairly limited as software is not regarded same as hardware (software do not degrade or break down with life). Another major reason for lack of monitoring of software in-operation performance in the past has been the un-availability of necessary skills at the service end to retrieve the data and easily feed it back to OEMs for analysis.

But with the advancements of new technology such as high speed data transfer, storage facilities, cloud storage and highly automated computer based diagnostics equipment's available across most of the service points offers unprecedented opportunity to collect, store and use the data from the in-operations phase and use it to feedback information that can further enhance the capabilities to design and develop even better, higher quality and safe automotive software.

We contend that the current technologies make it possible for OEMs to collect and analyse in-operations performance of software based systems very much like it has been the case for hardware components in the past. And much like how such monitoring helped design better hardware components, increase their life and reliability – monitoring the in-operations data of software systems performance will help design more robust, reliable and user friendly software functions in the future.

For example, following and analysing detailed performance metrics of software based system during their life-time operations will:

- Provide metrics for in-operations performance of software based systems.
- The qualitative and quantitative robustness and reliability measures from in-operations data will provide input (feedback) for experts and causal models on which software characteristics lead to most reliable performance.
- The current evaluation of performance of code and change metrics SDP models is based on their performance compared to defects found during development and testing. Using in-operations performance data and using code and change metrics data from their source code will help identify *"best practices"* for the software designers and developers to avoid actions that may lead to sub-optimal performance during operations.
- Insights from the in-operation phase are already used by certain OEMs for effective optimization/calibration. For example functional units such as powertrain use in-operations data to calibrate engines for achieving optimal balance between power and efficiency.
- With active monitoring and analysis of in-operations performance of software based systems will help isolate any potential performance related issues and offer quick updates whenever needed that will further enhance the overall dependability of automotive products during the actual operation.

Further in future where in-operation monitoring and feedback cycle is shortened would also enable OEMs to identify user satisfaction and usefulness of different features within their cars. This will allow for design and development of more user friendly features that will benefits the end customers.

4.2 Combining Different Models and Using Ground Up Approach to Prediction

In contrast to automotive domain, the telecom domain post release monitoring is done actively with strategic customers providing an active feedback channel for software development organization. Compared to the automotive domain, the telecom domain also usually have full access to source code and change metrics (developed internally) allowing use of some techniques that are not always feasible for other domains with limited access to these measures. On the other hand there are stringent requirements to develop and deliver features in shorter periods of time, still maintain high quality.

Two important areas for improving software defect predictions in this domain are identified as:

1. **Combining Different Software Defect Predictions Techniques:** as reviewed above different methods of defect prediction have their distinct advantages and also they are usually more appropriate at specific time point in the software development/testing phases. Using different techniques at different phases and combining strengths of different methods can help make defect predictions with higher effectiveness than using any single technique.

   For example expert opinions have been shown to provide software effort estimations better or at par with model estimates [20]. These estimates can be used in combination of other data based models compared to as competing techniques. Expert, analogy and/or causal models can be used to specify a probable high and lower limit for reliability growth models asymptote which can make the predictions more stable in comparison to using these models without such limits.

2. **Using Ground-up Approach for Defect Prediction:** another characteristic of defect predictions techniques are their applicability at only a certain level of software system. For example expert opinions and analogy based predictions works well at project or system level but do not scale down well. On the other hand regression and machine learning models provide useful estimates at file and module level. One way of making effective software defect predictions at higher level could be by using sampling and grounds up approach for making defect predictions. Defect predictions methods such as capture/recapture analysis or regression based models can be applied to a representative sample of files and modules and the predictions thus obtained could be projected for the full system/project. These predictions can also be validated or supported by predictions obtained from models (such as expert opinions and causal models) that work well at these higher levels, thus increasing the confidence in the predictions.

5   Conclusions

The role and importance of software in automotive and telecom domain has been rapidly increasing. The size, complexity and value software provides in these domains is ever increasing and expected to grow further. With trends moving towards connected society, more software enables functions, autonomous vehicles and active safety systems – ensuring dependability of software based systems is highest priority.

Software development in automotive domain is long and complex process, various software defect predictions models offer possibilities to predict expected defects thus providing early estimations that are useful for resource planning and allocations, release planning and enabling close monitoring of progress of given project. In the telecom domain the time to market and high quality of released software play a critical role.

In the paper we reviewed that different methods for SDP need different forms of input data, they also have different capabilities and limitations when it comes to their ability to make accurate and stable forecasts. Thus given at what phase of software development life cycle we are in and what kind of data is available, certain defect prediction models may be more appropriate than others and thus should be preferred.

For the automotive domain, we contend that unlike past, the present technology enables close monitoring, collection and analysis of detailed performance data of software based system during in-operations phase. This data now and in future will be much easy to collect, store, retrieve and analyse. We contend that analysis of such data will lead to development of more robust software based systems that will further help to enhance the reliability of automotive products and aid in development of features that provide superior overall user experience.

In case of telecom domain, we take a position that using different models in combination will provide better (more accurate and stable) predictions that using one method in isolation. It is further suggested that using sampling approach and predictions from lower granularity levels can be projected to higher granularity levels using ground-up approach which can further be complimented by predictions from defect prediction models that work best at higher granularity levels.

Acknowledgements. The research presented here is done under the VISEE project which is funded by Vinnova and Volvo Cars jointly under the FFI programme (VISEE, Project No: DIARIENR: 2011-04438). We are also thankful to companies involved (Volvo Car Group and Ericsson) for their participation in this study.

References

1. Jones, E.L.: Integrating testing into the curriculum—arsenic in small doses. ACM SIGCSE Bull. **33**, 337–341 (2001)
2. Rana, R., Staron, M., Hansson, J., Nilsson, M.: Defect prediction over software life cycle in automotive domain: state of the art and road map for future. Presented at the 9th International Joint Conference on Software Technologies - ICSOFT-EA, Vienna, Austria (2014)
3. Staron, M., Meding, W.: Predicting weekly defect inflow in large software projects based on project planning and test status. Inf. Softw. Technol. **50**(7), 782–796 (2008)
4. Almering, V., van Genuchten, M., Cloudt, G., Sonnemans, P.J.: Using software reliability growth models in practice. IEEE Softw. **24**(6), 82–88 (2007)
5. Rana, R., Staron, M., Mellegård, N., Berger, C., Hansson, J., Nilsson, M., Törner, F.: Evaluation of standard reliability growth models in the context of automotive software systems. In: Oivo, M., Jedlitschka, A., Baldassarre, M.T., Heidrich, J. (eds.) PROFES 2013. LNCS, vol. 7983, pp. 324–329. Springer, Heidelberg (2013)
6. Rana, R., Staron, M., Berger, C., Hansson, J., Nilsson, M., Törner, F.: Evaluating long-term predictive power of standard reliability growth models on automotive systems. Presented at the 24th Annual International Symposium on Software Reliability Engineering (ISSRE 2013), Pasadena, CA, USA (2013)
7. Wood, A.: Predicting software reliability. Computer **29**(11), 69–77 (1996)
8. Pham, H.: Software reliability and cost models: perspectives, comparison, and practice. Eur. J. Oper. Res. **149**(3), 475–489 (2003)
9. Khoshgoftaar, T.M., Allen, E.B.: Logistic regression modeling of software quality. Int. J. Reliab. Qual. Saf. Eng. **6**(04), 303–317 (1999)

10. Menzies, T., Greenwald, J., Frank, A.: Data mining static code attributes to learn defect predictors. IEEE Trans. Software Eng. **33**(1), 2–13 (2007)
11. Gondra, I.: Applying machine learning to software fault-proneness prediction. J. Syst. Softw. **81**(2), 186–195 (2008)
12. Ceylan, E., Kutlubay, F.O., Bener, A.B.: Software defect identification using machine learning techniques. In: 32nd EUROMICRO Conference on Software Engineering and Advanced Applications, SEAA 2006, pp. 240–247 (2006)
13. Fenton, N.E., Neil, M.: A critique of software defect prediction models. IEEE Trans. Software Eng. **25**(5), 675–689 (1999)
14. Fenton, N., Neil, M., Marsh, W., Hearty, P., Radliński, Ł., Krause, P.: On the effectiveness of early life cycle defect prediction with Bayesian Nets. Empir. Softw. Eng. **13**(5), 499–537 (2008)
15. Boehm, B.W.: A spiral model of software development and enhancement. Computer **21**(5), 61–72 (1988)
16. Dieterle, W.: Mechatronic systems: Automotive applications and modern design methodologies. Annu. Rev. Control **29**(2), 273–277 (2005)
17. ISO: International Standard-ISO 26262-Road vehicles-Functional safety. International Organization for Standardization (2011)
18. Tomaszewski, P., Berander, P., Damm, L.-O.: From traditional to streamline development—opportunities and challenges. Softw. Process Improv. Pract. **13**(2), 195–212 (2008)
19. Chillarege, R., Bhandari, I.S., Chaar, J.K., Halliday, M.J., Moebus, D.S., Ray, B.K., Wong, M.-Y.: Orthogonal defect classification-a concept for in-process measurements. IEEE Trans. Software Eng. **18**(11), 943–956 (1992)
20. Jørgensen, M.: A review of studies on expert estimation of software development effort. J. Syst. Softw. **70**(1–2), 37–60 (2004)

Time in the Domain Entities Access Architecture

Marco Covelli[1]([✉]), Daniela Micucci[2], and Marco Mobilio[2]

[1] TabulaeX, via Carducci 32, Milan, Italy
marco.covelli@tabulaex.com
[2] Department of Informatics Systems and Communication,
University of Milano Bicocca, Viale Sarca 336, Milan, Italy
{daniela.micucci,marco.mobilio}@unimib.it

Abstract. Domain Entities Access is an architecture that enables the realization of platforms supporting responsive environments in the interaction with instrumented physical environments through the observation and the control of meaningful domain entities. This results in an environment model that abstracts from any technological details. Domain entities are characterized by a set of pairs property-value. The value of a property is the last inferred one without any information with respect to when the data used in the inference have been acquired. Thus, the status of domain entities lacks of timeliness. The architecture has been revised so that end-user applications can rely on both inspection and control mechanisms whose results are driven by time. The new implementation of the framework have been validated in a real simplified scenario.

Keywords: Time · Perception flow · Action flow · Software architecture · Responsive environments

1 Introduction

Instrumented environments [1] are common environments enriched with devices able to gather information about them and to act on them. From a technological point of view, they constitute the milestone of responsive environments [2,3], systems able to sense the environment and to respond to it and to the users that inhabit it.

Those kind of systems primarily requires to intermix multiple components and integrated solutions that are highly heterogeneous, have different capabilities, and often rely on different communication protocols [4]. Due to this heterogeneity, many systems rely on *ad hoc* solutions that often are based on specific technologies and protocols.

The approaches to the integration of heterogeneous devices can be divided into two main groups: solutions that supply with enabling integration platforms [5–7], and solutions that provide platforms that allow applications to reason in terms of domain-related concepts [8,9]. Platforms of the first group provide an

© Springer International Publishing Switzerland 2015
A. Holzinger et al. (Eds.): ICSOFT 2014, CCIS 555, pp. 233–250, 2015.
DOI: 10.1007/978-3-319-25579-8_14

unified access to the heterogeneous devices. Thus, they can be used in any application domain, but they do not provide an abstract, domain-dependant model of the environment. On the opposite, solutions of the second group provide applications with a model of the environment that is closer to the application logic, thus filling the gap between the physical environment and how it is perceived by the applications. The main disadvantage of such solutions concerns the poor adaptability of the model to domains that differ from the one for which the model has been conceived. Moreover, time does not appear in the description of the analized approaches that maintain an environment model. On the contrary, in these kind of systems, time becomes crucial: an end-user application that uses information on the status of domain entities must be aware about its timeliness, that is, how old the data is [10]. For example, the position of a person without being enriched with the time at which it was acquired is an information potentially useless when the localization systems are not pervasive in the environment. With time-related information, end-user applications are able to determine the obsolescence and, therefore, the reliability of the information.

The paper presents an extension of the Domain Entities Access (DEA) [11], an architecture for the observation and the control of instrumented environments that is located halfway between the two main classes of approaches above described. DEA allows the integration of heterogeneous devices and provides end-user applications with a unified access to an abstract domain-related representation of the environment. The abstract representation of the environment (i) captures domain related issues by abstracting from the physical devices; (ii) can be inspected by end-user applications with the aim of identifying intelligent/ad hoc behavior; and (iii) can be used by end-user applications to deliver commands reifying the identified intelligent/ad hoc behavior.

The new contribution to DEA described in this article concerns the introduction of aspects related to time both in the environment model, and in the interaction between end-user applications and the model. In the new version of DEA, when the "real" environment represented by the model evolves, the corresponding status change is recorded in the model by placing it in a temporal context. The new mechanisms end-user applications exploit to observe and control the environment model take into account timing issues. End-user applications can inspect the model not only on the basis of information on the status of specific domain entities, but also for when these changes were recorded. In addition, end-user applications will control the environment model (i.e., the statuses of domain entities) by means of timed commands, that is, they can also specify when the change should take place. Finally, time has been included in the DEA architecture while preserving the logic of predicates that makes DEA independent of the specific application domain.

The paper is organized as follows: Sect. 2 overviews the DEA architecture and outlines the points of weakness of the model related to time; Sects. 3 and 4 present the new entity model and the new access layer respectively; Sect. 5 describes the implementation of a real simplified scenario; Sect. 6 compares DEA to the state of the art; and Sect. 7 outlines the conclusions and identifies future directions.

2   DEA Architecture Overview and Limitations

There is a semantic gap between the *environment model* used by end-user applications to observe and interact with the physical environment and the devices that produce *stimuli* and actuate *actions*. End-user applications reason in terms of *statuses of domain entities*. For example, *"Marco is located in room 27"*, "switch on the *main light* in *room 2006"*. On the opposite, sensing devices produce *stimuli* and actuating devices accept *actions* whose semantics and syntax is up to the devices. "DF6YH78KLO", "#01001#01", are respectively examples of a stimulus from a RFID reader and of an action to a BTicino light.

DEA (Domain Entity Access) is a layered architecture for the design of platforms supporting end-user applications that reason in terms of domain entities be they abstractions of physical devices (e.g., lamp) or inferred from events generated by sensing devices (e.g., people), thus filling the semantic gap. The architecture seamlessly integrates sensing and actuation devices, providing end-user applications with an *environment model* that they can exploit to control and observe the *status* of meaningful *domain entities*. The environment model is an abstract and unified representation of the *context of interest*, which ranges from the physical devices (e.g., lamps) to the people that inhabit the environment.

2.1   Overview

Stimuli from the sensing devices in the physical environment contribute in maintaining the environment model updated so that it can reflect the "real" situation. Symmetrically, *commands* from end-user applications possibly affect the "real" environment through *actions* that are performed by actuating devices. In turn, a change of the "real" environment is captured by sensing devices that produce stimuli, thus closing the loop. For example, an application that tracks people and activates cameras only when required, reasons on a model of the environment constituted by people and cameras whose status is updated by a set of physical cameras, RFID readers, and any kind of sensing device able to detect movements. Moreover, the application operates on the status of the camera in the environment model to control the corresponding physical camera, thus ignoring the specific technological dependant action required to switch on/off the physical camera. In turn, when the physical camera changes its status, the corresponding generated stimulus will update the status of the camera in the environment model. The two flows respectively realize the processes of perception [12].

Referring to Fig. 1, the first three layers of the architecture (from the bottom) deal with *data abstraction* that is responsible for maintaining the environment model updated with respect to the "real" environment, thus managing both the *perception* and the *action* flows. The upper layer deals with *access mechanisms* end-user applications can use to observe and control the environment model.

In detail, the *interface layer* is responsible for interfacing with the specific device; the *translation layer* translates *stimuli* as produced by the devices into a common vocabulary (*abstract stimuli*) and actions (*abstract actions*) into technological dependant actions; the *inference/reification layer* makes inferences about

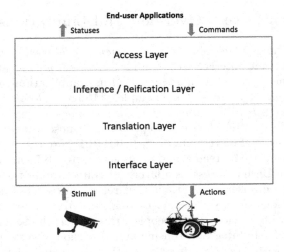

Fig. 1. Overall architecture.

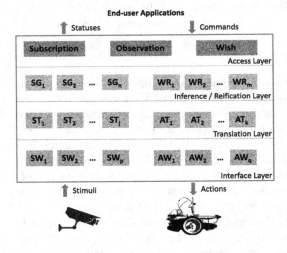

Fig. 2. Concrete architecture.

statuses of domain entities according to stimuli from the devices (and the actual statuses) and reifies commands into abstract actions (independent from any technological issues) that actuators have to perform; finally, the *access layer* provides mechanisms end-user applications exploit to observe and control statuses of domain entities.

2.2 Concrete Architecture

Figure 2 illustrates the overall architecture with emphasis on its concrete realization in terms of software components.

Each of the first three layers deals with well-defined data structures both in perception flow (from bottom to top) and in action flow (from top to bottom). This allows identifying software components characterized by compactness and insulation [13].

In detail and starting from the bottom, the component in charge of communicating with a device is the *sensor wrapper* (for sensing devices) and the *actuator wrapper* (for actuating devices). At least there are as many wrappers as the different typologies of the physical devices. In Fig. 2 they are represented by the components labeled SW_i (sensor wrappers) and AW_i (actuator wrappers).

The component in charge of operating translations is the *stimuli translator* (from stimuli to abstract stimuli) and the *action translator* (from abstract actions to actions) respectively. At least there are as many translators as the different typologies of protocols used by the physical devices. In Fig. 2 components labeled ST_i and AT_i are respectively stimuli translators and action translators.

Wrappers and translators depend on the specific devices that instrument the environment. Thus, they are domain-dependant components.

The inference and the reification activities in the inference/reification layer are respectively concretized by the *status guesser* and the *wish reasoner* components.

In Fig. 2, components labeled SG_i and WR_i are respectively status guessers and wish reasoners. How many guessers are needed depends both on the characteristics of the domain entities (i.e., their properties and dependencies) and on how much the guessers are compact and insulate. The same holds for the wish reasoners.

Guessers and reasoners depends on the specific domain entities that constitute the environment model and their properties. Thus, they are domain-dependant components.

In the access layer, three components reify the three supported interaction modes: the *observation* component is in charge of managing the observation interaction mode; the *subscription* component is in charge of managing the subscription interaction mode by capturing the status changes inferred by the status guessers and delivering them to the subscribed end-user applications; and the *wish* component is in charge of managing the status change requests, thus delivering them to the proper wish reasoners.

The identified components and layering allow to define a *framework* for what concerns the access layer and the structure of the components in the data abstraction layer. When an instrumented environment must be observed and controlled, then a platform is designed. Such a *platform* will relies on the framework for what concerns the domain-independent issues, and will include both the appropriate set of domain entities and the domain-dependant components.

2.3   Limitations

Domain entities realize the environment model. They are observable and possibly controllable units of interest in a "real" environment from the end-user application point of view.

In the previous version of the DEA architecture, an entity was defined as a set of *property-value* pairs, that entirely describes the entity itself. Each property models a piece of information. Which properties characterize an entity is a domain related issue. For this reason, DEA specifies only how they have to be defined.

The value of a property is the last inferred one without any information about *when* the stimuli that have been analyzed by the inference process have been acquired. Thus, the environment model maintains a snapshot of the "real" environment by relying on information with different timeliness [10], which describes how old is data.

Thus, time should be assigned to values associated to properties and made available to end-user applications. Any kind of aging policy should not be included in the model because the evaluation of the timeliness depends on the application domain. For example, an application that tracks persons in real-time needs information about their positions that has an associated timestamp close to the current time. On the opposite, an application that infers behavioral models of persons can also rely on information that is not properly updated.

The access layer provides mechanisms end-user applications can exploit to observe and control the environment model. Such mechanisms are based on messages and allow formulating requests about domain entities without the need to mention them explicitly. By exploiting a subset of the concepts of predicate logic, in the previous version of the architecture, end-user applications were able to refer to domain entities through their properties and their values. No consideration about time was taken into account. In detail, end-user applications were principally able to observe the statuses of the environment model and to make wishes about its evolution (i.e., to deliver commands). An observation returned values related to properties that were not enriched with time and were the last inferred ones. Thus, an application was not able to get to know the timeliness of the information received. Dealing with commands, they were executed as soon as they were received since no temporal scheduling was taken into account. This way, an end-user application must be aware about when to deliver commands so that their effects are implemented in the desired time. On the opposite, it would be desirable that an end-user application does not have to be aware of the technological details related to the actuators that fulfill the command: the application should only be aware about when it wants that the desired state is the current one. For example, if an end-user application wishes a mobile entity to be in a certain place at a specified time, it does not have to worry about when to send the command. The application must only specify it wants to get the mobile entity in that position to the desired time.

3   Time in the Data Abstraction Layer

An *entity* was previously defined in [11] as a set of *property-value* pairs, each one modeling a piece of information. Thus, each entity was described by the union of its current property values.

With the introduction of time, each piece of information is captured by a property having a set of *value-timestamp* pairs. Each pair represents the value of the property at a specific instant, usually discretized by the property value change. Thus, each entity is described by the changes of these values over time. In short, the introduced set represents the history of status changes over time.

Properties can be mutable and immutable: the former change over time, whilst the latter are fixed once for all. For example, the location of a person can vary over time; his name is fixed once for all.

Referring to a domotic domain, persons and lights are examples of domain entities. Each entity is characterized by its proper set of properties: a person has a position and a name, a light has a position too and is in an on/off status. Moreover, both the entities has a type and an unique identifier. Instances of those entities have registered values for their properties enriched with timestamps. For example, home at 7 AM, office at 9 AM, and lunch room at 1 PM are plausible values for the location property of person with identifier bob.

A property can also be controllable. For example, the on/off status of a light is typically controllable, the same cannot be asserted for a person's location. *Commands* are requests for changing the status of entities. Previously in [11], a command only specified the wished new value for a property. With the introduction of time, a command also specifies *when* the new property value is desired to be observable. For example, an end-user application can plan to turn the radio on at a specified time; or an end-user application can schedule a required temperature of 20 Celsius degrees when the user will come back at home.

The perception flow works as the previous version, with the addition of time in the data flow. For example, an RFID sensor detects a tag at 9:03 AM: this event is captured by the interface layer that exposes the data to the upper layer. Data is translated into the homogeneous syntax and propagated to its upper layer. The inference/reification layer infers the new value for the position property of the person with identifier m_covelli at 9:03 AM and then updates the persistent representation of the environment model, by adding a new *value-timestamp* pair to the Location property of m_covelli.

The action flow relies on the same stack too, with the addition of the concept of timed commands. For example, an end-user application wishes to turn a radio on at 6:30 AM. The radio is modeled by a domain entity with a set of properties including OnOffStatus, which is controllable and contains the status of the radio. The application delivers to the inference/reification layer a command stating that the value of the property OnOffStatus should be set to On at 6:30 AM (the user wishes the radio on when he wakes up in the morning). The layer is in charge of reifying the command by producing the proper abstract action for the corresponding radio switcher. Given that switching a radio on is an instant action, this command "sleeps" in the layer until few moments before 6:30. Then, the abstract action is delivered to the translation layer that produces an action that is understandable to the recipient radio switcher. The action is then managed by the interface layer that finally commands the device.

The approach can face more complex scenarios also, where the status changes can not be instantaneous. For example, ensuring 20 Celsius degrees at the time the user comes back home. In this case, the reification layer, by relying on the current temperature and other variables (such as the average time to warm the environment), is in charge to deliver to the translator layer the corresponding abstract actions at the right time to guarantee 20 Celsius degree at the desired time.

4   Time in the Access Layer

The inference/reification layer maintains entities (i.e., the environment model). With the introduction of time, this layer maintains *snapshots* of the environment status over time, which can be entirely or partially retrieved. This means that end-user applications can now refer to statuses in the past, in the present, and in the future.

As from the first version of the architecture, the access layer provides mechanisms end-user applications can exploit to observe and control the environment model. The interactions are based on messages and allow formulating requests about domain entities without the need to mention them explicitly. The delivery of the messages is formulated using a subset of the concepts of predicate logic, that allows to refer to domain entities through their properties and their values. Such a solution allows end-user applications to do not explicitly know the domain entities constituting the environment model. For example, an application can formulate a request like "switch on the lamp in room 27" without knowing which is the lamp in room 27. At a conceptual level, the approach is to send messages directly to domain entities, which respond individually on their merits. Reply messages are also characterized by a payload that contains the required information, and by a sender that identifies the entity to which the information is referred.

A *request message* consists of a *recipient*, which describes via predicate logic the properties of the entities to which the message is addressed, and a *payload*, which specifies the detail of the request. A *reply message* consists of a *sender* that is described via predicate logic and a *payload* with the information related to the sender.

We define a predicate $p(x)$, with x a domain entity, as a series of property-value pairs, linked by the common logical connectors (conjunction, disjunction, and negation). For example, the predicate $p_1(x)$ "x is a lamp located in sal2 lab" can be expressed in terms of property-value tokens like "x has property Type equals to Lamp AND x has property Location equals to sal2". Defining the environment model E as the set of all the domain entities and a given $p(x)$, it is possible to declaratively describe a set $E_p \subseteq E$, containing the entities having the characteristics described in p, as follows: $E_p = \{e \in E \mid p(e) \text{ is true}\}$. To be fully compliant with the domain model, the syntax includes the possibility to specify a minimum confidence, to filter values under a given trustworthiness threshold.

This approach effectively allows entity selection by the specification of property constraints.

The use of predicate enables the definition of dynamic sets of entities, by formalizing predicates that may include mutable property values.

For example, it is possible to define a predicate $p_2(x)$ "x is a person in sal2 lab": there will be a concrete possibility that an entity e could be in E_p at the moment t_0 but not at t_1. This makes possible to discriminate entities by their properties, without the need of enumerating them.

However, it is important to notice that this approach also fits the case an end-user application needs to explicitly refer to a specific entity, that could be done by defining a constraint on the Id property (if defined).

Leaving untouched the recipients and senders (the predicate logic part), that refers as before to current statuses of entities, time references to payloads have been introduced, which allow to retrieve past information and to schedule future environment changes.

Exploiting the above described message-based protocol, the access layer enables end-user applications

- to query the model about the punctual status of selected entities, in the present and in the past (*observation*)
- to express interest for status changes of selected entities, obtaining notifications at each occurrence (*subscription*)
- to express immediate or future desired statuses for entities, which are reified in changes to the physical environment made by suitable actuators (*wish*)

Observation and subscription are for observation purposes. In the first case the request concerns the status of an entity at a given time, thus allowing an end-user application to deal with past snapshots of the environment. In the second case, subscriptions refer to the status changes that occurs since the request. For example, observations allow to query the environment in order to obtain the names of the persons in a room at a given time; subscriptions allow to express interest for all the future changes of the status of the lights in a specific room, without having to list them.

Wish allows end-user applications to deliver commands (i.e., to change the entities status) so that the required status change can be observed at the requested time. Thus, end-user applications can *schedule* commands over time. For example, wishes allow to ask for switching off all the lights in a certain area at a certain time.

In the following details about the three supported interactions will be provided.

An *observation* consists in a request message specifying a logic predicate that defines the interested entities and a list L of properties and a time as payload.

For example, an end-user application needs to know the number of people that were present in a building composed by two rooms yesterday at 6:30 PM. Room is a domain entity characterized by the properties Id (the identifier), Type (the typology of the entity), and ContainedPeople (the number of contained people). Thus, the end-user application composes the observation request message:

```
Recipient:
    Type = Room
ObservationRequest:
    ContainedPeople, 15 Nov 2014 6:30PM
```

This message is delivered to all the entities who have the property **Type** equals to Room. The payload specifies that the request concerns the value of their property **ContainedPeople** on November the 15th 2014 at 6:30PM. The two rooms (**sal1** and **sal2**) *answer* the query by sending back to the requesting application, the messages:

```
Sender:
    Id = sal1
ObservationResponse:
    ContainedPeople = 1 0.9, 15 Nov 2014 5:34 PM

Sender:
    Id = sal2
ObservationResponse:
    ContainedPeople = 3 0.9, 15 Nov 2014 6:03 PM
```

The second value assigned to **ContainedPeople** in both the reply messages (0.9) is the confidence value. The date/time refers to the *age* of the information, namely it is the time that corresponds to the last update of the property value with respect to the time specified in the request. In this case, for example, the property **ContainedPeople** for **sal1** has changed for the last time at 5:34 PM with respect to 6:30 PM (the time specified in the request). Both confidence and time may help in reasoning on the aging of the statuses: given the nature of a specific property, a value can be evaluated as too old (thus, low reliable) by an end-user application, leading to further considerations for the business logic.

Subscription allows to observe the environment model asynchronously: end-user applications subscribe to entity status changes so that they will be notified each time a change occurs. Firstly the end-user application performs a subscription specifying the predicate p that describes the target entities and the list L of properties in which it is interested. Since the subscription, the end-user application will receive a notification whenever a status change involves one of the properties in L of an entity in E_p.

For example, an end-user application needs to be notified each time a student changes its location inside a university building. **Person** is a domain entity characterized by the properties **Id** (the identifier), **Type** (the typology of the entity), **Location** (the position inside the building), and **Role** (the role of the person). Thus, the end-user application composes the subscription request message:

```
Sender:
    CaseStudyApp
Recipient:
    Type = Person AND
    Role = Student
SubscriptionRequest:
    Location
```

From now on, the requesting application will be notified of any `Location` value change that involves entities of type `Person` and role `Student`. Differently from "standard" request messages, the subscription also includes a *sender* field, needed to identify the recipient of future notification messages. Suppose that the environment model has been updated as a result of a perception flow generated by an image captured by a camera. The `Location` value of the entity with `Id` equals to m_covelli has changed, meaning that the entity "has entered" a new location. Then, the entity itself sends to the applications that are subscribed to such event the notification message:

```
Sender:
   Id = m_covelli
StatusChange:
   Location = sal1 0.8, 16 Nov 2014 9:10 AM
```

Time in the payload refers to the time in which stimuli used to infer the location have been sensed.

Wish allows end-user applications to control the "real" environment through commands. Actuated commands can produce effects that are perceived by sensors, which activate a perception flow. Thus, the consequences of a command request will be observable by the applications if they properly observe the environment model, according to the previous introduced modes (observation and/or subscription). In other words, to perceive the change, the application must observe the entity it wants to control.

A wish consists in a request message that contains a predicate p that describes the target entities, and a property-value pair and a scheduled time as payload, that specifies the property and the new value the end-user application "wishes" to assign to the target entities and when the application "wishes" the new value to become effective.

For example, an end-user application needs to switch on all the lights in the `sal1` room today at 6:30 PM. `Light` is a domain entity characterized by the properties `Id` (the identifier), `Type` (the typology of the entity), `Location` (the position inside the building), and `OnOffStatus` (the on/off status). Thus, the end-user application composes the request message:

```
Recipient:
   Type = Light AND
   Location = sal1
WishRequest:
   OnOffStatus = On, 16 Nov 2014 6:30 PM
```

This request message selects the entities by the type (they should be lights) and the location (they should be in sal1), and asks them to switch on at 6:30 PM. This request activates an action flow that materializes the results at the specified time. Like for the observations, the time parameter is now mandatory.

Wishes can be not so trivial like switching on a light. In general, when the time interval between the request submission and the scheduled time is not enough for the materialization (e.g., warming a big cold room in less than 15 min), the general policy continues to be the best-effort one.

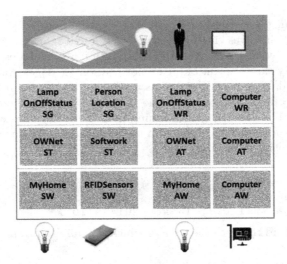

Fig. 3. Domain-related components for the applicative scenario.

5   Validation

The existing implementation of DEA has been extended to include time. The validation aimed to prove the effective advantages in the development of end-user applications using the presented architecture with the addition of time-related concepts.

5.1   The Case Study

The case study deals with a building that houses the offices of a company. Company employees use computers. The end-user application aims at making employees able to use their computers as soon as they reach their room avoiding both energy waste and time required to turn on the computer. Moreover, according to the policy of energy saving, when a employ leaves its office, the application turn the light off.

The behavior described above requires a specific instrumentation of the environments. In addition, the end-user application requires to know how long it takes for each employee to reach his office.

In the case study, only one employee (Mr. White) has been considered. The physical environment has been instrumented with RFID sensors produced by Softwork in proximity of the entrance and the exit of each involved rooms (i.e., the hall of the building and the office of Mr. White), with a BTicino system that controls the lights relying on the OWN protocol, and with a computer with a NIC (Network Internet Card) supporting the wake on LAN protocol (WOL). Once entered in the building, Mr. White takes 5 min to reach his office.

5.2   The DEA Configuration

The environment model consists of the following entities: Light, Person, and Computer. Each of them is characterized by the following properties: Location, Type, and Id. Moreover, Light and Computer have also OnOffStatus that states if they are switched on or off.

The above entities constitute the whole environment model since they entirely represent the "context of interest". Moreover, the model, by its own nature, handles the entities in the same way and does not specify any structural constraint between them. Possible physical/spatial considerations (e.g., the building topology) have to be done on one or more external physical space models.

The implemented components dealing with domain-related issues are sketched in Fig. 3. At a first look they may appear too many, but each one is actually very simple, reflecting a philosophy of high-cohesion and low-coupling. In particular, at the interface layer, MyHomeSW and RFIDSensorsSW respectively interfaces with the respective sensors to acquire the generated stimuli; MyHomeAW and ComputerAW respectively interfaces with the respective actuators to deliver actions. At the translation layer, OWNetST and SoftworkST translate stimuli from the respective sensors into abstract stimuli; OWNetAT and ComputerAT translate abstract actions from the wish reasoners into actions in a language that the target actuator is able to understand. Finally, at the inference/reification layer, LampOnOffStatusSG and PersonLocationSG are in charge of elaborating the abstract stimuli respectively from the OWNetST component to update the OnOffStatus property of each Light entity, and from the SoftworkST component to update the Location property of each Person entity; LampOnOffStatusWR and ComputerWR are in charge of reifying the commands from the end-user application into corresponding abstract actions and deliver them to OWNetAT and ComputerAT respectively.

5.3   The Interaction Between the End-User Application and DEA

The end-user application is a simple Java program that interfaces with the exposed web services of DEA platform. Its basic behavior is to initially send subscription requests and wait for status change notifications to trigger wish requests.

The following is the subscription request for observing changes in the location of employees:

```
Sender:
    CaseStudyApp
Recipient:
    Type = Person
SubscriptionRequest:
    Location
```

Thus, whenever a new person enters the hall, the application will receive a notification like the following:

```
Sender:
   Id = mr_white
StatusChange:
   Location = Hall 0.9, 16 Nov 2014 8:31 AM
```

The message notifies that Mr. White has entered at 8.31 AM the building with a confidence equals to 0.9. The application logic triggers a rule that sends a wish request like the following:

```
Recipient:
   Type = Computer AND
   Location =  OfficeOfMrWhite
WishRequest:
   OnOffStatus = On, 16 Nov 2014 8:36 AM
```

This message requests that the computer of Mr. White should be turned on at 8.36.

The ComputerWR will plan the actions with timing that are compliant with the computer involved. Considering that the computer of Mr. White requires two minutes for the boot, then the actions will be scheduled at 8:33 AM.

In this example, it was possible to save up two minutes of energy. On the contrary, if the application could only send the turn on command when notified about the entrance of Mr. White in the building, the computer would be unnecessarily turned three minutes in advance.

Finally, if the end-user application will receive the following command:

```
Sender:
   Id = mr_white
StatusChange:
   Location = Corridor 0.9, 16 Nov 2014 12:00 AM
```

the application will plan the following command to be executed immediately:

```
Recipient:
   Type = Light AND
   Location =  OfficeOfMrWhite
WishRequest:
   OnOffStatus = On, 16 Nov 2014 12:01 AM
```

6   Related Works

Devices interoperability is a well known issue [6,14]. Depending on the research field (more or less oriented to hardware integration), the proposed solutions can be classified in two main groups: the former composed by integration platforms that merely unify communication mechanisms from and to devices; the latter composed by more complex architectures that offer an environment representation to the applications, more suited to the application domain.

DEA fits in the middle of these two classes, reducing their drawbacks and exploiting their advantages.

6.1   Integration Platforms

Solutions in this scope focus on the technological problem of devices interoperability. Typically they offer platforms that abstract specific communication protocols and offer homogeneous mechanisms for interacting with the devices. The general approach is to define a set of communication requirements that applications have to use to interface with them. These requirements are often represented by the use of common vocabularies to uniform syntax and semantics of data and the adherence to a common communication mode.

The *CASAS Lightwight middleware* (CLM) [6], for example, is a solution based on message-passing between information sources (typically sensors) and consumers, that uses the *publish/subscribe* paradigm: the interested components subscribe to specific sources and consequently receive the produced information, expressed by a predefined XML syntax. Thomson et al. in [5] follows a *service-oriented* approach instead, proposing a framework that abstracts devices and exposes them as *web services* or through technologies like Java RMI.

Solutions of this kind often are foundations of research projects, in particular in the field of Ambient Intelligence and Ubiquitous Computing. *CLM*, for example, is used as a base for the communication system of the *smart home CASAS* (that, in the authors knowledge, has not public results yet); the framework by Thomson et al. constitutes instead the device abstraction infrastructure of *Amigo* [15], that proposes a *service-oriented* architecture for *smart homes.*

These integration platforms only deal with devices and their data (that may also include time or not), delegating the end-user applications to fit them into an appropriate environment representation. This allows these solutions to be potentially used in any application domain that concerns hardware components. However, defining and maintaining a proper environment model often is a nontrivial task.

DEA follows the general approach above described and takes inspiration from the CLM publish/subscribe model for its data abstraction layers, by allowing the communication between device components and inference/reification ones through the SIS framework. The syntax and semantic of the data are defined in a shared vocabulary, that models device raw data in a plain format. In addition, DEA allows to define and maintain an environment model, that could include the architecture into the "domain-oriented architectures" group.

6.2   Domain-Oriented Architectures

Domain-oriented architectures mainly focus on offering information models that fit particular application domains. These architectures usually include device interoperability mechanisms, that they use to infer domain knowledge from heterogeneous sources.

Usually information models refer to abstract representations of environments, whose complexity depends on the specific domain of the solution. In general, solutions in this scope add an abstraction layer to the previous group, with the goal of infer domain knowledge from device data.

In the field of home automation we found, for example, *DOG Gateway* [14], an architecture for "intelligent domotic environments", that abstracts hardware components into an ontological representation of the overall environment, which comprises appliances, various systems (e.g., HVAC, gas, lightning) and simple devices (e.g., lamps), and their spatial location into the environment topology. In this case, the gap between device data and domain knowledge is relatively small: most of the entities at domain level are devices or their aggregations.

In the field of Ambient Intelligence, and in more complex automation solutions, the richness of the models may increase, including more than just device entities and their statuses. In these scenarios, models are enriched by more abstract entities, like people or weather conditions; in general, using an Ubiquitous Computing term, these models deal with *context informations*.

Fernandez-Montes et al. in [16] propose a Smart Environments software reference architecture that implements a *perception-reasoning-action* cyclic flow. Through a component called *Ontologiser*, it organizes data, standardizing them into an environment model. This model includes devices information (i.e., their spatial location and status), inhabitants (like personal data, localization, and health status) and other environment information (e.g., room temperature and brightness). This perceived information is used to reason about the environment to possibly act on it.

In Ubiquitous Computing, the focus moves further on even more abstract environment representation, where devices may be mere information sources (e.g., RFID tags detecting people presence), thus sometimes directly excluded from the model. An example is *Gaia* [8], defined by its authors as a middleware for *Active Spaces*. An Active Space is an instrumented environment coordinated by a software infrastructure that extracts context information, that can be useful to adapt the environment itself to the user's needs.

The main common drawback of the solutions of this class is that each of them supports a specific domain and consequently defines a static information model, concretely excluding its reusability in different domains. Furthermore, the majority of the approaches doesn't deal with time as a primary aspect. DEA overcomes these issues by defining a plain and simple method for modeling domain information, based on property-value pairs, and its contextualization over time. Thus, we define how to model information, but not what, leaving to domain experts or anyone who wants to use the architecture the definition of its own environment model and how device data are linked to it.

Another aspect regards the *action* process, that is, how applications act on the environment to change its state. Although each of the presented architectures model in a clear way the *perception* of the environment (the transformation of device-related data into domain knowledge), there are not details for its symmetric process. The best expectation should be to express actions using the same syntax and semantic of the domain model. DEA complies this expectation by allowing the applications to express wishes on entity statuses at desired time, that will be transformed into feasible actions for the appropriate hardware components.

7   Conclusions and Future Directions

The paper presented an extension of an architecture that allows the integration of heterogeneous devices in order to offer end-user applications a representation of the environment at the right level of abstraction. The extension involves the inclusion of time-related concepts both in the model of the environment and in the mechanisms an end-user application can exploit to interact with the model. Such an inclusion both resolved the problem of information aging and both the problem in making the end-user application aware about when to deliver commands so that they can be fulfilled at the desired time.

The proposed architecture is independent from the application domain, highly modular and open. In fact, it is not designed for a specific scenario, but defines precise levels of abstraction in which placing well-defined components that are domain dependant. Such components are characterized by a high independence and have well-defined interfaces, which specify the structure of the data to be treated and how to communicate with the rest of the architecture. This enforces the openness of the solution, since it encourages the addition of components that adhere to the interfaces and that realize the needed abstraction flows, thus making easy to incrementally support new devices and entity models.

The implementation of a case study has also demonstrated the actual simplification in terms of access to the environment by end-user applications and the advantages in using timed commands.

Future developments will include the identification of solutions that can improve the performance of both the status guessers and wish reasoners reducing both their communication and computation overhead. This can be reached by applying the ALARM architecture [17] in the design of such components. ALARM is a layered architecture that improves software modularity and reduces computational and communication overhead for systems requiring data from sensors in order to perform domain-related elaborations (e.g., tracking and surveillance systems).

References

1. Butz, A., Krüger, A.: A generalized peephole metaphor for augmented reality and instrumented environments. In: Proceedings of The International Workshop on Software Technology for Augmented Reality Systems (STARS) (2003)
2. Negroponte, N.: Soft Architecture Machines. MIT Press, Cambridge (1975)
3. Bullivant, L.: Responsive Environments: Architecture, Art and Design (V&A Contemporaries). Victoria & Albert Museum, London (2006)
4. Kim, J.E., Boulos, G., Yackovich, J., Barth, T., Beckel, C., Mosse, D.: Seamless integration of heterogeneous devices and access control in smart homes. In: 2012 8th International Conference on Intelligent Environments (IE). pp. 206–213 (2012)
5. Thomson, G., Sacchetti, D., Bromberg, Y., Parra, J., Georgantas, N., Issarny, V.: Amigo interoperability framework: dynamically integrating heterogeneous devices and services. In: Mühlhäuser, M., Ferscha, A., Aitenbichler, E. (eds.) Constructing Ambient Intelligence, vol. 11, pp. 421–425. Springer, Berlin Heidelberg (2008)

6. Kusznir, J., Cook, D.: Designing lightweight software architectures for smart environments. In: 2010 Sixth International Conference on Intelligent Environments (IE), IEEE. pp. 220–224 (2010)

7. Ristau, H.: Publish/process/subscribe: message based communication for smart environments. In: 2008 IET 4th International Conference on Intelligent Environments. pp. 1–7 (2008)

8. Román, M., Hess, C., Cerqueira, R., Ranganathan, A., Campbell, R., Nahrstedt, K.: A middleware infrastructure for active spaces. IEEE Pervasive Comput. **1**, 74–83 (2002)

9. Aiello, M., Dustdar, S.: Are our homes ready for services? a domotic infrastructure based on the web service stack. Pervasive Mob. Comput. **4**, 506–525 (2008)

10. Wang, R.Y., Strong, D.M.: Beyond accuracy: what data quality means to data consumers. J. Manage. Inf. Syst. **12**, 5–33 (1996)

11. Covelli, M., Micucci, D., Mobilio, M.: An architecture for the design of platforms supporting responsive environments. In: Proceedings of the International Conference on Software Engineering and Applications (ICSOFT-EA). pp. 417–427 (2014)

12. Cook, D.J., Das, S.K.: How smart are our environments? an updated look at the state of the art. Pervasive Mob. Comput. **3**, 53–73 (2007)

13. Stevens, W., Myers, G., Constantine, L.: Classics in Software Engineering. Yourdon Press, Upper Saddle River, NJ, USA (1979)

14. Bonino, D., Castellina, E., Corno, F.: The DOG gateway: enabling ontology-based intelligent domotic environments. IEEE Trans. Consumer Electron. **54**, 1656–1664 (2008)

15. Janse, M., Vink, P., Georgantas, N.: Amigo architecture: service oriented architecture for intelligent future in-home networks. In: Mühlhäuser, M., Ferscha, A., Aitenbichler, E. (eds.) Constructing Ambient Intelligence. Communications in Computer and Information Science, vol. 11, pp. 371–378. Springer, Berlin Heidelberg (2008)

16. Fernandez-Montes, A., Ortega, J., Alvarez, J., Gonzalez-Abril, L.: Smart environment software reference architecture. In: Fifth International Joint Conference on INC, IMS and IDC, 2009, NCM 2009, IEEE. pp. 397–403 (2009)

17. Fiamberti, F., Micucci, D., Mobilio, M., Tisato, F.: A layered architecture based on previsional mechanisms. In: Proceedings of the International Conference on Software Engineering and Applications (ICSOFT-EA). pp. 354–359 (2013)

A Performance Prediction Model for Google App Engine Using Colored Petri Net

Sachi Nishida and Yoshiyuki Shinkawa[✉]

Ryukoku University, 1-5 Seta Oe-cho Yokotani, Otsu 520-2194, Japan
shinkawa@rins.ryukoku.ac.jp

Abstract. Recently, PaaS (Platform as a Service) type cloud services are widely accepted as platforms for various web applications. Google App engine (GAE) is one of the most popular ones of such services. However, as for mission critical applications, there are several obstacles to migrate into these cloud services like GAE. One of the crucial obstacles is that, while such applications require predictable stable response time, it is difficult to predicate or estimate it in these services, since only a little performance information on these cloud services is available. In addition, the structure of them is not opened to general public. Therefore, it seems difficult to build a performance estimation model based on the system structure. This paper proposes a Colored Petri Net (CPN) based performance prediction model or framework for GAE, based on the performance parameters obtained through the measurement by user written programs. The framework is build focusing on the application structure, which consists of a series of GAE APIs, and GAE works as a mechanism to produce the probabilistic process delays. These delays are modeled using the queuing theory which is embedded in the CPN model. The framework has high modularity to plug-in any kinds of applications easily.

Keywords: Cloud computing · Google App Engine · Performance prediction · Colored petri nets

1 Introduction

Google App Engine (GAE) [1,2] is one of the most popular PaaS (Platform As A Service) type cloud platform for scalable and economic information systems including database transaction processing. While GAE provides us with a easy way to implement considerably complicated transaction systems with low cost, little effort, and high quality, there are several obstacles for mission critical applications, especially for database transaction applications, to migrate into the GAE from their own on-premise systems or platforms. Among those obstacles, "data integrity", "security", and "system performance" seem most crucial.

While many attentions are paid to the first two topics during system and application design phases [3,4], the third topic is only focused on after the system operation. The major reason for this is that only a little information is

© Springer International Publishing Switzerland 2015
A. Holzinger et al. (Eds.): ICSOFT 2014, CCIS 555, pp. 251–265, 2015.
DOI: 10.1007/978-3-319-25579-8_15

available on the detail of the GAE, by which we can estimate the performance of the system currently designed, e.g. on the average response time of each GAE system component. However, the performance prediction in the design phase is important for the mission critical applications, since they usually have performance and throughput constraints, and if the problems with these concerns are detected after the cutover, an enormous amount of effort will be wasted to tune-up, re-design, and re-program the system. Therefore, the performance prediction is one of the critical tasks for such kinds of systems to run in the cloud.

In order to build a performance prediction model for the GAE, we need an alternative way to obtain the performance related information of the GAE. One practical way to gather such information is to measure the performance of the GAE under various configurations, to estimate the performance data.

This paper presents a simulation based approach to predicting the performance of GAE applications. In this approach, we focus on the APIs that the GAE provides, to compose the above performance prediction model, since they are easily measured by user written programs, and we can compose application process models using them. Colored Petri Net (CPN) [5] is used as a modeling and simulation tool, since it provides us with a vast capability for expressing the behavior and functionality of systems, with temporal characteristics. The rest of the paper is organized as follows. In Sect. 2, we introduce a CPN based performance prediction framework. Section 3 presents how the GAE applications and the GAE platform are modeled using CPN, along with the simulation data generation and resultant evaluation methods. Section 4 shows a way to obtain the performance parameters using user written measurement programs.

2   CPN Based Performance Prediction Framework

Google App Engine (GAE) is one of the most popular cloud services, which is categorized into the PaaS. GAE provides us with a variety of services, regarding web applications, databases, and software development environments. As a result, there could be a variety of system forms, using different program languages and databases.

Among them, one of the typical use of GAE is to deploy Java based *Datastore* applications in the form of servlets, developed under the Eclipse with the "Google Plugin". GAE *Datastore* is one of the NoSQL databsses [6], with simplified structure and manipulation, focusing more on the availability and scalability than the integrity and usability. The concepts of *"table"*, *"row"*, and *"column"* in the relational database are approximately mapped to *"kind"*, *"entity"*, and *"property"* in the *Datastore* respectively. We focus on this forms of application for the performance prediction.

Since the detailed internal structure of GAE is not opened to the general public, it seems impractical to predict the performance based on the temporal characteristics of each system component. Instead, an application structure oriented performance prediction seems more realistic, if we can obtain the required time with the statistical fluctuations for each API. These APIs include the *PersistenceManager* creation, the *Query* object creation, the data manipulation like data insertion, deletion, modification, and selection, transaction control, commit/abort, and so on.

From the performance viewpoint, each application program is regarded as a series of these APIs, which are passed to the GAE system. On the other hand, the GAE system is almost a black box, although several major components are partially opened to public, e.g. BigTable, GFS (Google File System), and Chubby [7,8]. Therefore, for the performance viewpoint, it seems better to regard GAE as a black-box mechanism to produce a temporal delay than to model the details of it.

In order to make a performance prediction model for GAE, we first have to choose an appropriate modeling tool having the capability of

1. expressing the behavior and functionality of each application program,
2. simulating the behavior and functionality of each application, along with the interactions with the GAE system, and
3. producing the temporal delay in the simulation.

Colored Petri Net (CPN) in conjunction with the CPN tools [9] is one of the most suitable modeling tools for these requirements.

CPN is formally defined as a nine-tuple $CPN=(P, T, A, \Sigma, V, C, G, E, I)$, where

P : a finite set of places.
T : a finite set of transitions.
  (a transition represents an event)
A : a finite set of arcs $P \cap T = P \cap A = T \cap A = \emptyset$.
Σ : a finite set of non-empty color sets.
  (a color represents a data type)
V : a finite set of typed variables.
C : a color function $P \rightarrow \Sigma$.
G : a guard function $T \rightarrow$ expression.
  (a guard controls the execution of a transition)
E : an arc expression function $A \rightarrow$ expression.
I : an initialization function : $P \rightarrow$ closed expression.

In the above definition, a "place" means some *location* or *mechanism* to hold some resources or data, which are represented by the "tokens". A "transition" means an occurrence of an *event* to manipulate the tokens. Each token is associated with a unique "color" that is defined as a *data type*. By introducing the data type into regular Petri Nets, CPN can perform explicit data processing to express the functionality of a model. An "arc" function and "guard function" are in charge of the above data processing. While an arc function can modify the relevant token values, a guard function examines the values to control the assigned transition firing.

CPN itself is not furnished with the temporal capability, however it have been enhanced to the *Timed* CPN [5], by incorporating the *"firing delay"* concept of the *timed* Petri Net [10] into it. In *Timed* CPN, each token can optionally be

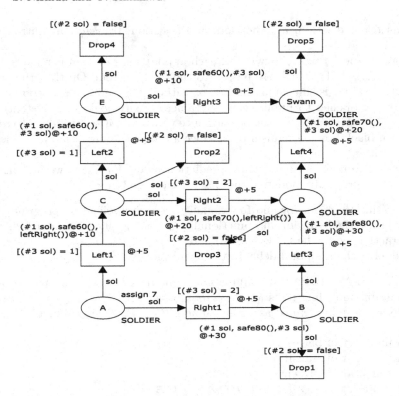

Fig. 1. An example of *Timed* CPN.

assigned a *timestamp* property along with a color set. By this timestamp, the firing of a transition by this token is postponed until the timestamp expires.

This property is declared at the "closet" (color set) definition time like

closet No = INT *timed*;

The actual timestamp is assigned by one of the three ways, namely, by the initial token marking, by the transaction firing, or by the arc function invocation. The assignment operation is designated by the symbol "@", e.g. "@ + 50". Figure 1 shows an example of such *Timed* CPN model.

In order to increase the modularity of the prediction model, we first build a high level framework using CPN, which is composed of functionally independent four major components, as shown in Fig. 2. In this figure, the "Generation" component generates all the application programs or transactions in the form of CPN tokens, which are to run in the GAE system. Each token is appended an appropriate *arrival time* as a CPN *timestamp*. The "Application" component performs the execution of each application at the given concurrency level.

The concurrency level is implemented as a maximum number of concurrently active *threads* to run each transaction. In order to control the concurrency level, the place "CLC" (an abbreviation for *Concurrency Level Control*) is marked

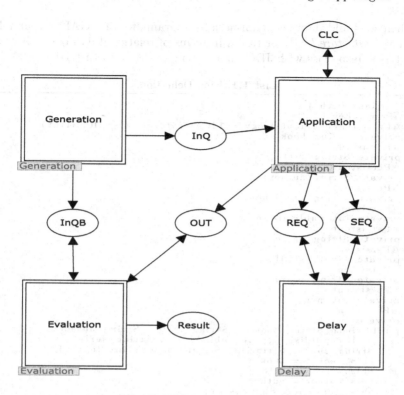

Fig. 2. High level framework.

with an integer list token, each element of which represent the thread availability, and the length of which represents the concurrency level, namely, the maximum number of concurrently active threads.

The "Delay" component produces the temporal delay with statistical fluctuation. The last component "Evaluation" examines the resultant tokens of the simulation marked in the "OUT" place, to calculate and report the performance indices, e.g. the mean response time, variance, waiting time, and throughput.

3   Performance Simulation and Evaluation Mode

Each component in the performance prediction framework is refined stepwise into the more detailed simulatable CPN model.

3.1   Refining the "Application" Component

As stated in Sect. 2, each application can be regarded as a series of GAE APIs from the performance prediction viewpoint, since the most of execution time is consumed for the processing of these APIs, and the rest part would be negligibly small.

When we build database transaction programs for the GAE, we first have to prepare *datastore kinds*, or tables in terms of relational databases. A *kind* is defined as a Java class with JDO annotation, as shown in List 1.1.

List 1.1. Kind Definition.

```
public class Buch {
    @PrimaryKey
    @Persistent(valueStrategy = IdGeneratorStrategy.IDENTITY)
    private String bookId;
    @Persistent
    private String title;
    @Persistent
    private String author;
    @Persistent
    private String publisher;
    @Persistent
    private int publishDate;
    @Persistent
    private String series;
    @Persistent
    private String shelf;
    @Persistent
    private String place;
    @Persistent
    private int price;
    @Persistent
    private int lent;
    public Buch(String bookId, String title, String author,
        String publisher, int publishDate, String series,
        String shelf, String place, int price, int lent) {
        this.bookId = bookId;
        this.title = title;
        this.author = author;
        this.publisher = publisher;
        this.publishDate = publishDate;
        this.series = series;
        this.shelf = shelf;
        this.place = place;
        this.price = price;
        this.lent = lent;
    }

    public String getBookId() {
        return bookId;
    }
    *
    *
    *   /* getters and setters follow */
    *
    *
}
```

A part of a simplified Java program to deal with this kind "Buch" is shown in List 1.2.

List 1.2. Sample GAE program.

```
public class BuchSuchen extends HttpServlet    {
            /* */
            /* Variable Definitions    */
            /* */
        public void doGet(HttpServletRequest req,
            HttpServletResponse resp)
```

```
                        throws IOException {
              resp.setContentType("text/html;charset=UTF-8");
              req.setCharacterEncoding("UTF-8");
              pm = PMF.get().getPersistenceManager();
              MemcacheService mcs = MemcacheServiceFactory.
                     getMemcacheService();
public void read () {
              filter = "";
              Query query = pm.newQuery(Buch.class);
              if (screen.equals("2")) {
                        filter = rt.getFilter();
              }
              else setFilterParameters();
              query.setFilter(filter); //
              rt.setFilter(filter);
              bookList = (List<Buch>) query.execute();
              System.out.println("size of booklist = " + bookList.
                     size());
}
public void update () {
          try {
                  Query query = pm.newQuery(Buch.class);
                  filter = "bookId == " + "'" + bookId + "'";
                  System.out.println("filter = " + filter);
                  query.setFilter(filter);
                  List<Buch> books = (List<Buch>) query.
                         execute();
                  System.out.println("Size == " + books.size()
                         );
                  for(Buch book: books) {
                     if (!book.getBookId().equals(bookId))
                         break;
                         book.setBookId(bookId);
                         if (title.length() > 0) book.
                                setTitle(title);
                         if (author.length() > 0) book.
                                setAuthor(author);
                         if (publisher.length() > 0) book.
                                setPublisher(publisher);
                         if (publishDate.length() > 0) book.
                                setPublishDate(Integer.parseInt(
                                publishDate));
                         if (series.length() > 0) book.
                                setSeries(series);
                         if (shelf.length() > 0) book.
                                setShelf(shelf);
                         if (place.length() > 0) book.
                                setPlace(place);
                         if (price.length() > 0) book.
                                setPrice(Integer.parseInt(price)
                                );
                         if (lent.equals("  ")) book.setLent
                                (1);
                  }
          } finally {
                  pm.close();
          }

}

     /* */
     /* Other Method Definitions    */
     /* */

}
```

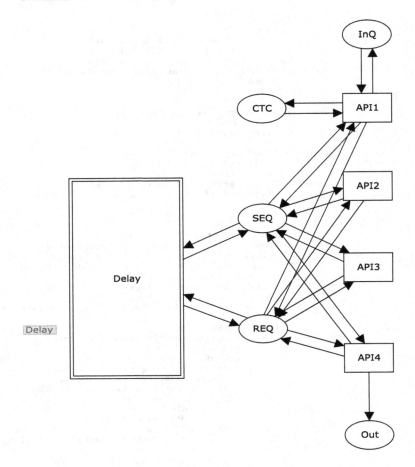

Fig. 3. "Application" component.

The typical GAE *Datastore* application, written by Java JDO, flows as follows.

1. Handle the *Session* and *Memcache* objects in its prologue.
2. Get the *PersistenceManager* instance.
3. Declare the beginning of the transaction.
4. Create and execute the *Query* objects to access the *Datastore* as many as required.
5. Close the *PersistenceManager*.
6. Commit or abort the transaction.

Each action of the above process is expressed as an "API". For each API that interfaces the GAE system, one CPN transition is assigned, in order to explicitly show the sequence of the issued APIs from a transaction. Since this sequence is different from each other between transactions, we have to create multiple instances of this "Application" component, each of which reflects the *application logic* of an individual transaction.

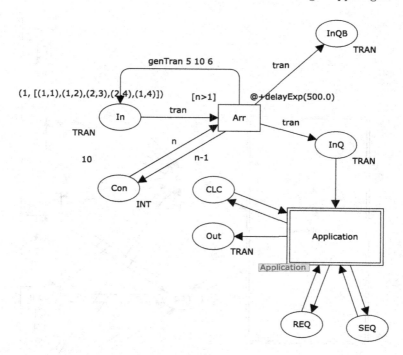

Fig. 4. "Generation" component.

As shown in Fig. 3, each transition in this component is connected to the two places "REQ" and "SEQ" that are interfaced with the "Delay" component. The "REQ" place holds the tokens each of which represents a single GAE API. Theses tokens are used to produce the temporal delay by the "Delay" component. On the other hand, the "SEQ" place holds a single token to control the firing sequence of the transitions. By this token we can implement the *if-then-else* branches and *while* loops to form the control structure of each application logic.

The color sets assigned to these places have the same name as the places, which are defined as

closet REQ = product OP * OptList;
closet SEQ = product OP * RC * SN;

Where "OP" represents the API name, "OptList" represents the option list or argument list of the API to derive the accurate delay time, "RC" is the return code from the API, and "SN" is the sequence number of the transition to be fired next.

3.2 Refining the "Generation" Component

The purpose of this component is to generate the transactions to be performed in the GAE system, at the appropriate arrival rate, following the appropriate distribution functions.

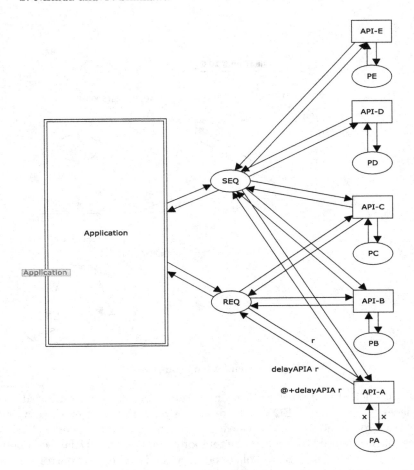

Fig. 5. "Delay" component.

In order to provide the transaction tokens at a desired arrival rate following a desired distribution pattern, we need to generate a set of the timestamps using the appropriate distribution function with the appropriate mean and variance values. The CPN ML language, which is a specification language for CPN models, provides us with a variety of distribution functions, e.g. *Exponential*, *Normal*, *Chi-square*, *Bernoulli*, and so on.

For example, in order to generate the transaction tokens at the arrival rate 500 per second, and each interval time between adjacent transactions follow the exponential distribution function, we first define the CPN ML function as,

fun delayExp (x) = round (exponential (1.0/x));

and add the timestamp by "@+delayExp(500.0)" to each initial transaction token with the "timestamp = 0". Figure 4 shows an example of "Generation" component for this arrival rate. In this figure, "Arr" transition add the above timestamps. This "Generation" component generates a *Poisson* arrival, since the time interval between events follows the exponential distribution function. The structure of "Generation" component for another transaction arrival pattern is basically the same.

The generated transaction tokens are marked in the "InQ" place, which interfaces with the "Application" component. The "InQB" place holds the copy of all the generated transaction tokens for the later performance evaluation.

3.3   Refining the "Delay" Component

The functionality of this component is rather simple in comparison with other components, since it simply adds the temporal delay to the received tokens which represents the GAE APIs. However, the delay could vary with many factors, some of which we cannot even forecast, e.g. the system reconfiguration, data replication, or recovery operations. Therefore, this component calculates the delay based on the mean and the variance values obtained through the system measurement. This approach is discussed in the next section.

Assuming this information is obtained, the component is implemented as a CPN model as shown in Fig. 5. In this figure, each transition "API-x" ($x = $ A, B, $\cdots$) represents a specific API. The delay would be different even for the same API, depending on the characteristics of the object to be handled and the API options such as *setFilter* options. Such information is embedded into the "OptList" field of the token "REQ" by the "Application" component, and is handled by the CPN ML functions in the "Delay" component. For example, if the delay of data insertion varies with the *kinds* of the *Datastore*, following the normal distribution functions with the different mean and variance values, we have to define the CPN ML function for the delay as List 1.3.

List 1.3. Delay Generation ML Program.

```
val tx = detTran t1
in
( uniqID , tx ,  ( genDBRL tx ) )
end ;
fun delaySelect db = case db of
        1 => round( normal( 2.6973 , 11.26709371 ) ) |
        2 => round( normal( 3.99365,  22.52153 ) ) |
        3 => round( normal( 3.54455,  10.54986359 ) ) |
        _ => 0;
fun delayUpdate db = case db of
        1 => round( normal( 76.099 , 9054.523299 ) ) |
        2 => round( normal( 48.38625,  1841.868 ) ) |
        3 => round( normal( 94.341,  3826.030719 ) ) |
        _ => 0;
fun delayInsert db = case db of
        1 => round( normal( 105.575 , 7693.153875 ) ) |
        2 => round( normal( 96.901,  6811.027 ) ) |
        3 => round( normal( 77.03,  4937.9957 ) ) |
        _ => 0;
fun delayDelete db = case db of
        1 => round( normal( 62.804 , 8665.071784 ) ) |
        2 => round( normal( 94.9975,  4257.376 ) ) |
        3 => round( normal( 73.1385,  2563.186393 ) ) |
        _ => 0;
fun f n = case ( t1 n ) of nil => [] |
        _ => ( t1 n );
```

This CPN ML function generates the different delay patterns for three different Datastore *kinds*, each of which follows the normal distribution function with different mean and variance values.

The transition "API-x" works a *server* in terms of *queuing theory* [11], therefore it should cease the firing while it processes the received request. It means if the transition generates the delay t, it never fires until the time t expires. On the other hand, the *Timed* CPN adopts a different mechanism. Even though the timestamp of a token postpones the firing of a transition, the firing ends instantaneously, and another token can fire it. In order to avoid this conflict, we use one more place "Px" for each transition "API-x" as shown in Fig. 5. The token in this place is initially marked with "timestamp = 0". Each time "API-x" fires, the timestamp value of the token in "Px" is increased by the delay time. Therefore, the token ceases the firing of "API-x" for the delay time.

3.4   Refining the "Evaluation" Component

After the simulation of the "Application" components ends, interacting with the "Delay" component, the "OUT" place contains all the scheduled transaction tokens with their *end* timestamps. Since the copy of the arrival transaction tokens with their *arrival* timestamps are marked in the "InQB" place, this module can calculate the elapsed time for each transaction, along with the mean response time, the variance, and the throughput. Each elapsed time is calculated by subtracting the arrival timestamp from the end timestamp, the mean response time is obtained by dividing the summation of these elapsed times by the number of transactions, and the variance is derived from this mean response time and each response time. The throughput is a number of the processed transactions per time unit, and is calculated similarly.

The resultant performance data obtained through the simulation are marked in the "Result" place as a report.

4   Measuring and Estimating the Base Parameters

The proposed framework regards the GAE as a black-box, therefore we need to obtain the base performance parameters, e.g. the mean and variance values of the elapsed time of each API, by measuring the system. For the obtainment of these parameters, a set of simple Java programs is used in this framework. Since an elapsed time of each API is usually too short to be measured by a program, each measurement program issues several hundreds of the same API, and calculates the mean value. This mean value is written to the GAE *log* as a *warning*. List 1.4 shows an example of such a Java code.

Each measurement program is performed many times to obtain the variance and to estimate the proper distribution function. As for the *Datastore* access APIs, the elapsed time would vary with the size of the *kind* and the number of the *properties* in the *kind*. Therefore, we have to measure the parameters varying these factors. Tables 1 and 2 show the sample results of such a measurement.

List 1.4. Measurement Program.

```
Query  query  =  pm.newQuery(Buch20.class);
long  start  =  System.currentTimeMillis();
for(int  i  =  1;i<=200;i++){
        String  s  =  "bookId==\""  +  i  +  "\"";
        query.setFilter(s);
        rt.setFilter(filter);
        bookList  =  (List<Buch20>)query.execute();
}
long  stop  =  System.currentTimeMillis();
long  t  =  stop  −  start;
log.warning("Elapsed  Time  =  "  +  t/200);
```

All the obtained parameters are embedded into the "Delay" component to produce the appropriate delay.

Table 1. Mean value – elapsed time.

Size	Sel	Mod	Del	Ins
3 × 10000	3.54455	94.341	73.1385	77.03
5 × 8000	2.744525	90.6515	71.7045	64.04
10 × 4000	3.99365	48.38625	94.9975	96.901
20 × 2000	2.8044	101.388	80.803	64.6795
50 × 1000	2.6973	76.099	62.804	105.575

Table 2. Distribution – elapsed time.

Size	Sel	Mod	Del	Ins
3 × 10000	10.54986359	3826.030719	2563.186393	4937.9957
5 × 8000	3.316131306	2586.511223	2847.611555	2751.954
10 × 4000	22.52153305	1841.868342	4257.375919	6811.027499
20 × 2000	9.33806114	10922.73706	2580.819791	1202.372305
50 × 1000	11.26709371	9054.523299	8665.071784	7693.153875

Since the above performance parameters vary over time, or in other words, they are time varying factors, we have to measure them periodically, and reflect them in the "Delay" component in order to keep the prediction framework up to date.

5   Conclusions

A simulation based performance prediction framework for GAE is proposed, which uses the *Timed* Colored Petri Net (*Timed* CPN). In order to increase the modularity, the framework is composed of four functionally independent components connected together by CPN places, namely, "Generation", "Application", "Delay" and "Evaluation" components.

Since GAE is almost a black-box from the performance prediction viewpoint, most performance parameters have to be obtained through the measurement using user written programs. Using the obtained parameters, that is, the mean and variance values with the estimated distribution functions, "Delay" components produces the delay for each API, then add it to the timestamp attribute of each token that has issued the API.

At the end of the simulation, the "Evaluation" component examines the resultant tokens to calculate the performance indices. The performance parameters change over time, or they are the time-varying factors, therefore the above measurement must be done periodically, so that the latest parameters are embedded into the "Delay" component.

The proposed approach estimates the performance from end-to-end basis for each transaction. However, for more precise prediction and performance analysis, we need component based estimation, that is, we have to take the delay of each component into account. For this purpose, we can use the monitoring facility of the CPN tools. However, we need to modify the prediction model to gather the monitoring data.

Acknowledgements. This work was supported by JSPS KAKENHI Grant Number 25330094.

References

1. de Jonge, A.: Essential App Engine: Building High-Performance Java Apps with Google App Engine. Addison-Wesley Professional, Boston (2011)
2. Sanderson, D.: Programming Google App Engine. Oreilly and Associates Inc., Cambridge (2009)
3. Garcia, J.L., Langenberg, R., Suri, N.: Bigtable: Benchmarking Cloud Security Level Agreements Using Quantitative Policy Trees. In: Proceedings of the 2012 ACM Workshop on Cloud Computing Security. Workshop, pp. 103–112 (2012)
4. Nishida, S., Shinkawa, Y.: Data Integrity in Cloud Transactions. In: Proceedings of the 4th International Conference on Cloud Computing and Services Science, pp. 457–462 (2014)
5. Jensen, K., Kristensen, L.M.: Coloured Petri Nets: Modeling and Validation of Concurrent Systems. Springer-Verlag, Heidelberg (2009)
6. Sadalage, P.J., Fowler, M.: NoSQL Distilled: A Brief Guide to the Emerging World of Polyglot Persistence. Addison-Wesley Professional, Cambridge (2012)
7. Chang, F., Dean, J., Ghemawat, S, Hsieh, W.C, Wallach, D.A., Burrows, M., Chandra, T., Fikes, A., Gruber, R.E.: Bigtable: A Distributed Storage System for Structured Data. In: Proceedings of the 7th Conference on USENIX Symposium on Operating Systems Design and Implementation, vol. **7**, pp. 205–218 (2006)
8. Howard, S.G., Gobioff, H., Leung, S.: The Google File System (2003). http://static.googleusercontent.com/media/research.google.com/ja//archive/gfs-sosp2003.pdf
9. Jensen, K., Kristensen, L.M., Wells, L.: Coloured petri nets and CPN tools for modelling and validation of concurrent systems. Int. J. Softw. Tools Technol. Transfer (STTT) **9**(3–4), 213–254 (2007)

10. Wang, J.: Timed Petri Nets: Theory and Application. The International Series on Discrete Event Dynamic Systems. Springer, Heidelberg (1998)
11. Gnedenko, B.V., Kovalenko, I.N.: Introduction to Queuing Theory. Mathematical Modeling. Birkhaeuser Boston, Boston (1989)

Software Paradigm Trends

A Case Study on Model-Driven Development and Aspect-Oriented Programming: Benefits and Liabilities

Uwe Hohenstein[1(✉)] and Christoph Elsner[2]

[1] Siemens AG, Corporate Technology,
Otto-Hahn-Ring 6, 81730 Muenchen, Germany
Uwe.Hohenstein@siemens.com
[2] Siemens AG, Corporate Technology,
Wladimirstr 3, 91058 Erlangen, Germany
Christoph.Elsner@siemens.com

Abstract. Model-driven development (MDD) and aspect-oriented programming (AOP) are two very different paradigms, having in common that they both aim at increasing development efficiency. In order to investigate their benefits and liabilities, we compared both in context of a case study on an industrial-grade software system, the Open SOA platform. Already having a model-driven XML/XSL-T implementation in place, we re-implemented the corresponding logic of the Open SOA platform with a corresponding AOP implementation in AspectJ. Considering several comparison criteria, the results of our case study indicate that the AspectJ implementation is less redundant, better testable, and improves on understandability and readability. The model-driven approach, in turn, is the more flexible one, as it allows for generating arbitrary artifacts and structures, without the need for compromising on design. Additionally, we expect that MDD can furthermore catch up on readability and understandability, when more advanced MDD tooling can be leveraged. As our case study mainly centers around implementing wrappers and boilerplate-code, which are rather common issues, our results may be transferred to similar problem settings. Furthermore, our evaluation criteria can guide others in making technology choices. To this end, we give an outlook on how combinations of MDD and AOP may leverage the best of both worlds.

Keywords: AOP · AspectJ · MDD · XSL-T · Case study

1 Introduction

Model-driven development (MDD) has the goal to develop software systems on a higher abstraction level than code [24]. Given some high-level form of input, more concrete output is generated, maybe even source code. Code generation not only saves time and effort, but also avoids programming errors and increases programmer productivity [21]. Moreover, the input has a higher level of abstraction, is simpler and shorter than the generated code, and makes concepts more explicit. One basic idea of MDD is a voluntary self-restriction, i.e., the input model uses a limited number of

© Springer International Publishing Switzerland 2015
A. Holzinger et al. (Eds.): ICSOFT 2014, CCIS 555, pp. 269–290, 2015.
DOI: 10.1007/978-3-319-25579-8_16

concepts that are defined by a metamodel. Common forms of input are domain-specific languages (DSL): graphical, textual, XML, or UML models. A lot of tooling can be used such as Xtext [28] or MPS [17] or pure::variants [3].

Aspect-orientation programming (AOP) is quite a different technology that provides new mechanisms to handle crosscutting concerns (CCCs). CCCs are those functionalities that are typically spread across several classes with conventional programming. Those CCCs usually cause duplicated and redundant code. This leads to lower programming productivity, poor quality and traceability, and a lower degree of code reuse. AOP provides new constructs to separate crosscutting concerns. This separation allows for a better modularization, thereby avoiding the well-known symptoms of code tangling and code scattering [25]. Aspect-oriented languages such as AspectJ [2, 12] support the separation of concerns by means of special language constructs. Even other languages such as Scala or Ruby are starting to offer means for handling CCCs such as abstractions or meta-programming.

Both technologies, MDD and AOP, can be used to avoid redundant code. As Normén, [18] states "code duplications smell badly" and should be avoided. However, there are always cases where they cannot be avoided using conventional programming languages. While MDD uses a generative approach, AOP extends an existing implementation language and modularizes common code in an aspect.

In this paper, we compare both technologies in a real industrial application. The comparison is done for XML-based code generation and the AspectJ language in the context of the OpenSOA project [22]. OpenSOA offers a service-oriented telecommunication middleware platform. It is an open service platform for the deployment and provision of communication services such as capturing user presence, management of calling domains, notifications, administration functionality for the underlying switch technology, and so forth. An OSGi container builds the technical basis.

A specific challenge within the OpenSOA framework is that several message-based interfaces have to be kept consistent. These interfaces are similar, however, having slight differences.

Since the development team spent about 50 % of its time to create and maintain interface code and inline documentation, an MDD approach has been implemented to avoid duplicated code in different layers and to achieve consistency between several closely related interfaces and Javadoc comments. The approach relies on XML input and XSL-T transformations producing Java code, similar to [20]. Although the approach is very helpful, developing and verifying XSL-T transformations has resulted to be tedious.

The content of this paper is to evaluate and compare the usage of AOP in such a typical MDD scenario. The work is based upon prior work that we presented in [8]. We started to re-implement the OpenSOA system with the language AspectJ to avoid code generation and to reduce code – even if it follows a different paradigm. The AspectJ implementation is a (non-obvious) alternative to the existing XSL-T code generation. Moreover, it could easily be integrated into the project infrastructure in contrast to other approaches. Using this basis, several facets of both solutions are compared and discussed.

At first, we compare the classical criterion of "lines of code". This is an indicator for the manual work to be done. "Code" does not only mean Java/AspectJ code but also writing XSL-T transformations and XML input in case of MDD: both comprise effort to be done.

We distinguish two major roles: The implementer provides the generative infra-structure, i.e., implements XSL-T scripts or codes aspects in AspectJ. In contrast, the user applies this infrastructure by providing XML input or defining pointcuts, respectively.

The more lines of code have to be written, the more work has to be done. But the code does not determine exclusively the effort. Therefore, we qualitatively and quantitatively evaluate several other measures. Understandability is a further mean for complexity and maintenance effort: The easier to apply, understand, and maintain a concept, the less effort an implementer or user has. Furthermore, testability is important for the implementer to check the correctness of the framework. For instance, XSL-T could generate code that is not accepted by a Java compiler. Further investigation criteria are usability, redundancy avoidance, and completeness of the approach. Our evaluation criteria have a strong industrial background and have been chosen due to their relevance for the involved OpenSOA software developers.

We use the case study to compare in detail the weaknesses and strengths of both approaches with regard to those criteria in order to give some guidance for choosing amongst the technologies and to make the best of both worlds.

In the following, we present in Sect. 2 the project OpenSOA, a telecommunication middleware [22], we used for our case study. Section 3 describes the model-driven approach, based upon XML and XSL-T, which was in productive use. We present in Sect. 4 an alternative AspectJ solution, which could serve the same purpose. Both approaches are compared in Sect. 5 using the above mentioned criteria. Moreover, it summarizes the limitations of both technologies and discusses what of our experiences can be generalized beyond the case study. Section 6 presents some related work, before Sect. 7 concludes the discussion.

2 The OpenSOA Framework

The OpenSOA framework consists of six services: DomainManagement, UserManagement, ResourceManagement, ProfileManagement, ApplicationManagement, and RoleManagement. These services offer CRUD functionality, i.e., create, find, update, and delete operations. There are 93 operations in total, i.e., 15.5 operations per service in average.

For each of these *Service*s, classes *Service*Skeleton and *Service*Trans-Skeleton implement essential middleware functionality, while a class *Service*-Impl implements the actual business logic. Figure 1 shows the important parts of these classes for the UserManagement service.

The classes *Service*Skeleton provide the entry point for service invocations. CRUD operations such as create expect both a dedicated parameter request object and a service context in its signature: OpReply op(OpRequest req, ServiceRequestContext ctx). Depending on whether persistence in a database is required or not, the call either delegates to the method op(*params*) of class *Service*TransSkeleton or to op(*params*, em) of class *Service*Impl.

```
public final class UserManagementSkeleton
              extends Service implements UserManagement {
  private UserManagementTransSkeleton trans = null; ...
  public void create(final UserRequest req,
                     final ServiceRequestContext srvCtx) {
    UserIdentity ret = null;
    try {
      if (LOG.isDebugEnabled())
       LOG.debug("Operation started: " + req.toString());
      final UserDTO user = req.getUser()
      boolean returnIdentity = req.getReturnIdentity();
      ret = trans.(user, returnIdentity, true);
      UserReply reply = new UserReply(ret);
      srvCtx.reply(reply);
      if (LOG.isDebugEnabled())
        LOG.debug("Return: " + reply.toString());
      if (LOG.isDebugEnabled())
        LOG.debug("Operation  completed successfully");
    } catch (DomainValidationException e) {
      if (LOG.isDebugEnabled())
        LOG.debug("missing or wrong arguments.");
      srvCtx.fail(e);
    } catch ...
} }
public final class UserManagementTransSkeleton {
  private UserManagementSkeleton skeleton;
  private UserManagementImpl impl = null;
  public UserIdentity create(final UserDTO user, final
     boolean returnIdentity, final boolean isValidated) {
    UserIdentity obj = (UserIdentity) skeleton
      .getOpenJPAConfiguration().getTemplate().execute (
        new OpenJPACallback() {
          public Object doInTransaction(final EM em) {
            UserIdentity result =
              impl.(user,returnIdentity,em,isValidated);
            return result;
  } } );
    return obj; } }
public final class UserManagementImpl  {
  private UserManagementSkeleton skeleton = null;
  public UserIdentity create(final UserDTO user, boolean
    retIdentity, EntityManager em, boolean isValidated) {
    if (!isValidated)  //---------- validate params
      DomainValidator.validate(user, "user");
    business logic to be implemented by the programmer
} }
```

Fig. 1. *Service* classes for the UserManagement service.

The parameter em provides an OpenJPA EntityManager to perform database operations. In both cases, a list of parameters (denoted as *params*) is extracted from the Request parameter by req.get...(). The *Service*Skeleton class catches technical exceptions and throws various service exceptions such as AuthorizationException or PersistenceDuplicateEntityException.

The *Service*Impl classes provide a code template to be filled out with the real business logic.

Classes *Service*TransSkeleton are used only by services that handle persistence. The class basically delegates to the *Service*Impl methods, but puts some logic around by a template mechanism, especially to let the Impl functionality run in a database session and transaction. The template is obtained by using the *Service*Skeleton object and used to execute an OpenJPACallback. The OpenJPACallback must implement a doInTransaction method, which invokes the *Service*Impl method that contains the logic to be executed in a session and transaction. That is, execute(OpenJPACallback) opens a database connection (which is represented by an EntityManager em in OpenJPA) and starts a transaction around doInTransaction. Moreover, when a database operation fails because of connection problems or database server crashes, a retry is performed taking a new connection, maybe from a failover server in order to achieve high availability.

Further classes *Op*Request and *Op*Reply are used in the signatures of *Service*Skeleton for operations *Op*.

Obviously, similar methods occur in different classes for one single service, having the same name but slightly different signatures. This should not be seen as a deficit of the architecture. A major reason for choosing the design with different signatures is to achieve better testability with shorter test cycles, since *Service*TransSkeleton/Impl can be tested without an OSGi container. Another reason for this type of architecture is to have a class *Service*TransSkeleton for a reusable session and transaction handling.

So, although we consider the architecture appropriate, a lot of method signatures and also code parts have to be kept consistent.

3 The MDD Approach

To ease the development and to handle consistency, an MDD approach has been established in the project. Its goal is to keep related signatures and documentation headers of different parts of a single service consistent.

The basic idea consists of specifying services in an XML-based description language in one place. The user has to specify a file *Service*.xml for each service. The corresponding metamodel is a predefined XML-Schema. Figure 2 presents such a file.

This XML input is taken for generating code by means of several XSL-T scripts. In particular, the documentation and the Javadoc description of parameters are generated in a consistent manner. The XML input specifies an XML element <service> with a certain name.

```
<service name="UserManagement" persistence="true"
          eventing="false">
  <operation name="create" id="#User01"
              deprecated="false" transaction="true">
    <description>
      <![CDATA[ * <p>Create a new user with all settings
                  from UserDTO.</p>
                * <p>The working domain is the user's
                  domain</p>]]>
    </description>
    <return type="com.siemens.project.UserIdentity">
      <description> <![CDATA[returns the identity object
                            of the user created.]]>
      </description>
    </return>
    <parameter name="user"
                type="com.siemens.project.UserDTO">
      <validation nullAllowed="false"/>
      <description> <![CDATA[DTO containing all
                      information about the new user.]]>
      </description>
    </parameter>
    <exception type=
        "com.siemens.project.DomainValidationException">
      <description> <![CDATA[if an argument value is
                    invalid; that means also null or
                    empty if not explicitly allowed.]]>
      </description>
      <logmessage>
        <![CDATA[missing or wrong arguments.]]>
      </logmessage>
    </exception>
    <!--other exceptions -->
  </operation>
  <!--other operations -->
<service>
```

Fig. 2. XML sample service description.

An attribute `persistence=true` controls the persistence infrastructure for using the OpenJPA persistence framework to access a DBS. Similarly, `eventing=true` prepares an eventing mechanism in the business logic.

Each `<service>` element specifies `<operation>`s with `<parameter>` types, `<return>` type, and `<exception>`s in XML. Several XML attributes affect the code generation:

- `deprecated=true` lets `@deprecated` occur in the Javadoc behind a parameter.
- `transaction=true` adds a session and transaction management. We call such an operation *transactional* in the following.
- Parameters can be validated by specifying a `<validation>` such as `nullAllowed` or `emptyAllowed`; checks are added on parameter values, e.g., whether null or empty strings are allowed.
- A `<description>` can be added to most XML parts to be used in Javadoc documentation.

3.1 XSL-T Scripts for Code Generating

There are three basic XSL-T transformations that are responsible for generating the code for the three types of classes mentioned before:

- `TransSkeleton.xsl` generates the complete code for *Service*-`TransSkeleton` classes.
- `Skeleton.xsl` generates the complete code for *Service*`Skeleton` classes.
- `Impl.xsl` generates the code frames for *Service*`Impl` classes, which have to be completed with business logic by programmers.

The overall principle of generation is straightforward. Each service in `Service.xml` results in three Java classes *Service*`TransSkeleton`, *Service*`Impl`, and *Service*`Skeleton`.

Each XSL-T implementation simply transforms XML elements and attributes to Java code and produces the classes. Each `<operation>` results in a corresponding Java method in each class, however, having slightly different signatures and implementations for the classes. The `<parameter>`s describe the signature of methods.

The `<description>` is used for adding a consistent documentation including Javadoc. `<description>` can occur at several levels (`<operation>`, `<exception>`, `<parameter>`).

Details about the output generated from the XSL-T scripts are described in the following. Figure 3 presents an excerpt of a script to generate a signature with documentation. These lines show how verbose and unreadable the XSL-T code is.

3.2 Classes *Service*Impl

The Java code for *Service*`Impl` classes and its methods are directly derived from the XML specification. *Service*`Impl` is the only class that is not fully generated. The user has to implement the business logic. Some specific points are (cf. Fig. 1):

- *Signature Changes*: The `create` method obtains two additional parameters `EntityManager em` and `boolean isValidated` if `transaction=true` and `<validation nullAllowed= "false"/>`, respectively, are specified for any operation. The first parameter `em` enables the method to use OpenJPA's

`EntityManager` functionality. The second parameter allows invokers to switch a parameter validation on or off.

- *Additional Code Fragments:* The validation of parameters of the form "`if (! isValidated)`...", if turned on by `<validation>`, is added at the beginning of the method. For instance, `nullAllowed=false` checks whether a parameter is null, then throwing a `DomainValidationException`.
- *Import Statements:* All required imports are generated, according to what classes are used.
- *JavaDoc:* The informal `<description>` text occurs in comments, particularly Javadoc `@param` and `@return` clauses are filled with the operation's `<description>` text as well as `@throws` for `<exception>` specifications. This avoids checkstyle warnings, which are reported in quality metrics. If an operation is marked with `deprecated=true`, then `@deprecated` will be added in Javadoc.

```
<xsl:param name="svc_name"/>
<xsl:template match=''//service''>
  <xsl:text>/* * </xsl:text>
  <xsl:value-of select=''$svc_name''/>
  <xsl:text>
    Skeleton.java * * Copyright (c) 2008 Siemens... */
    ...
  <xsl:for-each select=''operation''>
    <xsl:text> /* * Operation definition for message
                    based service interface. * *
    @param req    the service method's request object. *
    @param srvCtx the service methos's context object. *
    </xsl:text>
    <xsl:if test=@deprecated=''true''>
      <xsl:text> * @deprecated </xsl:text>
    </xsl:if>
    <xsl:text>*/ public void </xsl:text>
    <xsl:value-of select=''@name''/>
    <xsl:text (final </xsl:text>
    <xsl:value-of select=''@name''/>
    <xsl:text>
      Request req, final ServiceRequestContect srvCtx) {
    </xsl:text>
    <xsl:if test=''return/@type != 'void'''>
      <xsl:value-of select=''return/@type''/>
      <xsl:text ret;/>
      ...
    </xsl:if>
  </for-each>
  ...
</xsl:template>
```

Fig. 3. XSL-T excerpt from Skeleton.xsl.

3.3   Classes *Service*TransSkeleton

This type of class is only required for persistent classes, i.e., services that are specified as `persistence=true`. Their methods are allowed to access the database via OpenJPA. In contrast to `ServiceImpl` classes, the generated classes possess a complete implementation. The following points are specific:

- *Signature Changes*: The signatures differ since there is no parameter em.
- Again, headers with Javadoc are generated, taking into account the different signature.
- The same holds for *import statements*.
- *Code Variants:* The XML service description controls the code generation. For example, if `transaction=true` is specified for a method, OpenJPA is used to execute the database statements, and a session and transaction template is put around the logic, which also takes care of a retry in case connection problems.

3.4   Classes *Service*Skeleton

The `Service`Skeleton classes are completely generated according to the XML service specification, which controls the code generation. We again mention some specific points:

- *Signature Changes*: Compared to the other classes, signatures are changing again, e.g., operations possess a `Request`-object, which bundles parameter values instead of having individual parameters. This means that the parameters for invoking `trans.create` must be extracted from such a `Request`. Depending on the context, the right list of parameters is filled in.
- The relevant *import statements* are added, too. Again, headers with Javadoc are generated, taking into account the different signature.
- *Additional Class Fields:* If `persistence=true` is set for a service, then the class is prepared to use OpenJPA by providing an internal field `OpenJPA-Configuration openJPAConf` with get/set methods. Similarly, if `eventing=true` is specified for a service, the class is prepared for handling events by adding a field `EventingComponent myEC` with get/set methods. Any class with a transactional method also obtains an internal field `Service`TransSkeleton `trans`.
- *Code Variants:* Transactional methods such as `create` basically delegate to `trans.create`. Non-transactional methods directly delegate to the `ServiceImpl` class.

There are six exception types that can be specified for a method by means of `<exception>`: `DomainValidationException`, `AuthorizationException`, `DomainPersistenceException` etc. Every specified exception is caught, logged and re-thrown. Special database exceptions `DataAccessException` and `PersistenceException` are handled for `transaction=true`. In particular, several subtypes of `PersistenceException` are distinguished in order to throw service-specific exceptions such as `UserDuplicateEntityException` or `UserEntityNotFoundException`. The `<logmessage>` element for `<exception>` is used as text in `LOG.debug()`.

4 AspectJ Approach

The most popular aspect-oriented language is certainly AspectJ [2]. AspectJ programming is essentially done by adding aspects to Java source code. The main purpose of aspects is to concentrate crosscutting functionality. To this end, an aspect can intercept certain points of the program flow, called join points, and add logic by advices. Examples of join points are method and constructor calls or executions, attribute accesses, and exceptions.

Join points are syntactically specified by means of pointcuts. Pointcuts identify join points in the program flow by means of a signature expression. A specification can determine exactly one method by describing the complete signature including final, private, static, return and parameter types etc. Or it can use wildcards to select several methods of several classes by `* MyClass*.get*(.., String)`. A star "`*`" in names denotes any character sequence. Hence, `get*` means any method that starts with "get". A type "`*`" denotes any type. Parameter types can be fixed or left open (..).

The following aspect has a before advice that adds logic before executing those methods that are captured by the pointcut `myPC`:

```
aspect MyAspect {
    pointcut myPC(): execution(*MyClass*.get*(..));
    before() : myPC() { // advice:
          Java code to be executed before myPC join points  }
}
```

4.1 General Principle

Using AspectJ, we re-implemented the software system. We were able to replace the code generation with a pure homogeneous language approach. There is no XML input and no XSL-T transformation. It is just AspectJ code.

The basic idea is to let developers start with manually writing the `ServiceImpl` classes instead of `Service`.xml descriptions, including Javadocs and the business logic. The signatures in `ServiceImpl` now need to be specified as required, i.e., including *em* and `isValidated` parameters (which are added by XSL-T, cf. Section 3.2, if specified). This has to be done only once in the `Impl` classes.

AspectJ is used to add all the missing parts for the whole implementation. The aspects are described in more detail in the subsequent subsections.

4.2   One TransSkeletonAspect

A *TransSkeletonAspect* aspect is responsible for implementing the functionality of *TransSkeleton* classes (see Sect. 3.4 and Fig. 1), which provide the session and transaction handling. Instead of specifying *transaction=true* for specific methods, a pointcut *executeInTx()* determines the transactional methods to which the logic of *doInTransaction()* should be applied, i.e., all public methods of *Impl* classes that possess an *EntityManager* parameter:

```
pointcut executeInTx(EntityManager em)
   : execution(public *com.siemens.project.*Impl.*(..))
     && args(em);
```

A single around advice can then add the logic:

```
Object around(EntityManager em) : executeServiceInTx(em){
   Object ret = null;
   EntityManagerFactoryImpl emf
                             = openJPAConf.getEMFactory();
   em = emf.getEntityManager();
   ... retry loop around ...
   EntityTransaction tx  = em.getTransaction();
   ret = proceed(em);   /* execute Impl-method instead of
                            doInTransaction(em) */
   ... commit or rollback on tx ...
   return ret;
}
```

The advice obtains an EntityManager em, starts and ends a new transaction, invoking the intercepted method with proceed() in between, and putting the redo logic around (not shown here). Hence, the logic is done in a central place and becomes much easier since we get rid of the complicated OpenJPACallback template mechanism as shown in Fig. 1 and explained in Sect. 2. Please note this code is now defined once and no longer part of every transactional method. The pointcut defines where the code has to be executed.

4.3   One SkeletonAspect

In principle, there is no need for Skeleton classes since it is possible to put the logic around the Impl methods. However, we are faced with the problem that the Skeleton methods are invoked from outside. Moreover, the signatures refer to service-specific OpRequest and OpReply objects. Thus, we are forced to keep the Skeleton classes. But we are able to factor out common functionalities in aspects. The following code remains to be written for the user management service, for example:

```
public class UserManagementSkeleton extends Service {
  private UserManagementImpl impl = null;
  private UserManagementTransSkeleton trans = null;
  public void create(final CreateUserRequest req,
                     final ServiceRequestContext srvCtx) {
  if (LOG.isDebugEnabled()) {
    LOG.debug("Op create started");
  } // -> added by single before advice
  UserDTO user = req.getUser();
  boolean id = req.getReturnIdentity();
  UserIdentity ret = impl.create(user,id,true);
  CreateUserReply reply = new CreateUserReply(ret);
  srvCtx.reply(reply);
  if (LOG.isDebugEnabled()) {
    LOG.debug("Op create succeeded");
  } // -> added by after return advice
  return ret;
} }
```

This is basically the Skeleton method without logging functionality (see the strikethrough) and exception handling, both being extracted into aspects. In the original code, a method of the TransSkeleton or Impl is invoked inside depending on the transactional setting. Here, we call the Impl-method directly since the Trans-Skeleton behaviour (if necessary) is put around by means of an aspect. Thus, the reference TransSkeleton trans is no longer needed.

It remains to manually specify the signature, unpack parameters from a Create-UserRequest, and invoke methods impl.op of ServiceImpl classes.

If persistence is required, get/set methods for OpenJPAConfiguration and a corresponding internal field need to be added. This can simply be implemented in a dedicated superclass Persistence:

```
public class Persistence {
  private OpenJPAConfiguration jpaConf = null;
  public OpenJPAConfiguration getOpenJPAConfig()
    { return this.jpaConf; }
  public void setOpenJPAConfig (OpenJPAConfiguration cfg)
    { this.jpaConf = cfg; }
}
```

The following statement puts the Persistence superclass on top of persistent Skeleton classes and let derived classes inherit the above functionality:

```
declare parents: UserManagementSkeleton,... : Persistence
```

Similarly, another superclass Eventing and a declare parents statement are added if eventing is enabled. Please note there is no problem with multiple inheritance: Aspects can add two superclasses, Persistence and Eventing, to a Skeleton class.

A single SkeletonAspect aspect keeps all these declare parents statements and also concentrates the logging functionality in corresponding before/afterReturning advices:

```
public class SkeletonAspect  {
  declare parents: ... /* as above */
  private static final Logger LOG
               = Logger.getLogger(SkeletonAspect.class);
  before() : call(public *
               com.siemens.project.impl.*Skeleton.*(..)) {
    if (LOG.isDebugEnabled())
      LOG.debug("Operation " +
            thisJoinPoint.getSignature() + " started");
  }
  afterReturning() {
    Log.debug() for successful operation ... }
}
```

4.4 Aspect for Exception Handling

Another aspect takes care of exception handling, which was originally part of Skeleton classes. This aspect defines several advices. Each advice adds a further try-catch block around the invocation of Impl methods:

```
public aspect ExceptionAspect {
  Object around() : call(... any Skeleton method with a
                         DomainValidationException ...) {
    Object ret = null;
    ServiceRequestContext srvCtx
    = (ServiceRequestContext) thisJoinPoint.getArgs()[1];
    try {
      ret = proceed();
    } catch(DomainValidationException e) {
      if (LOG.isDebugEnabled())
        LOG.debug ("missing or wrong arguments.");
      srvCtx.fail(e);
    }
    return ret;
  } // ... for other exceptions
}
```

The `ServiceRequestContext`, which is used to signal a failure, is obtained by accessing the second parameter of the joinpoint by means of `thisJoinpoint.getArgs()[1]`.

`DataAccessException` and `PersistenceException`, which are thrown in case of transactional methods (`transaction=true`), are handled similarly, however, transforming exception types:

```
catch (PersistenceException e) {
  if (e instanceof PersistenceDuplicateEntityException) {
    if (LOG.isDebugEnabled())
      LOG.debug("Domain entity already exists in DB.");
    srvCtx.fail(new
        DomainDuplicateEntityException(e.getMessage()));
  } else if ... other exceptions ...
}
```

4.5   Validation Logic

Validation logic such as

```
if (!isValidated) DomainValidator.validate(user, ''user'')
```

is inserted whenever a validation is required. This adds a check for nullness for the given parameter name in the method of the `Impl` class. In XSL-T, this is specified for an operation by means of

```
<parameter name="user"
            type="com.siemens.project. UserDTO">
<validation nullAllowed="false"/>
```

The same behavior can be achieved by a `before` advice that adds the nullness check before method execution. The problem is how to get the parameter object to be checked, i.e., user above. As the kinds of validation checks the programmer would like to perform is known in advance, we can simplify the code by only referring to the position of the parameter in the signature. For example, we provide pointcuts `validateNotNullAtPosition`*i* that allow for adding a check for a certain position i. An advice can access the parameter at this position:

```
public aspect ValidationAspect {
  pointcut validateNotNullAtPos0(Object o, boolean
              isVal): execution(...) && args(o,..,isVal);
  before(Object o, boolean isVal) :
            validateNotNullAtPos0(o, isVal)  {
    if (!isVal) {
      MethodSignature sig = (MethodSignature)
                  thisJoinPointStaticPart.getSignature();
      String name = sig.getParameterNames()[0];
      DomainValidator.validate(o,name);
} } }
```

The parameter name, to be added to DomainValidator.validate, is obtained by means of reflection (MethodSignature); the isValidated parameter always occurs last and can simply be bound to a variable isVal.

To make code more readable, an annotation @Validate("user",nullAllowed="false") can mark every method to be validated: An aspect intercepts any usage of this annotation and inserts the validation logic. This makes usage easier.

5 Comparison

We compare the originally existing MDD with the new AOP approach with regard to several comparison criteria. The criteria have been selected due to their relevance for the OpenSOA developers. At first, we investigate the classical quantitative criterion of "lines of code". This is a measurement for the manual work to be done. "Code" here does not only mean Java or AspectJ code but also XSL-T transformations and XML input in case of MDD: This comprises effort to be done as well. Further, qualitatively evaluated, criteria are usability, understandability, testability (which all affect development time), and redundancy. We took those criteria without any weights since they all together have an impact on development time and cost. We asked the developers but did not obtain a precise weighting.

Please also note we ignored performance since the performance is mostly affected by database accesses. Anyway, the types of pointcuts we use are very simple and usually do not cause performance issues.

The results are partially subjective in the sense that the assessment of the original MDD infrastructure is done by the involved software developers.

5.1 Lines of Code

The XSL-T approach requires XML input files Service.xml. That is the specification effort for a user to apply the infrastructure for the six services ApplicationManagement, DomainManagement etc. All these XML files have **4339 lines** in total.

To provide the generative infrastructure, the implementer has to implement three XSLT scripts: `TransSkeleton.xsl` (220 lines), `Skeleton.xsl` (499 lines), and `Impl.xsl` (384 lines). We have mentioned briefly the classes `Request`/`Reply` for `Skeleton` operations. These are generated as well by XSL-T scripts `RequestObject.xsl` (205 lines) and `ReplyObject.xsl` (113 lines). These are 1421 lines for code generation.

In total, 5760 (=4339 + 1421) lines are required for the XSL-T approach.

In the AspectJ solution, an implementer has to code advices in AspectJ, while a user applies this infrastructure by defining pointcuts or placing annotations.

The user has to manually implement a class *Service*`Impl`. From a logical point of view, the specification parts in *Service*.xml are directly put into code in *Service*`Impl.java`; these are 1208 lines for 93 methods without business logic (which we do not count in either approach).

The infrastructure is given by aspects. One aspect `TransSkeletonAspect` handles the transactional behaviour for transactional methods. The decision which methods are transactional is done by means of method pointcuts. An `around` advice puts transactional logic around the relevant methods of the `Impl`-classes. This aspect has 259 lines.

A `SkeletonAspect` aspect adds `Persistence` and `Eventing` super classes by means of two declare parents pointcuts. Moreover, the aspect introduces logging with `before`/`afterReturning` advices. This aspect requires 12 lines of code. The two new superclasses `Persistence` and `Eventing` have 17 lines (9 and 8 lines).

For each Service, a *Service*`Skeleton` class must be implemented due to external usage. These are 93 methods with about 8 lines in average, which sums up to 744 lines.

An `ExceptionAspect` adds exception handling. It comprises 2 lines for the aspect declaration itself and 12 lines for each of 6 the exception types. Handling transactional exceptions requires additional 21 lines. This sums up to 95 lines.

One `ValidationAspect` handles the validation code for at most two positions: 8 * 2 positions à 13 lines. These are additional 208 lines.

Hence, the AspectJ approach requires 2543 lines thus saving more than 3600 lines, i.e., nearly 60 %.

Unfortunately, this calculation does not consider the 94 `Request` and 57 `Reply` classes for `Skeleton` operations. In the XSL-T approach, these 10418 and 4176 lines of code, respectively, are generated. But in the AspectJ approach, there is no mean to produce or to avoid these classes: We have to manually implement those 14594 lines of code: The previously calculated advantage of AspectJ is lost!

However, the classes contain a lot of trivial comments (28 lines for `Request` and 15 lines for `Reply` classes in average), i.e., 3487 lines could be left out. Since the classes are simple JavaBeans with a constructor, a `get`-method, and `toString` method, specifying the attributes is enough; Eclipse or any other IDE can generate the code by a mouse-click. This requires additional time to handle the IDE, but reduces the lines of code by further 735 lines (94 * 6 + 57 * 3). But the AspectJ approach still requires 10372 lines for handling `Request`/`Reply`-classes.

5.2 Understandability

There is another point that concerns the development time for providing the infrastructure: understandability. It also affects the evolution of the system.

XSL-T is quite different from an object-oriented programming language such as Java, since it defines a set of rules that apply to a given XML document recursively. Reading those rules and understanding the overall behavior is not easy even if one is familiar with XML and XPath. In particular, the rule-base approach makes it difficult to write or to extend XSL-T scripts. Moreover, programmers must handle a couple of unintuitive and error-prone details of XSL-T, such as a special handling of zero-parameter methods or leaving out a "," after the last parameter in parameter lists. Other MDD frameworks such as Xtend2 [27] or XPand [28] provide a better support.

These drawbacks are not present in the AspectJ approach. Indeed, its major advantage is its homogeneity: There is one language to learn, AspectJ, which extends well-known Java by a few constructs such as pointcuts and advices the semantics of which is clear and understandable. Advices, in turn, are implemented in pure Java. Having a little knowledge about AspectJ, it should be no problem to understand the advices we have presented.

The disadvantage is that some conceptual points cannot be handled appropriately. One example is adding validation logic, which becomes less intuitive because we cannot directly handle the parameter position (cf. Subsect. 4.5). Furthermore, we cannot generate Skeleton and Request/Reply classes easily. These parts must be hand-coded. And finally, import statements must be added manually or generated by using IDE support. In contrast, those parts are completely generated in the XSL-T approach.

5.3 Testability

Testability is the major disadvantage of the XSL-T approach. Since code is generated, syntactical correctness is not immediately visible. Thus, the effort to check correctness is high. Several cycles of generating code, compilation, testing, and debugging are necessary in order to check ultimate correctness. Moreover, debugging of XSL-T is very limited.

Moreover, the correct behavior must be proven by unit testing. This means particularly that any variation within XML service descriptions has to be checked and unit tested. This is difficult and increases complexity with the number of possible combinations. One possible but challenging approach is to generate unit tests as part of the XML-based generation. However, also because of the complexity of the XSL-T language, only manual testing of main use cases was performed for OpenSOA. The (inappropriate) strategy, we noticed in practice, is thus to let developers generate code and detect problems during tests; having their feedback, implementers can fix the problems. In turn, a new rollout of the MDD infrastructure is required, leading to slow turn-around cycles for bug fixing.

Using AspectJ, syntactical correctness is immediately given for both the infrastructural advices and the pointcuts thanks to special plug-ins such as AJDT for the Eclipse IDE. As a direct consequence of the integrated language approach and corresponding compiler support, any syntax errors in wildcards or aspects are detected by a compiler. The plugin also issues a warning if a pointcut does not match any joinpoint in the code base. Only the correct behavior has to be checked, but can be achieved by running unit tests in an ordinary Java IDE. Moreover, debugging AspectJ is similar to Java code thanks to IDE support.

5.4   Usability

In the XSL-T approach, it is very straightforward to write input.xml files. Moreover, an XML schema exists and indicates any syntactical errors in input files. Only the code generator has to be started to produce Java code.

In AspectJ, applying "code generation" means to specify corresponding pointcuts, e.g., to apply exception handling or the transaction template to methods. Despite not being part of the ordinary Java language, pointcuts are easy to understand. In fact, we only use a small subset of AspectJ pointcuts, more or less using obvious wildcard expressions in the sense of "all method of a Service class". Anyway, the simplest way is to enumerate methods. Applying aspects is mostly a one-line pointcut. Moreover, excellent support of the Eclipse AJDT plugin let one determine the effect of aspects immediately, e.g., where an advice will be inserted. Using annotations to apply an aspect certainly yields to a better separation of infrastructure and usage.

5.5   Redundancy

The XSL-T transformations are partially redundant because the redundancy of signatures moves from code to XSL-T scripts: Generating similar classes Impl, Skeleton, TransSkeleton etc. with similar methods requires similar XSL-T transformations. Furthermore, the exception handling in the generated code is crosscutting and scattered around classes in the final outcome.

AspectJ, from its nature, has a much better separation of concerns for handling the transaction skeletons and exception handling. The overall redundancy is less. There are no longer several similar classes, it is essentially the Impl Java class; the logic of other generated classes becomes part of aspects. However, there are some limitations. For instance, the Skeleton methods have to be manually written (with IDE support for generating import's). Even if some common logic can again be concentrated in aspects, e.g., by putting superclasses on top of classes, we cannot avoid these classes.

5.6   Completeness

The XSL-T approach allows for generating code including Javadoc comments and import statements.

In contrast, the AspectJ solution is not able to handle necessary import statements. The AO approach simply relies on IDE support such as "Organize import" functionality; which however often is just a mouse-click. Similarly, comments and Javadocs have to be manually added. From a logical point of view, those parts move from *Service*.xml to *ServiceImpl*.java, i.e., put directly into code. In the XSL-T approach, Javadoc is generated into several classes, but this is not necessary here: There will be only one Java class, besides additional aspects.

5.7 Comparison Summary

The results we obtained with our case study indicate that AspectJ reveals its major strengths in avoiding redundancy and better testability, while MDD with XSL-T is a more complete and flexible approach. In fact, XSL-T allows for generating arbitrary artifacts the design demands, whereas AspectJ cannot provide this functionality and would require changes in the design. AOP in turn is better understandable and readable, however, we see that other MDD tools offer more advanced and integrated features.

Table 1 provides a rough summary of the comparison results.

Table 1. Summary of comparison results.

	AspectJ - AOP	XSLT - MDD
Lines of code	− (requires add. OO classes)	o (duplicated XSLT code)
Understandability	+ (straight forward)	− (complex syntax/semantics)
Testability	+ (directly testable)	o (difficult for generated code)
Usability	o/+ (reasonable)	− (difficult)
Redundancy	+ (nearly not redundant)	o (partially redundant)

5.8 Limitations and Generality

As our case study focuses on a specific software framework, our study cannot serve as an extensive guide for the selection among the technologies for arbitrary use cases and software projects. Nevertheless, we think that our case study results can be of value for practitioners being in the situation to choose among them.

As our problem of generating wrapper classes and boilerplate-code is rather common, we believe that our results have potential to be transferred to other problem settings. Furthermore, we think that the dimensions our evaluation is based on will help others to guide their decision making when choosing amongst the technologies or to take benefit from the best of both worlds.

Whereas in our solution, understandability speaks in favor of AOP, we see that more advanced and integrated tooling could significantly improve the position of MDD here. More advance generator languages, for example Xtend2 [27], provide a more straight forward generation approach, without recursive generation rules, but with mature editor support and even debugging functionality.

6 Related Work

There are several case studies and a large body of papers that either only evaluate the benefits and liabilities of MDD (e.g., [11, 15] or AOP (e.g., [9]. For example, [9] take the Berkeley DB as a case study and refactored the code into 38 features. While other studies, e.g., [13], suggested that features of a product line be implemented by aspects, they find that AspectJ is not suitable to implement most of their features. Even if this work is not a comparison, it shows deficiencies of the language AspectJ, not necessarily of AO or AOP, with respect to their case study. In contrast, [5] shows how to successfully apply aspects to implement a persistence framework, which is usually controlled by code generation based upon annotations or XML.

Our work, in contrast, aims at a comparison of AOP with MDD, in order to support the selection among the technologies. Only few work exists that explicitly makes such a comparison. [23] argues that AOSD and MDD are alike since both adapt an input system in order to receive an augmented output system, however, using different approaches, weaving and transformation, respectively. They discuss the technical differences by means of an example. [10] compares AOP and MDD with regard to a better separation of concerns. They only investigate how to describe and how to apply both, concluding that a model-driven approach offers more flexibility.

Reference [14] uses a heart pacemaker product line to elaborate on modeling crosscutting variability with AO. They state that AO can benefit the MDD of product lines. The study identifies desired characteristics of AO modeling techniques for product lines and proposes similar evaluation criteria to ours such as feasibility, degrees of variability, evolution, tool support, and cost, however, miss to investigate those in their case study.

Reference [1] uses a mobile phone software product line to systematically evaluate AOP as a product line technology. Their result is that AOP is especially suitable for variability across several components. The study discusses several factors and the effort for various activities: implementing reusable code, reacting to evolutionary changes, reusing code, resolving variations, and testability. Our study discusses similar points, however, at a deeper level using a real industrial case study.

Indeed, there is further significant work on combining AOP and MDD. For instance, [7] notices that the generated code is not always adequate for a task at hand, and mentions following in-house coding conventions and missing import features as examples. These are particular problems we handle. Generating AspectJ code helps to give flexibility.

Reference [19] combines both approaches by describing an MDD approach that generates aspect-oriented models. That is, aspects are part of the outcome. This is especially useful to handle unanticipated variabilities by means of aspects as the MDD/AOP approach of [26] illustrates. In our work, we explicitly compare the two technologies, to avoid increasing the overall technical complexity and dependencies of the developed software, in our case, the OpenSOA framework.

7   Conclusions

In this paper, we compared two completely different approaches, model-driven development (MDD) and aspect-oriented programming (AOP) with AspectJ, by means of a real industrial software system and thus investigating several criteria. While MDD, here applying XSL-T, is straight forward and well-understood for code generation, the usage of AOP is not so obvious, but can serve the same purpose in a different manner [23].

We achieved some interesting results during an aspect-oriented re-implementation of the original XSL-T system. AOP is principally able to handle code generation and has some advantages over XSL-T: AspectJ is better understandable and usable, especially from an implementer's point of view. There is a huge advantage for testing, in particular, checking the syntactic and semantic correctness. We also notice a better separation of concerns and avoidance of redundancy, for instance, if logic is put around existing code (transactional skeleton) or after/before (logging). The most striking limitations appear if new classes have to be introduced. This is the main reason why the pure AspectJ-based solution requires more lines of code (LoC).

XSL-T has advantage if several code generators are producing several output files based upon the same input file. This leads to the mentioned LoC advantage. Thus, XSL-T is more extensible and has potential for creating further classes, in particular Request/Reply classes in this case study. Finally, XSL-T results in a rather weak understandability. This, however, seems to be a consequence of the technology choice than of the MDD approach in general. By using MDD approaches with more intuitive languages and mature IDE support based around Eclipse Ecore (e.g., Xtend2 [27] or XPand [28]), we believe the implementation and the evaluation would improve in this category. In particular, there are tools available that can be used to produce Java code, at least classes and method signatures as a model. This can build a basis to take the Java `ServiceImpl` file as input and produce Request and Reply classes. Indeed, [6] even developed an Ecore metamodel for Java 5.0 together with a parser and printer, so that plain Java statements could be produced.

A combination of XSL-T and AspectJ also seems to be a promising approach to combine the advantages of each technology. This particularly fits smoothly to the existing implementation. That is why we intend to investigate the combination of both approaches, i.e., following [7] to generate aspects within the code to get the best out of both worlds.

References

1. Muthig, D., Anastasopoulos, M.: An evaluation of aspect-oriented programming as a product line implementation technology. In: Krueger, C., Krueger, C., Dannenberg, R.B. (eds.) ICOIN 2004 and ICSR 2004. LNCS, vol. 3107, pp. 141–156. Springer, Heidelberg (2004)
2. AspectJ. Eclipse AspectJ Homepage. http://eclipse.org/aspectj/. Accessed 18 Mar 2014
3. Beuche, D.: Variant management with pure::variants. Technical report, pure-systems GmbH, 2006. http://www.pure-systems.com/fileadmin/down-loads/pv-whitepaper-en-04.pdf (2006). Accessed 25 May 2014
4. Groher, I., Krüger, C., Schwanninger, C.: A Tool-based approach to managing croscutting feature implementations. In: 7th International Conference on AOSD, Brussels (2008)
5. Hohenstein, U.: Using aspect-orientation to add persistency to applications. In: Proceedings of Datenbanksysteme in Business, Technologie und Web (BTW), Karlsruhe (2005)
6. Heidenreich, F., Johannes, J., Seifert, M., Wende, C.: Closing the gap between modelling and Java. In: Gašević, D., van den Brand, M., Gray, J. (eds.) SLE 2009. LNCS, vol. 5969, pp. 374–383. Springer, Heidelberg (2010)
7. Henthorne, C., Tilevich, E.: Code generation on steroids: enhancing code generators via generative aspects. In: 2nd International Workshop on Incorporating COTS Software into Software Systems: Tools and Techniques (IWICSS 2007) (2007)

8. Hohenstein, U., Elsner, C.: A case study for comparing of model-driven development and aspect-oriented programming. In: 9th International Conference on Software Technologies ICSOFT-PT Vienna (2014)
9. Kästner, C., Apel, S., Batory, D.: A case study implementing features using AspectJ. In: Proceedings of International Software Product Line Conference (SPLC), Kyoto (2007)
10. Kaboré, C., Beugnard, A.: Interests and drawbacks of AOSD compared to MDE – a position paper. In: 3rd Workshop on Aspects and Models, at 21st ECOOP 2007 (2007)
11. Kapteijns, T., Jansen, S., Houet, H., Barendse, R.: A comparative case study of model driven development vs traditional development: the tortoise or the hare. In: CTIT Proceedings of 5th European Conference on Model Driven Architecture (2009)
12. Kiczales, G., Hilsdale, E., Hugunin, J., Kersten, M., Palm, J., Griswold, W.G.: An overview of AspectJ. In: Lindskov Knudsen, J. (ed.) ECOOP 2001. LNCS, vol. 2072, pp. 327–357. Springer, Heidelberg (2001)
13. Lee, K.: Combining feature-oriented analysis and aspect-oriented programming for product line asset development. In: Proceedings of International Software Product Line Conference (2006)
14. Liu, J., Lutz, R., Rajan, H.: The role of aspects in modeling product line variabilities. In: Proceedings of 1st Workshop on Aspect-Oriented Product Line Engineering, GPCE, Portland (Oregon) (2006)
15. Lussenburg, V., van der Storm, T., Vinju, J., Warmer, J.: Mod4J: a qualitative case study of model-driven software development. In: Petriu, D.C., Rouquette, N., Haugen, Ø. (eds.) MODELS 2010, Part II. LNCS, vol. 6395, pp. 346–360. Springer, Heidelberg (2010)
16. Mezini, M., Ostermann, K.: Variability management with feature-oriented programming and aspects. In: Proceedings of 12th International Symposium on Foundations of Software Engineering (FSE), Newport Beach (CA) (2004)
17. MPS. JetBrains: Meta Programming System. http://www.jetbrains.com/mps/. Accessed 25 May 2014
18. Normén, F.: Remove code smell with AOP (2007). http://weblogs.asp.net/fredriknormen/archive/2007/11/29/remove-code-smell-with-aop.aspx Accessed 25 May 2014
19. Pinto, M., Fuentes, L., Fernández, L., Valenzuela, J.: Using AOSD and MDD to enhance the architectural design phase. In: Proceedings of OTM 2009 (2009)
20. Reichel, C., Oberhauser, R.: XML-based programming language modeling: an approach to software engineering. In: SEA 2004 (2004)
21. Smaragdakis, Y., Huang, S., Zook, D.: Program generators and the tools to make them. In: SIGPLAN Symposium on Partial Evaluation and Semantics-Based Program Manipulation. ACM Press (2004)
22. Strunk, W.: The symphonia product-line. In: Java and Object-Oriented (JAOO) Conference, Arhus, Denmark (2007)
23. Stein, D., Hanenberg, S.: Why aspect-oriented software development and model-driven development are not the same – a position paper. Electr. Notes Theor. Comput. Sci. **163**(1), 2006 (2006)
24. Stahl, T., Völter, M.: Model-Driven Software Development. Wiley, Hoboken (2006)
25. Tarr, P., Osher, H., Harrison, W., Sutton, S.: N degrees of separation: multi-dimensional separation of concerns. In: 21st International ICSE 1999 (1999)
26. Völter, M., Groher, I.: Product line implementation using aspect-oriented and model-driven software development. In: 11th International Software Product Line Conference (SPLC), Kyoto, Japan (2007)
27. Xtend2. Eclipse Xtend 2 Homepage. http://www.eclipse.org/Xtext/#xtend2. Accessed 18 Mar 2014
28. Xtext. Eclipse Xtext Homepage. http://www.eclipse.org/Xtext/. Accessed 25 May 2014

A Problem-, Quality-, and Aspect-Oriented Requirements Engineering Method

Stephan Faßbender, Maritta Heisel, and Rene Meis(✉)

Paluno - The Ruhr Institute for Software Technology,
University of Duisburg-Essen, Essen, Germany
{stephan.fabbender,maritta.heisel,rene.meis}@uni-due.de

Abstract. Requirements engineers not only have to cope with the requirements of various stakeholders for complex software systems, they also have to consider several software qualities (e.g., performance, maintainability, security, and privacy) that the system-to-be shall address. In such a situation, it is challenging for requirements engineers to develop a complete and coherent set of requirements for the system-to-be. Separation of concerns has shown to be one option to handle the complexity of systems. The problem frames approach address this principle by decomposing the problem of building the system-to-be into simpler subproblems. Aspect-orientation aims at separating cross-cutting functionalities into separate functionalities, called aspects. We propose a method called AORE4PF, which shows that aspect-orientation can be integrated into the problem frames approach to increase the separation of concerns and to benefit from several methods that exist on problem frames to develop a complete and coherent set of requirements. We validated our method with a small experiment in the field of crisis management.

Keywords: Early aspects · Problem frames · Requirements engineering

1 Introduction

Keeping an eye on good and sufficient requirements engineering is a long-known success factor for software projects and the resulting software products [1]. Nonetheless, larger software incidents are regularly reported, which originate in careless dealing with, for example, security requirements. Beside reputation damage, loss of market value and share, and costs for legal infringement [2,3], fixing defects that caused the incident is costly. Fixing a defect when it is already fielded is reported to be up to eighty times more expensive than fixing the corresponding requirements defects early on [4,5]. Therefore, it is crucial for requirements engineers to identify, analyze, and describe all requirements and related quality concerns. But eliciting good requirements is not an easy task [6], even more when considering complex systems.

Part of this work is funded by the German Research Foundation (DFG) under grant number HE3322/4-2.

© Springer International Publishing Switzerland 2015
A. Holzinger et al. (Eds.): ICSOFT 2014, CCIS 555, pp. 291–310, 2015.
DOI: 10.1007/978-3-319-25579-8_17

Nowadays, for almost every software system, various stakeholders with diverse interests exist. These interests give rise to different sets of requirements. These diverse requirements not only increase the complexity of the system-to-be, but also contain different cross-cutting concerns, such as qualities, which are desired by the stakeholders. In such a situation, the requirements engineer is really challenged to master the complexity and to deliver a coherent and complete description of the system-to-be.

One possible option to handle the complexity of a system-to-be is the concept of *separation of concerns* [7]. In its most general form, the separation of concerns principle refers to the ability to focus on, and analyze or change only those parts of a system which are relevant for one specific problem. The main benefits of this principle are a reduced complexity, improved comprehensibility, and improved reusability [7].

Both, *AORE (aspect-oriented requirements engineering)* and the problem frame approach implement this principle, but for different reasons. The approach of AORE, which originates from aspect-oriented programming, is to separate each cross-cutting requirement into an *aspect*. Instead of integrating and solving the cross-cutting requirement for all requirements it cross-cuts, the aspect is solved in isolation. Hence, aspect-orientation leads to a clear separation of concerns. To combine an aspect with a requirement, an aspect defines a pointcut (set of join points), which describes how the aspect and a requirement can be combined. The *problem frames approach* [8] generally also follows the separation of concerns principle. It decomposes the overall problem of building the system-to-be into small sub-problems that fit to a problem frame. Each sub-problem is solved by a machine, which has to be specified using the given domain knowledge. All machines have to be composed to form the overall machine. We will show that aspect-orientation gives guidance for the process of decomposing the overall problem and especially for the composition of the machines. As both ways of separating concerns seem to be complementary, it is promising to combine both. Hence, we propose the AORE4PF (Aspect-Oriented Requirements Engineering for Problem Frames) method that provides guidance for classifying requirements, separating the different concerns, modeling requirements for documentation and application of completeness and interaction analyses, and weaving the reusable parts to a complete and coherent system. Furthermore, AORE4PF provides tool support for most activities.

The rest of the paper is structured as follows. Section 2 introduces a smart grid scenario, which is used as a case study. In Sect. 3, we introduce the problem frames approach and UML4PF as background of this paper. Our method for the integration of AORE into the problem frames approach is presented in Sect. 4. A small experiment for validation is presented in Sect. 5. Work related to this paper is discussed in Sect. 6. Finally, Sect. 7 concludes the paper and presents possible future work.

2   Case Study

To illustrate the application of the AORE4PF method, we use the real-life case study of smart grids. As sources for real functional requirements, we consider diverse documents such as "Application Case Study: Smart Grid" provided by the industrial partners of the EU project NESSoS[1], the "Protection Profile for the Gateway of a Smart Metering System" [9] provided by the German Federal Office for Information Security[2], and "Requirements of AMI (Advanced Multi-metering Infrastructure") [10] provided by the EU project OPEN meter[3].

We define the terms specific to the smart grid domain and our use case in the following. The *smart meter gateway* represents the central communication unit in a *smart metering system*. It is responsible for collecting, processing, storing, and communicating *meter data*. The *meter data* refers to readings measured by smart meters regarding consumption or production of a certain commodity. A *smart meter* represents the device that measures the consumption or production of a certain commodity and sends it to the gateway. An *authorized external entity* can be a human or an IT unit that communicates with the gateway from outside the gateway boundaries through a *wide area network (WAN)*. The *WAN* provides the communication network that interconnects the gateway with the outside world. The *LMN (local metrological network)* provides the communication network between the meter and the gateway. The *HAN (home area network)* provides the communication network between the consumer and the gateway. The term *consumer* refers to end users of commodities (e.g., electricity).

We have chosen a small selection of requirements to illustrate our method. These requirements are part of the 13 minimum use cases defined for a smart meter gateway given in the documents of NESSoS and the open meter project. The considered use cases are concerned with gathering, processing, and storing meter readings from smart meters for the billing process. The requirements are described as follows:

(R1) Receive Meter Data. The gateway shall receive meter data from smart meters.

(R17) New Firmware. The gateway should accept a new firmware from authorized external entities. The gate shall log the event of successful verification of a new version of the firmware.

(R18) Activate New Firmware. On a predetermined date the gateway executes the firmware update. The gateway shall log the event of deploying a new version of the firmware.

(R28) Prevent Eavesdropping. The Gateway should provide functionality to prevent eavesdropping. The gateway must be capable of encrypting communications and data by the safest and best encryption mechanisms possible.

(R29) Privacy and Legislation. Many countries protect customers' and people's rights by laws, to ensure that personal and confidential information will not be disclosed easily within communicating systems. Grid systems shall not be a way to reveal information.

---

[1] http://www.nessos-project.eu/.

[2] www.bsi.bund.de.

[3] http://www.openmeter.com/.

3   UML-Based Problem Frames

Problem frames are a means to describe software development problems. They were proposed by Jackson [8], who describes them as follows: *"A problem frame is a kind of pattern. It defines an intuitively identifiable problem class in terms of its context and the characteristics of its domains, interfaces and requirement."* It is described by a *frame diagram*, which consists of domains, interfaces between domains, and a requirement. We describe problem frames using UML class diagrams extended by stereotypes as proposed by Hatebur and Heisel [11]. All elements of a problem frame diagram act as placeholders, which must be instantiated to represent concrete problems. Doing so, one obtains a *problem diagram* that belongs to a specific class of problems.

Figure 1 shows a problem diagram in UML notation. The class with the stereotype ≪machine≫ represents the thing to be developed (e.g., the software). The classes with some domain stereotypes, e.g., ≪biddableDomain≫ or ≪lexical-Domain≫ represent *problem domains* that already exist in the application environment. Jackson distinguishes the domain types *causal domains* that comply with some physical laws, *lexical domains* that are data representations, *biddable domains* that are usually people, and *connection domains* that mediate between domains.

Domains are connected by interfaces consisting of shared phenomena. Shared phenomena may be events, operation calls, messages, and the like. They are observable by all connected domains, but controlled by only one domain, as indicated by an exclamation mark. For example, in Fig. 1 the annotation WAN!{forwardUpdateFirmware} means that the phenomenon in the set {forward-UpdateFirmware} is controlled by the domain WAN and observable by the machine domain SMGFirmwareStorage, which is connected to it. These interfaces are represented as associations with the stereotype ≪connection≫, and the name of the associations contain the phenomena and the domains controlling the phenomena.

In Fig. 1, the lexical domain FirmwareUpdate is constrained and the Authorized-ExternalEntity is referred to, because the machine SMGFirmwareStorage has the role to store new FirmwareUpdates from AuthorizedExternalEntity for satisfying requirement R17. These relationships are modeled using dependencies that are annotated with the corresponding stereotypes.

The full description for Fig. 1 is as follows: The biddable domain Authorized-ExternalEntity controls the updateFirmware command, which is forwarded by the WAN and finally observed by the machine domain SMGFirmwareStorage. The SMGFirmwareStorage controls the phenomenon storeNewFirmware, which stores the received information in the lexical domain FirmwareUpdate.

Software development with problem frames proceeds as follows: first, the environment in which the machine will operate is represented by a *context diagram*. Like a problem diagram, a context diagram consists of domains and interfaces. However, a context diagram contains no requirements. Then, the problem is decomposed into subproblems. If ever possible, the decomposition is done in such a way that the subproblems fit to given problem frames. To fit a subproblem to a problem frame, one must instantiate its frame diagram, i.e., provide

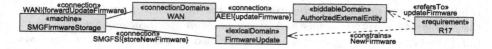

Fig. 1. Problem diagram R17: new firmware.

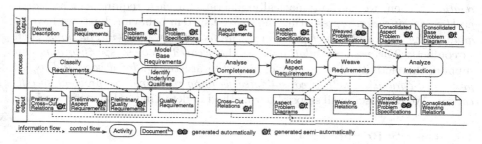

Fig. 2. The AORE4PF method.

instances for its domains, phenomena, and interfaces. The UML4PF framework provides tool support for this approach. A more detailed description can be found in [12].

4   Method

An illustration of our method is given in Fig. 2. The initial input for our method is a textual *informal description* of the requirements the system-to-be shall fulfill. These requirements are *classified* into *preliminary aspect requirements* (or short *aspects*), which are functional and cross-cutting, *preliminary quality requirements* (or short *qualities*), which are non-functional and cross-cutting, and *base requirements* (or short *bases*), which are not cross-cutting. Additionally, the relations between requirements and aspects or qualities are documented as preliminary cross-cut relations. Then all identified *base requirements* are *modeled* following the problem frames approach introduced in Sect. 3, such that for each *base requirement* a *base problem diagram* is created. Additionally, we create a sequence diagram for each problem diagram. The sequence diagrams serve as a *base problem specification*. To prepare the completeness analysis, we *identify* for all *preliminary aspect requirements* the underlying qualities they address. The already known *preliminary quality requirements* can aid the identification. As a result, we get a set of *quality requirements*. Based on the identified *quality and base requirements*, we can analyze whether there is a cross-cut relation between a quality requirement and a base requirement not discovered yet. Thus, we *analyze the completeness* of the *preliminary cross-cut relations* and update them if necessary. The results are a set of *cross-cut relations* and also updated *aspect requirements*. Next, the *aspect requirements* are *modeled* in a similar way as requirements using specialized problem diagrams, called *aspect problem diagrams*. Again, we specify the machine behavior using sequence diagrams, which results in *aspect problem specifications*. For the next step, *weave requirements*, the *base problem specifications* and *aspect problem specifications* are weaved to fulfill the base and aspect requirements as defined by the *base problem diagrams* and *aspect problem diagrams*. For the weaving, we have to accomplish two activities. First, we define the *weaving relations*. These relations refine the *cross-cut relations*. Then, we can automatically generate for each requirement a *weaved problem specification* representing the weaved system behavior. Last, we have to *analyze* the *base* and *aspect problem diagrams* for unwanted *interactions*, such as conflicts. The *weaving relations* and the *weaved problem specifications* can support this activity. The results of this step are *consolidated base and aspect problem diagrams* as well as *consolidated weaving relations and problem specifications*. We will discuss all steps of our method in detail in the following sections.

4.1   Classify Requirements

As a first step, we have to identify and analyze the requirements contained in the *informal description*. We have to separate and classify these requirements as they will be treated differently afterwards. A requirement can be (1) a base, which is functional and not cross-cutting, (2) an aspect, which is functional and cross-cutting, and (3) a quality, which is non-functional and cross-cutting. Note that we see quality requirements as requirements, which are not operationalized to an aspect right now. Hence, there is a clear relation between qualities and aspects, and we will later on refine qualities to aspects. Normally, statements in an informal description are not given that clear-cut as given by the three discussed classes of requirements. Hence, one can find requirements mixing different classes, for example, aspects are already combined with the corresponding bases or qualities are mentioned in the according bases. In consequence, identifying statements which constitute requirements is only half of the job, but also a separation of mixed requirements has to be performed.

First, we separate functional and quality requirements. A tool like OntRep [13] can support the requirements engineer in this step. This way we identify R29 as requirement containing two quality requirements (R29A and R29B) and R28 containing one quality (R28A) and one functional requirement (R28B):

(R28A) **Security.** The Gateway shall be protected against external attacks.

(R29A) **Privacy.** [...] personal and confidential information will not be disclosed easily within communicating systems. Grid systems shall not be a way to reveal information.

(R29B) **Compliance.** Many countries protect customers' and people's rights by laws.

Thus, we have identified and separated the *preliminary quality requirements*.

Second, we have to analyze the functional requirements for aspects and separate them. For this activity tools like EA-Miner [14], Theme/Doc [15] or REAssistant[4] can aid the requirements engineer. This way we identify the following two aspects:

---
[4] https://code.google.com/p/reassistant/.

(R28B) **Network Encryption.** [...] The gateway must be capable of encrypting communications and data by the safest and best encryption mechanisms possible.

(R30) **Logging.** The gate shall log the occurring important events.

Note that while eavesdropping is already formulated as separate aspect, logging is introduced as a new aspect that is extracted from **R17** and **R18** which both contain the logging aspect:

(R17B) **New Firmware: Logging.** The gate shall log the event of successful verification of a new version of the firmware.

(R18B) **Activate New Firmware: Logging.** The gateway shall log the event of deploying a new version of the firmware.

These two requirements describe how the aspect **R30** has to be integrated into the corresponding base requirements. This information is used later on during the weaving process. Thus, we have identified and separated the *preliminary aspect requirements.*

The remaining functional requirements form the *base requirements* for our system:

(R1) **Receive Meter Data.** The gateway shall receive meter data from smart meters.

(R17A) **New Firmware.** The gateway should accept a new firmware from authorized external entities.

(R18A) **Activate New Firmware.** On a predetermined date the gateway executes the firmware update.

We document the relations between the separated functional, quality, and aspect requirements in a *preliminary cross-cut relation table.* These relations are given in Table 1 with crosses in *italic* in the regions (Base,Quality), (Base,Aspect), and (Quality,Aspect). Note that everything given in **bold** is discovered later on in the annotated step (^{x}). Furthermore, the regions (Aspect,Quality) and (Aspect,Aspect) are considered in step 4, and (Quality,Quality) in step 7. If a requirement is separated into a functional requirement (base or aspect) and a quality, then we add a cross in the region (Base,Quality) of the table if the functional requirement is a base requirement, representing that the quality has to be taken into account for the base requirement, and in the region (Quality,Aspect) if it is an aspect requirement, representing that the aspect requirement addresses the software quality. In Table 1, we documented that the aspect **R28B** is related to the quality **R28A**. This kind of mapping will later on be used to provide guidance for the selections of mechanisms to address the quality requirements. If functional requirements are separated into base and aspect requirements, then we also add respective crosses in the upper right quadrant. In Table 1, we documented that the aspect **R30** cross-cuts the base requirements **R17A** and **R18A**.

Table 1. Requirements (Cross-cut) relation table for the smart grid scenario.

		Quality				Aspect		
		R28A	R29A	R29B	R31³	R28B	R30(R17B, R18B)	R32⁴
Base	R1	X^4	X^4	X^4	X^4	X^4	X^4	
	R17A	X^4			X^3	X^4	X	
	R18A				X^3		X	
Aspect	R28B							
	R30	X^4						X^4
	R32⁴							
Quality	R28A		I^7	I^7	I^7	X		X^4
	R29A	I^7		I^7	I^7	X^4		X^4
	R29B	I^7	I^7		I^7	X^4	X^4	X^4
	R31³	I^7	I^7	I^7			X^3	

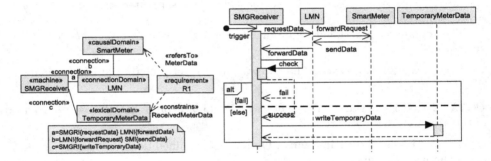

Fig. 3. Problem diagram for R1.   **Fig. 4.** Sequence diagram for R1.

4.2 Model Base Problems

In this step, we model the functional requirements identified in the previous step. For each functional requirement, we create a problem diagram as proposed by the problem frames approach introduced in Sect. 3. For reasons of space, we only show the problem diagrams for the requirements R1 and R17A, but these two problem diagrams are sufficient to understand the rest of the paper, even though we use the five selected requirements for exemplifying our method. The problem diagram for R17A is shown in Fig. 1 and explained in Sect. 3. Figure 3 shows the problem diagram for R1. The problem described in this diagram is that the machine SMGReceiver shall requestData via the LMN from the SmartMeter. In response, the SmartMeter will sendData that was requested via the LMN back to the machine. The machine does then writeTemporaryData received from the smart meter in the lexical domain TemporaryMeterData.

For every problem diagram, we have to provide a reasoning, called *frame concern* [8], why the *specification* of the submachine together with the knowledge about the environment (*domain knowledge*) leads to the satisfaction of the *requirement*. To visualize how frame concern is addressed in the specific problems, we create at least one sequence diagram for each problem diagram. These sequence diagrams describe the specification (behavior of the machine) and the domain knowledge (behavior of the domains) which is necessary to satisfy the requirement. How to systematically create the sequence diagrams is out of scope of this paper, but the approach presented by Jackson and Zave [16] can be used for this task. Figure 4 shows the sequence diagram for the sub-problem Receive Meter. The interaction is started the sub-machine SMGReceiver causing the phenomenon requestData (specification). This request is forwarded via the LMN to the SmartMeter (domain knowledge). The smart meter then answers the request and sends the meter data (requirement) using the phenomenon sendData (domain knowledge). The data is forwarded via the LMN to the sub-machine (domain knowledge). In the case of a successful check of the received data, the received data is stored in the lexical domain TemporaryMeterData (specification). Hence, the gateway stores the meter data received from smart meters (requirement).

4.3 Identify Underlying Qualities

In order to check whether the cross-cut relation is complete, we identify for all aspects the software qualities they address. Note that the relationship between aspects and qualities is many-to-many. That is, an aspect can address multiple software qualities. For example, the logging of system events possibly addresses the software qualities accountability, transparency, maintainability, performance, and traceability. On the other hand, a software quality can be addressed by multiple aspects, for example, the software quality confidentiality could be addressed by the following aspects: encryption, authentication and authorization, and data minimization. For the identification of underlying qualities tools such as QAMiner [17] can be used. This way we discover that in our case the aspect R30 has the underlying quality maintainability:

(R31) **Maintainability.** All events which are useful to trace a malfunction of the gateway shall be logged.

We document the relation between the aspect and the identified underlying quality in cross-cut relation table. In Table 1, we added the bold cross $\mathbf{X}^3$ in the lower right quadrant. Furthermore, we add the relations between the identified quality to the base requirements which are implied by the relations of the corresponding aspect. For our smart grid scenario, we added the bold crosses $\mathbf{X}^3$ in the upper left quadrant of Table 1. The consideration of the underlying qualities allows requirements engineers to access whether the selected mechanisms (aspects) sufficiently address the respective quality.

4.4 Analyze Completeness

Based on the identified qualities, we can re-use quality-dependent analysis techniques on problem frames to check the completeness of the cross-cut relation. For example, for privacy one can use the ProPAn method [18], the law (identification) pattern method [19] provides guidance for compliance, security is covered by the PresSuRE method [20], and so forth. These analysis techniques identify for a given problem frames model and the respective quality in which functional requirements the quality has to be considered. At this point of our method, we have all inputs that the analysis techniques need. Using the results of the analysis techniques, we can update the cross-cut relation and check whether the selected aspects together with the defined cross-cut relation guarantee the intended software qualities.

In this way, we identify that, for example, several qualities are relevant for R1. Privacy (R29A) is relevant as the consumption data metered by the smart meters enables one to analyze what the persons in the household are currently doing. Hence, the consumption data is an asset which has to be protected. As result, the security analysis also shows that the consumption data has to be protected against eavesdropping (R28A). Maintainability (R31) is also relevant for R1, as a malfunction can also occur while receiving consumption data. The compliance analysis (R29B) reveals and strengthens the importance of privacy because of different data protection acts. Additionally, the logging mechanism is not only relevant for maintainability but also for compliance as several laws require the fulfillment of accountability requirements whenever there is a contractual relation between different parties. This information is used to update the cross-cut relation table (see bold crosses $\mathbf{X}^4$ in Table 1). The already existing aspect requirements are sufficient to cover the newly found relations.

Furthermore, we have to check whether a software quality that was identified as relevant for a base requirement is also relevant for an aspect requirement that cross-cuts the base requirement. E.g., we have to check whether the logs written for the base requirements R1 and R17B contain confidential information that has to be protected against an external attacker. For presentation purpose, we assume that such an attacker has to be considered in the smart grid scenario and add an aspect requirement for the encryption of persistent data that cross-cuts the logging aspect.

(R32) **Data Encryption.** Persistent data shall be stored encrypted on the gateway.

We update the regions (Aspect,Quality) and (Aspect,Aspect) of the cross-cut relation table (see Table 1) to document that the quality R28A has to be taken into account for the aspect R30 (cross in region (Aspect,Quality)), and that the aspect R3 is cross-cut by the newly introduced aspect R32 (cross in region (Aspect,Aspect)).

4.5   Model Aspect Requirements

To model aspect requirements in a similar way as base requirements, we extended the UML profile of the UML4PF tool with aspect-oriented concepts. To differentiate aspect requirements, the machines that address them, and the diagram they are represented in, from base requirements and their machines and diagrams, we introduce the new stereotypes ≪Aspect≫, ≪AspectMachine≫, and ≪AspectDiagram≫ as specialization of the stereotypes ≪Requirement≫, ≪ProblemDiagram≫, and ≪Machine≫, respectively. In addition to problem diagrams, an aspect diagram has to contain a set of join points, which together form a pointcut. These join points can be domains and interfaces. Hence, we introduced the new stereotype ≪JoinPoint≫, which can be applied to all specializations of the UML meta-class NamedElement. During the weaving, join points are instantiated with domains of the diagrams the aspect cross-cuts.

To create an aspect diagram, we have to identify the join points which are necessary to combine the aspect with the problems it cross-cuts and to understand the problem of building the aspect machine. In most cases, we have a machine, besides the aspect machine, as join point in an aspect diagram. This machine will be instantiated during the weaving with the machine of the problem that the aspect is weaved into. The interface between this join point and the aspect machine describes how a problem machine can utilize an aspect and which context information is needed by the aspect machine. We have to derive the join points important for the problem described by the aspect from its description and the requirements it cross-cuts. Besides the specialized stereotypes for the machine and the requirement, and the definition of join points for the later weaving, the process of building an aspect diagram is similar to the process of building problem diagrams. As for problem diagrams, we also create sequence diagrams for each aspect. The sequence diagrams contain two kinds of information. First, the messages annotated with the stereotype ≪JoinPoint≫ describe the pointcut scenario. I.e., these messages describe when during the behavior necessary to accomplish the cross-cut requirement the behavior of the aspect can be integrated. Note that we can represent the common pointcut definitions used, e.g., in AspectJ, such as before, after and around, by a sequence diagram with the behavior description for the aspect before, after, or around the pointcut scenario, respectively. Second, all other messages describe the internal behavior necessary to accomplish the aspect requirement.

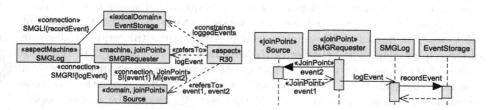

Fig. 5. Aspect diagram for aspect R30.   **Fig. 6.** Sequence diagram for aspect R30.

For reasons of space, we will only discuss the aspect requirement R30 in detail. The aspect R28B and the sequence diagram for the decryption of received data is described in [21]. R30 covers the logging of important events in the system. The corresponding aspect diagram is presented in Fig. 5. It contains the

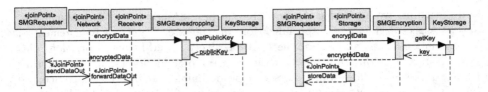

Fig. 7. Sequence diagram for aspect R28B.

Fig. 8. Sequence diagram for aspect R32.

aspect machine SMGLog, which is able to record events in the EventStorage. Furthermore, the aspect diagram contains two domains as join points. The machine SMGRequester will be instantiated by a problem machine and the domain Source by the origin of the event to be logged. The machine SMGRequester observes the phenomenon event1 of Source and is able to issue the phenomenon event2. These phenomena represent the events that shall be logged and need to be instantiated during the weaving. If an event that has to be logged is observed, then SMGRequester instructs the aspect machine SMGLog to log that event (logEvent). In general, we have to distinguish four cases for the event to be logged. The event could be issued using a synchronous or asynchronous message of the Source, or a synchronous or asynchronous message from the machine SMGRequester to the Source. For the sake of simplicity, we only consider the case shown in the sequence diagram in Fig. 6. This sequence diagram shows the case that SMGRequester sends a synchronous message to Source and receives a result (requirement). Then SMGRequester asks SMGLog to log the observed event (requirement). The machine SMGLog then records the event (specification). Hence, the observed event is logged (requirement). Figures 7 and 8 show the sequence diagrams for the behavior of aspect R28B for sending encrypted data via a network and aspect R32 for encrypting data that shall be stored persistently.

4.6   Weave Requirements

For each base requirement, we now create a sequence diagram that describes how the aspect requirements have to be weaved into it to address the cross-cut relations. The basis for the weaving sequence diagram is the sequence diagram of the requirement. The behavior of the sub-machine is extended with the invocation of the aspects given by the row of the base requirement in the cross-cut relation table (see Table 1). Furthermore, we have to consider whether the base requirement is cross-cut by an aspect a_1 that is itself cross-cut by another aspect a_2. If this is the case, we have to weave the aspect a_2 into the base requirement after the aspect a_1 was weaved into it.

The cross-cut relations are not sufficient to weave the aspect requirements into the base requirement. The reason is that the cross-cut relation does not define how and when an aspect has to be integrated into the base problem. Nevertheless, we can identify the situations during the dynamics of the base problem where an aspect could be integrated using the pointcut scenarios described in the sequence diagrams of the aspect. For each base requirement, we create a

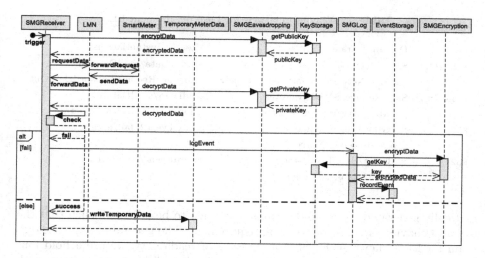

Fig. 9. Weaved sequence diagram for R17A.

table that defines the weaving relations, i.e., how and in which order the aspects have to be integrated into the base problem. A row in the table consists of the aspect sequence diagram that shall be weaved into the requirement, and the instantiation of the join points of the aspect with the domains and messages of the base sequence diagram. An instantiation of a join point j by a domain or message b of the base problem is denoted by b/j. The instantiated messages uniquely describe how and when the aspect is integrated into the base sequence diagram. Table 2 shows the weaving relations for base requirement R1.

Because of the aspect requirement R28B all communications have to be encrypted to prevent eavesdropping attacks. This implies that all external messages that a sub-machine sends have to be encrypted and the ones it receives have to be decrypted. Hence, we have to integrate the aspect R28B twice into the base requirement R1. The pointcut scenarios in the two sequence diagrams R28B (Out) (shown in Fig. 7) and R28B (In) can only be instantiated in one way, because in the sequence diagram for R1 (see Fig. 4) there is only one communication from the machine via a network (LMN) to a receiver (SmartMeter) and one back from the sender (SmartMeter) via the network (LMN). The first two lines of Table 2 describe these integrations. The pointcut scenario of the aspect R30 matches for all synchronous message calls with a reply (see Fig. 6). Hence, we have two possible situations in the sequence diagram for R1 where the aspect could be integrated. The event to be logged is a failed check of the received meter data and hence, we integrate aspect R30 as described by the third line in Table 2. Finally, we have to integrate aspect R32 that cross-cuts aspect R30. The pointcut scenario for R32 (see Fig. 8) has to be instantiated with the recording of the event (see Fig. 6) as described in line four of Table 2.

The weaving relations are used to generate the weaving sequence diagrams from the sequence diagrams of the problem and aspect diagrams. These auto-

Table 2. Weaving relations for base requirement R1.

Aspect	Domain Instantiations	Message Instantiations
R28B (Out)	SMGReceive/SMGRequester, LMN/Network, SmartMeter/Receiver	requestData/sendDataOut, forwardRequest/forwardDataOut
R28B (In)	SMGReceive/SMGRequester, LMN/Network, SmartMeter/Sender	sendData/sendDataIn, forwardData/forwardDataIn
R30	SMGReceive/SMGRequester, SMGReceive/Source	check/event2, fail/event1
R32	SMGLog/SMGRequester, EventStorage/Storage	recordEvent/storeData

matically generated sequence diagrams have then to be adjusted, such that the overall behavior satisfies the weaving requirement. The generated sequence diagram for R1 is shown in Fig. 9. For the sake of readability, we use a bold font for messages from the original problem specification of R1. In accordance with Table 2, the date sent to the smart meter is encrypted before sending and the received data is decrypted when received. Furthermore, in the case of a failed check of the received data an encrypted log is recorded.

4.7 Analyze Interactions

For reasons of space, we do not go into detail for this step. Alebrahim et al. provide methods for interaction analysis using problem frames. In [22] functional requirements are treated, and [23] describes how to analyze quality requirements for interactions. Both works use the smart grid as a case study. Hence, we re-used the methods and results also for this work. The results are documented in Table 1 using bold **I**.

Table 3. Effort spent (in person-hours/minutes) for conducting the method.

	Classify Requirements	Model Base Requirements	Identify Underlying Qualities	Analyze Completeness	Model Aspect Requirements	Weave Requirements	Analyze Interactions
Number of items	27 requirements	10 base requirements	6 aspect requirements	10 base requirements	5 aspect requirements	10 base requirements	16 functional requirements
Ø per item	11min	36min	7min	7min	34min	23min	6min
Total	5h 00min	6h 3min	45min	1h 15min	2h 51min	3h 53min	1h 45min

5 Validation

To validate our method, we applied it to the crisis management system (CMS) [24] that Kienzle et al. proposed as a case study for aspect-oriented modeling. We derived an informal scenario description and the textual use case descriptions from the original as input for our method[5]. The method was executed by a requirements expert, who did not know the case beforehand. From the

---

[5] For the inputs and the results see http://imperia.uni-due.de/imperia/md/content/ swe/aore4pf_cms_report.pdf.

information provided to the requirements analyst, he identified 13 base requirements that he modeled using 10 problem diagrams, 8 aspect requirements that he modeled using 5 aspect diagrams, and 6 quality requirements.

The effort spent for conducting our method on the CMS is summarized in Table 3. It took 5 h to classify the requirements. Note that for the case study this step was done manually. The reason was that tools such as, for example, OntRep [13] or EA-Miner [14] require some additional input like training documents or an existing ontology. But unfortunately, such inputs were not available. Hence, the first step can be sped up significantly using these tools. Another big block of effort is the modeling of base and aspect requirements. Here the tool support already helps to speed up the modeling, but is subject for further improvement. Note that the modeling steps do not only include the modeling itself, but also the analysis and improvement of the original requirements, which make the requirements more precise and unambiguous. Therefore, parts of the effort spent on the modeling steps are unavoidable even when using another method or notation. The modeling itself pays off as it allows the usage of the broad spectrum of methods and tools which need problem frame models as input. For example, the analysis of completeness uses these models and takes about an hour for different kinds of qualities. The weaving of aspects is quite time consuming right now. Here the tool support is on an experimental level, but the observations taken during the case study imply that a full fledged tool support will significantly drop the effort. The interaction analysis takes round about two hours, which is significantly below the effort of doing such an analysis without a problem frame model (see [22] for further information). All the effort spent sums up to 21,5 person hours, which is significant but reasonable with regards to the results one gets. And compared to efforts other authors report, the effort spent for our method seems to be even low. For example, Landuyt et al. [25] report an effort spent of 170 h for the requirements engineering related activities.

Table 4. Requirements identified.

		1) Functional	2) Availability	3) Reliability	4) Persistence	5) Real-Time	6) Security	7) Mobility	8) Statistic Logging	9) Multi-Access	10) Safety	11) Adaptability	12) Accuracy	13) Maintainability	14) Performance	15) Scalability	Sum
Same Class	Identified	100%	33%	50%	0%	0%	67%	0%	0%	0%	75%	0%	0%				30%
	Partly	0%	0%	0%	0%	0%	33%	0%	0%	0%	0%	0%	0%				3%
	Not Identified	0%	0%	0%	0%	0%	0%	33%	0%	0%	25%	0%	75%				13%
Other Class	Identified As		13)	2)	1)	14)		1)	1)	15)		1)	1)				
	Identified	0%	67%	50%	100%	67%	0%	67%	100%	100%	0%	25%	25%				45%
	Partly	0%	0%	0%	0%	33%	0%	0%	0%	0%	0%	75%	0%				10%
Aggregated	Identified	100%	100%	100%	100%	67%	67%	67%	100%	100%	75%	25%	25%				75%
	Partly	0%	0%	0%	0%	33%	33%	0%	0%	0%	0%	75%	0%				13%
	Not Identified	0%	0%	0%	0%	0%	0%	33%	0%	0%	25%	0%	75%				13%

To asses the sufficiency of the method and the used tools, the requirements and qualities found within our method were compared to the original document as described by Kienzle et al. Table 4 shows the comparison. Overall, the results are satisfying as most requirements were found and classified in the correct class (30 %) or in another, also correct, class (45 %). The high amount of requirements classified differently are due to specific classes given in the original documents. For example, persistence and statistical logging were completely described as functional requirements in the documents but treated as qualities. For such requirements it is a more general discussion if they are quality requirements or not. Hence, we accepted both views as correct. For some specific qualities, such as mobility or accuracy, the overall observation cannot be acknowledged. The reasons are subject to further investigations.

To asses the aspects identified, we compared the results of our method to the results given in other publications considering aspect-oriented requirements engineering using the same scenario [25,26]. The set of requirements identified with our method includes all requirements which are treated as aspects in the other works. 83 % of the aspects found and separated in [25] and 75 % of those in [26] were also separated as aspects by our method. The other 17 % of aspects in [25] and 25 % in [26] were identified as base requirements by our method. A detailed investigation showed that both views on these requirements are reasonable. Some of the aspects our method found were not mentioned in the other works. 38 % and 25 % of the requirements identified by our method where not mentioned in [25,26], respectively. Reasons for the missing requirements might be that they were not reported due to lack of space or that they were not found.

We could not asses our completeness analysis quantitatively as the other works using the scenario stick to the original requirements. But the qualitative investigation of the completeness analysis showed reasonable results. This observation is also true for the cross cut relations. We also compared the weaved specification with sequence diagrams or state machines given by the original document and works in [24]. Here we observed that the specifications produced by our method were at least as good as the chosen assessment artifacts. Again, the interaction analysis could not be assessed quantitatively due to missing benchmarks. But the found interactions seemed to be real problems which have to be resolved in a real case.

6   Related Work

There are many works considering early aspects [27–33]. Most of these approaches deal with goal-oriented approaches and use-case models. But goal or use-case models are of a higher level of abstraction than problem frames. Additionally, goal and use-case models are stakeholder-centric, while problem frames are system-centric. Therefore, refining functional requirements taking into account more detail of the system-to-be and analyzing the system-to-be described by the functional requirements is reported to be difficult for such methods [34]. Recently, there were papers which reported a successful integration of goal- and problem-oriented methods [35,36]. Hence, one might benefit from integrating goal-models in our method.

Conejero et al. [37] present a framework alike the method presented in this paper. Their process also starts with unstructured textual requirements. Then different tools and modeling notations are used along the frame work to identify and handle aspects. In difference to our process, they do not consider a completeness or interaction analysis and especially for the modeling of aspects they lack tool support.

Only few approaches consider the integration of early aspects in the problem frames approach. Lencastre et al. [38] also investigated how early aspects can be integrated into problem frames. Their method to model aspects in the problem frames approach differs from ours. For an aspect, the authors first select a problem frame as *PF Pointcut Scenario*. This pointcut scenario defines into which problems the aspect can be integrated. The pointcut scenario is then extended to the *PF Aspectual Scenario*, which is similar to our aspect diagrams, with the difference that the pointcut always has to be a problem frame. This reduces flexibility, because an aspect (e.g., logging of all system events) may have to be integrated into different problem diagrams.

7   Conclusions

In this paper, we presented the AORE4PF method which integrates aspect-orientation into the problem frames approach and utilizes many quality analysis method based on problem frames to be a problem-, quality-, and aspect-oriented requirements engineering method. We extended the UML4PF profile with stereotypes that allow us to create aspect diagrams. We further introduced a structured methodology to separate aspects from requirements, to model aspects, and to weave aspects and requirements together. We considered both the static and the behavioral view on the requirements, aspects, and their weaving. We exemplified our method using a smart grid scenario from the NESSoS project as case study and validated it using a crisis management system.

The contributions of this work are (1) the integration of aspects into the problem frames approach, (2) a structured way of separating base, quality and aspect requirements, starting from a textual description, (3) the detection of implicit qualities given by aspects, (4) identification of all base requirements relevant for a quality and the related aspects, (5) a structured method to weave base and aspect requirements, and (6) the integration of an interactions analysis between the resulting requirements. The AORE4PF method is (7) tool-supported in most steps. The resulting requirements model not necessarily leads to an aspect-oriented implementation of the software. The identified aspects can also help to define the structure of a component-based implementation.

For future work, we plan to improve the tool support. More steps of our method, such as the instantiation of pointcut scenarios during the weaving, can be automated to a higher degree and we want to provide an integrated tool chain for the requirements separation. Additionally, we will investigate how architectures can be derived from the aspect-oriented requirements model.

References

1. Hofmann, H., Lehner, F.: Requirements engineering as a success factor in software projects. IEEE Softw. **18**, 58–66 (2001)
2. Cavusoglu, H., Mishra, B., Raghunathan, S.: The effect of internet security breach announcements on market value: capital market reactions for breached firms and internet security developers. Int. J. Electron. Commer. **9**, 70–104 (2004)
3. Khansa, L., Cook, D.F., James, T., Bruyaka, O.: Impact of HIPAA provisions on the stock market value of healthcare institutions, and information security and other information technology firms. Comput. Secur. **31**, 750–770 (2012)
4. Boehm, B.W., Papaccio, P.N.: Understanding and controlling software costs. IEEE Trans. Softw. Eng. **14**, 1462–1477 (1988)
5. Willis, R.: Hughes aircraft's widespread deployment of a continuously improving software process. AD-a358 993. Carnegie-Mellon University (1998)
6. Firesmith, D.: Specifying good requirements. J. Object Technol. **2**, 77–87 (2003). http://www.jot.fm/issues/issue_2003_07/column7
7. Parnas, D.L.: On the criteria to be used in decomposing systems into modules. Commun. ACM **15**, 1053–1058 (1972)
8. Jackson, M.: Problem Frames. Analyzing and structuring software development problems. Addison-Wesley, New York (2001)
9. Kreutzmann, H., Vollmer, S., Tekampe, N., Abromeit, A.: Protection profile for the gateway of a smart metering system. Technical report, BSI (2011)
10. OPEN meter project: requirements of AMI. Technical report, OPEN meter project (2009)
11. Hatebur, D., Heisel, M.: A UML profile for requirements analysis of dependable software. In: Schoitsch, E. (ed.) SAFECOMP 2010. LNCS, vol. 6351, pp. 317–331. Springer, Heidelberg (2010)
12. Côté, I., Hatebur, D., Heisel, M., Schmidt, H.: UML4PF - a tool for problem-oriented requirements analysis. In: Proceedings of the 19th IEEE International Requirements Engineering Conference, pp. 349–350. IEEE Computer Society (2011)
13. Moser, T., Winkler, D., Heindl, M., Biffl, S.: Requirements management with semantic technology: an empirical study on automated requirements categorization and conflict analysis. In: Mouratidis, H., Rolland, C. (eds.) CAiSE 2011. LNCS, vol. 6741, pp. 3–17. Springer, Heidelberg (2011)
14. Sampaio, A., Rashid, A., Chitchyan, R., Rayson, P.: EA-Miner: towards automation in aspect-oriented requirements engineering. In: Rashid, A., Akşit, M. (eds.) Transactions on AOSD III. LNCS, vol. 4620, pp. 4–39. Springer, Heidelberg (2007)
15. Baniassad, E., Clarke, S.: Finding aspects in requirements with Theme/Doc. In: Early Aspects: Aspect-Oriented Requirements Engineering and Architecture Design, pp. 15–22 (2004). http://trese.cs.utwente.nl/workshops/early-aspects-2004/workshop_papers.htm
16. Jackson, M., Zave, P.: Deriving specifications from requirements: an example. In: ICSE, pp. 15–24. ACM Press, USA (1995)
17. Rago, A., Marcos, C., Diaz-Pace, J.A.: Uncovering quality-attribute concerns in use case specifications via early aspect mining. Requirements Eng. **18**, 67–84 (2013)

18. Beckers, K., Faßbender, S., Heisel, M., Meis, R.: A problem-based approach for computer-aided privacy threat identification. In: Preneel, B., Ikonomou, D. (eds.) APF 2012. LNCS, vol. 8319, pp. 1–16. Springer, Heidelberg (2014)
19. Faßbender, S., Heisel, M.: From problems to laws in requirements engineering using model-transformation. In: ICSOFT 2013, pp. 447–458. SciTePress (2013)
20. Faßbender, S., Heisel, M., Meis, R.: Functional requirements under security PresSuRE. In: ICSOFT-PT 2014 - Proceedings of the 9th International Conference on Software Paradigm Trends, pp. 5–16. SciTePress (2014)
21. Faßbender, S., Heisel, M., Meis, R.: Aspect-oriented requirements engineering with problem frames. In: ICSOFT-PT 2014 - Proceedings of the 9th International Conference on Software Paradigm Trends, pp. 145–156. SciTePress (2014)
22. Alebrahim, A., Faßbender, S., Heisel, M., Meis, R.: Problem-based requirements interaction analysis. In: Salinesi, C., van de Weerd, I. (eds.) REFSQ 2014. LNCS, vol. 8396, pp. 200–215. Springer, Heidelberg (2014)
23. Alebrahim, A., Choppy, C., Faßbender, S., Heisel, M.: Optimizing functional and quality requirements according to stakeholders' goals. In: Mistrik, I. (ed.) System Quality and Software Architecture. Elsevier, Amsterdam (2014)
24. Kienzle, J., Guelfi, N., Mustafiz, S.: Crisis management systems: a case study for aspect-oriented modeling. In: Katz, S., Mezini, M., Kienzle, J. (eds.) Transactions on Aspect-Oriented Software Development VII. LNCS, vol. 6210, pp. 1–22. Springer, Heidelberg (2010)
25. Van Landuyt, D., Truyen, E., Joosen, W.: Discovery of stable abstractions for aspect-oriented composition in the car crash management domain. In: Katz, S., Mezini, M., Kienzle, J. (eds.) Transactions on Aspect-Oriented Software Development VII. LNCS, vol. 6210, pp. 375–422. Springer, Heidelberg (2010)
26. Mussbacher, G., Amyot, D., Araújo, J., Moreira, A.: Requirements modeling with the aspect-oriented user requirements notation (AoURN): a case study. In: Katz, S., Mezini, M., Kienzle, J. (eds.) Transactions on Aspect-Oriented Software Development VII. LNCS, vol. 6210, pp. 23–68. Springer, Heidelberg (2010)
27. Rashid, A.: Aspect-oriented requirements engineering: an introduction. In: Proceedings of the 16th IEEE International Requirements Engineering Conference, pp. 306–309. IEEE Computer Society (2008)
28. Yu, Y., Cesar, J., Leite, S.P., Mylopoulos, J.: From goals to aspects: discovering aspects from requirements goal models. In: Proceedings of the 12th IEEE International Requirements Engineering Conference, pp. 38–47. IEEE Computer Society (2004)
29. Jacobson, I., Ng, P.W.: Aspect-Oriented Software Development with Use Cases. Addison-Wesley Professional, Englewood Cliffs (2004)
30. Whittle, J., Araujo, J.: Scenario modelling with aspects. IEE Proc. Softw. **151**, 157–171 (2004)
31. Sutton, Jr., S.M., Rouvellou, I.: Modeling of software concerns in cosmos. In: Proceedings of the 1st International Conference on Aspect-oriented Software Development, AOSD 2002, pp. 127–133. ACM, New York (2002)
32. Moreira, A., Araújo, J., Rashid, A.: A concern-oriented requirements engineering model. In: Pastor, Ó., Falcão e Cunha, J. (eds.) CAiSE 2005. LNCS, vol. 3520, pp. 293–308. Springer, Heidelberg (2005)
33. Grundy, J.C.: Aspect-oriented requirements engineering for component-based software systems. In: Proceedings of the IEEE International Symposium on Requirements Engineering, pp. 84–91. IEEE Computer Society, Washington (1999)

34. Alrajeh, D., Kramer, J., Russo, A., Uchitel, S.: Learning operational requirements from goal models. In: IEEE 31st International Conference on Software Engineering, pp. 265–275. IEEE Computer Society (2009)

35. Mohammadi, N.G., Alebrahim, A., Weyer, T., Heisel, M., Pohl, K.: A framework for combining problem frames and goal models to support context analysis during requirements engineering. In: Cuzzocrea, A., Kittl, C., Simos, D.E., Weippl, E., Xu, L. (eds.) CD-ARES 2013. LNCS, vol. 8127, pp. 272–288. Springer, Heidelberg (2013)

36. Beckers, K., Faßbender, S., Heisel, M., Paci, F.: Combining goal-oriented and problem-oriented requirements engineering methods. In: Cuzzocrea, A., Kittl, C., Simos, D.E., Weippl, E., Xu, L. (eds.) CD-ARES 2013. LNCS, vol. 8127, pp. 178–194. Springer, Heidelberg (2013)

37. Conejero, J.M., Hernandez, J., Jurado, E., van den Berg, K.: Mining early aspects based on syntactical and dependency analyses. Sci. Comput. Program. **75**, 1113–1141 (2010)

38. Lencastre, M., Moreira, A., Araújo, J., Castro, J.: Aspects composition in problem frames. In: Proceedings of the 16th IEEE International Requirements Engineering Conference, pp. 343–344. IEEE Computer Society (2008)

Problem-Based Security Requirements Elicitation and Refinement with PresSuRE

Stephan Faßbender[✉], Maritta Heisel, and Rene Meis

Paluno - The Ruhr Institute for Software Technology,
University of Duisburg-Essen, Essen, Germany
{stephan.fabbender,maritta.heisel,rene.meis}@paluno.uni-due.de

Abstract. Recently published reports on cybercrime indicate an ever-increasing number of security incidents related to IT systems. Many attacks causing the incidents abuse (in)directly one or more security defects. Fixing the security defect once fielded is costly. To avoid the defects and the subsequent need to fix them, security has to be considered thoroughly when developing software. The earliest phase to do so is the requirements engineering, in which security threats should be identified early on and treated by defining sufficient security requirements. In a previous paper [1], we introduced a methodology for Problem-based Security Requirements Elicitation (PresSuRE). PresSuRE provides a computer-aided security threat identification. The identification is based on the functional requirements for a system-to-be. Still, there is a need for guidance on how to derive security requirements once the threats are identified. In this work, we provide such guidance extending PresSuRE and its tool support. We illustrate and validate our approach using a smart grid scenario provided by the industrial partners of the EU project NESSoS.

Keywords: Security analysis · Problem frames · Requirements elicitation

1 Introduction

Recently, there has been an increase of reported security incidents hitting large software systems. For example, in the report on cybercrime for the year 2013 published by the federal criminal police office of Germany, the authors state that 64426 security incidents were reported in Germany [2]. This is an increase by 70 percent with respect to 2008 [3]. Moreover, particular types of attacks which aim at companies increased much more. For example, data manipulation and computer sabotage incidents in companies increased by 18 percent with respect to 2012 and 578 percent with respect to 2008. These numbers are limited to

Part of this work is funded by the German Research Foundation (DFG) under grant number HE3322/4-2 and the EU project Network of Excellence on Engineering Secure Future Internet Software Services and Systems (NESSoS, ICT-2009.1.4 Trustworthy ICT, Grant No. 256980).

Germany, but, for example, Norton reports a world wide damage of 113 billion US dollar in 2013 due to security incidents [4]. Hence, the need for secure IT systems is staggering.

Not all of the security incidents are directly related to security defects in an IT system, but many attacks abuse indirectly or directly one or more security defects. Hence, these security defects need to be fixed. But fixing the security defect causing the incident is costly. Fixing a defect when it is already fielded is reported to be up to eighty times more expensive than fixing the corresponding requirements defects early on [5,6]. Thus, security issues should be detected as early as possible for a system-to-be. Therefore, it is crucial for requirements engineers to identify security threats, and to refine the threats into security requirements. But eliciting good requirements is not an easy task [7], even more with regard to security, as most requirements engineers are not security experts in the first place.

In a previous work of ours, we proposed a method called problem-based security requirements elicitation (PresSuRE), which guides a requirements engineer through the process of eliciting a set of security requirements in collaboration with the stakeholders of the system-to-be and security experts [1]. PresSuRE has several benefits. It does not require the requirements engineer to have a security background. It does not require any preliminary security requirements and security relevant information. It lowers the effort by providing tool support for semi-automated modeling and an automated security analysis. Furthermore, PresSuRE is completely guided by a detailed process.

PresSuRE is based on the same idea of deriving information flows from functional requirements like the problem-based privacy analysis (ProPAn) [8], but changes the analysis to be suitable for security. The analysis and elicitation is based on a complete set of functional requirements for a system-to-be. The method is accompanied with tool-support[1]. PresSuRE is based on the problem frame notation introduced by Jackson [9]. Problem frames are suitable as input for a semi-automated analysis, as they have a predictable structure, underlying semantics, and support focusing on parts of the system-to-be.

But PresSuRE, as reported in the previous work, only gives detailed guidance for the steps which are necessary for analyzing the system-to-be for security threats. A description how to derive and model initial security requirements, and how to analyze if the security requirements are sufficient regarding the found threats, is still missing. Hence, in this paper we provide such guidance by extending PresSuRE.

We briefly describe the case study (Sect. 2) we use for the running example and the validation. The problem frame notation is explained in Sect. 3. Section 4 introduces the running example, which is used for the rest of the paper. The PresSuRE method as introduced in [1] is briefly explained in Sect. 5. In Sect. 6, we describe the our new extension for deriving security requirements and in Sect. 7 PresSuRE is validated. In Sect. 8 related work is discussed, and the final conclusion is drawn in Sect. 9.

---

[1] http://www.uml4pf.org/ext-pressure/installation.html.

2 Case Study

To illustrate the application of the PresSuRE method, we use the real-life case study of smart grids. As sources for real functional and quality requirements, we consider diverse documents such as "Application Case Study: Smart Grid" provided by the industrial partners of the EU project NESSoS[2], the "Protection Profile for the Gateway of a Smart Metering System" [10] provided by the German Federal Office for Information Security, and "Requirements of AMI (Advanced Multi-metering Infrastructure") [11] provided by the EU project OPEN meter[3].

To use energy in an optimal way, smart grids make it possible to couple the generation, distribution, storage, and consumption of energy. Smart grids use information and communication technology (ICT), which allows for financial, informational, and electrical transactions.

We define the terms specific to the smart grid domain and our use case in the following. The *smart meter gateway* represents the central communication unit in a *smart metering system*. It is responsible for collecting, processing, storing, and communicating *meter data*. The *meter data* refers to readings measured by smart meters regarding consumption or production of a certain commodity. A *smart meter* represents the device that measures the consumption or production of a certain commodity and sends it to the gateway. An *authorized external entity* can be a human or an IT unit that communicates with the gateway from outside the gateway boundaries through a *wide area network (WAN)*. The *WAN* provides the communication network that interconnects the gateway with the outside world. The *LMN (local metrological network)* provides the communication network between the meter and the gateway. The *HAN (home area network)* provides the communication network between the consumer and the gateway. The term *consumer* refers to end users of commodities (e.g., electricity).

3 Problem-Oriented Requirements Engineering

Jackson [9] introduced the concept of *problem frames*, which is concerned with describing, analyzing, and structuring software development problems. A problem frame represents a class of software development problems. It is described by a *frame diagram*, which consists of domains, interfaces between them, and a requirement. Domains describe entities in the environment. Jackson distinguishes the domain types *biddable domains* that are usually people, *causal domains* that comply with some physical laws, and *lexical domains* that are data representations. Whenever we have influence on the design of a domain it is a *designed domain*. To describe the problem context, a *connection domain* between two other domains may be necessary. Connection domains establish a connection between other domains by means of technical devices. Examples are video cameras, sensors, or networks. Note that one domain can have more than one type, for example a domain can be a connection and causal domain at the same time.

---

[2] http://www.nessos-project.eu/.
[3] http://www.openmeter.com/.

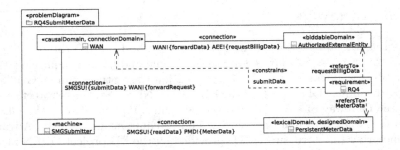

Fig. 1. Problem diagram RQ 4: submit meter data.

Interfaces connect domains, and they contain *shared phenomena*. Shared phenomena may be events, operation calls, messages, and the like. They are observable by at least two domains, but controlled by only one domain, as indicated by the abbreviation of that domain and "!". For example, the shared phenomenon *MeterData* in Fig. 1 is observable by the domains *SMGSubmitter* and *PersistentMeterData*, but controlled only by the domain *PersistentMeterData* (abbreviation PMD).

The objective is to construct a *machine* (i.e., software) that controls the behavior of the environment (in which it is integrated) in accordance with the requirements. Problem-oriented requirements analysis relies on a decomposition of the overall problem into sub-problems, which are represented by *problem diagrams*. Problem diagrams contain the requirements belonging to the sub-problem. When we state a requirement, we want to change something in the environment. Therefore, each requirement *constrains* at least one domain in the environment. A requirement may also *refer* to several domains in the environment of the machine.

The problem frames approach distinguishes between the *requirements (R)*, the *domain knowledge (D)*, and the *specification (S)*. The requirements describe the desired system after the machine is built. The domain knowledge represents the relevant parts of the problem world. The specifications describe the behavior of the software in order to meet the requirements.

We describe problem frames using UML class diagrams, extended by stereotypes, as proposed by Hatebur and Heisel [12]. Figure 1 shows a problem diagram in UML notation. The biddable domain (UML class with stereotype ≪biddableDomain≫) *Authorized External Entity* controls the *request billing data* phenomenon (Denoted by the *AEE!{requestBillingData}* in the name of the UML association with the stereotype ≪connection≫ between the classes *Authorized External Entity* and *WAN*), which is observed by the causal connection domain *WAN* (UML class with stereotype ≪causalDomain, connectionDomain≫). The *SMGSubmitter* controls the *read data* phenomenon, which is observed by the lexical domain *PersistentMeterData* (UML class with stereotype ≪lexicalDomain≫). Additionally, the *SMGProvider submits the data*. The *Persistent Meter Data* controls the *meter data* it contains. The *WAN forwards the data and commands* it observes. The requirement RQ 4 (for a textual description see Sect. 4) constrains the *WAN* for forwarding the submitted data and refers to the billing data requested by *Authorized External Entity*, and the meter data stored in the *PersistentMeterData*.

4 Running Example: Billing

We chose the use case *Meter Reading for Billing* given in the documents of NESSoS and the open meter project to exemplify our method. This use case is concerned with gathering, processing, and storing meter readings from smart meters for the billing process. Beside the billing use case, there are in total 13 use cases described for the minimal features of a smart meter gateway, which we all considered for our validation. The functional requirements for this use case are defined as follows:

(RQ 1)**Receive Meter Data.** The smart meter gateway shall receive meter data from smart meters.

(RQ 2)**Process Meter Data.** The smart meter gateway shall process meter data from smart meters.

(RQ 3)**Store Meter Data.** The smart meter gateway shall store meter data from smart meters.

(RQ 4)**Submit Billing Data.** The smart meter gateway shall submit processed meter data to authorized external entities.

(RQ 5)**Provide Consumption Data to Consumer.** The smart meter gateway shall provide meter data for consumers for the purpose of checking the consistency of bills.

The problem diagram for RQ 4 was already shown in Fig. 1 and explained in Sect. 3. Figure 2 shows the problem diagram for RQ 1. The causal domain *smart meter* controls the *send data* phenomenon, which is forwarded by the *LMN* and finally observed by the machine domain *SMGReceiver*. The *SMGReceiver* controls the phenomenon *writeTemporaryData*, which stores the received information in the lexical domain *temporary meter data*. Additionally, the *SMGReceiver* can *request data* which is forwarded by the *LMN* to the *smart meter*.

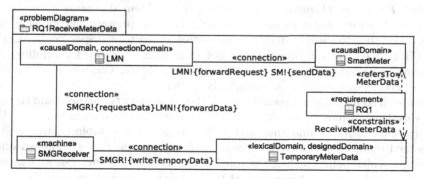

Fig. 2. Problem diagram RQ 1: receive meter data.

The causal connection domain LMN *forwards the data and commands* it observes. The requirement RQ 1 constrains the *temporary meter data* and refers to the *smart meter*. These two problem diagrams are sufficient to understand the rest of the paper, nevertheless we use all five functional requirements for our method.

Note that we will simplify this example in the following. We will not elaborate on all security elements but restrict ourselves to one example for each element, for example one asset, to improve the comprehensibility for the reader and for reasons of space. Nevertheless, for the validation we elaborated the full case study in means of 27 requirements and all possible assets and attackers.

5   The PresSuRE Method

The PresSuRE method as introduced in [1] consists of four phases and nine steps, which we will briefly explain in the following. For a detailed view we refer the reader to [1].

5.1   Model Functional Requirements

We assume that the functionality of the system-to-be is described completely, coherently and unambiguously. The functional requirements are a good starting point for a security analysis as the requirements engineer is used to deal with them, they are often already well defined, they already contain everything which has to be protected, and they also contain the entry points for possible attack vectors an adversary can use.

Model Problem Diagrams. In the first step of the PresSuRE method, the functional requirements have to be modeled using the *problem frame notation*. This can be done by the *requirements engineer* alone, based on a *textual description* of the *functional requirements*. The result is a set of *problem diagrams* as well as an automatically generated *connection domain discovery table*. *The functional requirements and corresponding problem diagrams are presented in Sect. 4.*

Adjust Problem Diagrams. As setting up problem diagrams allows some degree of freedom, adjustments might be needed to prepare the *problem diagrams*. For the PresSuRE analysis, connection domains are specifically important. But as connection domains are not of central relevance for fulfilling the functional requirements, they are often left out. Hence, one has to make sure that all connection domains are explicitly modeled.

For each connection between domains, the *requirements engineer* and the *system stakeholders* have to check if there is a connection domain in between. The *requirements engineer* and the *system stakeholders* use a table containing the connected domains pairwise, the phenomena in between and a standard questionnaire, which helps to elicit the missing connection domains. For an example of such a table see [1]. The result of this step are *adjusted problem diagrams*, which are modeled by the *requirements engineer* using semi-automated wizards.

For our example, using the table and answering the questions, we see that our problem diagrams have to contain WAN, HAN and LMN as connection domains. This information is already reflected by the problem diagrams shown in this paper.

5.2   Security Knowledge Elicitation

Before starting the security analysis, some security-specific knowledge has to be elicited. This information is crucial for the success of the analysis, as in most cases the functional requirements do not contain enough information for considering security thoroughly. The knowledge about assets in the system-to-be and attackers which might tamper with the system has to be made explicit. As this knowledge is not or only partially available for *requirements engineers*, they have to collaborate with the *stakeholders of the system* and *security experts*.

Prepare Knowledge Elicitation. Even though the functional requirements do not contain the information for security analysis, they do already contain some information, which is the starting point for eliciting the additional domain knowledge. We use *security element elicitation tables*, and *attacker elicitation tables* to elicit this information. Examples of such tables are given in [1]. The tables are automatically generated from the *problem diagrams*.

Identify Assets, Authorized Entities and Rights. The baseline questions for this step are "What has to be protected?" (*asset*), "Who is eligible to access the asset?" (*authorized entities*), and "Which actions are allowed for a stakeholder regarding an asset?" (*rights*). We use the previously generated *security element elicitation tables* to elicit this information. These tables are completed by the *stakeholders of the system-to-be* using the following description, while the *requirements engineer* models the results.

Assets. Identify those domains which have to be protected. Every domain beside the machine is an asset candidate. Most likely one wants to protect a lexical domain representing information or a causal domain. *For our example, we only select the persistent meter data as an asset, which contains information about the electricity consumption of the consumer. This information has to be protected for privacy reasons, as it, for example, allows to monitor the consumer. The full case study contains 13 further assets (see Sect. 7).*

Authorized Entities. An authorized entity to an asset is every domain which has an eligible interest in knowing the state / reading, or controlling / writing the asset. *Eligible entities of the meter data are the smart meters, which produce the meter data, the external entities, who need the consumption information for billing, and the consumer, who wants to check his/her electricity consumption.*

Rights. Authorized entities have different rights to access the asset. In case of a lexical domain, the rights are to read or write the information in the domain. In case of the causal domain, the rights are to control or know the state of the causal domain. For each right and authorized entity, one has to state if the entity is allowed to have the right or if the entity must have the right. *The smart* *meters must have the right to write the information, while the consumer and external entities must have the right to read the information. The smart meters do not need to read the stored consumption data, and the external entities and the consumer are not allowed to modify the consumption data.*

The elicited information has to be added to the model. For this purpose, we use *domain knowledge diagrams*. In domain knowledge diagrams additional knowledge about domains and relations between domains can be modeled. To support modeling security-related domain knowledge we developed UML profiles. The modeling is explained in detail in [1]. The diagrams are generated in the background while the *requirements engineer* completes a wizard which is similar to the security element elicitation table. The result of the step are *asset knowledge diagrams*.

Attacker(s) Elicitation. In this step, the *requirements engineer* and a *security expert* have to collaborate to define those *attackers* who might attack our system-to-be. While the *requirements engineer* has a deeper understanding of the system-to-be and its domain, the *security expert* adds his/her vital knowledge about attackers, attacker abilities, possible attack vectors, and so forth. Hence, it is not mandatory that the *requirements engineer* has a security background.

Beckers et al. [13] enumerate different *types of attackers*: *physical attacker, software attacker, network attacker,* and *social attacker.* Regarding their abilities, we have chosen the abilities as described by Dolev and Yao [14]: *read (read message / get state of domain), write (write message / change state of domain), interfere (intercept message / prevent the change of state).* For the purpose of eliciting the information about attackers, we use the generated *attacker elicitation tables*.

Attacker. First, we have to reason for each domain and type of attacker about the question if this type of attacker might exist for the domain at hand. *For simplicity's sake, we assume for the running example that we only have to defend against network attackers. We distinguish between two network attackers: The internal network attacker, who has access to the HAN and LMN, where the smart meters reside, and the external network attacker, who can attack via the WAN. Note that for the full case study we found and modeled 7 attackers in total, including all kinds of attackers.*

Abilities. For each attacker and each domain the attacker has access to, we have to state which abilities the attacker has. Whenever there is no detailed information about the attackers and their abilities regarding a domain they have access to, one should assume the strongest attacker. This might lead to an overestimation of the threats afterward. But adding an unnecessary security requirement is not so much of an issue, while missing one is critical. *After an assessment of all attackers of our example and their abilities, we could not exclude any of the basic abilities. Hence, our attackers have all abilities regarding the domains they have access to.*

The elicited information has to be added to the model to be available for our analysis, too. Again, the modeling can be done semi-automatically using the wizards our tool provides. The result are *attacker knowledge diagrams* (see [1] for more details).

5.3 Graph Generation

The automated part of the security analysis relies on graphs, which visualize information flows and access flows. The attacker asset access graphs, which contain the potential security threats towards the functional requirements, are generated stepwise. The steps and intermediate graphs are explained in the following.

Global Access Graph. All graphs $(\mathcal{V}, \mathcal{E})$ that we use for our security analysis in the PresSuRE method are labeled and directed. The set of vertices is a subset of the domains occurring in the model, formally $\mathcal{V} \subseteq Domain$. An edge is annotated with a diagram and a type. The diagram can be a problem diagram or a domain knowledge diagram. The type can be required (*req*), implicit (*imp*) or attack (*att*) (*Type* :: = req|imp|att). The type indicates if the edge is *required* or *implicitly* given by the problem diagram or if it shows a possible *attack* relationship defined in a domain knowledge diagram. The edges point from one domain to another, formally $\mathcal{E} \subseteq Domain \times Diagram \times Type \times Domain$. For the rest of the paper we will regard such an edge as an access flow. In the following, we describe a graph $(\mathcal{V}, \mathcal{E})$ only by its edges $\mathcal{E}$.

For the analysis of the threats towards an asset we will use the *global access graph*. This graph contains the information about access flows between domains, and which problem diagrams are the source of these flows. For the flows, we distinguish between required flows as stated by the requirement and implicit ones which are modeled due to the given environment. To set up the global access graph we use the problem diagrams as an input. The predicates $constrains, refersTo : \mathbb{P}(Domain \times Diagram)$ and $controls : \mathbb{P}(Domain \times Domain \times Diagram)$ can be derived from the problem frame model and are used to generate the global access graph. We have $(d, p) \in constrains$ and $(d, p) \in refersTo$ iff a requirement or domain knowledge in diagram p constrains the domain d or refers to it, respectively. $(d_1, d_2, p) \in controls$ is true iff the domain d_1 controls an interface that d_2 observes in the diagram p.

Using these predicates, we create the global access graph $\mathcal{G}$, which is an overapproximation of the access flows occurring in the system-to-be. An edge $(d_1, p, \text{req}, d_2)$ is in $\mathcal{G}$ iff the domains d_1 and d_2 are not equal, and the domain d_1 is referred to and the domain d_2 is constrained in p. *For example, the problem diagram for RQ 1 (see Fig. 2) contains the smart meter and the temporary storage. The smart meter is referred by RQ 1 and the temporary storage is constrained by RQ 1. Hence, we add a required access flow edge (solid arrow) between smart meter (node with name SmartMeter) and temporary meter data (node with name TemporaryMeterData) annotated with RQ 1 (see graph shown in Fig. 3).*

Additionally, an edge $(d_1, p, \text{imp}, d_2)$ is in $\mathcal{G}$ iff the $(d_1, p, \text{req}, d_2)$ is not already in $\mathcal{G}$, the domains d_1 and d_2 are not equal, and d_2 observes an interface controlled by d_1 in p. Note that machines are treated as transitive forwarders in this case. This means that whenever a machine m observes an interface controlled by d_1, and d_2 observes an interface controlled by m, we assume that

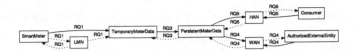

Fig. 3. Global access graph (also asset access graph for persistent meter data).

d_2 observes an interface of d_1. *For example, the domain LMN controls a phenomenon forwardMeterData which is observed by the machine (see Fig. 2). The domain temporary meter data observes a phenomenon writeTemporaryData from the machine. Hence, an implicit access flow edge (dotted edge) is added between the LMN and the temporal meter data annotated with* **RQ 1** *(see* Fig. 3*).* The complete formal definition is given in [1].

Because of the annotation of the edges we keep the information which problem diagram causes the access flow. Thus, our global access graph contains traceability links that are used in our further analysis. The semantics of an edge $(d_1, p, t, d_2) \in \mathcal{G}$ is that in problem diagram p there is possibly a required or implicit (depending on t) access flow from domain d_1 to domain d_2.

Asset Access Graph. As the global access graph can be huge for a complex system-to-be, we introduce an asset access graph which focuses the view on one asset only. It only contains access flows given by the requirements directly or indirectly concerning the asset. Thus, we get one asset access graph per asset. The asset access graph makes the information for the requirements engineer easier to comprehend. Hence, it improves the scalability of our method. An edge (d_1, p, t, d_2) is in $\mathcal{G}_{asset}$ iff p is in $\mathcal{P}_{access}$. A problem diagram p is in $\mathcal{P}_{access}$ iff there is an edge (d_1, p, t, d_2) which is required and d_1 and d_2 are both in $\mathcal{D}_{access}$. $\mathcal{D}_{access}$ is a union of $\mathcal{D}_{active}$ and $\mathcal{D}_{passive}$. A domain d_1 is in $\mathcal{D}_{active}$ iff there is a required access flow which starts at d_1 and the target domain d_2 is already in $\mathcal{D}_{active}$. Initially, only the *asset* is in $\mathcal{D}_{active}$. Hence, $\mathcal{D}_{active}$ contains all domains which have a required direct or indirect (via another domain) access flow towards the asset. A domain d_2 is in $\mathcal{D}_{passive}$ iff there is a required access flow which ends at d_2 and the source domain d_1 is already in $\mathcal{D}_{passive}$. Initially, only the *asset* is in $\mathcal{D}_{passive}$. Hence, $\mathcal{D}_{passive}$ contains all domains which are the target of a required direct or indirect (via another domain) access flow from the asset. The complete formal definition is given in [1].

The resulting asset access graph for the persistent meter data is shown in Fig. 3, as for our small example the global and the asset access graph do not differ. For a complex scenario the asset access graph is significantly smaller than the global access graph. The asset access graph can be used to check if a stakeholder can gain more rights than he/she should. For reasons of space, we do not go into detail on this matter.

Attacker Asset Access Graph. For each asset, we generate the attacker asset access graph, which visualizes the information and control flows from attackers to the asset and from the asset to the attackers. At this point, we focus on the basic information security goals confidentiality, integrity, and availability (short CIA), which are suggested by the Common Criteria [15] and ISO

27000 family of standards [16]. The problematic access flows are annotated with the information which CIA property(ies) are threatened (CIA:: = C|I|A|ε). First, the domains which are directly connected to attackers are identified. Note that for this purpose we use the information given in domain knowledge diagrams created during the step *Identify assets, authorized entities and rights* described in Sect. 5.2. From these diagrams, we can derive the predicates $read, write, interfere : \mathbb{P}(Domain \times Diagram)$. We have $(d, dk) \in read$, $(d, dk) \in write$, and $(d, dk) \in interfere$ iff domain knowledge in diagram dk has a read, write, or interfere dependency, respectively, to the domain d.

A domain d can be object to be attacked if it is in $\mathcal{D}_{access}$ for the asset at hand. That is, an attacker can access or influence information on the asset through the domain d. We define the sets $\mathcal{D}_w$, $\mathcal{D}_i$, and $\mathcal{D}_r$ as the sets of all domains for which an attacker has the ability to *write*, *interfere*, or *read* it, respectively. A domain d is in $\mathcal{D}_w$ iff there exists an attacker a and a domain knowledge diagram dk, in which d is written and a is referred to by the domain knowledge. The domain d is in $\mathcal{D}_i$ iff there exists an attacker a and a domain knowledge diagram dk in which d is interfered and a is referred as sources of the interference. The domain d is in $\mathcal{D}_r$ iff there exists an attacker a and a domain knowledge diagram dk in which the information in d is referred to and a reads this information. Based on the three sets of domains which might be attacked, the asset threat graph $\mathcal{G}_{threat}$ can be set up. $\mathcal{D}_w$, $\mathcal{D}_i$, and $\mathcal{D}_r$ are formally defined as follows.

$$\mathcal{D}_w = \{d : \mathcal{D}_{access} \mid \exists a : Attacker; dk : Diagram \bullet (d, dk) \in write \\ \wedge (a, dk) \in refersTo\}$$

$$\mathcal{D}_i = \{d : \mathcal{D}_{access} \mid \exists a : Attacker; dk : Diagram \bullet (d, dk) \in interfere \\ \wedge (a, dk) \in refersTo\}$$

$$\mathcal{D}_r = \{d : \mathcal{D}_{access} \mid \exists a : Attacker; dk : Diagram \bullet (a, dk) \in read \wedge (d, dk) \in refersTo\}$$

$\mathcal{G}_{threat}$ contains all edges, and therefore problem diagrams, of the corresponding asset access graph which might allow an attacker to successfully attack the asset at hand. An access flow $(d_1, p, t, d_2) \in \mathcal{G}_{asset}$ represents that information which is transferred from d_1 to d_2 that possibly comes from the asset or that possibly will be stored in the asset. Hence, such an access flow is a possible threat to the confidentiality of an asset if an attacker has the ability to read one of the domains d_1 or d_2 ($d_1 \in \mathcal{D}_r \vee d_2 \in \mathcal{D}_r$). In this case, we add the edge (d_1, p, t, C, d_2) to $\mathcal{G}_{threat}$. An access flow $(d_1, p, t, d_2) \in \mathcal{G}_{asset}$ is a possible threat to the integrity of an asset if an attacker has the ability to write the source d_1 of the access flow ($d_1 \in \mathcal{D}_w$), because an attacker could change the information of the asset or the information sent to the asset at domain d_1, which forwards it to domain d_2. In this case, we add the edge (d_1, p, t, I, d_2) to $\mathcal{G}_{threat}$. We have to consider an access flow $(d_1, p, t, d_2) \in \mathcal{G}_{asset}$ as a possible threat to the availability of an asset if an attacker has the ability to interfere one of the domains d_1 or d_2 ($d_1 \in \mathcal{D}_i \vee d_2 \in \mathcal{D}_i$), because an attacker is then able to threaten the availability of information flowing from or to the asset through the domains d_1 and d_2. In

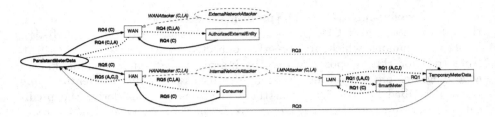

Fig. 4. Attacker asset access graph for persistent meter data.

this case, we add the edge (d_1, p, t, A, d_2) to $\mathcal{G}_{threat}$. $\mathcal{G}_{threat}$ is defined as follows.

$$\mathcal{G}_{threat} = \{(d_1, p, t, cia, d_2) : Domain \times Diagram \times Type \times CIA \times Domain \mid$$
$$(d_1, p, t, d_2) \in \mathcal{G}_{asset} \wedge [(d_1 \in \mathcal{D}_r \vee d_2 \in \mathcal{D}_r) \wedge cia = \text{C}$$
$$\vee d_1 \in \mathcal{D}_w \wedge cia = \text{I} \vee (d_1 \in \mathcal{D}_i \vee d_2 \in \mathcal{D}_i) \wedge cia = \text{A}]\}$$

The full attacker asset access graph $\mathcal{G}_{attack}$ is an extension of $\mathcal{G}_{threat} \subset \mathcal{G}_{attack}$. We add an edge $(d_1, p, t, \varepsilon, d_2)$ to $\mathcal{G}_{attack}$ iff (d_1, dk, t, d_2) is in $\mathcal{G}_{asset}$ but not in $\mathcal{G}_{threat}$. These edges visualize how the attacks on the access flows in $\mathcal{G}_{threat}$ might be propagated over the system due to the functional requirements. Additionally, the attackers are added to the attacker asset access graph. $\mathcal{G}_{attack}$ contains an edge (a, dk, att, cia, d) if a is an attacker and a domain knowledge diagram dk exists, in which d is referred to and d is written ($cia = \text{I}$) or interfered ($cia = \text{A}$). Additionally, $\mathcal{G}_{attack}$ contains an edge $(a, dk, att, \text{C}, d)$ if a is an attacker and a domain knowledge diagram dk exists in which d is referred to and a is read. Formally, we define $\mathcal{G}_{attack}$ as follows.

$$\mathcal{G}_{attack} = \{(d_1, p, t, \varepsilon, d_2) : Domain \times Diagram \times Type \times CIA \times Domain$$
$$\mid (d_1, p, t, d_2) \in \mathcal{G}_{asset} \wedge \forall st : CIA \bullet (d_1, p, t, st, d_2) \notin \mathcal{G}_{threat}\} \cup$$
$$\{(a, dk, att, cia, d) : Attacker \times Diagram \times Type \times CIA \times Domain \mid$$
$$(d, dk) \in refersTo \wedge [(a, dk) \in read \wedge cia = \text{C} \vee (a, dk) \in write \wedge cia = \text{I}$$
$$\vee (a, dk) \in interfere \wedge cia = \text{A}]\} \cup \mathcal{G}_{threat}$$

The generated attacker asset access graph for the persistent meter data is shown in Fig. 4. Note that for reasons of readability, the PresSuRE tool merges edges and their annotation if they have the same source and target, and are of the same type. The *asset* is now visualized as *ellipse with bold border* and the asset name (*PersistentMeterData*) is written in bold. The *attackers* internal and external network attacker are also added as *ellipses with dashed borders* and in italic font. Their *attack flow edges* are shown as dashed edges, which are annotated with the domain knowledge diagram they are described in and the security goals they may threaten. A bold (both, edge and annotation) access flow indicates a flow for which a security property might be threatened by an attacker. The threatened security property is annotated in brackets. For example, the implicit access flow edge between the nodes *LMN* and *TemporaryMeterData* is annotated with *RQ1 (A,C,I)*. Hence, it might be possible that for RQ1 the confidentiality, integrity and availability of persistent meter data is threatened.

6   Extending PresSuRE

For the last step of PresSuRE we have to *analyze the attacker asset access graphs* and derive initial security requirements. The input to this step are the attacker asset access graphs. As this step is sparsely described in [1], we elaborate this step and describe the extended tool support in the following. The attacker asset access graph contains all information regarding access flows to and from the asset at hand. And it contains the information where the asset might be threatened by an attacker. For each asset we identified previously, we check if we have to augment the original requirements related to the asset with security requirements. For each attacker asset access graph, we have to do the following as long as not all problematic access flows are treated:

Select Edge. Select a problematic required or implicit access flow (bold edge with bold annotation) not considered yet. *We select the implicit access flow edge between the nodes LMN and TemporaryMeterData annotated with RQ1 (A,C,I).*

Check Confidentiality. If there is a $(\ldots, C, \ldots)$ annotated, we have to check whether there is a threat to the confidentiality of the asset or not. If the threat can occur for the annotated requirement, we have to augment this requirement with a confidentiality requirement. *Indeed, the confidentiality is threatened by internal network attackers. If they are able to learn all data sent by the smart meters, they can derive the information contained in the persistent meter data by themselves. Hence, we have to add a confidentiality requirement complementing RQ1.*

Check Integrity. If there is an $(\ldots, I, \ldots)$ annotated, we have to check whether there is a threat to the integrity of the asset or not. If the threat can occur for the annotated requirement, we have to augment this requirement with an integrity requirement. *The integrity is threatened by internal network attackers. If they are able to add data or change data sent by the smart meters, they can change the information contained in the persistent meter data. This is a threat as the persistent meter data is the basis for the billing. Hence, we have to add an integrity requirement complementing RQ1.*

Check Availability. If there is an $(\ldots, A, \ldots)$ annotated, we have to check whether there is a threat to the availability of the asset or not. If the threat can occur for the annotated requirement, we have to augment this requirement with an availability requirement. *The availability can be threatened by internal network attackers. If they are able to deny the service of the LMN, no data can be sent by the smart meters. Thus, the persistent meter data cannot be computed and used for billing. Hence, we have to add an availability requirement complementing RQ1.*

The iteration over the assets, and the iteration over the edges in an according attacker asset access graph for the asset at hand, is guided by the tool. It indicates the asset and the edge in question and shows the according attacker asset access graph. The requirements engineer and security expert have to do

Table 1. SR template for connection domains, and integrity and confidentiality.

Input
domain accessed by the attacker, the attacker, and *threatened security property*
Precondition
Precondition 1: Domain accessed by the attacker is a connection domain
Precondition 2: Security property threatened is integrity or confidentiality
Template
Title: Secure access flows via [*domain accessed by the attacker*]
Text: The access flows via the [*domain accessed by the attacker*] must be secured in a way such that the [*the attacker*] is not able to threaten the [*threatened security property*] of the access flows

the reasoning and provide the result to the tool. From this information we collected for an edge, we can derive initial security requirements. The initial security requirements can be generated automatically, by using templates. For example, the template for a security requirement regarding a connection domain which can be accessed by an attacker to threaten the security properties confidentiality and integrity is shown in Table 1. Such a template defines the inputs for filling the templates. In this case, we need the attacker, the domain he/she can access and the security property threatened by the access of the attacker. To instantiate the template in a reasonable way some preconditions must be fulfilled. First, the domain accessed by the attacker must be a connection domain. Second, the security property threatened must be integrity or confidentiality. The template itself is given as gap-text in which the gaps are indicated by brackets. Within a bracket the input element is referenced, which will later on replace the bracket when instantiating the template. Such a template also contains the modeling rules to add the security requirement to the problem frames model. For sake of brevity, we do not show and discuss these rules in detail. An example model is shown in Fig. 5. In general, we stick to the profile and rules as defined in [17].

The templates for the different cases are implemented in the tool. *Hence, for our example we can generate the following requirement regarding confidentiality:* **SRQ 1.1 Secure access flows via LMN** *The access flows via the LMN must be secured in a way that the InternalNetworkAttacker is not able to threaten the confidentiality of the access flows. Fig. 5 shows the according modeling, in which the confidentiality requirement SRQ1.1 (UML class with stereotypes ≪requirement, confidentiality≫) complements (UML dependency with stereotype ≪complements≫) RQ 1 (UML class with stereotype ≪requirement≫). SRQ1.1 constrains (UML dependency with stereotype ≪constrains≫) the LMN (UML class with stereotypes ≪connectionDomain, causalDomain≫). SRQ1.1 considers the InternalNetworkAttacker (Property attackers of SRQ1.1). We treat the integrity and availability threat for the selected edge in the same way.*

Every newly added security requirement has an impact on the attacker asset access graph at hand. But it also has an impact on other attacker asset access graphs whenever an attacker asset access graph contains edges, which appear

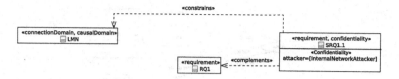

Fig. 5. Snipped from the problem diagram for RQ 1 augmented with SRQ1.1

due to the functional requirement that is complemented by the newly added security requirement. Hence, it is necessary to reduce all attacker asset access graphs to ensure that one only analyzes edges which are not already treated by a security requirement. For the specification of the reduction of attacker asset access graphs, we need two additional predicates. The predicate $isMitigated$: $\mathbb{P}(Requirement \times CIA \times Attacker)$ can be derived from the problem frame model. We have $(r, cia, a) \in isMitigated$ iff the requirement r is *complemented* by a cia security requirement, which refers to attacker a. The predicate $models$: $\mathbb{P}(Requirement \times Diagram)$ can be derived from the problem frame model. We have $(r, p) \in models$ iff a requirement r is part of the diagram p. Additionally, we define the set $\mathcal{R}_{access}$. $\mathcal{R}_{access}$ contains the tuples (r, cia, a) : $Requirement \times CIA \times Attacker$ which relate the requirement r to the attacker a who exploits r to threaten the security property cia. A tuple (r, cia, a) is in $\mathcal{R}_{access}$ iff an access flow (d_1, p, t, cia, d_2) exists in part of the attacker asset access graph $\mathcal{G}_{attack}$ for which the requirement r is modeled in the diagram p and $\mathcal{G}_{attack}$ additionally contains an edge $(a, dk, \text{att}, cia, d_1)$ or an edge $(a, dk, \text{att}, cia, d_2)$.

$$\mathcal{R}_{access} = \{(r, cia, a) : Requirement \times CIA \times Attacker \mid \exists(d_1, p, t, cia', d_2) : \mathcal{G}_{attack} \bullet$$
$$cia' = cia \wedge (r, p) \in models \wedge (\exists dk : diagram \bullet (a, dk, \text{att}, cia, d_1) \in \mathcal{G}_{attack}$$
$$\vee (a, dk, \text{att}, cia, d_2) \in \mathcal{G}_{attack}\}$$

Based on $\mathcal{R}_{access}$ and $\mathcal{G}_{threatOld}$, which is equal to $\mathcal{G}_{threat}$ calculated before we introduce a new security requirement, we can now update $\mathcal{G}_{threat}$. $\mathcal{G}_{threat}$ now contains all edges, and therefore problem diagrams, of the corresponding asset access graph which might allow an attacker to successfully attack the asset at hand and this attack is not mitigated by an according security requirement. An access flow $(d_1, p, t, cia, d_2) \in \mathcal{G}_{threatOld}$ is also contained in $\mathcal{G}_{threat}$ iff there exists an requirement r and an attacker a for which the requirement r is modeled in the diagram p, the requirement r enables the attacker a to threaten cia, and this access is still not mitigated by a complementing security requirement. Formally, we define the new $\mathcal{G}_{threat}$ as follows:

required $\mathcal{G}_{threatOld}$
$$\mathcal{G}_{threat} = \{(d_1, p, t, cia, d_2) : \mathcal{G}_{threatOld} \mid (\exists r : Requirement, a : Attacker \bullet$$
$$(r, p) \in models \wedge (r, cia, a) \in \mathcal{R}_{access} \setminus isMitigated)\}$$

The updated threat graph $\mathcal{G}_{threat}$ leads to an updated and reduced attacker asset access graph $\mathcal{G}_{attack}$. Hence, the tool ensures that only edges are analyzed which are not already treated. Additionally, the tool is now able to detect that an asset is not threatened anymore as $\mathcal{G}_{attack}$ is gradually reduced till it is empty. *As we have added security requirements for integrity, confidentiality, and*

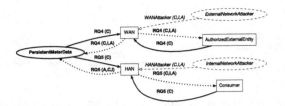

Fig. 6. Attacker asset access graph for persistent meter data after reduction.

availability complementing RQ 1 , the tool generates reduced attacker asset access graphs. Fig. 6 shows the graph for the persistent meter data after the reduction (the initial graph is shown in Fig. 4). The smart meters, the LMN, and the temporary meter data are no longer part of the graph, as the threats which made them relevant are already covered by security requirements.

7   Validation

We validated PresSuRE using two real-life case studies, the already introduced smart meter and a voting system. The voting system requirements were obtained from a Common Criteria profile for voting systems [18]. For more details on the voting system case study, see [19]. The results for applying PresSuRE are reported in the following in detail for the Smart Grid. The original functional requirements were obtained from [11] and the NESSoS case studies provided by the industrial partners of the project. For conducting our method, we selected 13 minimum uses cases, which embody 27 requirements in total. For these requirements, 14 assets and 7 attackers of all kinds, as described in Sect. 5.2, were identified. Based on this information, the graphs were generated, and the initial security requirements elicited.

We analyzed each attacker asset access graph for assessing the tool support, and we also analyzed the initial security requirements found for assessing the overall method. For the graph, we checked for each edge in the attacker asset access graph at hand if the annotated threats are existing according to the threats and security requirements of the original documents (e.g. [10,11] for smart meter). We also looked for threats and security requirements which are defined in such documents, but which were not identified using PresSuRE. In this way we were able to measure the precision and recall of our method. Unfortunately, we do not know which security analysis was used for eliciting the security requirements reported in those documents. But we assume that security experts were involved in writing the documents and the documents were reviewed thoroughly. Hence, these documents are a good benchmark.

Next, we aggregated the results of the edges of the attacker asset access graph for each requirement. Thus, we derived for each requirement the information if the requirement has to be complemented by security requirements according to PresSuRE. Again, we also checked if the found security requirements are

Table 2. Results of the assessment for the smart meter case study.

	Confidentiality	Integrity	Availability
Precision per attack asset access edges	36.14 %	66.35 %	62.52 %
Recall per attack asset access edges	100.00 %	100.00 %	100.00 %
Aggregated precision per attack asset access edges	55.00 %		
Aggregated recall per attack asset access edges	100.00 %		
Precision per requirement	92.59 %	96.30 %	96.30 %
Recall per requirement	100.00 %	100.00 %	100.00 %
Aggregated precision per requirement	95.06 %		
Aggregated recall per requirement	100.00 %		

compliant with the original documents. Last, we measured the precision and recall of PresSuRE on the requirements level.

The results of this analysis for the smart meter is shown in Table 2. Speaking of the precision on the level of edges of the attacker asset access graph, we have many false positives, especially for confidentiality. This is because the original documents do not demand a high level of confidentiality. Additionally, PresSuRE discovered potential indirect information flows between assets which will not occur in the system later on. Thus, PresSuRE is very strict and defensive, which is not appropriate in every case. Note that even though the indirect flows often turned out to be irrelevant, they have to be checked anyway. Often attacks use such indirect relations to tamper with a system. Overall, the precision on the level of edges of the attacker asset access graph is acceptable (55 %), but should be improved. The recall is perfect (100 %) as we did not find any false negatives. On the requirements level, our results are satisfying. Whenever PresSuRE suggested to add a complementing security requirement for a functional requirement, this suggestion was correct with a precision of 95 %, and no security requirement was missed (recall 100 %).

Similar results were obtained for the voting system case study. The precision on the level of edges of the attacker asset access graph is slightly higher, as the voting system documents are very strict regarding confidentiality. This fact is also reflected on the requirements level, but the difference to the smart meter case study is not significant. For the attacker asset access edge and the requirements level the recall was 100 % again.

Speaking of the effort, we spent 43 person hours, which is a significant effort, but seems to be reasonable. The effort for using PresSuRE was reported and discussed in detail in [1].

8 Related Work

Schmidt and Jrjens [20] propose to integrate the SEPP method, which is based on problem frames, and UMLSec [21], which is based on a UML profile and allows tool-based reasoning about security properties. In this way, they can express and refine security requirements and transfer the security requirements to subsequent design artifacts. A similar method is described by Haley et al. [22], which also relies on problem frames for security requirements analysis. The first method [20] starts after the initial security requirements are already known, while the latter one already embodies a step for security requirements elicitation. But this particular step is described very sparsely and informally. Hence, our work can complement and improve these works.

There are many publications concerning goal-oriented security requirements analysis (e.g. [23–26]). But goal models are of a higher level of abstraction than problem frames. Goal models are stakeholder-centric, while problem frames are system-centric. Therefore, refining functional requirements taking into account more detail of the system-to-be and analyzing the system-to-be described by the functional requirements is reported to be difficult for goal-oriented methods [27]. Alrajeh et al. try to tackle this problem by introducing refinement steps which rely on heavy weight formalizations. We offer an alternative way of bridging this gap. Thus, even though the goals of an attacker and their implication for the goals of stakeholders are already known, one might benefit from using our method.

9   Conclusions

In this paper, we extended a methodology for Problem-based Security Requirements Elicitation (PresSuRE). PresSuRE is a method for identifying security needs during the requirements analysis of software systems using a problem frame model. Our extension now enables a guided analysis of found threats. In consequence, security requirements can be derived in a structured way. In summary, the PresSuRE method extension has the following advantages: It introduces a method to reduce attacker asset access graphs successively by adding security requirements, which (1) allows to visualize the impact of a security requirement on the attacker asset access graphs, (2) visualizes the unmitigated threats, and (3) avoids analysis of threats which are already covered by a security requirement. And it is a re-usable requirements security analysis method which (1) investigates the threats gradually and relies on the analysis single access flow at a time, which the analyst can easily comprehend, (2) allows to derive security requirements in a structured way, (3) eases the formulation and modeling of the security requirements, (4) is applicable to different domains, and (5) is tool supported to ease analysis and the modeling tasks necessary for the method. We validated our method and tool with two real-life case studies in the fields of smart grids and voting systems. The results show the suitability of our method to detect initial security requirements. For the future, we plan to investigate how the basic CIA properties can be systematically refined further into more fine-grained security requirements such as authentification and authorization.

References

1. Faßbender, S., Heisel, M., Meis, R.: Functional requirements under security pressure. In: ICSOFT-PT 2014 - Proceedings of the 9th International Conference on Software Paradigm Trends, Vienna, Austria, 29–31 August 2014
2. Bundeskriminalamt (federal criminal police office): Bundeslagebild Cybercrime 2013 (report on cybercrime 2013). Technical report, Germany (2014)
3. Bundeskriminalamt (federal criminal police office): Bundeslagebild Cybercrime 2012 (report on cybercrime 2012). Technical report, Germany (2013)
4. Norton: Norton Report 2013. Technical report, Norton (2013)
5. Willis, R.: Hughes Aircraft's Widespread Deployment of a Continuously Improving Software Process. AD-a358 993. Carnegie-mellon university, Pittsburgh (1998)
6. Boehm, B.W., Papaccio, P.N.: Understanding and controlling software costs. IEEE Trans. Softw. Eng. **14**, 1462–1477 (1988)
7. Firesmith, D.: Specifying good requirements. J. Object Technol. **2**, 77–87 (2003)
8. Beckers, K., Faßbender, S., Heisel, M., Meis, R.: A problem-based approach for computer-aided privacy threat identification. In: Preneel, B., Ikonomou, D. (eds.) APF 2012. LNCS, vol. 8319, pp. 1–16. Springer, Heidelberg (2014)
9. Jackson, M.: Problem Frames: Analyzing and structuring software development problems. Addison-Wesley, Boston (2001)
10. Kreutzmann, H., Vollmer, S., Tekampe, N., Abromeit, A.: Protection profile for the gateway of a smart metering system. Technical report, BSI (2011)
11. Requirements of AMI. Technical report, OPEN meter project (2009)
12. Hatebur, D., Heisel, M.: Making pattern- and model-based software development more rigorous. In: Dong, J.S., Zhu, H. (eds.) ICFEM 2010. LNCS, vol. 6447, pp. 253–269. Springer, Heidelberg (2010)
13. Beckers, K., Hatebur, D., Heisel, M.: A problem-based threat analysis in compliance with common criteria. In: ARES 2013, IEEE Computer Society (2013)
14. Dolev, D., Yao, A.C.: On the security of public key protocols. IEEE Trans. Inf. Theor. **29**, 198–207 (1983)
15. ISO/IEC: Common Criteria for Information Technology Security Evaluation. ISO/IEC 15408, International Organization for Standardization (ISO) and International Electrotechnical Commission (IEC), Geneva, Switzerland (2009)
16. ISO/IEC: Information technology - Security techniques - Information security management systems - Overview and Vocabulary. ISO/IEC 27000, International Organization for Standardization (ISO) and International Electrotechnical Commission (IEC), Geneva, Switzerland (2009)
17. Hatebur, D., Heisel, M.: A UML profile for requirements analysis of dependable software. In: Schoitsch, E. (ed.) SAFECOMP 2010. LNCS, vol. 6351, pp. 317–331. Springer, Heidelberg (2010)
18. Volkamer, M., Vogt, R.: Common Criteria Protection Profile for Basic set of security requirements for Online Voting Products. Bundesamt f"ur Sicherheit in der Informationstechnik (2008)
19. Faßbender, S., Heisel, M.: From problems to laws in requirements engineering using model-transformation. In: ICSOFT 2013, SciTePress. pp. 447–458 (2013)
20. Schmidt, H., Jürjens, J.: Connecting security requirements analysis and secure design using patterns and UMLsec. In: Mouratidis, H., Rolland, C. (eds.) CAiSE 2011. LNCS, vol. 6741, pp. 367–382. Springer, Heidelberg (2011)
21. Jürjens, J.: Secure Systems Development with UML. Springer, Heidelberg (2005)

22. Haley, C.B., Laney, R., Moffett, J.D., Nuseibeh, B.: Security requirements engineering: a framework for representation and analysis. IEEE Trans. Softw. Eng. **34**, 133–153 (2008)

23. Liu, L., Yu, E., Mylopoulos, J.: Security and privacy requirements analysis within a social setting. In: RE 2003. pp. 151–161 (2003)

24. Mouratidis, H., Giorgini, P.: Secure Tropos: a security-oriented extension of the tropos methodology. Int. J. Softw. Eng. Knowl. Eng. **17**, 285–309 (2007)

25. Salehie, M., Pasquale, L., Omoronyia, I., Ali, R., Nuseibeh, B.: Requirements-driven adaptive security: protecting variable assets at runtime. In: RE 2012. pp. 111–120 (2012)

26. Van Lamsweerde, A.: Elaborating security requirements by construction of intentional anti-models. In: ICSE 2004. pp. 148–157 (2004)

27. Alrajeh, D., Kramer, J., Russo, A., Uchitel, S.: Learning operational requirements from goal models. In: ICSE 2009. pp. 265–275 (2009)

Model Refactorings for and with Graph Transformation Rules

Sabine Winetzhammer$^{(\boxtimes)}$ and Bernhard Westfechtel

Applied Computer Science I, University of Bayreuth,
Universitätsstraße 30, 95440 Bayreuth, Germany
{sabine.winetzhammer,bernhard.westfechtel}@uni-bayreuth.de
http://btn1x4.inf.uni-bayreuth.de/modgraph/homepage

Abstract. Refactoring denotes the activity of improving the structure of software by applying a series of transformations without affecting its externally observable behavior. Refactoring has been applied extensively at the source code level. In the context of model-driven software engineering, refactoring has to be applied consistently to both structural and behavioral models. In this paper, we present tool support for model refactoring in ModGraph, a tool which employs Ecore class diagrams for structural modeling and graph transformation rules for declarative behavioral modeling. A refactoring transformation restructures the structural model — an Ecore class diagram — and propagates the changes consistently to the behavioral model — a set of graph transformation rules. Since the refactoring transformations are implemented with graph transformation rules, ModGraph supports model refactoring both for and with graph transformation rules.

Keywords: Refactoring · Graph transformation rules · ModGraph

1 Introduction

Model-driven software engineering reduces the effort of developing software by replacing low-level programming with the construction of high-level executable models. To this end, both structural and behavioral models have to be developed. In the context of object-oriented modeling, there seems to be a general consensus to employ some variant of class diagrams for structural modeling, e.g., EMF, MOF, or UML class diagrams. In contrast, there is a wide spectrum of languages for behavioral modeling which are based on different computational paradigms (e.g., state machines, activity diagrams, or rule-based transformation languages). In this paper, we will focus on behavioral modeling with *graph transformation rules* [22]: Models are considered as graphs, and transformations of these graphs are specified declaratively by graph transformation rules.

Software evolution [14] is a discipline which provides concepts, methods, and tools for evolving software in response to changing requirements, platforms, technologies, etc. A prerequisite for evolving software according to these changes is

---

This paper is an extended and revised version of [27].

© Springer International Publishing Switzerland 2015
A. Holzinger et al. (Eds.): ICSOFT 2014, CCIS 555, pp. 331–348, 2015.
DOI: 10.1007/978-3-319-25579-8_19

that the software is well structured and prepared for changes. In the context of object-oriented software development, this problem is addressed in a variety of different ways, including e.g. design patterns [10] and refactorings (the focus of this paper).

According to [9], *refactoring* denotes the activity of improving the structure of software by applying a series of transformations without affecting its externally observable behavior. The transformations proposed in [9] were developed for and applied to (object-oriented) programs. In the context of model-driven software engineering, refactoring has to be applied to both structural and behavioral models. Previous work on model refactoring focused on structural models [3,13,16]. However, when the structural model is refactored, the respective changes have to be propagated into the behavioral model; otherwise, the behavioral model is no longer consistent with the structural model.

In this paper, we close the gap identified above, resulting in comprehensive support for model refactoring. We present tool support for model refactoring in ModGraph[1], a tool which employs Ecore class diagrams for structural modeling and graph transformation rules for behavioral modeling. For the structural model, ModGraph offers a set of refactoring transformations along the lines of Fowler's work [9]. The tool support goes beyond previous work since the refactorings are propagated from the structural model into the behavioral model. Thus, graph transformation rules are updated in response to the changes of the underlying Ecore model. Furthermore, tool support for model refactoring is implemented in ModGraph with the help of graph transformation rules. Thus, ModGraph supports *model refactoring* both *for* and *with graph transformation rules*.

Altogether, our work provides an important contribution to *model evolution*, which is an essential prerequisite for putting model-driven software engineering to work. The term model evolution is used in a variety of different contexts. Frequently, model evolution is concerned with the changes of model instances in response to changes of the underlying metamodel [20] (analogously to schema evolution in databases [2]). In contrast, the work presented in this paper has a different focus: It deals with the consistent refactoring of a set of interdependent models, which requires propagation of the changes of the structural model into the behavioral model. The *migration* of *model instances* is not considered here.

Section 2 provides some background information on ModGraph. Section 3 gives an overview of our approach to the consistent refactoring of structural and behavioral models. Section 4 introduces an example which serves to illustrate our refactoring approach. Section 5 deals with the model-driven implementation of refactoring transformations. Section 6 discusses related work. Section 7 concludes the paper.

2   ModGraph

The work reported in this paper was carried out in the context of the *ModGraph* project [26]. ModGraph is a tool for model-driven software engineering which is

---

[1] http://btn1x4.inf.uni-bayreuth.de/modgraph/homepage.

based on the Eclipse Modeling Framework (EMF, see [23]). Structural modeling is performed with *Ecore*. For behavioral modeling, ModGraph follows a hybrid approach: Complex model transformation rules are specified declaratively as graph transformation rules. Graph transformation rules may be organized into control structures with the help *Xcore*[2], which provides a textual language for Ecore models and a procedural and functional language for model transformations (*Xbase* [8]). Furthermore, Xbase may be used to realize simple operations directly.

In Ecore, a structural model essentially consists of a set of *classes* owning structural and behavioral features. *Structural features* are partitioned into attributes, which have (collections of) simple values, and references to target classes. By default, references are unidirectional (from instances of the source class to instances of the target class); however, a pair of unidirectional references may be grouped into a bi-directional reference. *Behavioral features* are modeled by operations. The structural model merely describes the signature of operations, but not their behavior.

In ModGraph, the behavior of an operation may be specified declaratively by a graph transformation rule. Model instances are considered as graphs whose nodes and edges correspond to objects and links, respectively. A *graph transformation rule* describes an in-place model transformation and essentially consists of a left-hand side and a right-hand side. The left-hand side describes the pattern to be matched, the right-hand side describes the replacing subgraph. Nodes and edges occurring only on the left-hand side and right-hand side are deleted and created, respectively.

Traditionally, the left-hand side and the right-hand side are displayed separately. For example, the left part of Fig. 1 shows a *divided view* of a graph transformation rule which describes a simple refactoring on a structural model: The attribute a is moved from the class C1 to the class C2. The right part illustrates the notation used in ModGraph: The left-hand side and the right-hand side are shown in a single *merged view*, which eliminates the redundancies of the divided view. Elements belonging only to one side are marked: Elements to be deleted are shown in red color and are annotated with --, while inserted elements are displayed in green color and are annotated with ++.

Figure 1 shows a very simple example of a graph transformation rule. In Mod-Graph, a graph transformation rule consists of a *precondition*, a *graph pattern*,

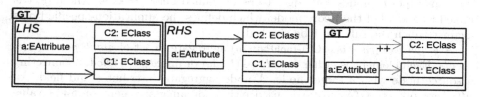

Fig. 1. A graph transformation rule shown as divided view and merged view.

[2] https://wiki.eclipse.org/Xcore.

a set of *negative application conditions (NAC)*, and a *postcondition*. A negative application condition is a graph pattern the presence of which inhibits the application of the rule. If the precondition holds, the graph pattern has been matched and none of the NACs has been matched, the transformation is applied and must guarantee the postcondition.

Altogether, the ModGraph tool has to deal with different *types of models*, as illustrated in Fig. 2. The blue boxes represent the models which are created by the ModGraph user: The structural model is defined by an Ecore class diagram. The behavioral model consists of a set of graph transformation rules specifying the behavior of operations introduced in the structural model. At runtime, graph transformation rules will be applied to model instances by matching and replacing subgraphs. Internally, a graph transformation rule is represented as a model, too (namely an instance of the graph transformation metamodel, which in turn is an instance of the Ecore metamodel).

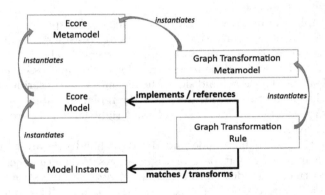

Fig. 2. Models and metamodels in ModGraph.

An excerpt from the *graph transformation metamodel* is shown in Fig. 3. The graph pattern of a graph transformation rule essentially consists of nodes and edges, all of which are represented as objects. Each object is typed in two ways: First, it is typed by a class from the graph transformation metamodel. The metamodel for the graph pattern provides a class hierarchy which defines different types of nodes and edges to be explained below. Second, the object is linked to a class of the Ecore model which defines the application-specific types against which the rule must be checked.

A *graph pattern* (class GTGraphPattern) aggregates a set of *graph pattern elements*. Each element is either a *node* (GTNode) or an *edge* (GTNode) connecting a source node with a target node. A node aggregates attributes and field. An *attribute* object (GTAttribute) is used either for an assignment or for a value comparison. A *field* (GTField) specifies a constraint (in OCL or Xcore) or an operation call.

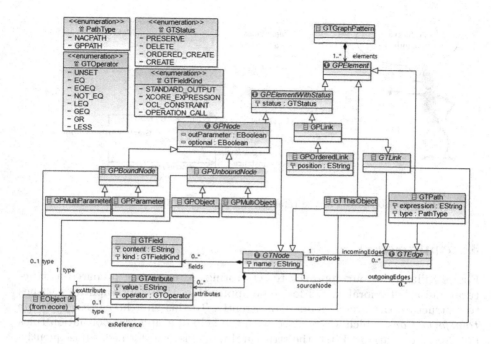

Fig. 3. Metamodel for the graph pattern of a graph transformation rule.

Pattern elements may have a *status* (GPElementWithStatus) which defines whether the element is created, deleted, or preserved. The class GPNode serves to represent graph pattern nodes with a status. If a node is designated as *optional*, it is not required for a successful match. Pattern nodes are either *bound* or *unbound* (classes GPBoundNode and GPUnboundNode, respectively). Both bound and unbound nodes are classified into *single nodes* and *multi-nodes*, which are matched against single nodes and sets of nodes, respectively. The node for the *current object* (GTThisObject) may be neither be created nor deleted. Edges with a status are modeled by the class GPLink. *Paths* (GTPath) define derived edges by a path expression. Paths constitute positive application conditions and can neither be created nor destroyed.

ModGraph provides a single type of *graph rule* which may be used for different purposes. The rule specifies a *graph transformation* if it contains elements to be inserted or deleted or attribute assignments. A graph rule which does not specify any changes is a *graph test* which checks whether the graph pattern is present or not. Rules may also represent *graph queries*; to this end, graph pattern nodes may be designated as *output parameters*. A graph rule may serve simultaneously as a transformation and a query.

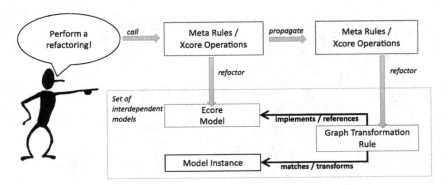

Fig. 4. Interaction of the refactoring engine with the affected models.

3   Approach

Figure 4 illustrates our approach to refactoring. After having prepared a structural and a behavioral model for some application, the ModGraph user wishes to restructure the overall model consistently. To this end, he calls *refactoring transformations*, which are realized with the help of graph transformation rules and Xcore operations. First, the structural model is transformed. Subsequently, the performed changes are propagated to all affected graph transformation rules. Due to our *reflective approach*, refactoring transformations could be applied to themselves (at least as far as the graph transformation rules are concerned; see below). All refactoring transformations are typed over a refactoring metamodel (not shown in Fig. 4) which extends both the Ecore metamodel and the graph transformation metamodel.

Please notice that refactoring support is confined to the Ecore model and the graph transformation rules. In addition, the ModGraph user may have written procedural Xcore operations which currently have to be refactored manually. Furthermore, progating changes to Ecore models to their instances goes beyond the scope of ModGraph's tool support, as well. This propagation is called *model migration* and has already been addressed extensively in the scientific literature (see [20] for an overview and see also work on schema evolution support for database systems [2]).

Table 1 describes a few refactoring transformations which we implemented in ModGraph; see [27] for a complete list. For each refactoring, the table lists its name and describe its effect on the Ecore model and the graph transformation rules. The refactorings were inspired by the work of Fowler [9], who proposed a comprehensive set of refactorings for object-oriented programs. We adapted these refactorings to operate on Ecore models and ModGraph's transformation rules (examples see Figs. 6 and 7).

Table 1. Refactoring transformations: Changes to the Ecore model and propagations to graph transformation rules.

Name	Change bi- to unidirectional reference
Ecore model	Delete one of a pair of opposite references
ModGraph rules	Replace each instance of the deleted reference with an instance of its previously opposite reference
Name	**Change uni- to bidirectional reference**
Ecore model	Add a reference to a class and set its opposite
ModGraph rules	—
Name	**Extract class**
Ecore model	Create an extracted class and a reference from an existing class. Move selected features from the existing class to the extracted class
ModGraph rules	If a node is typed with the existing class, check whether it uses features moved to the new class. In this case, create a node of the extracted class and an edge from the old node. Move the elements referencing the extracted class to the new node
Name	**Extract subclass**
Ecore model	Extract a set of features of an existing class to a new subclass
ModGraph rules	Retype nodes typed with the existing class to the new subclass provided that they use features moved to the new subclass
Name	**Pull up attribute**
Ecore model	Move an attribute which is defined identically in all subclasses to their common superclass
ModGraph rules	—
Name	**Replace inheritance by delegation**
Ecore model	Replace the inheritance relationship between a subclass *sub* and a superclass *sup* by a reference from *sub* to *super*
ModGraph rules	If a node typed with *sub* uses features of *super*, add a new node and an edge from the old node to the new node. Move the elements referencing *super* from the old node to the new node

4   Example

We applied refactoring transformations to a sample project — *Bug Tracker* — which may be retrieved from the ModGraph homepage. The state of the Ecore model before the refactoring is displayed in Fig. 5. The class BugTracker models a bug tracking database which composes users, user groups, and projects. Each project maintains a set of reported tickets, each of which evolves into a sequence of revisions. In the following, we will discuss two refactoring transformations on the Ecore model and its attached graph transformation rules.

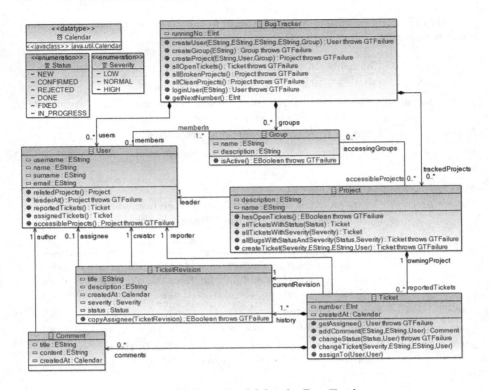

Fig. 5. The Ecore model for the Bug Tracker.

4.1 Changing a Bi- to a Unidirectional Reference

With one exception, all containment references in the Ecore model are unidirectional. This style of modeling is common since the EMF implementation maintains links from contained objects to their containers anyway. This is achieved in a generic way, independently of the application-specific Ecore model. Thus, there is no need to model opposite references explicitly.

The user who created the Bug Tracker model wishes to apply this modeling style consistently throughout the whole Ecore model. To this end, (s)he invokes the refactoring transformation for *changing a bi- to a unidirectional reference* on the reference owningProject from Ticket to Project.

The upper part of Fig. 6 shows the cutout of the Ecore model to be modified, as well as a ModGraph rule which will be affected by the intended change. The sample rule defines a graph query rather than a graph transformation rule. The rule implements an operation on the class Project which returns a set of tickets with given severity and status for a given project. Its graph pattern includes a node named this, which denotes the current object on which the rule is invoked. The node tickets is a multi-node (shaded rectangle) which is matched against a set of nodes. The node is marked with out, implying that the matched set will be

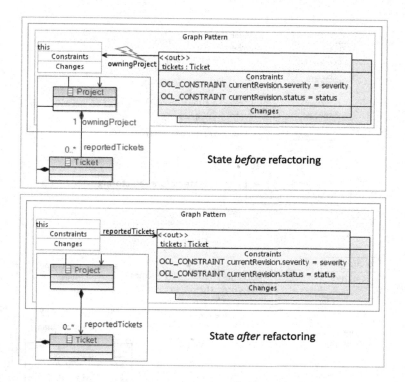

Fig. 6. Example: Changing a bi- to a unidirectional reference.

returned by the rule. The Constraints compartment contains two OCL constraints: Both the status and the severity of the current revision of a matched ticked must have the values which are passed as parameters to the rule.

If the changes in the Ecore model were not propagated to the rule, the link labeled owningProject would become inconsistent because its type (the removed reference) does not exist any more. The lower part of Fig. 6 shows the consistent state which will be produced by applying ModGraph's refactoring transformation for changing a bi- to a unidirectional reference: The link is inverted and retyped automatically to the containment reference reportedTickets.

4.2   Extracting a Class

Our second transformation deals with the *extraction of a class*: Features of an existing class are moved to a new class which is referenced from the existing class. The upper part shows an excerpt from the Ecore model of the Bug Tracker (class User) and a graph transformation rule which adds a user to a given group and assigns its attributes. The lower part shows the updated excerpt from the Ecore model: The name attributes of the class User are moved to the new class Names. This change introduces inconsistencies into the createUser rule shown on the top:

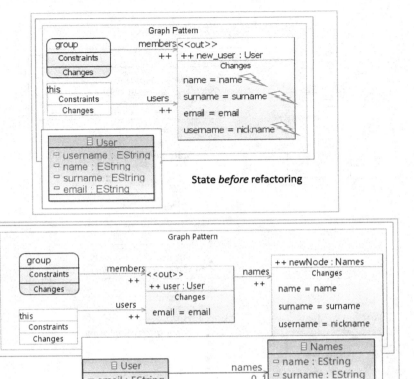

Fig. 7. Example: Extracting a class.

Listing 1.1. Changing a bi- to a unidirectional reference in the Ecore model.

```
1   class Refactoring{
2     ...
3     op void changeBidirectionalToUnidirectionalReference(EReference ref) {
4       if(ref.EOpposite != null)
5         EcoreUtil::remove(ref)
6     }
7     ...
8   }
```

Assignments to the moved attributes are no longer valid. The refactoring transformation reestablishes consistency by updating the graph pattern: A newNode
is inserted which is referenced from user through a names link, and the attribute
assignments are moved to newNode.

Listing 1.2. Propagation of the change of a bi- to a unidirectional reference.

```
1   class Propagation {
2   ...
3     op void propagateChangeBidirectionalToUnidirectionalReference(
4        EReference formerOpposite , GraphTransformationRule rule) {
5     try {
6       var pattern =
7          propagateChangeBidirectionalToUnidirectionalReferenceGraphPattern(
8             formerOpposite , rule)
9       for (GTNegativeApplicationCondition nac :
10            rule.negativePattern as GTNegativeApplicationCondition[]) {
11         this.propagateChangeBidirectionalToUnidirectionalReferenceNAC(
12            formerOpposite , nac)
13       }
14     } catch (Exception e) {
15       e.printStackTrace()
16     }
17     // Propagate changes to textual elements of the rule
18   }
19   ...
20   }
```

5 Refactoring Transformations

We implemented refactoring transformations in ModGraph with the help of graph transformation rules and Xcore operations. To illustrate this approach, we resume the examples which were presented in the previous section.

5.1 Changing a Bi- to a Unidirectional Reference

The transformation for changing a bi- to a unidirectional reference is structured into two parts dealing with the structural and the behavioral model, respectively.

The *structural refactoring transformation* is realized by a simple Xcore operation (Listing 1.1); it does not pay off to write a graph transformation rule. If the supplied reference ref has an opposite reference, it is deleted by calling the remove method provided by the utility class EcoreUtil.

The *behavioral refactoring transformation* is performed after the structural refactoring transformation. To this end, the change is propagated to all rules attached to the structural model. Listing 1.2 shows the Xcore operation for propagating the change to a single rule. The operation is supplied with two parameters (shown as rounded rectangles): the formerOpposite reference, i.e., the reference whose opposite was deleted, and the rule to which the change is to be propagated. In the body, the propagation is applied to all components of the rule, including the graph pattern, the set of NACs, and textual elements such as pre- and postconditions, etc.

The repair of an affected link in a graph pattern is realized by a graph transformation rule (Fig. 8); change propagation to a NAC is handled similarly. The meta rule receives the rule to be updated, the former opposite reference, and the name of the deleted reference as parameters. The node delLink at the bottom stands for the link to be deleted. Its OCL constraint checks that it has been an instance of the deleted reference. The link is reached by navigating from

Listing 1.3. Xcore operation for propagating a class extraction.

```
1   op EObject [] propagateExtractClassNEW (EClass extractedClass,
2       EClass existingClass, GraphTransformationRule rule) {
3     var GTGraphPattern pattern = rule.pattern
4     var EList<EObject> objectsToRemove = newBasicEList()
5     var GTNode existingNode
6     var EList<GTField> gTFields = newBasicEList()
7     var EList<GTAttribute> gTAttributes = newBasicEList()
8     var EList<GPLink> gTInLinks = newBasicEList()
9     var EList<GPLink> gTOutLinks = newBasicEList()
10    for (GPElement gpu : pattern.elements) {
11      if (gpu instanceof GPUnboundNode && ((gpu as GPUnboundNode).^type as
12          EClass).name.equals(existingClass.name)) {
13        existingNode = gpu as GPUnboundNode
14      } else if (gpu instanceof GTThisObject &&
15          ((gpu as GTThisObject).^type as EClass).name
16          .equals(existingClass.name)) {
17        existingNode = gpu as GTThisObject
18      }
19    }
20    if (existingNode != null) {
21      for (EAttribute ea : extractedClass.getEAttributes()) {
22        for (GTAttribute gta : existingNode.attributes) {
23          if (gta.exAttribute.eIsProxy() && getNameFromURI(gta.exAttribute)
24              .equals(ea.name)) {
25            gTAttributes.add(gta);
26          }
27        }
28      }
29      for (EOperation eo : extractedClass.getEOperations()) {
30        for (GTField gtf : existingNode.getFields()) {
31          if (gtf.getKind().getName().equals("OPERATION_CALL")) {
32            var String content = gtf.content
33            var String operationName =
34                content.split(Pattern.quote("(")).get(0)
35            if (operationName.equals(eo.name)) {
36              gTFields.add(gtf)
37            }
38          }
39        }
40      }
41      for (EReference er : extractedClass.getEReferences()) {
42        for (GPLink gtl : existingNode.outgoingEdges
43            .filter(e|e instanceof GPLink) as GPLink[]) {
44          if (gtl.exReference.eIsProxy() &&
45              getNameFromURI(gtl.exReference).equals(er.name)) {
46            gTOutLinks.add(gtl)
47          }
48        }
49        for (GPLink gtl : (existingNode.incomingEdges
50            .filter(e| e instanceof GPLink))
51            as GPLink[]) {
52          if (gtl.exReference.eIsProxy()
53              && getNameFromURI(gtl.exReference).equals(er.name)) {
54            gTInLinks.add(gtl)
55          }
56        }
57      }
58      try{ if(!gTAttributes.isEmpty() || !gTFields.isEmpty() ||
59          !gTInLinks.isEmpty() || !gTOutLinks.isEmpty() )
60          propagateExtractClassSF(extractedClass, existingClass, rule,
61              gTAttributes, gTInLinks, gTOutLinks, gTFields)
62      }catch(GTFailure f){}
63    // Update NACs and textual elements
64  }
```

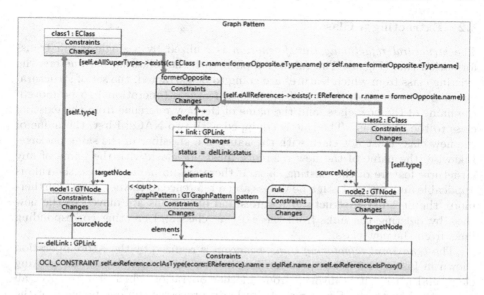

Fig. 8. Rule propgagating a change of a bi- to a unidirectional reference to an affected link in a graph pattern of a graph transformation rule.

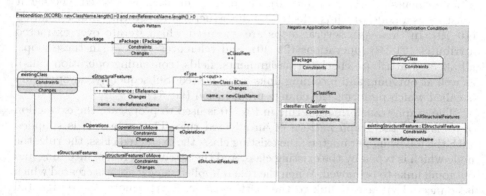

Fig. 9. Rule for extracting features into a new class in the Ecore model.

the rule to the elements of its graph pattern. The new link link instantiates the formerOpposite reference and swaps the source and the target node of the old link. Finally, the nodes class1 and class2 ensure that the new link is type consistent: It must connect two nodes whose types conform to the source and target class of the formerOpposite reference. These checks are realized with the help of path expressions (represented by thick grey arrows).

5.2   Extracting a Class

The *structural refactoring transformation* is realized by a single graph transformation rule (Fig. 9). The rule is supplied with the following parameters: the existing class from which features are going to be extracted, the set of structural features to be moved, the set of behavioral features (operations) to be moved, the name of the new class, and the name of the new reference from the existing class to the new class. The rule is equipped with two NACs: First, the name of the new class must not clash with the name of a classifier in the same package. Likewise, the name of the new reference must not clash with the name of any structural feature of the existing class. If there are no name clashes, the rule is applicable and creates both a new class and a reference to the new class. Furthermore, the designated structural features and operations are moved to the new class by deleting the links from the existing class and creating corresponding links from the new class.

The *behavioral refactoring transformation* is realized by the Xcore operation shown in Listing 1.3. The operation is called on an extracted class, an existing class, and a rule; it is invoked from another operation which iterates over all rules attached to the Ecore model. Its body processes the components of the rule (graph pattern, NACs, pre- and postconditions) in turn. The listing shows only the propagation to the graph pattern, which is performed in a loop over all of its elements (starting in line 10). For each element, it is checked whether it constitutes a node which is affected by the structural refactoring transformation (10–19). In this case, several loops are executed which iterate over extracted attributes (21–28), operations (29–40), and references (41–57). In these loops, all affected attribute checks or assignments, fields (containing operation calls), as well as outgoing and incoming links are collected. Subsequently, an operation is called which performs the change propagation (60–61).

The graph transformation rule in Fig. 10 is used to propagate the extraction of a class to the graph pattern of an affected rule. The meta rule is supplied with the following parameters: the existing class, the extracted class, the rule, the node which is typed by the existing class, and the attributes, fields, incoming and outgoing links to be moved. When the rule is applied, a new node is created which is connected via a new link to the existing node. Furthermore, the designated attributes, fields, incoming and outgoing links are moved to the new node. Please notice that the creation of containment links from the new node implicitly deletes old containment links, since each object may have at most one container.

6   Related Work

Mens [17] provides a comprehensive survey of software refactoring. Fowler's book probably constitutes the most cited reference in this domain [9]. The refactorings presented in this book all apply to object-oriented programs, i.e., they are applied to source code rather than models. Furthermore, refactorings are described in an informal way. A formalization which is based on program graphs and graph transformation rules is presented in [15]. A major restriction of this work consists

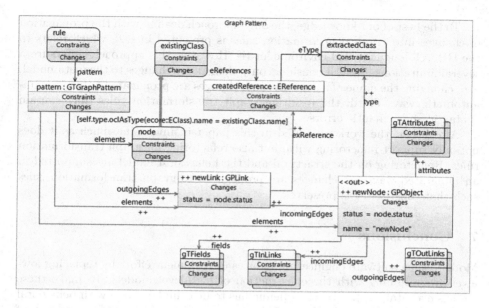

Fig. 10. Propagation of the extraction of a class to a graph pattern.

in the fact that each transformation has to be realized by a single rule. In general, programmed graph transformation rules are required for specifying refactorings. This is demonstrated e.g. by [11], in which a refactoring case prepared for the GraBaTs 2008 workshop was realized in Fujaba [28]. The refactoring case included three refactorings on program graphs.

Research on model refactoring primarily focuses on the structural model (class diagrams). For example, in [3] refactoring of Ecore models is specified with graph transformation rules in the AGG environment [24]. Mens [13] demonstrates how refactoring transformations on UML class diagrams may be specified in different graph transformation languages (AGG and Fujaba). In [16], critical pair analysis is applied to AGG rules for refactoring Ecore models in order to detect dependencies between refactoring transformations. Based on this analysis, the user is guided in the application of these transformations.

Bottoni [4] goes beyond these approaches by providing integrated refactoring transformations: A refactoring transformation is applied not only to a UML class diagram, but also to the source code implementing the structural model. Our work differs from this approach inasmuch as we consider behavioral models rather than source code.

We are aware of only a few approaches dealing with the propagation of changes from the structural model into the behavioral model. Rosner and Bauer [21] propose an approach to update model transformations in response to metamodel changes. The approach requires an ontology mapping between metamodel versions and is applied to evolve QVT-R [18] transformations. The evolution of model transformations constitutes an example of a higher order transformation [25].

To the best of our knowledge, the only approach dealing with the propagation of changes into graph transformation rules is presented in [12], which refers to the GReAT language and environment [1]. However, this approach suffers from several limitations. First, it considers only elementary changes to the metamodel, e.g., changing the name of a class. Second, changes are propagated only in a semi-automatic way. Third, the resulting graph transformation rules may contain syntactic and semantic errors.

Altogether, the work presented in this paper is unique inasmuch as it does not only support refactoring with, but also refactoring for graph transformation rules. Refactoring on the structural and the behavioral model are supported in an integrated way, and changes are propagated to graph transformation rules such that consistency is preserved.

7   Conclusions

Model-driven software engineering reduces development effort by replacing low-level programming with the construction of high-level models. To make these models executable, structural modeling has to be complemented with behavioral modeling. During their lifetime, models undergo many changes for a variety of different reasons. Thus, it is crucial to support model evolution. Refactoring of models provides an important contribution to model evolution since it aims at restructuring models such that future changes are facilitated.

In this paper, we presented tool support for model refactoring in the Mod-Graph environment. ModGraph employs Ecore models for structural modeling and graph transformation rules for behavioral modeling. Refactorings are supported in an integrated way: Each refactoring transformation on the structural model is consistently propagated into the behavioral model. In this way, our work goes considerably beyond previous work on model refactoring which was confined to the refactoring of the structural model. Furthermore, while several other approaches use graph transformations for refactoring (i.e., refactoring with graph transformations), our work is unique inasmuch as it addresses refactoring for graph transformations, as well.

Altogether, we implemented 19 refactoring transformations; see [27] for a complete list. The transformations provided to the end user were realized with

Table 2. Average number of elements per rule, compared to data from [6].

language	Fujaba	ModGraph
project	MOD2-SCM	Refactoring
single nodes	1,71	4,43
multi-nodes	0,03	3,06
links	0,73	5,74
paths	0,01	0,91

a total of 35 graph transformation rules and 71 Xcore operations. According to our findings from [6], we followed a hybrid approach to behavioral modeling, mixing procedural and rule-based operations. The rightmost column of Table 2 lists the average number of single nodes, multi-nodes, links, and paths in graph patterns of the transformation rules for refactoring. These data demonstrate that our refactoring rules are fairly complex, in particular if they are compared against the numbers from [6] (referring to the MOD2-SCM project [5,7], which was implemented in Fujaba rather than in ModGraph). This complexity results from our style of modeling: First, graph transformation rules are used only when they really pay off. Second, as illustrated in Subsect. 5.2, graph transformation rules usually perform complex modifications in a single step after all required data have been collected in preceding Xcore operations.

References

1. Agrawal, A., Karsai, G., Neema, S., Shi, F., Vizhanyo, A.: The design of a language for model transformations. Softw. Syst. Model. 5(3), 261–288 (2006)
2. Banerjee, J., Kim, W., Kim, H.J., Korth, H.F.: Semantics and implementation of schema evolution in object-oriented databases. In: Proceedings of the 1987 ACM SIGMOD International Conference on Management of Data (SIGMOD 1987), pp. 311–322. ACM Press, San Franciso (1987)
3. Biermann, E., Ehrig, K., Köhler, C., Kuhns, G., Taentzer, G., Weiss, E.: EMF model refactoring based on graph transformation concepts. In: Favre, J.M., Heckel, R., Mens, T. (eds.) Proceedings of the Third Workshop on Software Evolution Through Transformations: Embracing the Change. Electronic Communications of the EASST, vol. 3. Natal, Rio Grande del Norte, Brazil, 16 p., September 2006
4. Bottoni, P., Parisi-Presicce, F., Taentzer, G.: Specifying integrated refactoring with distributed graph transformations. In: Pfaltz et al. [19], pp. 220–235
5. Buchmann, T., Dotor, A., Westfechtel, B.: MOD2-SCM: a model-driven product line for software configuration management systems. Inf. Softw. Technol. 55(3), 630–650 (2013)
6. Buchmann, T., Westfechtel, B., Winetzhammer, S.: The added value of programmed graph transformations – a case study from software configuration management. In: Schürr, A., Varró, D., Varró, G. (eds.) AGTIVE 2011. LNCS, vol. 7233, pp. 198–209. Springer, Heidelberg (2012)
7. Dotor, A.: Entwurf und Modellierung einer Produktlinie von Software-Konfigurations-Management-Systemen. Ph.D. thesis, University of Bayreuth, Germany (2011)
8. Efftinge, S., Eysholdt, M., Köhnlein, J., Zarnekow, S., Hasselbring, W., von Massow, R., Hanus, M.: Xbase: Implementing domain-specific languages for Java. In: Proceedings of the 11th International Conference on Generative Programming and Component Engineering (GPCE 2012), pp. 112–121. ACM Press, Dresden (2012)
9. Fowler, M.: Refactoring: Improving the Design of Existing Code. Addison-Wesley, Boston (1999)
10. Gamma, E., Helm, R., Johnson, R., Vlissides, J.: Design Patterns - Elements of Reusable Object-Oriented Software. Addison-Wesley, Reading (1994)

11. Geiger, L.: Graph transformation-based refactorings using Fujaba. In: Rensink, A., van Gorp, P. (eds.) 4th International Workshop on Graph-Based Tools: The Contest, Leicester, UK (2008)
12. Levendovszky, T., Balasubramanian, D., Narayanan, A., Karsai, G.: A novel approach to semi-automated evolution of DSML model transformation. In: van den Brand, M., Gašević, D., Gray, J. (eds.) SLE 2009. LNCS, vol. 5969, pp. 23–41. Springer, Heidelberg (2010)
13. Mens, T.: On the use of graph transformations for model refactoring. In: Lämmel, R., Saraiva, J., Visser, J. (eds.) GTTSE 2005. LNCS, vol. 4143, pp. 219–257. Springer, Heidelberg (2006)
14. Mens, T., Demeyer, S. (eds.): Software Evolution. Springer, Heidelberg (2009)
15. Mens, T., Eetvelde, N.V., Demeyer, S., Janssens, D.: Formalizing refactorings with graph transformations. J. Softw. Maint. Evol. Res. Pract. **17**(4), 247–276 (2005)
16. Mens, T., Taentzer, G., Runge, O.: Analysing refactoring dependencies using graph transformation. Softw. Syst. Model. **6**(3), 269–285 (2007)
17. Mens, T., Tourwé, T.: A survey of software refactoring. IEEE Trans. Softw. Eng. **30**(2), 126–139 (2004)
18. OMG: Meta Object Facility (MOF) 2.0 Query/View/Transformation Specification. Object Management Group, Needham, MA, formal/2011-01-01 edn., January 2011
19. Pfaltz, J.L., Nagl, M., Böhlen, B. (eds.): AGTIVE 2003. LNCS, vol. 3062. Springer, Heidelberg (2004)
20. Rose, L.M., Herrmannsdoerfer, M., Williams, J.R., Kolovos, D.S., Garcés, K., Paige, R.F., Polack, F.A.C.: A comparison of model migration tools. In: Petriu, D.C., Rouquette, N., Haugen, Ø. (eds.) MODELS 2010, Part I. LNCS, vol. 6394, pp. 61–75. Springer, Heidelberg (2010)
21. Roser, S., Bauer, B.: Automatic generation and evolution of model transformations using ontology engineering space. In: Spaccapietra, S., Pan, J.Z., Thiran, P., Halpin, T., Staab, S., Svatek, V., Shvaiko, P., Roddick, J. (eds.) Journal on Data Semantics XI. LNCS, vol. 5383, pp. 32–64. Springer, Heidelberg (2008)
22. Rozenberg, G. (ed.): Handbook of Graph Grammars and Computing by Graph Transformation: Foundations, vol. 1. World Scientific Publishing, Singapore (1997)
23. Steinberg, D., Budinsky, F., Paternostro, M., Merks, E.: EMF: Eclipse Modeling Framework, 2nd edn. Addison-Wesley, Boston (2009)
24. Taentzer, G.: AGG: A graph transformation environment for modeling and validation of software. In: Pfaltz et al. [19], pp. 446–453
25. Tisi, M., Jouault, F., Fraternali, P., Ceri, S., Bézivin, J.: On the use of higher-order model transformations. In: Paige, R.F., Hartman, A., Rensink, A. (eds.) ECMDA-FA 2009. LNCS, vol. 5562, pp. 18–33. Springer, Heidelberg (2009)
26. Winetzhammer, S.: ModGraph – generating executable EMF models. In: Krause, C., Westfechtel, B. (eds.) Proceedings of the 7th International Workshop on Graph Based Tools. Electronic Communications of the EASST, vol. 54, pp. 32–44. EASST, Bremen (2012)
27. Winetzhammer, S., Westfechtel, B.: Propagating model refactorings to graph transformation rules. In: ICSOFT-PT 2014 - Proceedings of the 9th International Conference on Software Paradigm Trends, Vienna, Austria, pp. 17–28, Aug 2014
28. Zündorf, A.: Rigorous object oriented software development. Technical report, University of Paderborn, Germany (2001)

A Tool-Supported Approach for Introducing Aspects in UPPAAL Timed Automata

Dragos Truscan[1]([⊠]), Jüri Vain[2], Martin Koskinen[1], and Junaid Iqbal[1]

[1] Åbo Akademi University, Joukahaisenkatu 3–5 A, Turku, Finland
{dragos.truscan,martin.koskinen,junaid.iqbal}@abo.fi
[2] Tallinn University of Technology, Tallinn, Estonia
vain@ioc.ee

Abstract. In this paper, we suggest an approach which combines aspect-oriented concepts with UPPAAL timed automata (UPTA), in order to provide a systematic constructive approach with tool support for model weaving and verification. Using our approach one may develop independently different aspects of the system as timed automata and then weave them later on into a complete specification. In order to facilitate the weaving process, we suggest explicit composition patterns which allow us to fully automate the weaving process via model transformations. The composition patterns are accompanied by generic verification rules which ensure that the weaving of an aspect does not conflict with the original behaviour of the base model. Preliminary results show that the weaving process can be fully automated while preserving the modularity of the specifications.

Keywords: Aspect-oriented modeling · UPPAAL Timed Automata · Model transformation

1 Introduction

Aspect-oriented modeling (AOM) [1,2] is a paradigm inspired from *aspect-oriented programming* [3,4], which promotes the idea of *separation of concerns* in order to build more modular and easy to update specifications. An *aspect* describes a particular *concern* of the system from a particular *viewpoint*, allowing the developers to focus on individual features of the system in isolation.

An *aspect model* consists of an *advice model* (a model fragment describing a new functionality), a *pointcut model* (a model fragment specifying where the aspect can be composed to a base model) and a *composition protocol* (how the advice model is connected via the pointcut model). An aspect model can be woven with the base model in many places (called *join points*) and in different ways. The result of composing advice models and a *base model* is called *composite model*. The composition process is also called *model weaving*.

According to Sutton, *aspect-oriented software development* (AOSD) provides improved separation of concerns, ease of maintenance, evolution and customization, and greater flexibility in development [5]. Other researchers report in a

© Springer International Publishing Switzerland 2015
A. Holzinger et al. (Eds.): ICSOFT 2014, CCIS 555, pp. 349–364, 2015.
DOI: 10.1007/978-3-319-25579-8_20

survey of industrial projects [6] that the main benefits of AOSD are the substantial reduction in model size and improved design stability. However, the main body of AOSD and AOM technologies provides a conceptual framework, leaving room for relatively loose semantic interpretation. Nevertheless, the main research challenges remain in hiding from users the complexities of the composition mechanisms and in developing associated tool support.

In this paper, we suggest the use of aspect-oriented methods in the context of *UPPAAL timed automata* (UPTA) with the focus on providing a constructive approach accompanied by automated tool support for model weaving. Our suggestion would allow for decoupling the design of different aspects of the system and the use of explicit composition patterns to weave the aspects together via model transformations. The composition patterns are accompanied by generic verification rules which are used to verify that the weaving process does not conflict with the behavior of the base model. The approach will take advantage of the precise semantics of UPTA and their expressiveness when specifying behavioural aspects: incorporate timing constraints explicitly, multi-processes, synchronization and data structures. In addition, one can take advantage of the good tool support for model-checking in UPPAAL and of the available test generation tools built on top of UPPAAL, which have been used in many industrial projects.

In the following, we discuss related works in Sect. 2. Section 3 will provide a short introduction to timed automata. Our aspect-oriented modeling approach is described in Sect. 4. Section 5 exemplifies the approach with an example, followed by a description of tool support in Sect. 6. We conclude with a preliminary analysis of the approach and discuss future work.

2   Related Work

The Unified Modeling Language (UML) [7] has been used as the *de facto* modeling language in the AOM community and several language extensions have been proposed in e.g., [8–12] along with corresponding weaving mechanisms. For a more complete overview, the reader is referred to [13]. However, aspect operations used in the context of UML lack clear semantics and constructive definitions. Although UPTA is less expressive than UML, they allow more rigourous semantic definition. In our approach, we suggest the use of UPPAAL timed automata for specifying aspect models and their weaving without extending the formalism.

Several researchers have studied the verification of AO programs [14–16] and of the AO designs. For instance, D. Xu [17] translates a woven state model into *finite state processes* (FSP), which is verified in the Labeled Transition System Analyzer (LTSA) tool [18] using manually specified verification properties. This approach is similar to our approach in the sense that it allows the verification of the specification. However, in our case, both the advice models and the woven model are specified using UPPAAL timed automata and then simulated and verified in the UPPAAL tool.

To our best of knowledge the only attempt to combine aspect-orientation and UPPAAL timed automata has been suggested by Sarna and Vain [19]. They provide an approach for including aspects in the construction of test models by formal refinements of UPTA specifications. The difference to our paper is that they used aspects for refining the system specification in place, whereas in this paper the aspects are used for extending the functionality of the system with new features. Such an approach allows one to define features aspect-wise, while aspect weaving rules provide discipline for structural modeling.

3   Preliminaries of UPTA

An UPTA model M is a *closed network of extended time automata* $\mathcal{A}_1, \ldots, \mathcal{A}_n$, that are called processes. The processes are combined into a single system by the CCS[1] parallel composition $\mathcal{A}_1 \parallel \ldots \parallel \mathcal{A}_n$ [20, Sect. 5.1,pp.25]. Synchronous communication between the processes is done by hand-shake synchronization links that are called channels. Each process may have input actions denoted $ch?$, where ch is the name of a channel, output actions denoted $ch!$, and internal actions Act of $\mathcal{A}_1, \ldots, \mathcal{A}_n$. Asynchronous communication between processes is done by shared variables.

Each UPTA process $\mathcal{A}_i$ is given as a tuple $(L; E; V; Cl; Init; Inv; TL)$ where L is a finite set of locations, E is the set of edges defined by $E \subseteq L \times G(Cl; V) \times Sync \times Act \times L$, where $G(Cl; V)$ is the set of enabling conditions - guards. $Sync \subseteq \Sigma$ is a set of synchronisation actions over the channels the process $\mathcal{A}_i$ is linked to the network. In the graphical notation, the locations are denoted by circles and edges by arrows (see Fig. 2). The set Act of internal actions is a set of sequences of assignment actions with integer and boolean expressions as well as with clock resets r. V denotes the set of integer and boolean variables. Cl denotes the set of real-valued clocks $(Cl \cap V = \oslash)$. $Init \subseteq Act$ is a set of assignments that assigns the initial values to variables and clocks. $Inv : L \to I(Cl; V)$ is a function that assigns an invariant I to each location, $I(Cl; V)$ is the set of invariants over clocks Cl and variables V. $T_L : L \to \{\text{ordinary, urgent, committed}\}$ is the function that assigns the type to each location of the automaton.

The semantics of UPTA $M = \mathcal{A}_1 \parallel \ldots \parallel \mathcal{A}_n$ is given in terms of *labelled transition systems* (LTS) [20]. A state of a network is a pair $\langle L, u \rangle$, where L denotes a vector of current locations of the network, one for each process $\mathcal{A}_1, \ldots, \mathcal{A}_n$ and u is a clock assignment reflecting the current values of the clocks in M. A network may perform two types of transitions, delay transitions and discrete transitions.

There are two rules for discrete transitions defining local actions where one of the processes makes a move on its own, and synchronizing actions where two processes synchronize on a channel and move simultaneously. Let l_i stand for the ith element of a location vector l and $l[l_i'/l_i]$ for the vector l with l_i being

---

[1] Calculus of Communicating Systems.

substituted with l_i'. The transition rule is as follows:

$$\langle L, u \rangle \rightarrow_{Act} \langle L[l_i'/l_i], u' \rangle$$
$$\text{if } l_i \rightarrow_{g,Act,r} l_i', u \in g, u' \in I(L[l_i'/l_i]) \quad (1)$$

$$\langle L, u \rangle \rightarrow_{Act} \langle L[l_i'/l_i], L[l_j'/l_j], u' \rangle,$$
if there exists $i \neq j$ such that
1. $l_i \rightarrow_{gi,ch?,ri} l_i', lj \rightarrow_{gj,ch!,rj} l_i'$ and $u \in g_i \wedge g_j$, and
2. $u' \neq u[r_j \mapsto 0(r_i \mapsto 0)]$ and $u' \in I(L[l_i'/l_i], L[l_j'/l_j])$ $\quad (2)$

Delay transitions apply uniformly to the set u of clocks of M:

$$\langle L, u \rangle \rightarrow_d \langle L, u + d \rangle \text{if } u \in I(L) \text{ and } (u + d) \in I(L),$$
$$\text{where } I(L) = \cap I(l_i). \quad (3)$$

Besides clock variables, UPTA may have boolean and integer variables, each with bounded domain and initial value. Predicates over these variables can be used as guards of the edges and they can be updated using resets on the edges. The semantics of the models that include such variables is extended in natural way, i.e. for an action transition to be enabled, the extended clock assignment must also satisfy all integer guards on the corresponding edges and when a transition is taken the assignment is updated according to the boolean, integer and clock resets.

To model atomic sequences of actions, e.g. atomic broadcast or multicast, UPTA support a notion of *committed locations*. A committed location is a location where no delay is allowed. In a network, if any process is in a committed location then only action transitions starting from such a committed location are allowed. Thus, processes in committed locations may be interleaved only with processes in a committed location.

Let $C(L)$ denote the set of committed locations in L and $\rightarrow_c$ denote the transition relation for a network with committed locations, then the conditions in formula 1 and 2 are strengthened respectively with a condition:

1. either $l_i \in C(L)$ or $C(L) = \emptyset$,
2. either $l_i \in C(L), l_j \in C(L)$ or $C(L) = \emptyset$.

In the rest of the paper, we explain the weaving operations by referring only to syntactic notions of UPTA and rely on the transition semantics of parallel components defined herein.

4   Introducing Aspects in UPTA

As discussed in the introduction, the concerns of a system are developed in weakly related parts (models) called aspects. An aspect model is composed of a

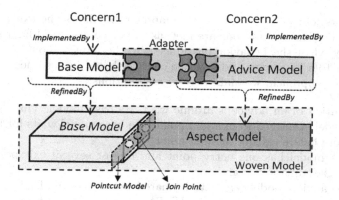

Fig. 1. Generic weaving architecture for UPTA.

pointcut and an advice. Pointcuts identify points in the execution model referred to as join points.

With respect to UPTA, a pointcut can be a guard or set of guards applied to any combination of UPTA elements (model fragments) that are accessible via the edges to which the pointcut guards are attached. Consequently, a join point is a place in the base UPTA model where the advice model is superimposed and the pointcut defines under what conditions the advice can be inserted in the base model.

Both the base model and advice model are assumed to be UPTA and this model class is conservative under weaving operations described in this section. A *composed model* or *woven model* is a network of automata interacting via join points. The composition protocol is specified by generic adapters corresponding to each type of advice. During the composition the same aspect can be woven in several places (join points) in the base model.

4.1   Generic Process

The generic weaving process is shown in Fig. 1. In this figure, two independent timed automata *Base Model* and *Advice Model* implement two cross-cutting concerns *Concern1* and *Concern2*, respectively. When the two models are composed a *woven model* is created. The weaving process is regarded as a model transformation in which two independently developed models are composed via generic adapters.

Let *Base Model* be the base model to which the functionality of *Advice Model* is composed, resulting in a UPTA network. We define an *Adapter* as a model fragment which introduces weaving information in both models. Basically, the adapter introduces a *JoinPoint* in the base model, and the corresponding entry and exit points of the advice that matches to the join point. The adapter encodes one of the following composition rules: *before*, *after*, *around*, and *conditional*. The first three follow the semantics of the AspectJ aspect-oriented programming language [21], that is a piece of code of the aspect is executed before, after, or in place of its join points. The fourth adapter type allows the execution of an aspect only if certain conditions are met, as it will be discussed later on. These rules specify when the behavior introduced by the advice should be executed with respect to a join point and how the control should be returned to the base model. In our approach, we make several assumptions:

- The execution of an advice is atomic w.r.t. its base model. That is, once an aspect model is entered from a join point, the base model waits for the aspect to complete before exiting the join point;
- An advice model has one entry point and one or several exit points which return to the same join point;
- The same advice model template is shared between several join points of a base model if it includes only one UPTA process. If more than one parallel processes constitutes a base model, the waiting and race conditions for an advice are avoided due to the assumption that the number of advice model instances needs to be equal to the number of base model processes that have join points with given advice. The number of advice instances may be less in special cases where simultaneous execution of join points in parallel processes is excluded.
- The base model and the advice model can be woven using UPTA-specific communication and synchronization assumptions, e.g. synchronizing the entry and exit of advice model with wait in the base model, sharing or refining data between base and advice model, etc.

4.2   Join Point Adapters

For the purpose of making weaving operators constructive, we suggest several join point adapters which allow for a systematic and mechanized weaving of aspects into the base models. These adapters allow one to decide, based on the pointcut condition, whether the aspect should be executed at a given join point.

The adapters we define can be applied for refining a channel synchronization, generically shown as the model fragment in Fig. 2. The *channel** represents a synchronization between edges of parallel automata, whereas the direction of the synchronization is specified by suffixes of the channel name, e.g. *channel!* denotes the sending and *channel?* the receiving side of the channel. The synchronization can take place whenever both edges linked with a channel are enabled by their guards. During the synchronization, the variable updates specified on the synchronized edges are performed. In the following, in order to save space, we only present the adapters that can be applied to a receiving model fragment, however the adapters to be applied to a sending model fragment are similar.

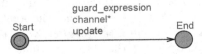

Fig. 2. Model fragment with channel synchronization.

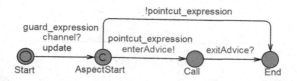

Fig. 3. Generic *after* adapter.

The *after adapter* (Fig. 3) allows the execution of an advice after a channel synchronization. It refines the *End* location with two new locations *AspectStart* and *Call*, as well as with two new channels *enterAdvice!* and *exitAdvice?*. Whenever the *pointcut_expression* is true, the advice is executed, otherwise the base behavior is executed.

The corresponding adapter introduced to the advice model during the weaving is shown in Fig. 4. As one may notice, the execution of the advice model is triggered from the base model via the join point by receiving the *enterAdvice?* synchronization and, after executing the advice functionality, it returns the control via the *exitAdvice!* synchronization.

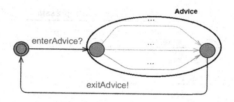

Fig. 4. Generic advice.

The *before adapter* (Fig. 5) allows the execution of the advice model before the base model reaches its fragment. The same generic advice model as in Fig. 4 can be used.

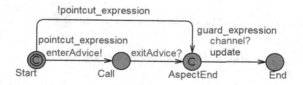

Fig. 5. Generic *before* adapter.

The third adapter, the *around adapter* (Fig. 6), allows the weaving of around advices by starting the execution of the advice model before the one of the base model fragment and returning from the advice model afterwards. The same generic advice model as in Fig. 4 can be used. This is the most complex adapter type, and it can be used to both overload and override the functionality of the base model fragment.

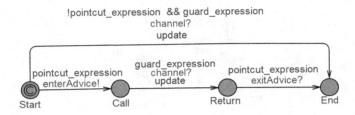

Fig. 6. Generic *around* adapter.

Finally, the *conditional adapter* (Fig. 7) introduces new functionality to the same base model fragment in Fig. 2. The new functionality decides whether the execution of the base model continues after executing the advice or returns to a previous location. Compared to the previous adapters, the conditional adapter will allow the base model to consume the *channel?* synchronization, but the advice will decide if the same synchronization should be executed again via *exitAdviceRepeat* or the base model should proceed to the next location via *exitAdviceContinue*.

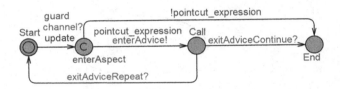

Fig. 7. Generic *conditional* adapter.

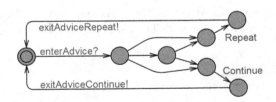

Fig. 8. Generic conditional aspect.

The corresponding generic aspect model for this advice is shown in Fig. 8. As one may notice, this model can return to the join point via two different channels. If needed the adapter may be extended with more complex behavior, for instance with multiple exit points, which we defer for future work.

4.3 Generic Verification Rules for the Weaving

Extending the base models with new functionality may imply changing of the liveness conditions or of the timing behaviour of the woven models. Thus it is important to check that after the weaving of an aspect at a given join point the original properties of the base model are not affected. Therefore, for each type of adapter defined in the previous section we associate two generic verification rules, similar to *contracts*, which have to hold before and after weaving an aspect model into the base model.

These rules are specified as liveness properties using TCTL (Timed Computation Tree Logic) [22] queries. For instance, if we consider the model fragment in Fig. 2, the first generic query can be specified as:

$$Start \rightarrow Stop$$

which allows one to verify that the model fragment, once it reaches location *Start* it will inevitably lead to location *Stop*. This rule should hold before and after weaving an aspect into a base model. Thus the rule is associated with the generic join point adapters of type (Fig. 3), *before* (Fig. 5), *after*, and (Fig. 6) *around*.

With respect to the conditional adapter (Fig. 7), the rule is refined in order to allow the model to inevitably progress to the *Stop* location or return to the *Start* state, as follows:

$$AspectStart \rightarrow Stop \textbf{ or } Start$$

The above rules allow one to verify local deadlock freeness. In order to ensure global deadlock freeness, for each new woven model we verify the following rule:

$$A\square \textbf{ not } deadlock$$

Additional verification rules, including time related ones, can be specified on a case-by-case basis.

5   Case Study: Auto-Off Lamp

We exemplify our approach with an example originally found as a demo model in the documentation of the UPPAAL TRON tool [23], under the name *auto-off lamp controller*.

5.1   Base Model - Revisited

The purpose of the lamp controller is that, once it is tuned on, it will wait for a given time period before turning off, unless there are user inputs ("touches") which reset its auto-off function. The demo is composed of two models: a lamp and a user model. The lamp model (Fig. 9-left) reacts to events, on the *touch* channel, and synchronizes to the user via the *done* channel. When the lamp is in the *OFF* location and the touch synchronization arrives, the internal clock x of the lamp is set to zero at the same time as the lamp transitions to the *switchON* location. The lamp is allowed to stay in this location for *tolerance* time units, during which it has to change the lamp-state modeling variable n to value 10 and synchronize its location to the environment on the *done* channel. After that, the lamp is in *ON* location, where it can accept new touch events.

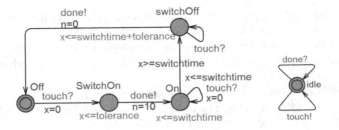

Fig. 9. Original lamp (left) and user (right) models.

The lamp will stay in the *ON* location for *switchtime* time units, unless a touch event is received during its allowed stay and the clock is reset. When *switchtime* time units have elapsed the lamp transitions to *switchOFF* location and the *n* variable is set to zero. In this location the lamp will continue to accept touch events, even though these have no effect. A location change synchronization on *done* channel will take place from the *switchOFF* location to the *OFF* location within *switchtime + tolerance* time units. This implies that the lamp is allowed to stay in the *switchOFF* location for *tolerance* time units.

The model of the environment is presented in Fig. 9-right. Its functionality is to emit touch events when the lamp is in a receiving state or to accept confirmation that the lamp level has changed.

5.2 Introducing New Functionality

We introduce two new orthogonal concerns to the lamp specification:

– *Authentication:* only authenticated users may change the state of the lamp;
– *Logging:* authentication attempts should be logged.

Each concern will be implemented separately as a stand-alone advice and woven in the base model of the lamp using the adapters described in Sect. 4.

Authentication Aspect. The first step is to create an advice model which implements the authentication. Since the authentication can result either in a successful or in a failed attempt, the advice model will have two exit points and thus should be compatible with a conditional adapter. The *authentication* advice (Fig. 10) is entered via the *enAuth?* synchronization, after which, depending on the result of the authentication, it will exit via either *exAuthCon!* or *exAuthRep!*. For simplicity, the authentication is discriminated by a *pass* variable shared with the user model.

Intuitively, we would like to extend the behavior of our lamp model, to accept touch events only from authenticated users. If the user is not authenticated, the touch event is received but it has no effect on the lamp. In order to weave the authentication advice with the base model, the conditional adapter has to be applied to the base model in all possible locations. The target locations are

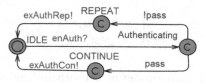

Fig. 10. Advice handling authentication.

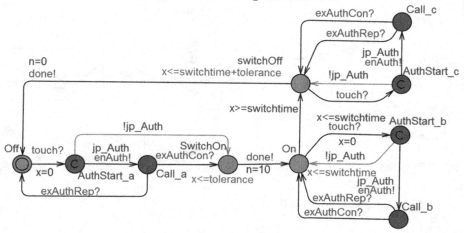

Fig. 11. Lamp woven with authentication advice.

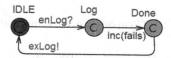

Fig. 12. Logging advice.

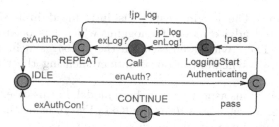

Fig. 13. Weaving the logging advice into authentication.

all those edges having a *touch?* channel synchronization. The result of weaving authentication using the conditional adapter is shown in Fig. 11.

The behavior of the lamp model is the same with the base model whenever the authentication is successful or the jointpoint condition is not satisfied. When

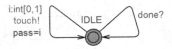

Fig. 14. Environment model with authentication.

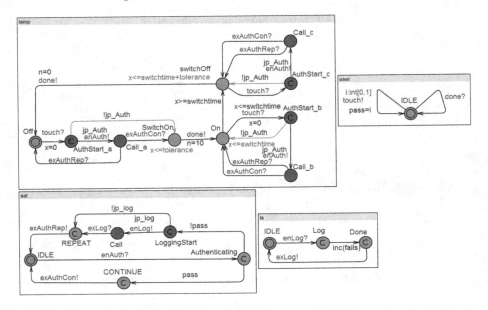

Fig. 15. Complete woven lamp model.

the authentication fails, the control is returned to the location preceding *touch*, ignoring the user touch.

Logging Aspect. The logging aspect is introduced in a similar manner. Figure 12 shows and advice model for logging which has been already refined with an adapter. The advice is entered via the *enLog?* synchronization and it exits via the *exLog!* synchronization after incrementing the number of failed authentications.

In order to weave this aspect with its base model, in this case the Authentication advice model, we refine *exAuthRep!* edge in Fig. 10 using the before adapter defined in Fig. 5, obtaining the model shown in Fig. 13.

Based on the new advice, whenever the authentication fails, the event is logged by invoking the Logging advice via the *enLog!* synchronization and after receiving *exLog?*, the original *exAuthRep!* is synchronized to the lamp model.

Environment with Authentication. The original user model in Fig. 9 is updated to provide simple, both valid and invalid, authentication credentials via the global integer variable *pass*, as shown in Fig. 14. Instead of having a complete set of correct and incorrect authentication credentials, we used only two values (0 and 1), one to represent all the successful cases and one to represent the unsuccessful cases. We also consider the authentication to take place at the same time as the touch event. Therefore the *touch* channel has not changed name. The new functionality could have been also introduced via a new aspect, but we decided to keep the example simple.

5.3   Complete Woven Model

The resulting UPTA after weaving both the authentication and logging aspects into the original lamp model is shown in Fig. 15. As one may notice, at runtime, the aspects can be enabled or disabled statically by the use of the *jp_Auth* and *jp_log* variables. When both these variables are set to *false*, the model in Fig. 15 will be equivalent with the original lamp model in Fig. 9. This approach allows us to include or exclude the aspects using one single UPTA model.

6   Tool Support

6.1   Aspect Weaving

Since the composition mechanisms are specified explicitly via generic adapters, the aspect weaving was completely automated via a tool implemented in the Python programming language [24]. In order to implement the graphical user interface (GUI), an open source, cross-platform, light-weight *wxPython* library is used. In the GUI, the user can select a template from UPPAAL model files as the base model template, the advice model template, the channel pinpointing a join point and the type of weaving adapter (Fig. 16).

The tool parses the base model and identifies the locations and edges where advice model has to be woven. By using this information, the advice model is then woven at identified model fragments according to the type of advice. The corresponding synchronizations are then added to the base model, in order to synchronize the entry and exit of the advice model.

As a result of weaving process, a new UTPA model and the accompanying verification rules are generated. The composite model is an UPTA model which can be used to simulate and verify the composite specification. The woven aspect behavior can be completely bypassed by setting the pointcut variables, which results in the behavior of original base model. The newly generated composite model can also act as base model to weave other advice models as described earlier, supporting thus an incremental development approach.

6.2   Verification

After weaving the Authentication aspect into the original lamp model, the following verification rules have been generated by the tool, corresponding to each join point related to a *touch?* synchronization.

$lamp.AuthStart\_a \rightarrow lamp.SwitchOn$ **or** $lamp.Off$

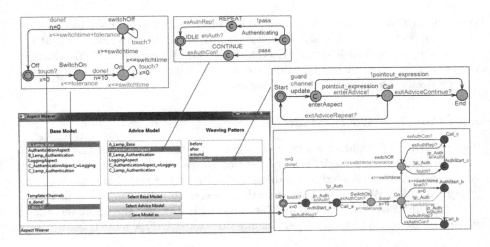

Fig. 16. Screen caption of the model weaver GUI.

$$lamp.AuthStart\_b \rightarrow lamp.On \text{ or } lamp.On$$
$$lamp.AuthStart\_c \rightarrow lamp.switchOff \text{ or } \overline{lamp.switchOff}$$

Due to the source and target location being the same for the touch channel, the underlined part of the second and third verification rules is redundant and thus it can be discarded. In case where more precision is needed in distinguishing the path taken in the join point, one can augment the join point with auxiliary boolean variables which will be reset to *true*, whenever an edge (labelled with that reset) of the join point is traversed.

Subsequently, when weaving the Logging advice into the Authentication model, the following rule is generated:

$$aal.LoggingStart \rightarrow aal.IDLE,$$

where *aal* is an instantiation of the Authentication aspect woven with Logging aspect as previously shown in Fig. 15.

Last but not least, the tool generates the verification query for deadlock freeness. All the generated rules including case specific ones are then verified in the UPPAAL verifier.

7   Conclusions and Future Work

In this paper, we proposed an approach in which we introduce aspects-oriented concepts in the context of UPTA models with the purpose of creating more modular, manageable and easy to update specifications. More specifically, we have proposed a set of generic adapters that can be used for systematic and tool-supported weaving and verification of UPTA-based aspect models. Our approach allows one to employ aspect-oriented concepts without modifying the underlying UPTA formalism. In addition, it allows one to take advantage of the verification engine of UPPAAL to ensure the validity of the resulting models.

The use of generic weaving adapters allowed to implement weaving as a model transformation. Due to the way the adapters are defined, the weaving does not replace the original model fragment where the join point is applied, allowing thus for multiple aspects to be woven consecutively at the same model fragment.

Preliminary evaluation shows that creating and updating aspect models becomes easier following our approach and that weaving of the models does not have a dramatic effect on the symbolic state space of the resulting models. However a more thorough evaluation is subject to future work.

Future work also includes an evaluation on what are the benefits of using UPTA-based aspect-oriented models for testing. More specifically we will look at the impact of using aspect models on the test suite updates and will investigate new aspect-based test coverage criteria which will exploit the modularity of the models.

References

1. Clarke, S., Baniassad, E.: Aspect-Oriented Analysis and Design. The Theme Approach. Addison-Wesley, Boston (2005)
2. France, R.B., et al.: An aspect-oriented approach to design modeling. In: IEE Proceedings - Software, Special Issue on Early Aspects: Aspect-Oriented Requirements Engineering and Architecture Design, vol. 151 (2004)
3. Filman, R.E., et al.: Aspect-Oriented Software Development. Addison-Wesley, Boston (2005)
4. Kiczales, G., et al.: Aspect-oriented programming. In: Matsuoka, S., Akşit, M. (eds.) ECOOP 1997. LNCS, vol. 1241, pp. 140–149. Springer, Heidelberg (1997)
5. Sutton Jr., S.M.: Aspect-oriented software development and software process. In: Li, M., Boehm, B., Osterweil, L.J. (eds.) SPW 2005. LNCS, vol. 3840, pp. 177–191. Springer, Heidelberg (2006)
6. Rashid, A., et al.: Aspect-oriented software development in practice: tales from AOSD-Europe. Computer **43**, 19–26 (2010)
7. Rumbaugh, J., Jacobson, I., Booch, G.: Unified Modeling Language Reference Manual, 2nd edn. Pearson Higher Education, Upper Saddle River (2004)
8. Ali, S., et al.: Modeling robustness behavior using aspect-oriented modeling to support robustness testing of industrial systems. Softw. Syst. Model. **11**, 633–670 (2012)
9. Aldawud, O., et al.: UML profile for aspect-oriented software development. In: Proceedings of Third International Workshop on Aspect-Oriented Modeling (2003)
10. Han, Y., et al.: A meta model and modeling notation for AspectJ. In: The 5th AOSD Modeling with UML Workshop (2004)
11. Stein, D., et al.: A UML-based aspect-oriented design notation for AspectJ. In: Proceedings of the 1st International Conference on Aspect-oriented Software Development, AOSD 2002, pp. 106–112. ACM, New York (2002)
12. Tkatchenko, M., Kiczales, G.: Uniform support for modeling crosscutting structure. In: Briand, L.C., Williams, C. (eds.) MoDELS 2005. LNCS, vol. 3713, pp. 508–521. Springer, Heidelberg (2005)
13. Wimmer, M., et al.: A survey on UML-based aspect-oriented design modeling. ACM Comput. Surv. **43**, 28:1–28:33 (2011)

14. Ubayashi, N., Tamai, T.: Aspect-oriented programming with model checking. In: Proceedings of the 1st International Conference on Aspect-oriented Software Development, AOSD 2002, pp. 148–154. ACM, New York (2002)

15. Denaro, G., Monga, M.: An experience on verification of aspect properties. In: Proceedings of the 4th International Workshop on Principles of Software Evolution, IWPSE 2001, pp. 186–189. ACM, New York (2001)

16. Krishnamurthi, S., Fisler, K.: Foundations of incremental aspect model-checking. ACM Trans. Softw. Eng. Methodol. **16**, 7 (2007)

17. Radu, V.: Application. In: Radu, V. (ed.) Stochastic Modeling of Thermal Fatigue Crack Growth. ACM, vol. 1, pp. 63–70. Springer, Heidelberg (2015)

18. Magee, J., Kramer, J.: Concurrency: State models and java programs. Wiley, New York (1999). [IBMb 02] IBM, "Business Process Execution Language For Web Services" (1) 6

19. Sarna, K., Vain, J.: Exploiting aspects in model-based testing. In: Proceedings of the Eleventh workshop on Foundations of Aspect-Oriented Languages, FOAL 2012, pp. 45–48. ACM, New York (2012)

20. Bengtsson, J.E., Yi, W.: Timed automata: semantics, algorithms and tools. In: Desel, J., Reisig, W., Rozenberg, G. (eds.) Lectures on Concurrency and Petri Nets. LNCS, vol. 3098, pp. 87–124. Springer, Heidelberg (2004)

21. Kiczales, G., Hilsdale, E., Hugunin, J., Kersten, M., Palm, J., Griswold, W.G.: An overview of aspectJ. In: Lindskov Knudsen, J. (ed.) ECOOP 2001. LNCS, vol. 2072, pp. 327–354. Springer, Heidelberg (2001)

22. Alur, R., et al.: Model-checking for real-time systems. In: LICS 1990, Proceedings of Fifth Annual IEEE Symposium on e Logic in Computer Science, pp. 414–425. IEEE (1990)

23. Hessel, A., Larsen, K.G., Mikucionis, M., Nielsen, B., Pettersson, P., Skou, A.: Testing real-time systems using UPPAAL. In: Hierons, R.M., Bowen, J.P., Harman, M. (eds.) FORTEST. LNCS, vol. 4949, pp. 77–117. Springer, Heidelberg (2008)

24. van Rossum, G.: The Python Programming Language. http://www.python.org (Accessed Sep 2015)

A Timed Semantics of Workflows

Marcello M. Bersani[1], Salvatore Distefano[1,2], Luca Ferrucci[3],
and Manuel Mazzara[4]([✉])

[1] Dipartimento di Elettronica Informazione e Bioingegneria,
Politecnico di Milano, Milano, Italy
{marcellomaria.bersani,salvatore.distefano}@polimi.it
[2] Kazan Federal University, Kazan, Russia
[3] ISTI-CNR, Pisa, Italy
luca.ferrucci@isti.cnr.it
[4] Innopolis University, Kazan, Russia
m.mazzara@innopolis.edu.ru

Abstract. We formalize timed workflow with abnormal behavior management (i.e. recovery) and demonstrate how temporal logics and model checking are methodologies to iteratively revise the design correct-by construction system. We define a formal semantics by compiling generic workflow patterns into an extension of LTL with dense time clocks (CLTLoc). CLTLoc allows us to define the first logical formalization of workflows that can be practically employed in verification tools and to avoid the use of well-known automata based formalisms dealing with real-time. We use an ad-hoc bound model checker to prove requirements validity on a business process. The working assumption is that lightweight approaches easily fit into processes that are already in place so that radical change of procedures, tools and people's attitudes are not needed. The complexity of formalisms and invasiveness of methods have been demonstrated to be one of the major drawback and obstacle for deployment of formal engineering techniques into mundane projects.

Keywords: Workflow · Recovery framework · Formal methods ·
Temporal logic · Semantics

1 Introduction

Workflows are logical, abstract artifacts able to describe or implement patterns of activities required to perform real works. Any type of resources is considered in this definition, both human and mechanical, including electronic, automation and computer-based devices or systems. The general concept of workflow has been adopted and characterized in several contexts such as economics (knowledge economy, business process), management (manufacturing, job shop), mathematics (queueing systems, decision making, operations research), engineering (quality engineering, service engineering). With specific regard to computer science, workflows are used in several contexts such as algorithms, business processes,

© Springer International Publishing Switzerland 2015
A. Holzinger et al. (Eds.): ICSOFT 2014, CCIS 555, pp. 365–383, 2015.
DOI: 10.1007/978-3-319-25579-8_21

Web services, machine learning, service oriented computing, software product lines, human machine interaction.

Workflows are therefore applied in different contexts and also in different ways: in design phase, where their representations are used to evaluate specific properties (both functional and non-functional) of the corresponding systems; to represent and evaluate the effectiveness of scheduling systems and policies; in document management and imaging; in service composition and orchestration (service oriented architecture/infrastructure, bioinformatics and cheminformatics scientific workflows); to study human machine interactions.

This work can be framed into the workflow representation techniques, proposing a formal approach based on CLTLoc [1] semantics for modelling the real-time workflow executions and for the verification of dependability properties. In fact, as CLTLoc extends LTL [2] by allowing timing constraints into formulae, both instantaneous (zero time) and time consuming activities can be taken into account in the workflow model, thus providing an effective tool for dependability verification of workflows.

On Methods and Tools. Logics and model-checking have been successfully used in the last decades for modelling and verification of various types of hardware and software systems and have a stronger credibility in the scientific community when compared with other formalisms. We here give an CLTLoc-based semantics of workflow execution and use Zot [3] model checker for requirement verification. By applying model-checking on the case study presented in this paper, we demonstrate the feasibility of the verification approach and how temporal logics can work for both modelling and verification of (simple but realistic) business workflows inclusive of exception handling. This work has to be intended as complementary to what has been done in [4] where a similar problem was approached in term of Process Algebra.

Differently from several others formalizations only offering languages without methods – for a detailed discussion see [5,6] – our approach, together with software tools, aims at offering a complete practical toolkit for software and systems engineers working in the field of workflow design. Following the line of [7] this approach goes under the correct-by-construction paradigm and the idea of developing dependable systems by integrating specific approaches well-suited to each development phase.

The ideal process of workflow verification is an iterative process. In this work, we aim at providing an instrument for workflow revision, i.e. a procedure to follow until the requirements are finally met. To do this, we encode the workflow into a formal language and, at the same time, we formally describe specific requirements on the system. This is discussed in Sect. 3. At this point, as shown in Sect. 4, correctness can be automatically determined via the Zot model checker. As an outcome of model checking we may need to revise the workflow in order to meet the requirements.

A Descriptive Semantics. The role of temporal logics in verification and validation is two-fold. First, temporal logic allows abstract, concise and convenient expression of required properties of a system. In fact, temporal logic is often used with this goal in the verification of finite-state models, e.g., in model checking [8]. Second, temporal logic can be used as a descriptive approach for specifying and modelling systems (see, e.g., [9,10]). A descriptive model is based on axioms, written in some (temporal) logic, which define the system through its general properties, rather than by an operational model based on some kind of machine behaving in the desired way. In this case, verification typically consists of satisfiability checking of the entailment between the model and the desired property [11].

Specifying temporal relations among events that do not inherently behave in an operational way may become rather hard when operational models are employed. This is the case for the system recovery considered here. Exception handling is an event-based paradigm that implements the asynchronous exchange of warning events among actors that are part of the system. The typical implementation of exception handling mechanisms – through logical rules of the form *if (cond) then* throw(*e*) and *try-catch* blocks – requires ad-hoc extensions of operational-based formalisms by means of the definition of message-passing primitives. Specifying exception handling mechanisms through temporal logic can be easily achieved by the logic itself and also allows modelling of classes of exceptions endowed with a specific semantics (see Sect. 3) in a coherent and uniform way.

Other Approaches and Novelty. Several approaches have been adopted in recent years to provide formal semantics of business processes. Most of them are very much bound to a specific formalism accordingly extended to better cope with modelling issues. These attempts mostly belong (but not limited) to the process algebras, Petri nets or model-based philosophies, with some raid into temporal logics et similia too.

Mobile process algebra have been successfully used in [4] that this work intend to complement. Limitations of process algebras approaches like the previous ones and, for example, [12] are related to the fact that process algebras are based on equational reasoning. From a practical perspective, this makes verification tricky, difficult and certainly not user-friendly, because verification is mainly carried out by specific proof techniques that are used to prove behavioural equivalence among processes. Furthermore, all these approaches mostly focus on the verification of reachability-based properties (with some exceptions like [13]) and tool support is very limited (see [14]). On the other side, other works like [15] provide a methodology and tool support for the modelling phase, but do not cope with the verification phase and either do not belong to the correct-by-construction paradigm.

Petri Nets supporters and van der Aalst approaches like Workflow Petri Nets (WPN) [16] reached the objective of verification and tool support to a much larger extent than other communities. This approach is based on extensions of previously existing formalisms and still represents an operational model, which also inherits the relative overhead. A successful attempt to overcome this issue has been provided by [17] where acyclic WPN are translated into a finite-state automaton and verified against a suitable LTL property in order to verify soundness.

Model-based approaches have also been used, though to a much lesser extent and often in combination with testing, for validation of business critical systems. The B-model is one of the most popular together with its reactive-systems extension Event-B [18]. B and Event-B are not lightweight methods. They do come with a refinement-based methodology, which however cannot easily be embedded into already existing industrial processes [7].

In the domain of temporal logics, CTL has been used to specify and enforce intertask dependencies [19], and LTL for UML activity graphs verification [20]. Other temporal logics have also been used for similar objectives. In particular, in [21] a complete and coherent semantics based on the TRIO logic [22] has been proposed for a more consistent set of UML diagrams.

Recovery frameworks have been more rarely formalized in similar manners instead. This was the main contribution of [23]. One of the first works formally discussing business recovery in terms of long-running transactions is [24]. In [25] a simplified and clarified semantics of WS-BPEL recovery framework has been presented in terms of Process Algebras. In [26] the state-of-the-art in formalizing fault, compensation and termination mechanisms of WS-BPEL 2.0 has been deeply investigated. More recently, another model has been formulated for the description of composite web services orchestrated by WS-BPEL and with resources associated. The key contribution of [27] is the integration of WS-BPEL with WSRF [28], a resource management language, taking into account the main structural elements of WS-BPEL with event handling and fault handling.

The main contribution of the paper is a timed semantics for workflows which extends the one in [23] with the definition of timing constraints bounding delays of activities and transitions. CLTLoc, being the first extension of LTL with constraints over Reals, allows us to define a descriptive semantics based on a temporal logic, along the line of that we proposed in [23], without resorting to Timed Automata [29], the de-facto standard formalism for dealing with real-time reasoning. So, to the best of the authors' knowledge, the proposed semantics is the first descriptive formalization of workflows with recovery over real-time.

The working assumption is that a lightweight solution would easily fit into processes that are already in place without the need for a radical change of procedures, tools and people's attitudes, which is actually the case for most of the aforementioned techniques. The complexity of formalisms and invasiveness of methods have been demonstrated to be one of the major drawback and obstacle for deployment of formal engineering techniques into mundane projects [7,30].

The rest of the paper is organized as follows: Sect. 2 describes the case study of a workflow for order processing. The semantics of workflows and exception handling is given using temporal logic in Sect. 3 where a general encoding into CLTLoc is provided. In Sect. 4 the implementation of this translation is illustrated and tests have been carried out to validate its correctness. Finally, Sect. 5 draws conclusive remarks and focus on future developments.

2   Timed Workflows with Recovery

A business process is a set of logically related tasks performed to achieve a well defined business outcome. Examples of typical business processes are elaborating a credit claim, hiring a new employee, ordering goods from a supplier, creating a marketing plan, processing and paying an insurance claim, and so on. Many computer systems are already available in the commercial marketplace to address the various aspects of Business Process Management (BPM) and automation.

An automated business process is generally called *business workflow*, i.e. a choreographed and system-driven sequence of activities directed towards performing a certain business task to completion. By *activity* we mean an element that performs a specific function within a process. Activities can be as simple as sending or receiving a message, or as complex as coordinating the execution of other processes and activities. A business process may encompass complex activities some of which run on back-end systems such as, for example, a credit check, automated billing, a purchase order, stock updates and shipping, or even such frivolous activities as sending a document and filling a form.

Workflow is commonly used to define the dynamic behaviour of business systems and originates from business and management as a way of modelling business processes that could wholly or partially be automated. It has evolved from the notion of process in manufacturing and offices because these processes are the result of trying to increase efficiency in routine work activities since industrialization.

The view on a workflow which is inherited from the BPM perspective – i.e. the way in which workflow designers may see a system – is somehow different from the way formalists see it. Therefore, to fill the gap between the formal and informal world, we will provide the reader with a precise understanding introducing a formal definition of a business workflow. However, our notation is suitably abstract enough to represent a large number of different modelization formalisms, such as those based on State Machines (Statecharts [31], UML Activity Diagrams [32] and Petri Nets) or specialized to represent business processes, such as BPEL [33]. In fact, one of the purposes of this work is defining a general notation able to include most of the specialized constructs of these languages, by abstraction. How this abstraction is performed is out of the scope of the paper.

A workflow is a directed graph defined by pair (A, T), where A is a finite non empty set of places (or *activities*) and T is a relation that is defined as $T \subseteq A \times A \times \mathbb{N}$. Elements of T are pairs (p, q, d), with $p, q \in A$ and $d \in \mathbb{N}$, that are called *transitions* (later indicated by t_{pq}^d). When d is zero, the transition is called zero-time and it is simply written t_{pq} otherwise d is the delay of executing t_{pq}^d. Let a be a place of A and $time : A \to \mathbb{N}$ be a function labelling activities of the workflow. We write a_c, with $c = time(a)$, for the activity a which lasts c time units. We assume that activities have non null duration, i.e., function $time$ never nullifies. Set $out(a)$ is the set of *outgoing transitions* starting from a which is defined as $\{(a, q) \mid q \in A, (a, q) \in T\}$. Set $in(a)$ is the set of *ingoing transitions* leading to p which is defined as $\{(q, a) \mid q \in A, (q, p) \in T\}$.

We assume that $|out(a)| \geq 1$, for all $a \in A$, except for place end, and that $|in(a)| \geq 1$, for all $a \in A$, except for place $start$.

A *finite path* from a to a' is a (finite) sequence of pairs $(a_0, a_1) \ldots (a_{n-1}, a_n)$ with $a_0 = a$ and $a_n = a'$, such that $(a_i, a_{i-1}) \in T$, for all $1 \leq i \leq n$. An *infinite path* from a is an (infinite) sequence of pairs $(a_i, a_{i-1}) \in E$, for all $i \geq 1$, where $a_0 = a$. As in [23], we assume that workflows are structurally correct, that is, such that there exists at least one path from place $start$ to (any) place end. The CLTLoc modelling allows us to define precisely all the executions of a timed workflow that, informally, are the superposition of paths of the workflow starting from the initial place.

Conditional cases and *split-join* activities have been already considered in [23]. In this paper, we refine their modelling to make it compliant with the real-time semantics. We briefly recall their intuitive meaning. Conditional cases model *if-then-else* blocks provided with the usual semantics. If the condition holds the "then" branch is executed otherwise the execution flow follows the "else" branch. Split-join activities model the parallel execution of two (or more) branches of the workflow that starts concurrently when activity *split* is executed and eventually synchronize their computations in correspondence with the associated *join* activity. We assume that conditional cases and split-joins are fictitious activities with non relevant time duration. Therefore, the execution of conditional cases and split-join is considered instantaneous with no time consumption and causes the related activity to start at the same instant where they occur. However, a non null duration may still be associated with these activities by defining a non-zero time incoming transition.

We consider workflows that are endowed with *exceptions*, which are events (or signals) representing erroneous configurations that occur during the workflow execution and that may prevent it from reaching a final place. With no loss of generality, we assume that an exception (raised at some moment throughout the execution) that is not managed forces the running activities that monitor that exception not to terminate. The termination of an execution, and then of all the activities occurring therein, can only be guaranteed if end is reached. The assumption is not too strong and does not prevent modelling an activity, say a, that terminates with an error configuration. In fact, one can introduce an exception to represent the wrong termination of a and a special activity that detects it and that is specifically devised for managing faulty termination of a. In addition, workflow executions are not restricted only to finite paths (from $start$ to end) and infinite iterations of finite paths of the workflow are still allowed. In fact, infinite executions are representative of wrong behaviours only when there is one (ore more) activity, over some paths, that can not terminate and does not allow the workflow to proceed further and reach end. To guarantee that a workflow is correctly designed, all the exceptions that may raise during an execution have to be caught and solved. Designers should prevent anomalous situations by defining suitable recovery actions that restore the workflow execution.

Exceptions associated with a workflow are partitioned into the set of permanent (i.e., non-punctual) exceptions and the set of punctual exceptions, as in [23].

Informally, we say that an exception is *punctual* when its duration is negligible, whereas we say that an exception is *non-punctual* when it may have a duration lasts from a position where it is raised until a position where it expires. In this paper, since we extend the modelling through real-time constraints we allow permanent exception to have an exact duration by which it must be handled. If this is not the case, then the workflow does not terminate. Punctual exceptions are not associated with any duration as they must be solved by some activity that is already underway. Activities in the workflow can be associated with three, possibly empty, sets of exceptions: (i) the set of exceptions that activity can notify whenever a potential dangerous error may compromise the workflow execution and that have to be suitably handled by some other activity which is able to repair the fault; (ii) the set of exceptions that activity can handle and the set of exceptions that may compromise the workflow execution because they let activity switch to an error state, if no activity catching them is active at the same time.

3   Formal Semantics

Constraint LTL (CLTL [34,35]) is an extension of LTL allowing atomic formulae over a constraint system. Let V be a finite set of variables and let $\mathcal{D} = (\mathbb{R}, \{<, =\})$ be a constraint system over which formulae are interpreted. In this paper, we consider a fragment of CLTL where temporal terms α are defined as: $\alpha := c \mid x$, where c is a constant in $\mathbb{N}$ and x is a variable in V.

An atomic constraint is a term of the form $\alpha_1 \sim \alpha_2$, where $\sim \in \{<, =\}$, α_1 and α_2 are temporal terms. Well-formed CLTL formulae are defined as follows:

$$\phi := p \mid \alpha_1 \sim \alpha_2 \mid \phi \wedge \phi \mid \neg\phi \mid \mathbf{X}(\phi) \mid \mathbf{Y}(\phi) \mid \phi\mathbf{U}\phi \mid \phi\mathbf{S}\phi$$

where $p \in AP$, every α_i' is a temporal term, $\sim \in \{<, =\}$, $\mathbf{X}$, $\mathbf{Y}$, $\mathbf{U}$ and $\mathbf{S}$ are the "next", "previous", "until" and "since" operators of LTL. The semantics of CLTLoc is defined with respect to $\mathcal{D}$ and the order $(\mathbb{N}, <)$ representing positions in time. An interpretation is a pair (π, σ), where $\sigma : \mathbb{N} \times V \to D$ is a mapping assigning for every variable $x \in V$ its value $\sigma(x, i)$ at each position $i \in \mathbb{N}$ and $\pi : \mathbb{N} \to \wp(AP)$ is a mapping associating a set of propositions with each position in $\mathbb{N}$. The semantics of CLTL at a position $i \in \mathbb{N}$ over an interpretation (π, σ) is defined in Table 1 (Boolean connectives are omitted for brevity). A formula $\phi \in$ CLTL is satisfiable if there exists a pair (π, σ) such that $(\pi, \sigma), 0 \models \phi$. In this case, we say that (π, σ) is a model of ϕ and we write simply $(\pi, \sigma) \models \phi$.

CLTLoc [1] is a special case of CLTL, where the arithmetical variables behave as clocks, as in Timed Automata [29]. The logic is the first decidable extension of LTL that embeds the notion of dense time through explicit clocks in the language for which there is an implemented decision procedure freely available. Intuitively, a clock x measures the time elapsed since the last time when $x = 0$, i.e., the last "reset" of x. To ensure that time progresses at the same rate for every clock, σ must satisfy the following condition: for every position $i \in \mathbb{N}$, there exists a "time delay" $\delta > 0$ such that for every clock $x \in V$ either time

Table 1. Semantics of CLTL.

$$(\pi,\sigma), i \models p \Leftrightarrow p \in \pi(i) \text{ for } p \in AP$$
$$(\pi,\sigma), i \models \alpha_1 \sim \alpha_2 \Leftrightarrow \sigma(i, x_{\alpha_1}) \sim \sigma(i, x_{\alpha_2})$$
$$(\pi,\sigma), i \models \neg\phi \Leftrightarrow (\pi,\sigma), i \not\models \phi$$
$$(\pi,\sigma), i \models \phi \wedge \psi \Leftrightarrow (\pi,\sigma), i \models \phi \text{ and } (\pi,\sigma), i \models \psi$$
$$(\pi,\sigma), i \models \mathbf{X}(\phi) \Leftrightarrow (\pi,\sigma), i+1 \models \phi$$
$$(\pi,\sigma), i \models \mathbf{Y}(\phi) \Leftrightarrow (\pi,\sigma), i-1 \models \phi \wedge i > 0$$
$$(\pi,\sigma), i \models \phi\mathbf{U}\psi \Leftrightarrow \exists j \geq i : (\pi,\sigma), j \models \psi \wedge (\pi,\sigma), n \models \phi \, \forall \, i \leq n < j$$
$$(\pi,\sigma), i \models \phi\mathbf{S}\psi \Leftrightarrow \exists j \leq i : (\pi,\sigma), j \models \psi \wedge (\pi,\sigma), n \models \phi \, \forall \, j < n \leq i$$

progress, i.e., $\sigma(i+1, x) = \sigma(i, x) + \delta$, or the clock is reset , i.e., $\sigma(i+1, x) = 0$. The initial value of a clock, $\sigma(0, x)$, may be any non-negative value. If needed, a clocks x may be initialized to c just by adding a constraint of the form $x = c$.

Workflow Model. Workflows model execution of systems as sequences of activities. Transitions, conditional case and split-join interleave the activities and determine uniquely the execution flow, i.e., the sequence of activities that realizes the computation. An activity is an abstraction of a compound of actions that are performed by the real workflow. Although they can be modelled as atomic computations, we adopt a different perspective for which the activities, being actions in the real world, have a non-punctual duration. To translate workflows into an CLTLoc formula, we assume that all the activities (except for the activities *start* and *end*) are always followed by a transition, and viceversa, and that conditional case and split-join are special activities that have punctual duration. When an activity is performed, the firing of the outgoing transition lets the system change allowing it to execute the next activity.

Let (A, T) be a workflow. With no loss of generality, we assume that no element in the graph is duplicated. By this assumption, we associate each activity with an atomic proposition that uniquely identifies it. We write t_{pq} to indicate an element $(p, q) \in T$, i.e., a transition between activities $p, q \in A$. If activity $a \in A$ holds at position i then the workflow is performing activity a at that position; similarly for t. We introduce $\|$ and $\oplus$ to indicate a split-join activity and a conditional case activity, respectively; *start* and *end* to indicate the starting and the final activity of the workflow. Workflow diagrams are translated according to rules in Table 2.

Let $t_{out}(a)$ be the disjunction $\bigvee_{t \in out(a)} t$ and $t_{in}(a)$ be the disjunction $\bigvee_{t \in in(a)} t$.

Table 2 summarizes the CLTLoc formulae defining the translation of the workflow. We slightly depart from the formalization provided in [23] to model zero-time transitions and the duration of activities. We now describe all formulae defining such aspects while motivations for formulae that are not detailed here can be found in [23].

Table 2. Workflow LTL encoding. For convenience, transitions are labeled with numeric pedices.

$[a]_{t_{out}(a)}$	$a \Rightarrow (a \wedge \neg t_{out}(a))\mathbf{U}(t_{out}(a)) \vee \mathbf{G}(a)$ (1) $\displaystyle\bigwedge_{t \in out(a)} (t \Rightarrow \mathbf{Y}(a) \wedge \neg a)$ (2)	$\xleftarrow{t_1} \boxed{a} \xrightarrow{t_2}$ $\Big\downarrow t_i$
$t_{in}(a)[a]$	$a \Rightarrow (a \wedge \neg t_{in}(a))\mathbf{S}(t_{in}(a))$ (3) $\displaystyle\bigwedge_{t^d \in in(a)} (t^d \Rightarrow \mathbf{X}(a) \wedge \neg a)$ (4) $\displaystyle\bigwedge_{t \in in(a)} (t \Rightarrow \neg \mathbf{Y}(a) \wedge a)$ (5)	$\Big\downarrow t_i$ $\xrightarrow{t_1} \boxed{a} \xleftarrow{t_2}$
$[\cdot + \cdot]$	$t_1 \Rightarrow \neg t_2$ (6) $\oplus \Rightarrow \neg \mathbf{Y}(\oplus) \wedge \neg \mathbf{X}(\oplus)$ (7) $t_1 \vee t_2 \Leftrightarrow \oplus$ (8)	$\xleftarrow{t_1} \langle + \rangle \xrightarrow{t_2}$
$[\cdot \| \cdot]$	$\displaystyle\bigwedge_{t_1,t_2 \in out(\|)} (t_1 \Leftrightarrow t_2)$ (9) $\| \Rightarrow \neg \mathbf{Y}(\|) \wedge \neg \mathbf{X}(\|)$ (10) $t_i \Leftrightarrow \|$ (11)	$\xleftarrow{t_1} \langle \| \rangle \xrightarrow{t_2}$ $\Big\downarrow t_i$
$[\cdot \| \cdot]$	$\displaystyle\bigwedge_{t_1,t_2 \in in(\|)} (t_1 \Leftrightarrow_2)$ (12) $\| \Rightarrow \neg \mathbf{Y}(\|) \wedge \neg \mathbf{X}(\|)$ (13) $t_i \Leftrightarrow \|$ (14)	$\Big\downarrow t_i$ $\xrightarrow{t_1} \langle \| \rangle \xleftarrow{t_2}$
t^d	$t^d \Leftrightarrow x_t = 0 \wedge \mathbf{X}(x_t = d)$ (15)	$\Big\downarrow t^d$
	$a \wedge \neg \mathbf{Y}(a) \Leftrightarrow x_a = 0$ (16) $\mathbf{Y}(a) \wedge \neg a \Rightarrow x_a = time(a)$ (17)	$\boxed{a_{=time(a)}}$

Zero-time transitions are modelled through Formula 5. Let t be a transition reaching activity a, i.e., such that $t \in in(a)$. When t fires at position i then a is true in i but it does not at position $i-1$ where an activity b such that $t \in out(b)$ was active. Formula 4 and 5 are different, as the former, combined with Formula 2, forces the absence of the two activities a and b when t_{ab} occurs; the latter lets t_{ab} fire exactly at the first position where b holds. In other words, a transition t_{ab} between activity a followed by b, is non zero-time when, if i is the position where it fires, activity a holds at position $i-1$, where it ends, and activity b holds at position $i+1$, where it starts, but none of them at position i. Conversely, a transition t_{ab} between activity a followed by b, is zero-time when activity a

holds at position $i-1$ and activity b holds at position i, where it starts exactly at the same position when t_{ab} holds.

Figure 1 shows an example of a zero-time and non zero-time transition.

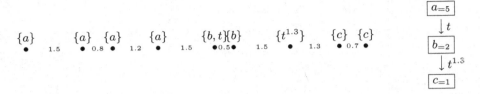

Fig. 1. Portion of an execution (left) of the sequence of activities a, b and c (right) where t is a zero-time transition between a and b and $t^{1.3}$ is a non zero-time transition that lasts 1.3 time units. The delays between two consecutive positions of the CLTLoc representation of the execution are shown in the picture between any pair of bullets. For instance, the time elapsing between position 2 and 3 is 0.8 time unit. Zero-time transition t occurs in the first position of the execution of activity b which, therefore, begins exactly when activity a terminates. Transition $t^{1.3}$ has a non null duration and then it separates activity b from c.

Given an activity $a \in A$, the CLTLoc semantics that we associated with $[a]_{t_{out}(a)}$ and $t_{in}(a)[a]$ does not impose any constraint on the firing of transitions in the sets $out(a)$ and $in(a)$, making the execution flow non-deterministically determined. Formulae (1)-(4) are the same of those presented in [23]. The only difference is in Formula (4) which is now written for non zero-time transitions.

Conditional case $[\cdot + \cdot]$ and split-join $[\cdot \mid \cdot]$ activities are modelled similarly to [23] by formulae (1)-(5) . However, we introduce formulae (8), (11) and (14) to model the zero duration of split/join activities and conditional cases. They enforce the contemporaneity of the activities $\oplus$ and $\parallel$ with the outgoing transitions, that are assumed to be zero-time. Therefore, their behaviour is modelled by Formula (5).

Adding time to workflows requires care in modelling split-join activities and the duration of their branches. It is, in fact, possible to write unfeasible split-join blocks that do not allow any execution to reach the join when the branches are not "temporally synchronized", that is, when there is at least a pair of paths in the split-join block whose duration (the sum of the duration of all the activities and non zero-time transitions over the path) is not equal. In such a case, the designer must introduce special activities, that are not functionally related to the workflow, to delay the execution of those paths in the split-join which have different duration. In Sect. 4, we show how our approach can be used to refine the model and design split-join activities that are correctly synchronized.

Formulae (15)-(17) are new and not part of [23] as they model the real-time temporal behaviour of activities and transitions. Figure 2 shows an example of constraints on clocks measuring delays for activities and non zero-time transitions. Formula (15) defines the duration of non-zero time transitions. For each non-zero time transition t_i^d, we introduce a clock x_i that is reset when t_i^d fires

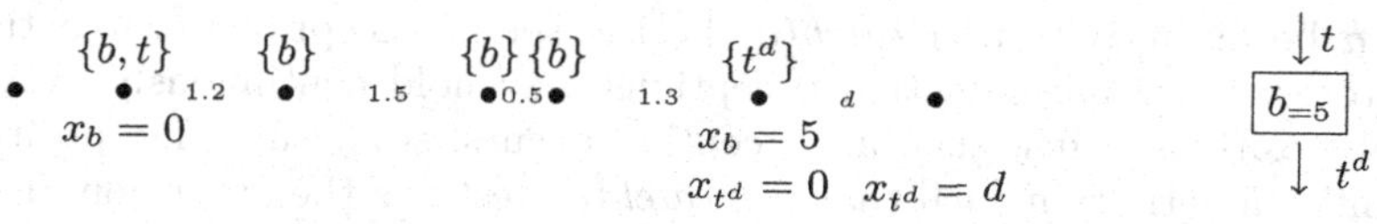

$$\{b,t\} \qquad \{b\} \qquad \{b\}\{b\} \qquad \{t^d\}$$

$$\bullet \quad \underset{1.2}{\bullet} \quad \bullet \quad \underset{1.5}{} \quad \underset{0.5}{\bullet}\bullet \quad \underset{1.3}{} \quad \bullet \quad \underset{d}{} \quad \bullet$$

$$x_b = 0 \qquad\qquad\qquad\qquad x_b = 5$$

$$x_{t^d} = 0 \quad x_{t^d} = d$$

$$\downarrow t$$

$$\boxed{b_{=5}}$$

$$\downarrow t^d$$

Fig. 2. Execution (left) of activity b and transitions t and t^d depicted on the right, where t is a zero-time transition preceding b and t^d is a non zero-time transition that lasts d time units. The delays between two consecutive positions of the CLTLoc representation of the execution are non-deterministically determined to meet the constraint on the duration of the activity imposed in Formula (17). In position 2, activity b starts and clock x_b is reset. The constraint $x_b = 5$ on the duration of activity b is met in the next position where b terminates (in the example this holds when t^d occurs). Formula (15) models temporal constraints on t^d. When t^d occurs, clock x_{t^d} is reset. In the next position, it meets the constraint $x_{t^d} = d$.

and whose value is exactly d in the next position. To measure activity delays, we introduce clock x_a for activity $a \in A$. Formula (16) defines the condition for resetting x_a that occurs when activity a starts. The formula states that if, at the current position, activity a holds and in the previous position a was not underway, then clock x_a is reset. This allows the clocks to initiate the measuring of the duration of a. When activity finishes then, at that moment, clock x_a must evaluate to $time(a)$. In a terminating run, all activities terminate and eventually are such that $\mathbf{Y}(a) \wedge \neg a$. Then, all the executions meet the temporal constraints on the duration of the activities by enforcing the consequent of Formula (17). In case of workflow errors, some activities of the workflow may loop forever.

In such a case, the antecedent of the implication is false, as the activity satisfies $\mathbf{G}(a)$, and does not constraint the value of clock x_a to any specific value. Along the execution of activity a, its clock x_a has a value which is less than the duration $time(a)$ of the activity itself.

As in [23], we assume that when a workflow terminates, it never resumes, by adding to the model formula $end \Rightarrow \mathbf{G}(end)$.

Encoding Exceptions. Let E be a (finite) set of exceptions associated with the workflow and P and S be two subsets of E such that $P \cup S = E$ and $P \cap S = \emptyset$ where P is the set of permanent exceptions and S is the set of punctual exceptions. In this section, with abuse of notation, we restrict set A only to activities that are not *start*, *end*, split-join and conditional activities with which no exception is associated.

Informally, we say that an exception is punctual when it holds exactly one time instant whenever it occurs. Conversely, an exception is non-punctual when it may have a duration and it lasts from a position where it is raised until a position where it expires. In this paper, we focus on non-punctual exceptions for which the modelling is modified with respect to [23] to deal with time constraints. Formulae defining the behaviour of punctual exceptions are not shown here as they are the same as those presented in [23].

Let a be an activity and $catch(a)$ be the set of exceptions that activity a can restores. Since non-punctual exceptions may hold continuously over some adjacent positions, when such an exception occurs, say e, at some position, it holds until an activity a such that $e \in catch(a)$ restores the exception. To store the time elapsed since its generation, we introduce a clock x_e, for all $e \in P$. Formula (18) imposes that clock x_e is reset when exception e is thrown.

$$\bigwedge_{e \in P} (e \wedge \neg \mathbf{Y}(e) \Leftrightarrow x_e = 0). \tag{18}$$

We extend function $time$ to element of set E. Formula (19) is different from the one presented in [23] as it also includes the timing constraint on clock x_e to meet the deadline $time(e)$. It states that if, at the current position, e holds then there is a position in the future where an activity restores it before the deadline $time(e)$, otherwise it will hold indefinitely. In fact, if the right-hand formula holds, i.e., the exception is managed correctly before the deadline, then $\neg \mathbf{G}(e)$ holds and e will not hold indefinitely. Conversely, if the right-hand formula does not hold then $\neg \mathbf{G}(e)$ does not holds, that is, e will hold indefinitely.

$$\bigwedge_{e \in P} (e \Rightarrow (\neg \mathbf{G}(e) \Leftrightarrow \bigvee_{\substack{a \in A \\ e \in catch(a)}} (e\mathbf{U}(a \wedge x_e \leq time(e))))). \tag{19}$$

Any non-punctual exception which is not properly resolved by some activities of the workflow before its deadline causes the workflow to fall into an error configuration and lets the execution loop forever. Formula (20) states that in exception e is active and its clock is greater than its deadline then the exception remains active and endures indefinitely. Formula (20), conjoined with Formula (19), avoids the occurrence of an already managed exception e after its deadline, because otherwise $\mathbf{G}(e)$ holds which, by Formula (19), is equivalent to not having an activity that managed e (Fig. 3).

$$\bigwedge_{e \in P} (e \wedge x_e > time(e) \Rightarrow \mathbf{G}(e)). \tag{20}$$

Let $probe(a)$ be the set of exceptions associated with activity a that may let a loop indefinitely. If a is active at a certain position of the time, then the occurrence of (i) an exception e in $probe(a)$ causes an abortion of a if, at that moment, there is no activity b that restores e, such that $e \in catch(b)$ or (i) an exception e has not met its deadline. The abortion represents a configuration of error that can not be restored, i.e., a loops infinitely or terminates with a system error. Formula (21) is the same as the one in [23] and is defined for all activities $a \in A$ of the workflow with a non empty set $probe(b)$

$$\bigwedge_{e \in probe(a)} (a \wedge (\mathbf{G}(e) \vee e \wedge \bigwedge_{\substack{b \in A \\ e \in catch(b)}} \neg b)) \Rightarrow \mathbf{G}(a) \tag{21}$$

Formula (22), which is introduced for all activities $a \in A$ appearing in the workflow, defines the necessary conditions to have infinite execution. It is modified

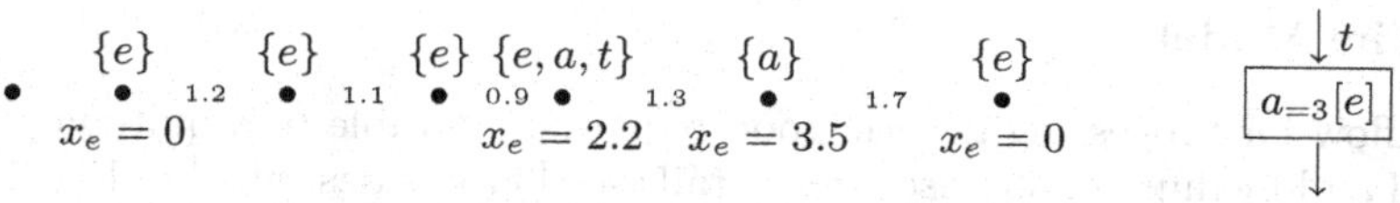

Fig. 3. Portion of the execution (left) of exception e with deadline $time(e) = 3$ caught by activity a, i.e., such that $e \in catch(a)$. In position 5, where $x_e = 2.2$, activity a solves the exception before its deadline. Therefore, e does not occur in the next position, that occurs after 3 time units since the generation of e, because of Formula (20) and Formula (20). Exception e is newly thrown in the last position of the sub-execution where clock x_e is reset.

with respect to the correspondent one in [23] because the disjunct $\bigvee_{e \in P} \mathbf{G}(e)$ is added to the formula. At a certain position, if activity a is active and it never terminates, i.e., $\mathbf{G}(a)$ holds at that position, then (i) there exists an activity c of the workflow, possibly different from a, that eventually loops indefinitely because an exception $e \in probe(c)$ is not correctly handled or (ii) there is an exception e whose deadline has not met which continues indefinitely (due to Formula (20)). If activity a holds forever, then there is an activity c (which may possibly be a) and a non-punctual exception $e \in probe(c)$ that holds indefinitely, because no activity b, that actually could manage e, ever catches it.

$$\mathbf{G}(a) \Rightarrow \mathbf{F}\left(\bigvee_{\substack{c \in A \\ e \in probe(c)}} \left(\mathbf{G}\left(c \wedge e \wedge \bigwedge_{\substack{b \in A \\ e \in catch(b)}} \neg b \right) \right) \vee \bigvee_{e \in P} \mathbf{G}(e \wedge c) \right) \quad (22)$$

Observe that when $probe(c)$, for some $c \in A$, is empty the formula within $\mathbf{F}$ is trivially false. In this case, the activity appearing in the antecedent of the formula always terminates and no looping executions are admitted for it, because $\mathbf{G}(a)$ is false.

An exception $e \in E$ is *internal* if it is thrown by some activity appearing in the workflow whereas it is *external* otherwise. The same formalization in [23] holds in this context, so the reader may refer to [23] for further details.

We can now, formally, define the executions of a workflow. Let W be a workflow and ϕ_W the CLTLoc formula translating W that is defined by conjunction the formulae above, globally quantified over the time. We define *execution* of W an CLTLoc interpretation (π, σ) for formula ϕ_W such that $(\pi, \sigma), 0 \models \phi_W$.

4   An Example

To demonstrate the soundness and effectiveness of the proposed approach, it has been applied to the investigation of an example taken from literature and related to an office process. This way, in the following, we first describe the office workflow and then we report on how to apply our framework to the verification of some basic properties of the overall process.

4.1   The Model

A workflow for processing generic good requests, referable to a quite large class of small and medium enterprises (for details see [36]), is described in Fig. 4. Even if simple, it could represent, from a high level perspective, a broad class of actual e-commerce or similar (remote) purchase systems. In the corresponding workflow model we included some design flaws on exception handlers that may drive to neverending executions.

More specifically, the office workflow is composed of ten activities, drawn as rectangles, which could generate three types of exceptions: *HF* (Hardware Failure), *SF* (Software Failure) and *TF* (Transport Failure). The first two of them

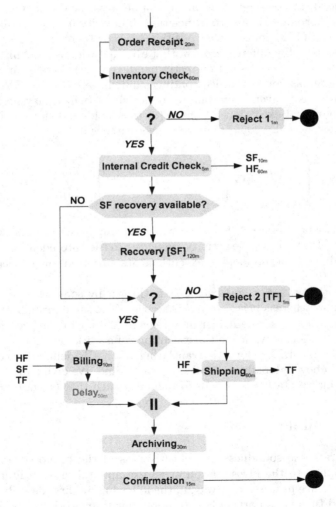

Fig. 4. Office workflow representation.

(HF and SF) are permanent exceptions, while TF ones are punctual exceptions. The *probe* and *throw* exception sets related to an activity are identified by all its ingoing or outgoing labelled arrows, respectively. This way we have $throw(InternalCreditCheck) = \{HF, SF\}$ and $throw(Shipping) = \{TF\}$. The set of exceptions caught by an activity is specified within square brackets close to its name in the rectangle ($catch(Recovery) = \{SF\}$ and $catch(Reject_2) = \{TF\}$). Conditions are represented by diamonds and labelled with ? or with $< Condition\ Name >?$ (*SF recovery available?*). Similarly, split-join concurrent activities are depicted by diamonds labelled with $\|$. Both condition and split-join activities are instantaneous activities thus characterized by zero-time durations. Finally, the number specified as subscript of labels represents the time spent in an activity with the corresponding time unit (m stands for minutes), i.e. the activity time durations. With regard to exceptions, this time represents a timeout: once expired the exception can no longer be handled and/or recovered.

Verifying the reachability property $\mathbf{G}\,(\neg Arch)$, we prove that *Archiving* activity is not reachable. So, to synchronize the execution of the two branches, we have introduced a new dummy activity *Delay* to equal the duration of activity *Shipping*.

4.2   Verification

To demonstrate the effectiveness of our approach in this section we verify (the CLTLoc model of) the workflow described above to identify wrong execution patterns taking into account different, alternative scenarios characterized by the exceptions, thus obtaining hints able to drive the model refinement towards a correct design. In this section, we discuss on the performance results of the verification process and the satisfiability of properties.

To validate the CLTLoc model, we exploit the Bounded Satisfiability Checking (BSC) [11] approach similarly to [23].

Table 3 shows time – in seconds – required by Zot to verify a set of functional user-defined properties, memory occupation – in MBytes – and the result, i.e. whether the property is satisfied or not.

Formula $\mathbf{G}\,(\neg tf \wedge \neg hf \wedge \neg sf \Rightarrow \mathbf{F}\,(end))$ states that, if no exceptions occur, the workflow must terminate, as in [23]. As reported in Table 3, the property holds also in the timed version of the workflow, since there are no traces which satisfy its negation.

Formula $(\mathbf{G}\,(\neg hf \wedge \neg sf) \wedge \mathbf{F}\,(tf \wedge x_{Shipp} = 5)) \Rightarrow \mathbf{F}\,(end)$ checks the occurrence of the *TransportFailure* punctual exception, which is thrown by *Shipping* activity and models a shipping problem, such as a truck accident. The variable x_{Shipp} is the clock associated to activity *Shipping*, which counts the time elapsed since the beginning of the execution of the activity: in this formula, we want to simulate the thrown of the *tf* exception after 5 time units – minutes, in the case study – from the beginning of the activity. As reported in Table 3, the property does not hold: the counterexample trace shows, as in [23], that the activities *Billing* and *Shipping* loop forever. Having a look at the workflow, we observe that some activities never terminate since the exception *tf* can be caught only

Table 3. Test results.

Formula	Time (s)	Memory (Mb)	Result
$\mathbf{G}\,(\neg tf \wedge \neg hf \wedge \neg sf \Rightarrow \mathbf{F}\,(end))$	7.545	25	UNSAT
$(\mathbf{G}\,(\neg hf \wedge \neg sf) \wedge \mathbf{F}\,(tf \wedge x_{Shipp} = 5)) \Rightarrow \mathbf{F}\,(end)$	8.536	180	SAT
$(\mathbf{G}\,(\neg hf \wedge \neg sf) \wedge \mathbf{F}\,(tf \wedge x_{Shipp} = 25)) \Rightarrow \mathbf{F}\,(end)$	7.846	28	UNSAT

by activity *Reject2*, which can not be executed in parallel with *Shipping*, and because activity *Billing* catches the exception before its deadline, which is 10 time units.

Formula $(\mathbf{G}\,(\neg hf \wedge \neg sf) \wedge \mathbf{F}\,(tf \wedge x_{Shipp} = 25)) \Rightarrow \mathbf{F}\,(end)$ checks, again, the occurrence of the *TransportFailure* punctual exception, but in a scenario where it is thrown after activity *Billing* has finished its execution. In this case, there are no parallel activities that catch the exception, since activity *Delay* is only a placeholder to wait for synchronization, so the workflow terminates.

All tests have been carried out on a 3.3 Ghz quad core PC with 16 Gb of RAM. The bound k, which is a user-defined parameter representing the maximal length of runs analysed by Zot, corresponds to the number of discrete positions that are used to build the bounded representation of the model. The value chosen is $k = 35$. By analysing the longest path of the workflow of Fig. 4, one can see that this value for k is big enough to guarantee the definition of meaningful workflow executions, i.e., interpretations over the symbols appearing in the workflow that are model of the LTL formula translating it (partly shown in and defined through rules of Sect. 3).

To verify properties like the one modelled by Formula $\mathbf{G}\,(\neg tf \wedge \neg hf \wedge \neg sf \Rightarrow \mathbf{F}\,(end))$, Zot must exhaustively analyse all possible runs to return UNSAT, which is the worst case in terms of time and memory consumed; taking it into account, we can conclude that it is feasible, using modern model checking tools such as Zot, to perform formal verification of non-trivial functional real-time properties, in a limited amount of resources, allowing designer to execute the analysis in an interactive real-time manner.

5   Conclusions and Future Work

The major objective of this paper is demonstrating how temporal logics are effective in giving semantics and iteratively enforce requirements into the process. To this purpose, starting from [23], we extended the previous LTL semantics formalization of workflows to include timed activities. To model timed workflow we exploit CLTLoc [37], which is an LTL based logic where atomic formulae are both atomic propositions and constraints over dense clocks. The implemented solution is able to verify time behavior of a wide class of workflows, as also demonstrated by an example of a generic office business process.

The workflow patterns here analyzed are limited with respect to a real scenario, where more complex patterns, as the ones identified in [38], need to be investigated and encoded into our approach. Once workflows are intended as graphs and transitions are treated like in this paper, similarities emerge with the Petri Nets approach, in particular with Workflow Petri Nets [16]. Other formalisms such as the business process modeling notation (BPMN) [39] could be considered as starting point for our approach. Indeed, in [40] BPMN has been exploited for workflow design since it includes the concept of partition (modeled as pools and swimlanes), an essential features for business processes modeling not considered here. This will need to be investigated later.

Zero-time modeling is also an open issue. When some workflow activities have a negligible duration with respect to the other ones, they may be modeled as having a logical zero time duration. This implies Zeno behaviours and other counterintuitive consequences. [10] introduces a new metric temporal logic called *X-TRIO*, which exploits the concepts of *Non-Standard Analysis* [41]. The way to "glue" together CLTLoc with X-TRIO is a promising research strand.

Finally, runtime evolution in business processes [42] and, more in general, the idea of self-reconfiguring systems are related issues we intend to further explore.

Acknowledgements. The authors acknowledge the support and advice given by Marina Carvalho, Miticus Flamejante, Vínicius Pereira, Diego Pérez, Michele Ciavotta, Marco Miglierina and all the other Friends at Politecnico di Milano, which represent a moving force, an actual égrégore capable of always moving ideas forward to the next level.

References

1. Bersani, M.M., Rossi, M., Pietro, P.S.: A tool for deciding the satisfiability of continuous-time metric temporal logic. In: 2013 20th International Symposium on Temporal Representation and Reasoning, 26–28 September, 2013, Pensacola, FL, USA, pp. 99–106 (2013)
2. Lichtenstein, O., Pnueli, A., Zuck, L.: The glory of the past. In: Parikh, R. (ed.) Proceedings of Logics of Programs. LNCS, vol. 193, pp. 196–218. Springer, Heidelberg (1985)
3. Pradella, M., Morzenti, A., San Pietro, P.: Refining real-time system specifications through bounded model- and satisfiability-checking. In: ASE, pp. 119–127 (2008)
4. Lucchi, R., Mazzara, M.: A pi-calculus based semantics for ws-bpel. J. Logic Algebraic Program. **70**, 96–118 (2007)
5. Mazzara, M.: Deriving specifications of dependable systems: toward a method. In: 12th European Workshop on Dependable Computing (EWDC) (2009)
6. Mazzara, M.: On methods for the formal specification of fault tolerant systems. In: Proceedings of the 4th International Conference on Dependability (DEPEND 2011) (2011)
7. Gmehlich, R., Grau, K., Iliasov, A., Jackson, M., Loesch, F., Mazzara, M.: Towards a formalism-based toolkit for automotive applications. In: Formal Methods in Software Engineering (FormaliSE) (2013)
8. Baier, C., Katoen, J.P.: Principles of Model Checking. MIT Press, Cambridge (2008)
9. Morzenti, A., San Pietro, P.: Object-oriented logical specification of time-critical systems. ACM Trans. Softw. Eng. Methodol. (TOSEM) **3**, 56–98 (1994)

10. Ferrucci, L., Mandrioli, D., Morzenti, A., Rossi, M.: A metric temporal logic for dealing with zero-time transitions. In: Proceedings of 19th International Symposium on Temporal Representation and Reasoning, pp. 81–88. IEEE Computer Society (2012)
11. Pradella, M., Morzenti, A., San Pietro, P.: Bounded satisfiability checking of metric temporal logic specifications. ACM Trans. on Soft. Eng. Meth. (TOSEM) (2013)
12. Vaz, C., Ferreira, C.: On the analysis of compensation correctness. J. Log. Algebr. Program. **81**, 585–605 (2012)
13. Calzolai, F., De Nicola, R., Loreti, M., Tiezzi, F.: TAPAs: a tool for the analysis of process algebras. In: van der Aalst, W.M.P., Billington, J., Jensen, K. (eds.) Transactions on Petri Nets and Other Models of Concurrency I. LNCS, vol. 5100, pp. 54–70. Springer, Heidelberg (2008)
14. Mazzara, M., Bhattacharyya, A.: On modelling and analysis of dynamic reconfiguration of dependable real-time systems. In: DEPEND, International Conference on Dependability (2010)
15. Montesi, F., Guidi, C., Zavattaro, G.: Service-oriented programming with jolie. In: Web Services Foundations, pp. 81–107 (2014)
16. van der Aalst, W.M.P.: Verification of workflow nets. In: Azéma, P., Balbo, G. (eds.) ICATPN 1997. LNCS, vol. 1248, pp. 407–426. Springer, Heidelberg (1997)
17. Yamaguchi, M., Yamaguchi, S., Tanaka, M.: A model checking method of soundness for workflow nets. IEICE Trans. **92**(A), 2723–2731 (2009)
18. Augusto, J.C., Howard, Y., Gravell, A.M., Ferreira, C., Gruner, S., Leuschel, M.: Model-based approaches for validating business critical systems. In: STEP, pp. 225–233 (2003)
19. Attie, P.C., Singh, M.P.: Specifying and enforcing intertask dependencies. In: Proceedings of the 19th VLDB Conference, pp. 134–145 (1993)
20. Eshuis, R., Wieringa, R.: Verification support for workflow design with uml activity graphs (2002)
21. Baresi, L., Morzenti, A., Motta, A., Rossi, M.: A logic-based semantics for the verification of multi-diagram uml models. ACM SIGSOFT Softw. Eng. Notes **37**, 1–8 (2012)
22. Ghezzi, C., Mandrioli, D., Morzenti, A.: Trio: A logic language for executable specifications of real-time systems. J. Syst. Softw. **12**, 107–123 (1990)
23. Ferrucci, L., Bersani, M.M., Mazzara, M.: An LTL semantics of businessworkflows with recovery. In: ICSOFT-PT 2014 - Proceedings of the 9th International Conference on Software Paradigm Trends, Vienna, Austria, 29–31 August, 2014, pp. 29–40 (2014)
24. Butler, M.J., Ferreira, C.: An operational semantics for stac, a language for modelling longrunning business transactions. In: Meredith, G., Ferrari, G.-L., De Nicola, R. (eds.) COORDINATION 2004. LNCS, vol. 2949, pp. 87–104. Springer, Heidelberg (2004)
25. Dragoni, N., Mazzara, M.: A formal semantics for the ws-bpel recovery framework. In: Laneve, C., Su, J. (eds.) WS-FM 2009. LNCS, vol. 6194, pp. 92–109. Springer, Heidelberg (2010)
26. Eisentraut, C., Spieler, D.: Web services and formal methods. Springer, Heidelberg (2009)
27. Díaz, M., Valero, V., Macía, H., Mateo, J., Díaz, G.: Bpel-rf tool: An automatic translation from ws-bpel/wsrf specifications to petri nets. In: ICSEA 2012 : The Seventh International Conference on Software Engineering Advances (2012)

28. Foster, I., Frey, J., Graham, S., Tuecke, S., Czajkowski, K., Ferguson, D., Leymann, F., Nally, M., Storey, T., Weerawaranna, S.: Modeling stateful resources with web services (2004)

29. Alur, R., Dill, D.L.: A theory of timed automata. Theor. Comp. Sci. **126**, 183–235 (1994)

30. Romanovsky, A., Thomas, M. (eds.): Industrial Deployment of System Engineering Methods. Springer, Heidelberg (2013)

31. Harel, D.: Statecharts: a visual formalism for complex systems. Sci. Comput. Program. **8**, 231–274 (1987)

32. OMG: Unified modeling language 2.0 (2005). http://www.omg.org/spec/UML/2.0/

33. OASIS: Web services business process execution language version 2.0 (2007). http://docs.oasis-open.org/wsbpel/2.0/wsbpel-v2.0.pdf

34. Demri, S., D'Souza, D.: An automata-theoretic approach to constraint LTL. Inf. Comput. **205**, 380–415 (2007)

35. Bersani, M.M., Frigeri, A., Rossi, M., San Pietro, P.: Completeness of the bounded satisfiability problem for constraint LTL. In: Delzanno, G., Potapov, I. (eds.) RP 2011. LNCS, vol. 6945, pp. 58–71. Springer, Heidelberg (2011)

36. Ellis, C., Keddara, K., Rozenberg, G.: Dynamic change within workflow systems. In: Proceedings of Conference on Organizational Computing Systems. COCS 1995, pp. 10–21. ACM, New York (1995)

37. Bersani, M.M., Rossi, M., San Pietro, P.: A tool for deciding the satisfiability of continuous-time metric temporal logic. In: Proceedings of the International Symposium on Temporal Representation and Reasoning (TIME), pp. 99–106 (2013)

38. van der Aalst, W., ter Hofstede, A., Kiepuszewski, B., Barros, A.: Workflow patterns. Distrib. Parallel Databases **14**, 5–51 (2003)

39. OMG: Business process model and notation (bpmn) (2011). http://www.bpmn.org/

40. Mazzara, M., Dragoni, N., Zhou, M.: Implementing workflow reconfiguration in ws-bpel. Security **2**, 73–92 (2012)

41. Robinson, A.: Non-standard analysis. Princeton University Press, Princeton (1996)

42. Baresi, L., Guinea, S., Manna, V.P.L.: Consistent runtime evolution of service-based business processes. In: Liu, A., John Klein, A.T. (ed.) Working IEEE/IFIP Conference on Software Architecture (WICSA) (2014)

Author Index

Printed in the United States
By Bookmasters